BIOLOGY FOR LIFE

TEACHER'S GUIDE

JOHN FINAGIN
BSc M.I.Biol
Head of Science, Rhyl High School

and

NEIL INGRAM
BSc PhD
Clifton College, Bristol

Nelson

To Vicky and Helen

Thomas Nelson and Sons Ltd
Nelson House Mayfield Road
Walton-on-Thames Surrey
KT12 5PL UK

Nelson Blackie
Wester Cleddens Road
Bishopbriggs
Glasgow G64 2NZ UK

Thomas Nelson Australia
102 Dodds Street
South Melbourne
Victoria 3205 Australia

Nelson Canada
1120 Birchmount Road
Scarborough Ontario
M1K 5G4 Canada

First published by Thomas Nelson and Sons Ltd 1988

I(T)P Thomas Nelson is an International Thomson Publishing Company.

I(T)P is used under licence.

ISBN 0-17-448156-X
NPN 9 8 7 6 5

Printed in China

Preface

The aim of this book is to help teachers to use *Biology for Life* effectively as a GCSE textbook. The advent of GCSE courses has placed new demands upon teachers and their pupils. The emphasis placed upon teaching and assessing scientific skills is new to many teachers, and few of those who have some experience of it have ever undertaken it on the scale upon which it is now being performed.

One of the major problems confronting the teacher is the burden of the additional marking required. Much of the practical work completed in the laboratory generates written product, which must be marked carefully if it is to be used to develop or assess practical skills. This marking is additional to the routine marking of homework and class exercises. This book contains comprehensive mark schemes for all of the Assignments in *Biology for Life*, together with suggestions on how they could be used and developed. These schemes should help the teacher mark the routine work more efficiently, allowing more time for the other marking.

There are no simple answers to the problems generated by practical assessment, and certainly there is no single universal solution that will suit everybody. The professional styles of teachers, departments, schools and examination boards differ so widely that a single prescriptive solution is neither possible nor desirable. This book will allow teachers to develop their own style of assessment, within the framework of the scheme outlined by their own GCSE examination board.

Many opportunities for teaching and assessing scientific skills arise when performing the Investigations in *Biology for Life*. Each has been checked against the requirements of the examination boards. The apparatus required by each group of pupils, and useful general comments on the Investigations, have been included, together with reminders on points of safety. There is also a set of copyright-free worksheets which will allow teachers to assess a wide range of scientific skills within a biological context.

This book is rather like a cookery book. When first trying a recipe it is best to follow the instructions carefully. After a while, however, it is possible to amend the recipe by adding or subtracting a few ingredients to suit the tastes of the guests. A favourite cookery book soon becomes lined with pencilled comments, and inserted ideas, as we adapt it to our needs. It is hoped that this book will prove to be as useful as that cookery book, and that teachers will feel able to modify and develop ideas, and add new ones as they try the many recipes for teaching and assessment found here.

This book was originally the idea of Dr Michael Roberts, the author of *Biology for Life*. Michael read and commented on the manuscript of the *Teacher's Guide* throughout its development, and we are especially grateful to him for the many constructive suggestions which he made. His guidance, support and friendship have been a great encouragement to us both.

We are very grateful to Peter Bright who kindly contributed one of the worksheets, and spent many hours discussing the problems of assessing practical skills. We are also grateful to many other friends and colleagues who have discussed the contents of this book with us, and who have made perceptive and helpful comments. They include: David Barrett, George Davidson, Linda Gunary, Jane Jenkins, Debbie Judd, Patrick McGuire, Grace Monger and Simon Reece. Any errors and inconsistencies that remain are the fault of the authors.

Thomas Nelson and Sons Ltd have dealt with the vagaries of two novice authors with good humour and patience. We are grateful to them, particularly Chris Coyer and Sharon Jacobs.

Finally, we must thank Vicky Finagin and Helen Ingram for their extraordinary patience and consideration in allowing their husbands to disappear for long hours as they wrote this book. We hope that they feel the effort has been worthwhile.

John Finagin
Neil R. Ingram
Abergele and Clifton
March 1988

Contents

The Development And Assessment Of Scientific Skills

—The aims of practical work

Traditionally, the principal aim of practical has been to help the pupil to understand the theoretical ideas being taught by the teacher. This was a perfectly valid aim and is one that should still be encouraged. There are now, however, additional aims for practical work which the new GCSE courses have emphasised.

Teachers of GCSE biology courses need to ensure that all of their pupils are given opportunities to develop certain skills associated with practical work before any final assessments are made, since pupils can only develop these skills by attempting practical tasks, making mistakes, asking for help and learning from their mistakes.

Practical work has assumed a new importance since the advent of GCSE, and it has become increasingly important that teachers work out their aim for a particular investigation before they use it. It could be for developing an understanding of theoretical principles, or for developing scientific skills, or for the final assessing of those skills. It is probably wise to inform the pupils of the purpose of the investigation as they begin it, so they do not become unnecessarily distracted.

The Investigations in *Biology for Life* (*BFL*) contain many opportunities to allow pupils to experience biological phenomena, solve problems, and develop laboratory and analytical skills. Most of the Investigations can also be used for assessment purposes, as can the worksheets at the end of this guide.

—The scientific skills used in this guide

Each of the Investigations in *BFL* and the worksheets in this guide has been analysed in terms of 37 specific scientific skills. Each skill has been given a code, and the code has been used to indicate where a particular Investigation provides an opportunity to develop or assess that skill. These skills are as follows:

Handling materials and apparatus

HMA 1 Following instructions to complete a procedure
HMA 2 Showing appropriate initiatives
HMA 3 Working safely

HMA 4 Assembling common apparatus
HMA 5 Using a light microscope
HMA 6 Preparing a temporary microscope slide
HMA 7 Using materials and apparatus correctly

Making accurate measurements and observations

AMO 1 Measuring temperature accurately
AMO 2 Measuring length accurately
AMO 3 Measuring volume accurately
AMO 4 Measuring time accurately
AMO 5 Measuring mass accurately
AMO 6 Counting accurately

AMO 7 Assigning objects to groups
AMO 8 Observing major similarities and differences between specimens
AMO 9 Observing detailed similarities and differences between specimens
AMO 10 Making accurate observations

Recording observations and results

REC 1 Drawing
REC 2 Completing tables
REC 3 Recording accurately
REC 4 Plotting graphs
REC 5 Selecting the appropriate methods of presenting results

Interpreting experimental results

INT 1 Drawing appropriate conclusions
INT 2 Extracting relevant information from tables and charts
INT 3 Extracting relevant information from graphs
INT 4 Performing simple calculations
INT 5 Recognising experimental error and variation in results
INT 6 Recognising patterns in experimental results

Designing and conducting experiments

EXP 1 Forming hypotheses
EXP 2 Devising an experiment to test a hypothesis
EXP 3 Specifying the apparatus for an experiment
EXP 4 Specifying the sequence of an experiment
EXP 5 Suggesting appropriate experimental controls
EXP 6 Suggesting appropriate levels of replication
EXP 7 Conducting the experiment
EXP 8 Interpreting the results of the experiment
EXP 9 Evaluating the experiment

—Assessment schemes

The assessment schemes of most of the examination boards describe skills that are composed of several of the 37 discrete skills, and this guide therefore provides opportunities to assess the skills used by the examination boards in a variety of different contexts and ways. Detailed guidance on how the skills used in this guide relate to those used by each of the examination boards is now presented.

London and East Anglian Group (LEAG)

LEAG operates a common scheme of assessment for each of its three Biology syllabuses (A,B,C) and for its Biology (Human) syllabus.

Category A: Making And Recording Accurate Observations

(i)	Drawings of biological materials	REC 1
(ii)	Comparisons of biological material	AMO 8,9
(iii)	Measurements with apparatus:	
	mass	AMO 5
	length	AMO 2
	volume	AMO 3
	time	AMO 4
	temperature	AMO 1

Category B: Performing Experiments And Interpreting The Results

(i)	Procedure and use of apparatus	HMA 1, 3, 4, 7
(ii)	Record of results	REC 2, 3, 4, 5
(iii)	Interpretation of results	INT 1, 5, 6

Category C: Designing And Evaluating An Experiment

(i)	Plan of an investigation	EXP 1, 2, 3, 4, 5, 6
(ii)	Evaluation of experiment	EXP 8, 9

Two additional skills, 'Using a compound microscope' (HMA 5) and 'Preparing a temporary microscope slide' (HMA 6) could be used to assess B(i), 'Procedure and use of apparatus'.

Midland Examining Group (MEG)

Two MEG Biology syllabuses (A and B) and the Human Biology syllabus share a common assessment scheme.

1. Following instructions	HMA 1, 2
2. Handling apparatus and materials	HMA 3, 4, 7
3. Observing and measuring	AMO 1, 2, 3, 4, 5, 10
4. Recording and communicating	REC 2, 3, 4
5. Interpreting data	INT 1, 5
6. Experimental design problem solving	EXP 2, 3, 4, 5, 6, 7, 8, 9

Two additional skills, 'Using a compound microscope' (HMA 5) and 'Preparing a temporary microscope slide' (HMA 6) could be used to teach and assess Skill 2. 'Handling apparatus and materials'. Three skills (AMO 7, 8, 9) refer to observation exercises which can be used to teach and assess Skill 3, 'Observing and measuring'. Four skills (INT 2, 3, 4, 6) refer to skills that can be used to teach and assess Skill 4. 'Recording and communicating'.

Northern Examination Association (NEA)

NEA specify 32 skills for assessment, which are related closely to the skills used in this guide.

Measurement	
1. Reading whole number scales	AMO 1, 2, 3
2. Reading multiple/fractional scales	AMO 1, 3
3. Measuring out quantities	AMO 3, 5
4. Scaling	HMA 5
5. Systematic counting	AMO 6
Observations	
6. Matching	AMO 7
7. Describing gross features	AMO 10
8. Describing fine details	AMO 10
9. Finding gross differences	AMO 8
10. Finding detailed differences	AMO 9
Handling materials and apparatus	
11. Assembling of common apparatus	HMA 4
12. Handling of common apparatus	HMA 7
13. Using the compound microscope	HMA 5
14. Preparing temporary mounts	HMA 6
Recording	
15. Using diagrams	REC 1
16. Completing prepared tables	REC 2
17. Devising a table	REC 2
18. Plotting a graph	REC 4
19. Constructing a graph	REC 4
Data and its interpretation	
20. Extracting information from tables and charts	INT 2
21. Extracting information from graphs	INT 3
22. Performance of calculations	INT 4
23. Identifying anomalous results	INT 5
24. Identifying areas of experimental error and explaining variation in results	INT 5
25. Recognising patterns	INT 6
26. Drawing valid conclusions	INT 1
Experimental design	
27. Identification of an uncontrolled variable	EXP 5
28. Suggested appropriate control	EXP 5
29. Formulating a hypothesis (1)	EXP 1
30. Formulating a hypothesis (2)	EXP 1
31. Specifying apparatus	EXP 3
32. Planning the sequence	EXP 4

Skills 7 and 8 of the NEA scheme are treated in this guide as AMO 10, 'Making accurate observations'. It should be noted, however, that only some of the occurrences of AMO 10 are suited to the assessment of these two skills. A selection of those Investigations that are appropriate are shown below. The *BFL* reference is the topic number followed by the Investigation number:

NEA Skill	7	8
BFL reference	12/1	2/1
	15/1	6/2
	28/1	11/1
	53/1	54/2
	103/1	103/5

Northern Ireland Schools Examination Council (NISEC)

There are five skill areas, each divided into two or more different skills, which correspond closely to those used in this guide. In some cases only a few Investigations are relevant to a particular skill, and these have been included in the table below. In all cases the *BFL* topic number precedes the Investigation number (e.g. 12/1).

Skill area	*Skills in this guide*
I	
A	HMA 7 (4/1, 5/3, 30/1)
B	HMA 7 (4/1, 26/1, 30/1)
C	HMA 7 (7/1, 23/1, 57/1)
D	HMA 5
E	HMA 7
II	
A	HMA 1, 2, 4
B	HMA 1, 2, 7
III	
A	AMO 1, 2, 3, 4, 5
B	AMO 1, 2, 3, 4, 5
C	AMO 1, 2, 3, 4, 5
D	HMA 3
E	AMO 10 (47/1, 51/2, 58/2)
F	AMO 8, 9
IV	
A	REC 3
B	AMO 10 (5/1, 5/2, many Assignments)
C	REC 2,5
D	REC 2, 4; INT 2, 3, 4
E	INT 1, 5, 6
V	
A	EXP 1
B	EXP 3
C	EXP 5
D	EXP 7
E	EXP 7
F	EXP 7
G	EXP 9

Southern Examining Group

SEG specifies seven skills for assessment, which correspond to the following skills in this guide:

1. To follow written and diagrammatic instructions	HMA 1
2. To handle apparatus and materials	HMA 4, 7
3. To make and convey accurate observations	AMO 10
4. To record results in an orderly manner	REC 1, 3
5. To formulate a hypothesis	EXP 1
6. To design experiments to test a hypothesis	EXP 2, 3, 4, 5
7. To carry out safe working procedures	HMA 3

Two additional skills, 'Using a compound microscope' (HMA 5) and 'Preparing a temporary microscope slide' (HMA 6), could be used to teach and assess Skill 2, 'To handle apparatus and materials'. Three skills (AMO 7, 8, 9) refer to observation exercises which can be used to teach and assess Skill 3, 'To make and convey accurate observations'.

Welsh Joint Examination Committee

WJEC specifies five skills for assessment:

1. Observational and recording skills	AMO 7, 8, 9, 10 REC 1
2. Measurement skills	AMO 1, 2, 3, 4
3. Procedural skills	HMA 1
4. Manipulative skills	HMA 3, 4, 7
5. Formulation of hypotheses and experimental design	EXP 1, 3, 4, 5

Two additional skills, 'Using a compound microscope' (HMA 5), and 'Preparing a temporary microscope slide' (HMA 6), could be used to teach and assess Skill 4, 'Manipulative skills'.

—Selecting practical work for teaching and assessing scientific skills—

BFL consists of 111 topics, most of which contain one or more Investigations that can be used to teach or assess the scientific skills. In this guide the opportunities for assessment are presented for each Investigation, together with lists of equipment needed and suggestions to teachers on ways to complete the Investigations.

A set of copyright-free worksheets appears at the end of the guide. The worksheets have been carefully designed to enable each of the 37 profile skills to be assessed at least once, in exercises that are relevant to the topic being taught. Equipment lists and general comments are presented for each worksheet.

It will be clear that HMA 3 (Working Safely) can be assessed on every occasion that the pupils are in the laboratory. Furthermore, the teacher has a legal requirement to make sure that pupils work safely. In the guide, HMA 3 is only mentioned when there is some special reason why precautions should be taken. In this way it serves as a reminder to teachers about the safety implications of a particular practical.

Special mention also needs to be made of the exercises involving making comparisons between the structure of two specimens (AMO 8 and AMO 9). Four examination boards specify the use of this exercise (LEAG, NEA, NISEC and WJEC), and the exercise can be used to assess making observations in all of the schemes of the other examination boards.

The NEA assessment is concerned with differences between specimens, whilst LEAG, NISEC and WJEC pupils can consider both similarities and differences. Furthermore, the NEA scheme is concerned with differentiating between major features and fine detail. This is not the case with LEAG, NISEC and WJEC.

As far as teachers of LEAG, NISEC and WJEC are concerned, AMO 8 and AMO 9 assess the same skill, and all occurrences of these skills in the text can form the basis of a comparisons exercise. NEA teachers should use AMO 8 to refer to differences between major features and AMO 9 to differences between fine detail.

In this guide, the experimental design skills have normally been considered together, because a suggested hypothesis will allow all the relevant EXP skills to be assessed. Exceptions occur where an investigation allows a particular point about experimental design to be emphasised. In such cases, the citation of a particular EXP skill will mean that the teacher can use it as material for teaching (but not necessarily assessing) the design skills.

There are so many opportunities to develop and assess each skill in the *BFL* Investigations that an index of skills would not be particularly helpful. Teachers should select those investigations that they consider to be most relevant to their teaching, and then analyse the distribution of skills within them.

Table 1

	Skill	Suitable practicals for its assessment
HMA 1	Following instructions to complete a procedure	24/2, 47/1, 64/2
HMA 2	Showing appropriate initiatives	26/1, 47/2, 70/1
HMA 3	Working safely	18/1, 49/1, 70/3
HMA 4	Assembling common apparatus	44/1, 58/2, 71/1
HMA 5	Using a compound microscope	29/2, 31/1, 91/4
HMA 6	Preparing a temporary microscope slide	42/2, 43/2, 90/1
HMA 7	Using materials and apparatus correctly	54/1, 66/1, 81/7
AMO 1	Measuring temperature accurately	49/1, 55/3, 72/1
AMO 2	Measuring length accurately	29/3, 50/6, 55/3
AMO 3	Measuring volume accurately	49/1, 70/2, 72/1
AMO 4	Measuring time accurately	48/1, 61/2, 61/3
AMO 5	Measuring mass accurately	49/1, 29/4, 91/1
AMO 6	Counting accurately	23/1, 70/5, 108/1
AMO 7	Assigning objects to groups	3/1, 4/1, 5/2
AMO 8	Comparing the structure of two specimens	10/1, 15/1, 19/2
AMO 9	Comparing the detailed structure of two specimens	10/1, 15/1, 103/1
AMO 10	Making accurate observations	22/1, 44/3, 93/2
REC 1	Drawing	4/1, 6/1, 77/3
REC 2	Completing tables	110/1, 55/3, 58/3
REC 3	Recording accurately	66/1, 70/1, 29/4
REC 4	Plotting graphs	44/1, 47/2, 66/1
REC 5	Selecting the appropriate methods of presenting results	22/1, 55/3, 72/1
INT 1	Drawing appropriate conclusions	44/2, 48/1, 51/2
INT 2	Extracting relevant information from tables and charts	58/4, 24/2, 110/1
INT 3	Extracting relevant information from graphs	91/1, 100/1, 66/1
INT 4	Performing simple calculations	104/3, 55/3, 29/5
INT 5	Recognising experimental error and variation in results	23/1, 50/6, 66/1
INT 6	Recognising patterns in experimental results	66/1, 61/4, 51/3
EXP:	These skills are considered together:	9/1, 24/1, 36/2
EXP 1	Forming hypotheses	
EXP 2	Devising an experiment to test a hypothesis	
EXP 3	Specifying apparatus for an experiment	
EXP 4	Specifying the sequence of an experiment	
EXP 5	Appropriate use of controls	
EXP 6	Suggesting appropriate levels of replication	
EXP 7	Conducting the experiment	
EXP 8	Interpreting the results from the experiment	
EXP 9	Evaluating the experiment	

Even so, some teachers might like to refer to a table of some of the most useful practicals for assessing a particular skill. This information appears in Table 1: the practicals are referred to by their 'topic number/investigation number'.

Developing a system for teaching and assessing scientific skills

The demands of practical assessment on the teacher are great, particularly with regard to accurate record keeping. Detailed recommendations can be obtained from each examination board on the form of the records required, and these should be studied carefully.

One approach to the problem is to use a pupil profile as a basis for record keeping. A profile is a record of the performance of a pupil for a range of different skills. Several levels of achievement can be included on the profile, which is updated regularly when a pupil improves the performance of a particular skill. A typical profile might be as shown in Figure 1.

Using a profile as a system of record keeping can be time consuming, but it has the potential to be extremely valuable because it enables the teacher to:

- monitor how the skills of each pupil are developing;
- discuss with each pupil how their skills are developing;
- produce an appropriate assessment mark for the examination board at the end of the course, using the pupils' best performances.This eliminates need for formal assessment exercises.

If a pupil profile is to be used for these purposes, it must be understood by the teacher and the pupil. At any point in the course, the profile is an accurate description of what the pupil has achieved. It can, therefore, help teachers to make pupils aware of their progress in a very positive way.

Each pupil should have access to the profile, and should be encouraged to discuss its content regularly with the teacher, who should indicate what is needed to develop the skills further. It is necessary, therefore, that the skills listed on the profile are simple, unambiguous, and are worded in such a way that both pupils and teachers understand their meaning.

Name________________ Form/Set________________________

A B C

FOLLOWING INSTRUCTIONS
Following instructions (HMA 1)
Working safely (HMA 3)

HANDLING APPARATUS AND MATERIALS
Assembling apparatus correctly (HMA 4)
Using materials and apparatus correctly (HMA 7)
Using the compound microscope (HMA 5)
Preparing a temporary microscope slide (HMA 6)

OBSERVING AND MEASURING
Measuring temperature (AMO 1)
Measuring length (AMO 2)
Measuring volume (AMO 3)
Assigning objects to groups (AMO 7)
Making accurate observations (AMO 10)

RECORDING AND COMMUNICATING
Designing and using tables for experimental results (REC 2)
Recording results and observations accurately (REC 1/REC 3)
Plotting graphs, histograms or bar charts (REC 4)

INTERPRETING DATA
Extracting relevant information from tables or graphs (INT 2/INT 3)
Drawing appropriate conclusions (INT 1)

EXPERIMENTAL DESIGN AND PROBLEM SOLVING
Turning a problem into an idea for an experiment (EXP 2)
Specifying apparatus and materials for a new experiment (EXP 3)
Specifying the sequence of the experiment (EXP 4)
Evaluating the experimental methods and suggesting improvements (EXP 9)

Figure 1 A typical pupil profile.

It is also important that the results of the profile can eventually be converted into a final assessment mark. Ideally, this process should be as simple as possible, and it is important to design profiles which allow this to occur. The pupil profile is not a confidential document, but the examination mark derived from the profile is confidential, and should not be communicated to the pupil. It is important that the pupil is not aware of the mechanism by which examination scores are obtained from the profile.

Most of the examination boards (other than NEA) use descriptions of skills that contain several different ideas. A typical description might read:

> *Handling materials and apparatus*
> A pupil can handle apparatus and materials correctly and confidently, usually recognising and correcting errors of assembly and safety.

The teachers may then be expected to assess the pupil according to the amount of help given in achieving these objectives: no assistance receives the highest level (3), some assistance is the mid-level (2) and considerable assistance is the lowest level (1).

Such a skill description is inappropriate to a pupil profile because it is difficult to assess unambiguously. One can envisage a situation where a pupil requires assistance in assembling a piece of apparatus, but then, unaided, manipulates it correctly for most of the lesson, and later needs a warning about becoming careless with the apparatus. It is difficult for the teacher to grade the pupil unambiguously for this skill, as a grade somewhere between the high and mid-levels is needed, and it may be hard for the pupil to understand how the assessment was made.

It is possible to overcome this problem by treating 'Assembling apparatus', 'Working safely' and 'Using apparatus' as separate skills on the profile. The pupil would achieve scores of 2, 2, 3 for these three skills, and it would be easy to explain why.

It is also easy to convert the profile scores into a score appropriate for the examination board. Suppose, by the end of the course, the pupil had not improved the performance for these three profile skills, and that the board require a score (maximum of 3) for the skill 'Handling materials and apparatus'. An average of the three scores could be used to produce the final mark.

Teachers interested in this approach are recommended to select a number of the 37 *BFL* skills as a basis for a pupil profile. The skills should be those that are most directly relevant to the assessment scheme of the examination board being used. The composition of a profile is a compromise between that which is desirable and that which is practical.

Observing and assessing skills in the laboratory

It is not advisable to try to write directly upon the record sheets of pupils whilst assessing in the classroom. Practical assessment is, at best, a frenetic activity, and it is not the ideal place to produce neat marks on a piece of paper that is of great significance.

What is needed instead is a second piece of paper with the pupils' names down the left-hand side and columns for the various skills across the top. There should also be space to give details of the practical that is being used for assessment. The skills used in this guide have convenient code names, which can be used to head the columns. A copy of the instructions accompanying the practical can be supplied if different from those in *BFL*.

This form could have the format shown in Figure 2. The marks made on the laboratory record sheet will vary from board to board, and should be identical to those required by the pupil profile.

DATE: _______ FORM: ___ PRACTICAL: ______________

Name	HMA 5	HMA 6	REC 1	REC 5	INT 1	Notes
Brian Carter Sharon Carter John Elliott David Inmann Carole Perkins Ann Sotiris						

Figure 2 Example of a laboratory record sheet.

It will be necessary to transfer the contents of this form onto the separate pupil records as soon as possible after the practical has finished. It is advisable to file these original sheets in case they need to be referred to at a later stage of the course.

It will also be necessary to store representative samples of pupils' work so that moderation of standards within the department can occur. Further details of these procedures should be obtained directly from the examination boards themselves.

The teacher must also decide which pupils are to be assessed. Pupils who consistently achieve the highest level of assessment for a particular skill need not be assessed again for that skill. Pupils who are particularly weak will need more assistance.

A few of the skills need to be observed by the teacher whilst the pupil is performing the practical. These are the 'process skills', namely handling materials and apparatus skills (HMA 1–7), and the measuring skills (AMO 1–6). The remainder of the skills can be assessed from written work produced *independently* during the lesson with the teacher present during the whole time.

It is possible to assess the whole class at the same time for the profile skills assessed from written product, and several such skills can be assessed at the same time. This is not the case for the process skills where only a few pupils can be observed in each lesson. The teacher will need to select the pupils in advance. It needs to be understood by pupils that they will not be assessed on every occasion.

The number of process skills that can be assessed on any one occasion needs to be carefully determined. Many of the investigations in *BFL* can be used to assess several process skills. Only the most relevant ones should be selected on any particular occasion.

When selecting a number of skills to be assessed together, care needs to be taken to ensure that a failure at one stage does not allow the pupil to fail altogether. For example, suppose two skills are selected for assessment: HMA 4 and AMO 10. Failure of a pupil to complete HMA 4 must not automatically prevent the pupil from making accurate observations of the outcome of the experiment. It may be that the teacher needs to have a set of assembled apparatus ready for this pupil to use.

If assessments are being made regularly, it should not be necessary to make a final assessment of each skill in a 'formal' manner as suggested by some of the examination boards. Rather, the highest performances of the pupil for each skill can be used to produce the final assessment mark. This has the advantage of assessing the pupil only in the context of 'normal' practical classes. If assessment occurs regularly throughout the course, the pupil gets used to it and is not made self-conscious by it. The only times when formal 'practical examination-style' lessons could be of value are when it would be impossible to assess the pupils in the course of a normal lesson, for example with difficult classes or when resources are limited and a circus arrangement of apparatus is needed.

The attitudes of the class when assessments are being made is important, and the teacher must take steps to ensure that the atmosphere is as relaxed and normal as possible. There will be many opportunities for the pupils to develop the confidence and competence to work at the highest level of their skills, and each pupil is encouraged to ask for help if it is needed.

It is better to ask for help and complete the task, than to ask for no help and fail to complete the task. Assessments can only be made if the pupil completes the task successfully. There are many pupils, however, who ask questions as an excuse for not thinking for themselves. In such circumstances, the pupils need to be gently discouraged from seeking help. It is clear that the whole question of giving help to pupils is one in which a delicate balance is needed. All pupils should aim to work independently of the teacher whenever possible.

Safe working practices in the laboratory

The Department of Education and Science has stated in the document *AIDS, Some Questions and Answers* (available from the publication departments of regional DES offices) that the practice of using samples of human blood and other cellular material should be discontinued in class practicals. This is because of the risk of transmitting certain diseases (primarily hepatitis and AIDS). WE THEREFORE RECOMMEND THAT THE FOLLOWING PRACTICALS SHOULD NOT BE PERFORMED: 'Looking at cheek cells' (*BFL* p. 137), 'Looking at blood' (*BFL* p. 207), 'To find out how long blood takes to clot' (*BFL* p. 211) and 'Looking at blood groups' (*BFL* p. 211).

In addition, certain examination boards have recommended that investigations involving the use of body fluids should also not be performed. This eliminates a number of investigations involving saliva, and one involving urine. It seems that this goes beyond the policy of the DES, and concerned teachers might wish to consult their local examination board for further clarification. This guide contains a number of suggestions for suitable alternative investigations.

Marking schemes for the assignments

The assignment exercises at the end of each topic fulfil three main purposes. First, they are formative in developing the various skills and understanding necessary for answering questions. Secondly, they are evaluative in monitoring the understanding a pupil has for biology and diagnosing particular areas of strength and weakness. Thirdly, they can form the basis for valuable class discussion. Such questions are identified in this guide by an asterisk (*), and additional discussion questions are suggested at the end of each marking scheme.

The assignments are intended to do more than narrowly simulate examination questions. Learning biology at GCSE-level should ideally achieve more than pupils 'performing' well within the restricted limits defined by an examination syllabus. However, the assignments should help pupils to tackle most types of GCSE examination questions.

It is hoped that the marking schemes will serve as a guide and time saver. Don't feel that because the mark allocations are in print that they have some mystical and irrevocable quality – they don't! The answers, too, may sometimes be a matter of opinion. Consider the answers and marking schemes to be a starting point, not an end-product. You should feel free to modify them to suit your own requirements.

Developing conceptual skills and understanding

The assignment questions do much more than test factual recall. The selection of questions that you set will no doubt reflect not only the content of that topic but also broader skills and understanding. Questions can be divided into the following categories:

1 Comprehension and factual recall. These are based on material in *BFL*.
2 Understanding and reasoning. The ability to apply biological concepts to everyday situations.
3 Research, both from within *BFL*, via the index, and from other sources.
4 Calculation, involving simple mathematical processes applied to biological data: using a pocket calculator, showing all working, and working to an accuracy of 1% are all to be encouraged (check INT 4).
5 Hypothesis formation (check EXP 1).
6 Understanding experimental procedures (check EXP 3).
7 Designing experiments and other investigations (check EXP 2)
8 Plotting graphs from data (check REC 4).
9 Interpreting graphs (check INT 3).
10 Interpreting data tables (check INT 2).
11 Interpreting experimental results (check EXP 8).
12 Interpreting diagrams and photographs (check AMO 8, 9).

Most questions require relatively short answers and conciseness in pupils' answers is to be strongly encouraged. The first two categories (comprehension and factual recall, understanding and reasoning) constitute the greatest proportion of the assignment questions and it is largely possible for a pupil of average ability to tackle these types of question with success by referring only to the information within that particular topic. Almost all of the end of topic assignments have questions of these categories and no reference to particular questions is made in this guide.

The remaining categories might prove of interest or value beyond the context of a particular topic. For example, suppose that several pupils in a class have difficulty in plotting the line graph in question 6 of Topic 66. It would be useful for the teacher to have a list of other examples of line graphs which could be used to develop this particular skill. In order to make this possible, a reference list is given for categories 3 to 12 above. The numbers indicate: Topic number – question(s)

Research (Category 3) (i) Elsewhere in textbook: 7–5; 25–1. (ii) From other sources: 3–1; 5–3; 18–3; 25–1; 28–7; 58–5.

Calculation (Category 2) (Check INT 4) 1–3; 7–2; 8–5; 29–5; 32–4; 34–3; 36–6; 42–1; 49–1,2,3,7; 55–5; 59–3,7; 61–4; 63–6; 77–3; 87–4; 90–1; 91–4.

Hypothesis formation (Category 5) (Check EXP 1) 9–2; 14–2; 15–3; 16–1,2; 19–3; 20–6,8; 21–5; 24–2,3; 25–2,4,5,6; 26–3; 28–3; 30–3; 31–2,3; 32–6; 33–4; 34–2; 37–6; 38–3; 41–3; 42–5; 44–1,2; 49–4; 53–6; 54–6; 56–4; 58–3; 60–3; 61–2,4; 62–4,5; 63–7; 66–3,5; 67–3,4,5; 68–5; 70–2,5; 71–2; 72–2; 74–1; 76–4,6; 78–4; 79–6; 82–4; 83–5; 85–6; 87–2; 88–7; 89–3; 95–4,5; 98–3,4; 101–3; 104–2,3.

Understanding experimental procedures (Category 6) (Check EXP 3); 4–2, 3; 23–1; 29–5; 30–3; 50–3; 51–6; 58–1; 64–4; 65–1,3,4,5; 67–6; 68–4; 70–4; 91–5; 104–1.

Designing experiments and other investigations (Category 7) (Check EXP 2) 4–4; 15–3; 23–4,5; 24–2,3; 25–5,6; 27–5; 28–3; 30–3,4; 33–4,6; 36–5; 40–4; 44–2; 46–2; 47–11,12; 48–5; 50–2; 51–5; 52–3; 54–5; 56–4,5; 57–5; 61–2; 63–5; 66–3,5; 67–2,5; 73–3; 74–4; 78–5; 79–5; 81–5; 84–5; 85–5; 93–1; 100–7; 104–2,3; 110–5.

Plotting graphs from data (Category 8) (Check REC 4) (i) Line graphs: 1–2; 22–5; 47–13; 49–8; 66–6; 91–4. (ii) Bar graph/histogram: 1–2; 23–6. (iii) Pie chart: 1–2

Interpreting graphs (Category 9) (see also category 8) (Check INT 3) Graphs from data: 31–4; 32–1,3,5; 38–7; 47–14; 48–6; 49–5; 50–6; 61–1,6; 63–6; 66–5; 72–4; 76–5; 81–7; 95–6; 96–5; 98–5; 99–3; 104–3.

Interpreting data tables (Category 10) (see also category 8) (Check INT 2) Graphs from data 32–4; 33–5; 49–2,3,7; 55–3,5; 56–4; 63–7; 66–4; 97–4.

Interpreting experimental results (Category 11) (Check EXP 8) 44–2; 55–5; 56–4; 60–5; 61–1; 63–7; 65–2; 66–5; 70–4,5; 71–6; 72–3; 75–4; 76–5; 81–7; 89–3; 92–5; 104–3.

Interpreting diagrams and photographs (Category 12) (Check AMO 8,9) 17–3; 30–2; 37–9; 40–3; 41–7 – map; 42–5; 51–6; 53–6; 65–6; 69–6; 71–6; 77–3; 82–2; 83–1; 87–4,5; 92–3,5; 93–4; 94–3; 103–3,4; 104–1; 105–4; 107–3,4; 108–5.

While much can be covered by the assignment questions, other activities can effectively supplement the development of conceptual skills and understanding. Designing games (e.g. to deter would be smokers or drug abusers, or to simulate feeding relationships), writing letters (e.g. to a confectionery firm manufacturing 'sweet cigarettes' – few in the United Kingdom, but certainly some on the continent), and designing their own biological models are some suggestions.

Biology is a deceptive subject. Superficially it seems easy, but pupils frequently discover that the subject is much more demanding than first expected. It probably requires a greater diversity of skills, both conceptual and practical, than any other subject they study. By being able to identify where weak spots occur in any of the categories, it is hoped a pupil's individual coping of the subject can be developed.

Evaluation and monitoring

Evaluation matters to a pupil because it gives a clear indication of his/her own strengths and weaknesses. To be effective it must be:

(a) **Positive.** Assignments must show what the pupil can do, rather than what he/she cannot do.
(b) **Supportive.** Assignments should encourage the successful and assist the unsuccessful. Comments matter more than ticks, crosses and marks.
(c) **Differentiated.** The most capable should be stretched. The less capable should achieve something.
(d) **Regular.** Skills and understanding need to be reinforced when there is most impact.
(e) **Diagnostic.** It should be possible for a teacher to recognise the individual strengths and weaknesses of the pupil.
(f) **Workable.** A compromise also has to be struck between a highly detailed but time-consuming 'profile' and a manageable working system within the typical teacher's hectic week.

The marks allocated to questions are largely notional. They don't add up to 'easy numbers' because this would artificially weight some parts of questions over others of similar value. The general principle is to award a mark for each point or logical step made (as far as this is workable!). A total out of 37, for example, can easily be converted to a mark out of 10 by using a pocket calculator. If marks are going to be allocated it is advisable to put the mark in the margin next to each question or part of a question. If the pupil has attained a lower mark than that allocated, then indicating the maximum mark is constructive in showing that a question was tackled reasonably well, but not completely. For example, the mark 3 (5) would tell a pupil that he/she has made some headway but the ideal answer should have gone a little further.

Scaling might be necessary if groups are of high or low ability. The most able pupils should not earn full marks too easily and lower ability pupils do need some positive reinforcement. Readjusting the mark allocation might prove necessary at times. The individual teacher needs to use discretion on such occasions. The mark allocations in this guide do seem to work on the many occasions when the marking schemes have been tried out.

As mentioned before, the marking schemes are a starting point, not an end-product. They cannot include all of the possible correct answers that pupils may produce. Sometimes a wrong answer has value (category 5 Hypothesis formation) because of the thought processes behind it, and this should be rewarded. A problem often found hard to resolve is when an assignment question states 'give reasons', or 'give examples'. Giving credit for too few reasons or examples means that the more able are not stretched. But if too many are required, they become unattainable. In cases such as this it is best to use your own discretion in deciding what the reasonable number is for any able pupil to deliver. Sometimes it is one, at other times two, three or more! Use your own judgement as to what is reasonable in the light of your own pupils' abilities, mark accordingly and award additional (bonus) marks for those who deliver more than you expected. Hopefully, the notional mark allocation with the possibility of bonus marks creates a flexible system which can be freely adapted to various needs.

Note on mark allocations

It is virtually impossible to devise a mark allocation system which will work perfectly in every assignment, simply because of the diversity of styles of question. However, a general system has been devised which works as follows:

(i) Each point made is allocated a mark in brackets immediately next to it, i.e. (*1*).

(ii) The total mark for a question which has not been broken up into sections either in the textbook or in the marking scheme is represented by a mark in brackets with the word marks after it, ranged to the right, e.g. (*6 marks*)

(iii) Where a question has been broken down into sections, either in response to the structure of the question in the textbook ((a), (b), (c), etc.), or in an implied structure within a paragraph question (shown in the marking scheme as (i), (ii), (iii), etc.), or where the pupil is expected to produce an elaborate answer which needs a lot of structure in the marking scheme to process it, then the total for each section is represented by a mark in brackets at the end of each section, e.g. (*4 marks*).

(iv) The total mark for a structured question which can only be marked in sections is represented as a question total, e.g. (*Total 14 marks*)

(v) Since marks are to an extent notional, where bonus marks are clearly awarded (i.e. (+*1*)) they are in no way reflected in the question total.

Vehicles for discussion

There is an element of discussion in many assignment questions, and going through the assignment questions done by a class is a worthwhile exercise. Those particularly suited for additional discussion have been labelled with an asterisk (*).

2–8; 5–2; 6–5; 7–4; 8–1,6; 9–4; 10–2; 13–5,6: 16–2,3; 17–1,3; 18–1,2; 20–3,5; 22–2,3,4; 27-5; 28–4,7,8; 30–3; 31–4; 32–1,2,3; 34–2,4; 35–1; 37–5; 41–3; 45–4; 47–10,11,13; 50–2,5,6; 54–5; 56–2,4; 58–1; 61–3; 63–1,4,5; 64–4,5; 65–2,5; 66–4,6; 70–5; 76–6;78–5;86–5;91–4;92–5;95–5;98–4;100–7;101–3,4;110–5.

In addition, discussion questions related to each topic are included with the marking schemes. These explore ethical, social, technological, economic, aesthetic and purely imaginative dimensions within each topic. They are designed to prompt, provoke, stretch the minds and increase the awareness of pupils in the true spirit of *Biology for Life* (in *both* senses!!). Notes of guidance are given but many discussion questions have no answers – this is deliberate and the authors make no apology.

Topic 1
Studying Living Things

This topic outlines many of the skills that the pupil will need to acquire during this course. They form the basis of many of the skills used in the profiles in this guide, particularly the REC and INT skills. It is probably best to refer to many of the ideas in this topic as and when they are required, since they will mean very little to the pupil at the start of the course. The paragraphs with immediate relevance are those on microscopy.

Investigation 1

Learning to use the microscope

Requirements
Light microscope with low and high power objective lenses; prepared slide of a specimen (e.g. TS leaf); light source.

Practical skills
HMA 1, HMA 5

General Comments
This is a fundamental exercise in biology, in which pupils should show competence. It is essential that they learn not to allow the high power objective lens to touch the microscope slide, and never to put the microscope away with the high power objective lens in position. Microscope slides used with the high power lens must be covered with a coverslip.

Once clear instructions have been given, HMA 1 can be assessed. This practical exercise provides the opportunity to develop the skills for HMA 5. A summary of the basic techniques used in this investigation is desirable at the end of the lesson. Pupils should be able to carry a microscope safely to the work surface, to adjust it so that a prepared slide can be viewed using the lower power objective lens, and to readjust it to view under high power.

This exercise could be combined with Topic 42, Investigation 1 (making slides of cheek cells).

Investigation 2

The magnifying power of the microscope

Requirements
Light microscope with low and high power objective lenses; microscope slide; coverslip; plastic ruler with millimetre scale.

Practical skills
AMO 2, REC 1, INT 4.

General Comments
This simple exercise introduces the concept of scale, and the relationship between µm and mm. It enables pupils to develop a feel for scale factors, which is a part of REC 1. Pupils should be able to calculate the magnification of the microscope and understand its significance – a simple application of INT 4. The use of the ruler could introduce the concept of measuring length (AMO 2).

Investigation 3

Seeing is believing

Requirements
Light microscope with low power objective lens; microscope slide; coverslip; mounted needle; dropping pipette; a supply of newsprint; plastic ruler with millimetre scale.

Practical skills
HMA 5, HMA 6, AMO 2, INT 4.

General Comments
The exercise develops the concept of a scale factor on a drawing, and the skills needed to make microscope slides (HMA 6), but not staining procedures. Pupils should measure the width of the letter before it is magnified (AMO 2). They will be surprised at the fuzzy edges of the enlarged familiar letter of newsprint.

Following this exercise it is possible to allow the pupils to make their own slides (Topic 42, Investigation 1) or to allow them to make a proper scale drawing of a prepared slide, following the criteria of REC 1.

Assignments

1 **Note:** answers should include those branches of biology that are asterisked.

This question could form the basis for a class discussion.

(i) Farmer: nutrition*, heredity, zoology, botany, ecology.
At least two – 1 mark each (2)

(ii) Gardener: botany*, ecology.
At least one (1)

(iii) Nurse: anatomy*, physiology*, nutrition.
At least two – 1 mark each (2)

(iv) Family doctor: anatomy*, physiology*, nutrition, heredity.
At least two – 1 mark each (2)

(v) Game warden: zoology*, ecology*, nutrition.
At least two – 1 mark each (2)

(vi) Dog breeder: heredity*, nutrition, zoology.
At least two – 1 mark each (2)

(vii) PE teacher: anatomy*, physiology*, nutrition.
At least two – 1 mark each (2)

(viii) Forester: botany*, ecology*.
Both – 1 mark each (2)

(ix) Surgeon: anatomy*, physiology*.
Both – 1 mark each (2)

(x) Zoo keeper: zoology*, nutrition, ecology.
At least two – 1 mark each (2)

(Total 20 marks)

2 Marking a line graph; look for:
(i) correctly drawn and labelled axes; (*2*)
(ii) accurate plotting; (*2*)
(iii) curve or line (as appropriate); (*2*)
(iv) presentation. (*2*)
(8 marks)

Marking a bar graph; look for:
(i) correctly chosen and labelled axes; (*2*)
(ii) bars correctly and accurately drawn; (*2*)
(iii) *x*-axis indices in the appropriate positions beneath bars; (*1*)
y-axis indices on the left of the horizontal lines; (*1*)
(iv) presentation. (*2*)
(*8 marks*)

Marking a pie chart; look for:
(i) circular shape; (*1*)
(ii) accurate division into segments; (*3*)
(iii) segments appropriately labelled; (*2*)
(iv) presentation. (*2*)
(*8 marks*)

Correct choice of line graph/bar graph/pie chart (*2*)
(*Total 10 marks*)

3 (a) 500 micrometres (μm) (*2*)
(b) 500 000 micrometres (μm) (*2*)
(*4 marks*)

—*Discussion*

1 Of course biological experiments always work. They just don't give the results we expect.
Note: an experiment is a means of testing hypothesis. Results can be negative as well as positive. Complex living systems are usually influenced by many variables, some of which are beyond our control.

2 What skills should the 'ideal biologist' have?
Note: consider activities that pupils on a GCSE course are likely to be involved in. Some experience is likely from past courses. Skills vary enormously depending on the branch of biology.

Topic 2
The Characteristics of Living Things

—*Investigation 1*

Detecting movement inside a plant

Requirements
Light microscope with low and high power objective lenses; microscope slide; coverslip; dropping pipette; *Elodea*; scissors.

Practical skills
HMA 5, AMO 10, REC 1, EXP.

General Comments
This can be an unpredictable practical as the movement of chloroplasts within the leaf can usually be detected only by careful observation. It occurs most rapidly if the cells are warm. It is important to use fresh healthy pieces of *Elodea*, or, better still, its tropical relative *Hydrilla*, which is available from aquarium shops. Alternative materials are the staminal hairs of the flowers of *Tradescantia*.

The use of the compound microscope can be assessed (HMA 5) and the preparation of simple microscope slides reviewed, although the assessment of this skill (HMA 6) should be delayed until staining techniques are familiar. The careful observation of movement of chloroplasts can be reported orally or in writing (AMO 10). Thorough accounts should include some indication of the direction of movement, its relative rate (within a cell or between cells), whether it is permanent or eventually slows down and stops, and if so the final orientation of the chloroplasts.

Pupils could be encouraged to keep a slide of *Elodea* in the dark for ten minutes and then view it under a microscope with sub-stage lighting. They should be asked whether this treatment has any effect on the rate and direction of movement compared with a specimen that has not been pretreated, and whether these differences are due to temperature changes or to light intensity changes. This allows open-ended activities to begin, and the range of EXP skills to be developed. One way into this is to ask the pupils to think about a possible cause for this orientation of chloroplasts. A possible hypothesis is that it enables the chloroplasts to optimise their response to the available light. Under intense light, the chloroplasts may orientate themselves with the long axes parallel to the light source, which could be a way of *reducing* their surface area of exposure to it. Pupils might consider whether dimmer lights cause a different effect and whether destarched *Elodea* behaves differently. An alternative hypothesis to consider is that it provides a mechanism for distributing the products of photosynthesis around the cell.

Astute observers may occasionally see chloroplasts apparently move from cell to cell. This is an optical trick, caused by the cells being deeper than the optical focal depth of the microscope. So that not all of the cell is in focus. A chloroplast moving away from the eye and passing beyond the point of focus may occasionally be replaced by a chloroplast in an adjacent cell moving towards the eye. If the disappearance of the one chloroplast coincides with the emergence of the second, then a chloroplast appears to cross from cell to cell. This is an opportunity to discuss the problem of optical illusions and artefacts when studying the structure and function of cells.

—*Investigation 2*

Getting a plant to respond to touch

Requirements
A healthy *Mimosa pudica* plant which has been well watered; mounted needle; dropping pipette; water.

Practical skills
AMO 10, REC 1, EXP.

General Comments
This practical provides a fascinating demonstration of movement in plants. *Mimosa pudica* responds quickly to touch. A response brought about by rapid changes in turgor in the cells at the base of the petiole. It is reversed after a few minutes. Accurate observations can be assessed (AMO 10), either with diagrams (REC 1) or without them. The relationship of the recovery time to the strength of the initial stimulus is a useful topic for extended investigation, and for assessing EXP skills. Showing a time-lapse film, if available, of plants making tropic or nastic movements would reinforce this point.

Investigation 3

Recognising the characteristics of life in organisms

Requirements

Living or preserved organisms, photographs or videotape sequences of a number of organisms, for example: gerbil, tortoise, horse, human, rosebush, fir tree, earthworm, locust, toad, mouse, snail, mould, lichen, or fresh yeast; a clam.

Practical skills

AMO 8, AMO 10.

General Comments

The aim of this practical is to allow pupils to interpret the structures of living things in terms of their functions, whilst recognising the limitations of what they are doing.

Photographs and preserved materials do not reveal any of the *characteristics* of living things: they show *structures* (e.g. gills, legs, etc.) which may be adaptations for staying alive, although we could not prove this without studying *living* specimens. Some characteristics are obvious just by looking at specimens (e.g. movement in locusts); others are much less so and can only be investigated through a combination of experiments and dissection.

Accurate descriptions of the characteristics of some of these organisms could be assessed (AMO 10).

Step 3 provides the first opportunity to compare similarities and differences in gross structure, and introduces AMO 8. Later investigations (e.g. in Topics 6–18) will provide opportunities to assess this skill further, as well as that concerned with detailed similarities and differences (AMO 9).

Assignments

1 Movement, detecting stimuli, growth, breathing/respiration, reproduction, feeding (!), excretion.
Any three (*3 marks*)

2 (a) Sensitivity (*1*)
(b) Movement, sensitivity (*1 each*)
(c) Movement, sensitivity (*1 each*)
(d) Reproduction (*1*)
(e) Sensitivity or growth (*1*)
(f) Respiration (*1*)
(g) Sensitivity (*1*), growth (*1*).
(*10 marks*)

3 Respiration (*1*), sexual reproduction (*1*), growth (*1*).
(*3 marks*)

4 e.g. A detectable (*1*) change (*1*) in an organism's surroundings (*1*).
(*3 marks*)
e.g. potted plant name: geranium. (*1*)
e.g. Stimuli: light, gravity, water. *Any two* (*2 marks*)
(*Total 6 marks*)

5 No. Reasons (e.g.):
(i) No increase in mass (*1*)
(ii) No materials have been assimilated (*1*)
(iii) Increase in volume only temporary. (*1*).
Any two (*2 marks*)

6 Dead — was once living (*1*)
Non-living — was never alive (*1*).
(*2 marks*)

Is death a characteristic?: Either yes or no — depends on the reason given (e.g.):
Yes: it applies to all living things/part of life cycles of all living things.
No: once dead all other characteristics don't apply/some creatures e.g. amoeba, don't clearly die.
Note: the plausibility of the answer is the key criterion, rather than being absolutely right biologically.
'Yes'/'no' (*1*); reason (*1*). (*2 marks*)
(*Total 4 marks*)

7 Similar:
releases energy ('respires'); (*1*)
produces waste ('excretes'); (*1*)
consumes petrol ('feeds'); (*1*)
moves. (*1*)
Different:
doesn't grow; (*1*)
doesn't reproduce; (*1*)
isn't sensitive (as a general rule!). (*1*)
(*7 marks*)

8*(a) (a) Feeding: animals cannot synthesise food, so need to feed on ready-made organic food. (*1*)
(b) Feeding structures: since plants have no need to feed, feeding structures (e.g. mouth, gut) are unnecessary). (*1*)
(c) Chlorophyll: since animals cannot photosynthesise, chlorophyll is unnecessary. (*1*)
(d) Leaves: since animals cannot photosynthesise they do not possess leaves. (*1*)
(e) Roots: since animals move, they do not have roots. (*1*)
(f) Moves around: animals need to move around to feed; plants can photosynthesise, which does not require moving around. (*1*)
(g) Nerves and muscles: nerves are necessary for speedy co-ordination, muscles for movement; only essential if an organism needs to move around. (*1*)
(h) Receptors: only animals need to respond quickly. (*1*)
(*8 marks*)

Note: in each case the wording may differ substantially.

(b) Exceptions (all e.g.s)
(a) Feeding: animal – green hydra 'photosynthesises' (mutualism with photosynthetic protists in body wall).
Note: the term 'symbiosis' is gradually being replaced by the term 'mutualism'.
Plant – Venus fly trap, sundew, pitcher plant.
(b) Feeding structures: animal – tapeworm;
plant – Venus fly trap, sundew, pitcher plant.
(c) Chlorophyll: animal – green hydra (see above);
plant – dodder, broomrape (parasitic plants).
(d) Leaves: animal – none (although there are 'leaf' insects!);
plant – *Spirogyra*, seaweeds.
(f) Moves around: animal – barnacle, marine mussel (*Mytilus*).
Note: sessile animals almost always have a motile larval form. It might be worth discussing why this is the case.
Plant – *Euglena* is counted as a plant.

(g) Nerves and muscles: animal – none, unless *Amoeba* is counted as an animal; plant – none.
(h) Receptors: animal – tapeworm, sponge; plant – *Euglena* has 'eye spot'.

Note: the exceptions are few if the five-kingdom system is adopted. In the five-kingdom system *Amoeba* and *Euglena* are *not* included in the animal and plant kingdoms, but are placed in a separate kingdom, the Protists.

One mark each (*8 marks*)

(c) No – (*1*)
Exceptions are a minority of cases, so the table is generally true. (*1*)
(*2 marks*)

(*Total 18 marks*)

—Discussion

1 Before this century it was not unusual for live persons to be diagnosed as dead and buried alive. This gave rise to all sorts of folk tales about the dead rising from the grave, ghouls, vampires and the like. How could doctors have made such horrifically wrong diagnoses?
Note: what signs would the pupil look for? What advances have there been in a doctor's ability to distinguish life from death? Modern diagnosis ultimately considers brain stem inactivity determined electrically as the base line for death. It is therefore possible to keep a 'corpse' alive.

2 Is there life elsewhere in the universe? If so would we always be capable of telling if an alien organism was alive?
Note: must life be carbon based? It certainly looks as though life as we know it is very likely to be. The vast number of stars and some current evidence that we are not the only planetary system suggest life elsewhere to be almost inevitable. Whether it would be intelligent is another matter.

Topic 3
Classifying, Naming and Identifying

—Investigation

Making a key for identifying organisms

Requirements
Appropriate specimens (e.g. leaves of sycamore, plane, oak, elm, willow, beech, ash, horse chestnut).

Practical skills
AMO 7.

General Comments
Keys can be made from a collection of leaves; a simple one is given below:

1	Leaf simple (i.e. not divided into separate leaflets	go to 2
	Leaf divided into separate leaflets	go to 7
2	Leaf with three large lobes	go to 3
	Leaf not lobed or with many small lobes	go to 4
3	Leaf toothed all around its margin	Sycamore
	Leaf with few teeth, mainly near leaf stalk	Plane
4	Leaf with teeth or small lobes	go to 5
	Leaf without teeth or lobes	go to 6
5	Leaf with small, irregular lobes, giving wavy margin	Oak
	Leaf toothed along margin	Elm
6	Leaf spear-shaped, about four times as long as broad	Willow
	Leaf oval, about twice as long as broad	Beech
7	Leaf divided into leaflets in opposite pairs	Ash
	Leaf divided into leaflets radiating from leaf stalk	Horse chestnut

This topic can be revised when the classification of the animal kingdom has been completed in Topic 5; the table in this topic is suitable for producing a key to the invertebrates. Worksheet 1 in this guide enables pupils to use a prepared key to identify a wide range of tree leaves.

Pupils usually find a spider key easier to make and use because the statements are arranged in a sequence down the page and are connected by arrows. A spider key can be transformed into a numbered key by giving each group a number and labelling the two contrasting statements *a* and *b*. The key can be reworded into a linear sequence by using the numbers of each group.

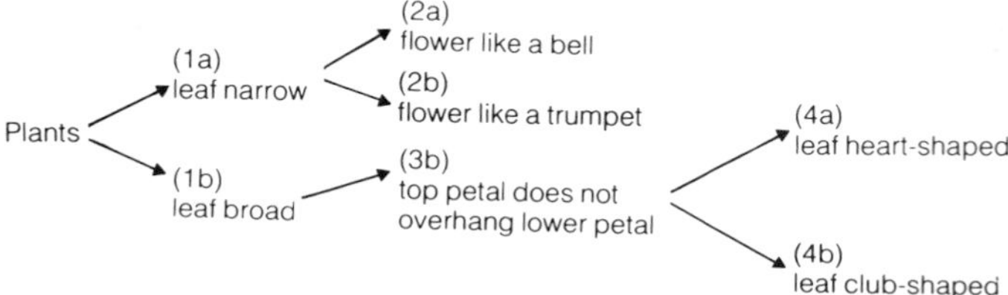

A numbered key is easier to use than a spider key if the number of identifying group is large. A spider key involving more than ten different steps would need to be written on a very wide piece of paper!

AMO 7 can assess the ability to use a numbered dichotomous key. Designing keys is a skill that many pupils find difficult. For some classes it might be better to concentrate on using learning to use prepared keys properly.

—Assignments

1 Any five organisms (animals, plants or a mixture of both), e.g.: *Lumbricus terrestris* (common earthworm), *Asterias rubens* (common starfish), *Vulpes vulpes* (red fox), *Fagus sylvatica* (beech), *Bellis perennis* (daisy).
Note: Generic (first) name starts with capital letter, specific (second) name starts lower case.
1 mark each (*5 marks*)

2 (a) Flowers are much more noticeably different than leaves (*1*).
(b) Many possible answers, e.g. lesser celandine has eight petals, primrose has five/lesser celandine has pointed petals, primrose has rounded (bilobed) petals/centre of flower exposed in lesser celandine, receded in primrose (*1*). 2 marks if a comparison occurs (*2*). (*3 marks*)

(*Total 4 marks*)

3 There are many possible keys (e.g.):

1 Body broad ________ go to 2
Body narrow ________ go to 5

2 Antennae feathered ________ go to 3
Antennae straight ________ go to 4

3 Antennae short ________ shortfeather shield-beetle
Antennae long ________ longfeather shield-beetle

4 Body spotted ________ spotted shield-beetle
Body striped ________ jack o'stripey

5 Sting at rear ________ go to 6
No sting ________ go to 7

6 Short sting ________ lesser stingpill
Long sting ________ greater stingpill

7 Claspers at rear ________ clasper-ended pillbug
No claspers ________ common pillbug

Marking the key: 4 criteria, each worth up to 3 marks:
Criteria:
(i) single identifiable feature used;
(ii) always a two-way separation;
(iii) go to instructions logical and clear;
(iv) insects biologically or creatively named.

Marks per criterion:
(a) always applicable (*3*)
(b) largely applicable (*2*)
(c) partially applicable (*1*)
(d) not apparent in pupil's key (*0*)

(*Total 12 marks*)

—Disscussion—

1 Proper names are much less misleading than common names but biologists can still disagree what the proper name of a newly discovered organism ought to be. When do you think this happens?
Note: recognising a species is not easy. Features such as structural homology (Topic 25, Adaptation and survival'; Topic 111, 'How do new kinds of organisms arise?') and analogy (e.g. wings of bird, bat and pterosaur) must be considered very closely. Biochemical homology is probably the most reliable modern indicator (e.g. similarities between particular proteins).

2 Can identification keys have uses outside biology?
Note: computer data processing, police files and supermarket warehouses all use the same process of identification.

Topic 4 Collecting Living Things

—Investigation—

Collecting and examining living things

Requirements

Appropriate sampling apparatus (from Figure 3 in *BFL*); identification keys; dishes, forceps and preserving fluid (e.g. 50% ethanol or 1% formalin).

Suitable published identification keys include:
Belcher, H. and Swale, E. (1976). *A beginners' guide to freshwater algae.* Institute of Terrestrial Ecology.
Elliot, J.M. and Mann, K.H. (1979). *A key to British freshwater leeches.* Freshwater Biological Association. Scientific publication 40
Leadley Brown, A. (1970) *A key to pond organisms.* Nuffield Advanced Science.Biological Sience. Penguin.
Darlington, A. and Smyth, J.C. (1970). *Keys to small organisms in soil, litter and water troughs.* Nuffield Foundation. Longmans/Penguin.

Practical skills

AMO 7, REC 1, EXP.

General Comments

It is not necessary to go to great lengths to collect living material from the countryside for this exercise. A bucket of pond water should provide sufficient organisms. Small pitfall traps can provide soil invertebrates for investigation. The use of the school grounds for this exercise is probably more suitable than a widespread assault on a natural habitat. If pitfall traps are emptied at different times of the day, it is possible to investigate the diurnal activity of the various invertebrates that fall in. Such activities are more open ended and could be used to develop various EXP skills.Considerable help will be needed in identifying the various organisms found.

The removal of organisms from their natural habitat for school study raises important conservation issues that are avoided with the use of another technique. A plastic tank containing mineral salts (e.g. Knop's culture solution) left outside for 10 weeks will provide abundant organisms for study. This could be used in conjunction with Topic 20.

The activity could also be done in conjunction with investigation 3 of Topic 5. Alternatively, some of the organisms could be preserved in 50% alcohol or 1% formalin and used again in that topic.

—Assignments—

1 e.g. (i) Large enough to catch fish; (ii) mesh fine enough to prevent fish escaping; (iii) net strong enough to hold fish.
Any two – 1 mark each

(*2 marks*)

2 (a) e.g. (i) Twist net with each sweep; (ii) ground clear of obstructions; (iii) well clear of fellow students!
Any one (*1*)
(b) e.g. (i) Free hand well away from penknife; (ii) make sure knife does not damage animal.(*1*)
Any one (*1*)
(c) e.g. Don't squeeze forceps too hard.(*1*)
(d) e.g. (i) The insect is small enough; (ii) there is a gauze on the sucking tube.
Any one (*1*)
(e) e.g. (i) Trap covered to shelter from rain; (ii) well away from possible vandalism/interference.
Any one (*1*)

(*Total 5 marks*)

3 (i) Collecting water animals: examples could include jam jar on string, fishing line, lobster pot, sieve net.
Any example – 1 mark

e.g. Jam jar on a string (e.g. for catching minnows):
tie string round neck of jam jar; (*1*)
put bait (e.g. bread) inside; (*1*)
allow to stand in water; (*1*)
until minnows enter; (*1*)
and pull string.(*1*)
(*5 marks*)

(ii) Collecting land insects: examples could include sticky tape, a sheet smeared with petroleum jelly or coloured water-filled trays for trapping winged insects.
Any example – 1 mark
e.g. sticky tape:
lay down a piece/strip of paper cloth; (*1*)
smeared with sticky substance; (*1*)
e.g. grease, gum; (*1*)
insects stumble across trap; (*1*)
and get caught by being stuck. (*1*)
(*5 marks*)

(*Total 12 marks*)

Note: differences between various trap designs suggest some discretion is needed here.

4 e.g. Small box-like trap; (*1*)
with food at one end; (*1*)
and open 'triggered' door at other; (*1*)
mammal sets off trigger in reaching bait; (*1*)
and door shuts behind it. (*1*)

(*5 marks*)

Note: my example is obviously a Longworth trap. Reward ingenious alternatives accordingly!

Discussion

1 When is it morally right and when is it morally wrong to collect living things?
Note: is it ever right to kill an animal? Is it ever right to keep it captive? Zoos conserve species endangered in their natural habitats. Discuss protected species. Consider the damage done to the environment by collecting.

2 What economic value might be in collecting living things?
Note: pet and skin trades can be discussed as the 'dark side' of collecting. Tropical plants as sources of medicines (e.g. cinchona bark – quinine – malaria) and specimens for biological knowledge are possibly the 'lighter side'. However, even biologists have threatened species (e.g. the common frog!) by over-collecting.

Topic 5 Who's Who in the World of Living Things

These three activities provide a major opportunity to teach and assess the observation skills AMO 7–9.

Investigation 1

Putting some familiar animals and plants into groups

Requirements

A variety of organisms, or photographs of organisms, as illustrated in *BFL* Topic 5; copies of *BFL* for each pupil or group.

Practical skills

AMO 7.

General Comments

This activity is designed to allow pupils to become familiar with the text and diagrams in Topic 5 of *BFL*. It can lead on to Investigation 2. This provides an alternative way of measuring AMO 7 for those who cannot use keys. Credit should be given only for precise matching, for example being able to identify a woodlouse as a crustacean or distinguishing between a scorpion and a lobster.

Investigation 2

Putting some unfamiliar animals and plants into groups

Requirements

Museum specimens, photographs, and/or video extracts of a range of living organisms, for example *Stylonichia*, fir twig, daffodil, limpet, *Cyclops,* prawn, pycnogonid, housefly, salamander (video tapes of the BBC's 'Life on Earth' and 'Living Planet' are obtainable from BBC Education and Training, BBC Enterprises, Woodlands, 80 Wood Lane W12 0TT); hand lenses and microscopes, where appropriate.

Practical skills

AMO 7, AMO 8, AMO 9.

General Comments

AMO 8 and AMO 9 assess the ability of a pupil to be able to report on the similarities and/or differences between any two selected organisms. It is important that pupils are not hampered in their attempts at this exercise by lack of appropriate vocabulary. AMO 9 refers to fine detailed differences between specimens, such as can only be seen with a hand lens or a microscope. Sufficient time should be devoted to this activity if it is being assessed.

AMO 7 assesses the ability to match a specimen with others of the same major group. Teachers must decide whether to allow pupils access to the tables in Topic 5 of *BFL*. Specimens could be coded and arranged around the room in a circus. Pupils moving around the room could attempt to classify the organisms in their correct group, *explaining why* (on paper or orally) they have made that decision. This exercise could lead naturally to Assignments 1 and 2 for homework.

Investigation 3

Collecting and naming organisms

Requirements

Appropriate collecting apparatus as used in Topic 4, Investigation 1 of *BFL*; etherising bottle; cotton wool; forceps; binocular and monocular microscopes; hand lenses. The etherisers should be set up before the lesson begins by the teacher or technician. The room should be adequately ventilated, because ether fumes are dangerous when inhaled in a confined space.

Practical skills

AMO 7.

General Comments

This follows on from Investigation 1 of the previous topic, where a number of organisms were collected. It might be appropriate to delay the teaching of that topic until this point has been reached. Pupils need to realise that sampling of rare organisms is not permitted. AMO 7 can be assessed by matching specimens to their correct group.

Assignments

1 In each case the organism is listed first; the group follows after the dash:
moss – mosses and liverworts/bryophytes; (*1*)
jellyfish – coelenterates; (*1*)
turtle – reptiles; (*1*)
tapeworm – flatworms/platyhelminthes; (*1*)
whale – mammals; (*1*)
mushroom – fungus kingdom; (*1*)
mould – fungus kingdom; (*1*)
tube worm – ringed worms/annelids; (*1*)
seaweed – algea; (*1*)
newt – amphibians. (*1*)
(*10 marks*)

2 (a) e.g. Arthropod has exoskeleton (*1*); vertebrate has internal skeleton (*1*).
(b) e.g. Insect has six legs (*1*); arachnid has eight (*1*).
(c) e.g. Amphibian has moist skin (*1*); reptile has dry skin (*1*).
(d) e.g. Alga contains chlorophyll (*1*); fungus does not (*1*) (i.e. alga is green, fungus is not).
(e) e.g. Conifer's reproductive structures are cones (*1*); flowering plant's are flowers (*1*).
Note: comparison must be made
(*10 marks*)

3 (i) Algae: e.g.
giant kelp; (*1*)
up to 62 metres tall. (*1*)
(ii) Ferns: e.g.
tree ferns; (*1*)
up to 25 metres tall (usually 15 metres). (*1*)
(iii) Conifers: e.g.
giant redwood; (*1*)
over 112 metres tall. (*1*)
(iv) Flowering plants: e.g.
giant eucalyptus; (*1*)
at least 80 metres tall. (*1*)
(*8 marks*)

4 (a) Jellyfish. (*1*)
(b) e.g. Lizard (reptile). (*1*)
(c) e.g. Kangaroo (marsupial). (*1*)
(d) Starfish. (*1*)
(e) e.g. Grasshopper (insect). (*1*)
(f) Frog (amphibian). (*1*)
(g) e.g. Octopus (cephalopod mollusc). (*1*)
(h) e.g. Butterfly. (*1*)
(i) e.g. Spider (arachnid). (*1*)
(j) e.g. Minnow (fish). (*1*)
(*10 marks*)

Note:
(i) The group in brackets after some named animals is a guide to alternative answers.
(ii) In (h) metamorphosis is displayed by many different animals in many phyla. The butterfly is just one of many possible examples.

5 (a) e.g. Foxglove (angiosperm). (*1*)
(b) e.g. Bracken (fern). (*1*)
(c) e.g. *Euglena* (protist). (*1*)
(d) e.g. *Streptococcus* (bacteria), but also check other groups. (*1*)
(e) e.g. mushroom (fungus)/almost any animals (only the most perverse pupil would put 'hydra'!). (*1*)
(*5 marks*)

6 Possessed only by insects:
(c) six legs; (*1*)
(e) two pairs of wings. (*1*)
Possessed by arthropods in general:
(a) hard cuticle; (*1*)
(b) joints; (*1*)
(c) feelers. (*1*)
(*5 marks*)

7 Missing are:
(i) eyes; (*1*)
(ii) wings. (*1*)
Reasons:
(i) soil is dark so eyes unnecessary; (*1*)
(ii) soil surroundings are too confined for wings. (*1*)
(*4 marks*)

Discussion

1 The simplest life forms are the most successful. Do you agree?
Note: the answer depends on whether one defines 'success' in terms of producing offspring and surviving, or of the organism's position in the 'evolutionary tree'.

2 Why should living things come in so many shapes and sizes?
Note: refer to Topic 25 'Adaptation and Survival', Topic 110, 'Variation' and Topic 111 'How do new kinds of organisms arise?'.

Topic 6
Amoeba *and other Protists*

Investigation 1

Looking at *Amoeba*

Requirements

Light microscope with low and high power objective lenses; microscope slide; coverslip; mounted needle; dropping pipette; prepared slide of *Amoeba* and living material; drawing paper.

General Comments

Amoeba can be obtained from ponds and ditches or from biological suppliers. If abundant supplies are available, the pupils can try to sample them for themselves. If time or specimens are scarce, then the teacher can sample them beforehand, storing them in individual pipettes with a small volume of water or placing them directly onto the cavity slides. A video tape called 'Biovideo', showing locomotion in protists is available from the BBC (see p. 14 of this guide).

Investigation 2

Looking at *Euglena* and other protists

Requirements

As above, a sample of protists; a mineral tank (see p. 13 of this guide) ought to provide a variety of protists, as will pond or ditch water during the spring and summer; the video tape mentioned in Topic 5, Investigation 2 features a range of protists, and would make a useful back-up; coverslip; microscope slide; dropping pipette.

Practical skills

AMO 9, AMO 10, REC 1.

General Comments

These organisms can move quite rapidly, so care will be needed if valuable observations are to be made. *Amoeba* and *Euglena* are both unicellular protists, with a nucleus and other cytoplasmic inclusions. *Euglena* is photosynthetic and contains chloroplasts, whilst *Amoeba* and *Paramecium* extract small particles of food from the water. All the organisms are sensitive to changes in their environment: *Euglena* is sensitive to changes in light intensity (see Topic 24, Investigation 3), whilst *Amoeba* and *Paramecium* will respond to changes in water temperature and chemical substances in the water.

All three organisms have contractile vacuoles, and different methods of locomotion – *Amoeba* using pseudopodia, *Euglena* using a single flagellum, and *Paramecium* using numerous cilia (see Topic 89 for movement in *Amoeba*).

These above features could be used as a basis of a detailed comparison exercise (AMO 9). Detailed descriptions of these organisms can be used to assess AMO 10, and appropriate diagrams can be assessed as REC 1.

Assignments

1 Contractile vacuole. (*1*)
Pseudopod. (*1*)
Food vacuole. (*1*)
Ectoplasm and endoplasm (as opposed to 'simply cytoplasm'. (*1*)

(*4 marks*)

2 Contractile vacuole – water. (*1*)
Pseudopod – movement. (*1*)
Food vacuole – digestion. (*1*)
Endoplasm – runny. (*1*)
Splitting – reproduction. (*1*)

(*5 marks*)

3 (a) Guide *Euglena* towards light. (*1*)
(b) Make up *Amoeba*'s cytoplasm. (*1*)
(c) Nutrition: food vacuole – *Amoeba;* chloroplast – *Euglena.* (*1*)
(d) Outer boundary: cell membrane – *Amoeba;* pellicle – *Euglena.* (*1*)

(*Total 4 marks*)

4 (a) Cell membrane (gas exchange). (*1*)
(b) Cell membrane. (*1*)
(c) Cell membrane (excretion)/contractile vacuole (osmoregulation) (either/or). (*1*)
(d) Pseudopod. (*1*)
(e) Food vacuole. (*1*)

(*5 marks*)

5 *e.g.
(i) *Amoeba*: single cell; (*1*)
human: many cells. (*1*)
(ii) *Amoeba*: no nervous system; (*1*)
human: advanced nervous system. (*1*)
(iii) *Amoeba*: no clear permanent structure; (*1*)
human: all features permanent and highly organised. (*1*)
(iv) *Amoeba*: reproduces by splitting in two; (*1*)
human: complex process of sexual reproduction. (*1*)
(v) *Amoeba*: excretes by simple diffusion; (*1*)
human: excretes in a complex way (by filtering blood and reabsorbing useful substances). (*1*)

(*10 marks*)

6 Plant like: e.g. chloroplasts (*1*), photosynthesis (*1*).
Animal-like: e.g. movement (*1*), very sensitive (*1*) (light-sensitive swelling and pigment spot).

(*4 marks*)

Discussion

1 Does *Amoeba* live forever?
Note: How can we reconcile life and death with reproduction by binary fission? Does one 'parent' split off many daughters before it itself ages and dies? Do strains lose vitality over time? How could these hypotheses be tested?

2 What advantages are there in protists being so small?
Note: protists have a wide choice of niches that are unavailable to larger organisms. On the other hand there are obviously disadvantages in being small, especially for many predators.

Topic 7 Bacteria

Investigation

Culturing bacteria

Requirements

A pure culture of *Escherichia coli* or *Bacillus subtilis* obtainable from biological suppliers; two petri dishes with lids containing sterile agar; wire loop; bunsen burner; sellotape; scissors; access to an incubator at 37°C.

Practical skills

HMA 1, HMA 3, HMA 7, EXP 5.

General Comments

It is important to exphasise the safety aspects of this practical. The plate containing the bacterial culture should be opened for as short a time as possible. Correct aseptic techniques need to be demonstrated and could then be assessed as HMA 3 and 7. It is important that the culture of bacteria given to the pupil should contain only harmless bacteria. If there is any doubt over this the culture should not be used. Additional precautions could be taken to incubate all the plates at a temperature less than 37°C to reduce the chances of culturing any bacteria harmful to humans, and to insist that the plates prepared by the pupils are sealed and not opened when inspected.

Pupils could be asked to design controls for this experiment (developing skills to be assessed as EXP 5), such as keeping an agar plate from the same batch unexposed to the air as a check on the sterility of the agar. A plate that is exposed to the air for the same length of time as the experimental plate, but which lacks the added bacteria, can be used to indicate the approximate level of airborne contamination.

—*Assignments*

1 Any two differences, e.g.
- (i) bacterial cell has cell wall, animal cell hasn't (cell membrane only);
- (ii) bacterial cell enclosed by slimy capsule, animal cell isn't;
- (iii) bacterial cell has no proper nucleus;
- (iv) bacterial cell is smaller (c.1 μm), animal cell is larger (c.10–20 μm);
- (v) bacterial cell has no mitochondria, these are present in animal cell.

2 marks per comparison – brackets show additional (bonus?) information

(*4 marks*)

2 Length of second line = 42 mm (*1*)
Micrometres per mm = 1000 (*1*)
Therefore there would be 42 × 1000 (*1*) = 42 000 (*1*) bacteria laid side by side.

(*4 marks*)

3 Any three ways, e.g.:
- (i) shape;
- (ii) single or in groups;
- (iii) flagella present or absent;
- (iv) size;
- (v) colour;
- (vi) stain or don't stain with certain dyes;
- (vii) grow or don't grow on a particular nutrient medium.

1 mark each

(*3 marks*)

4 *Two ways in which bacteria feed:
- (i) saprotrophs (feed on dead organisms); (*1*)
- (ii) parasites (feed on living organisms). (*1*)

Two ways in which bacteria survive bad conditions:
- (i) by becoming dormant spores; (*1*)
- (ii) by reproducing rapidly when conditions are good (thus increasing odds for survival). (*1*)

Note: some pupils are likely to give spore formation and dormancy as two answers. Use discretion to award marks and follow up with discussion.

(*4 marks*)

5 e.g.:
- (i) to develop ways of destroying disease bacteria;
- (ii) to find out more about the disease bacteria;
- (iii) to identiiy which bacteria cause a particular disease.

Any one *answer*

(*2 marks*)

—*Discussion*

1 How would you explain to a primary school pupil that there are bacteria all around us?
Note: framing a question in this way does test understanding. An active learning approach could include role playing the parts of: (i) the person giving the explanation and (ii) the primary school child receiving it (who could be encouraged to ask all sorts of awkward questions!).

2 All weapons of war are horrific. Why should bacterial warfare agents be especially horrifying? We know that such agents have been made, so why is so little said about them?
Note: it is reputed that 500 grams worth (i.e. enough to fill a large coffee jar) of a germ warfare botulinus bacterium could, if evenly dispersed, wipe out the human race. In World War II the British had plans to bomb German cities with anthrax bacilli. Only a shortage of materials from the United States prevented such plans from going into action.

Topic 8
Viruses

—*Assignments*

1 *e.g. Diseases of humans: flu, common cold, poliomyelitis, sore throat, measles, german measles, chickenpox, rabies, AIDS.
Note: smallpox is a virally caused disease which has been eradicated worldwide. An answer including smallpox is worth the mark with subsequent discussion and/or reference to Topic 37 of *BFL*.
Any four diseases (*4 marks*)
e.g. Disease of plants: tobacco mosaic virus. (*1*)

(*Total 5 marks*)

2 (a) 1 micrometre = 1/1000 millimetre (a thousandth). (*1*)
(b) 1 nanometre × 1/1000000 millimetre (a millionth). (*1*)
Because they are so small. (*1*)

(*3 marks*)

3 (a) In 1900 a Dutch professor call Beijerinck (*1*) took some juice (*1*) from leaves (*1*) of tobacco plants (*1*) with mosaic disease (*1*). He filtered juice (*1*) to remove bacteria (*1*) and rubbed juice (*1*) on to leaves (*1*) of a healthy plant (*1*) and transmitted the disease (*1*). (*11 marks*)
(b) Unglazed porcelain forms a very fine sieve (*1*) which can filter (*1*) bacteria from a liquid (*1*), so any infection resulting from the liquid (*1*) was caused by a virus (*1*). (*5 marks*)

(*Total 16 marks*)

4 They can only reproduce inside the cells (*1*) of living organisms (*1*). This destroys the cells (*1*).

(*3 marks*)

5 Line 5 = 54 mm (*1*)
Line 5 = 54 million nanometres (*1*)
Width of cold virus = 70 nanometres
Number of viruses = 54 000 000 ÷ 70 (*1*)

Number of viruses = 771 429
Answer: 750–800 thousand (*1*).

(*4 marks*)

Note: prior advice to the pupils whether a good estimate or an accurate answer is expected is worth considering. Accurate answers can be easily obtained from pocket calculators. Good estimates might actually require more skill.

6 *e.g. They are not living:
Their only characteristic of life is reproduction; (*1*)
This is not enough to conclude that a virus is alive. (*1*)
e.g. They are living:
They show the characteristics of life; (*1*)
but only when inside other cells, i.e. they are an extreme form of parasite.(*1*)
Notional marks for either answer

(*2 marks*)

—Discussion—

1 Professor Beijerinck believed that a virus was an infectious fluid. What ideas might he have had about how tobacco mosaic virus was able to infect other plants?
Note: ideas could include 'virus washed into soil by rain', 'virus in water evaporated from leaves', 'virus carried by vectors', 'virus carried in droplet form'.

2 The type of virus which attacks bacteria is shown in Topic 7, Figure 3 of *BFL*. It is perfectly designed to carry out its function. How do you think it works?
Note: clues you could give might be 'it looks like a lunar lander' or 'compare it with a hypodermic syringe'.

Topic 9
Pin Mould

—Investigation 1—

To find out if pin mould needs moisture to grow

Requirements
Two small slices of dry bread; two petri dishes with lids; distilled water in bottles; a warm cupboard or incubator.

Practical skills
AMO 10, EXP.

General Comments
A description of the appearance of the two slices of bread can be used to assess AMO 10. This simple demonstration could be developed to enable the pupils to develop experiments to test various hypotheses, for instance: Does the mould come from the air, or from the bread itself? Does temperature influence the growth rate? How much water is needed before the mould will grow? Will it grow on solid starch? Will it grow on plain agar or on agar containing glucose? Are the spore cases reproductive structures? How resistant are the spores to temperature? Will the mould grow in the absence of oxygen? Will the mould produce carbon dioxide when respiring? Aseptic techniques should be used throughout, and efforts need to be made to prevent accidental contamination of plates by spores. Hands need to be washed regularly.

—Investigation 2—

Looking at pin mould

Requirements
Bread containing pin mould; forceps; microscope slide; cover-slip; distilled water; light microscope with low and high power objective lenses; drawing paper.

Practical skills
HMA 5, HMA 6, AMO 10, REC 1.

General Comments
This exercise will enable pupils to examine for themselves the growth of the mould, and to investigate the spore cases. Written descriptions of the mould, with accompanying diagrams, can be used to assess AMO 10 and REC 1. It also allows the microscope skills to be assessed (HMA 5 and HMA 6).

—Assignments—

1 It feeds (*1*) on dead material (*1*).

(*2 marks*)

2 Mould cytoplasm (*1*) needs water (*1*).

(*2 marks*)

3 Spores are dispersed at random. (*1*)
They will not always land on a suitable surface. (*1*)
So large numbers must be produced. (*1*)

(*3 marks*)

4 *e.g. Argument for fungi as plants:
Note: points are listed here but pupils should write their answers as continuous prose.
(i) they lack feeding structures;
(ii) hyphae absorb nutrients – like plant roots;
(iii) do not move around;
(iv lack nerves and muscles;
(v) lack receptors;
(vi) some plants reproduce asexually by spores (e.g. ferns);
(vii) some simple plants (e.g. *Spirogyra*) reproduce sexually by conjugation;
(viii) large central vacuole inside hyphae (rather like large central vacuole in plant cell).

e.g. Argument against fungi as plants:
(i) heterotrophic rather than autotrophic nutrition.
(ii) lack chlorophyll;
(iii) lack leaves;
(iv) lack roots;
(v) lack discrete cells;

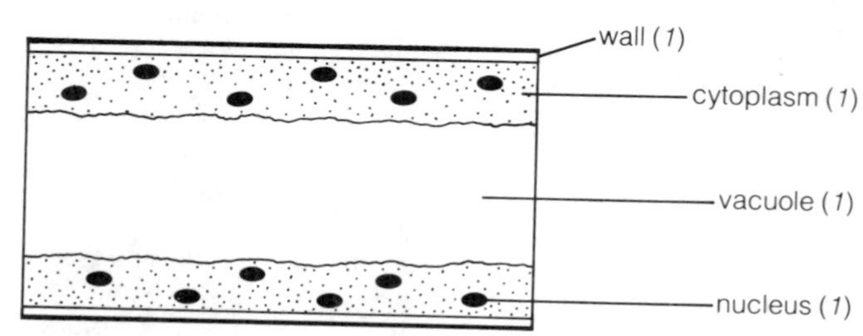

(vi) digest food with enzymes;
(vii) do not need light;
(viii) always need an outside source of oxygen – cannot produce own.
At least five good points (*5 marks*)
Continuous prose used well (*2 marks*)
Clarity of argument (*2 marks*)
Presentation (*1 mark*)
Note: The above marking scheme for the short essay question is intended as a guide only. Be flexible in awarding marks as pupil responses cannot always be predicted!

(*Total 10 marks*)

5 *This is a test of the pupil's ability to turn a verbal description (*BFL*, p. 28, lines 21–23) into a diagram.

(*6 marks*)

The wall is not mentioned in *BFL* but could be inferred. I would be tempted to allow a membrane with discussion. A membrane and wall are well worth a bonus mark.

—Discussion

1 Some biologists classify fungi as plants. Others claim that fungi are much more like bacteria. How could you show which is more likely to be the case?
Note: pupils could draw up tables of characteristics of green plants, bacteria and fungi and find ways of comparing them. A debate is another possibility.

2 Why does white bread go mouldy much faster than wholemeal bread?
Note: processed flour is obviously more digestible. Comparing both wholemeal and white bread/flour will probably yield clues. Texture, fibre content, moisture are all possible reasons. The validity of the above assumption could be tested by designing an experiment.

Topic 10 Spirogyra

—Investigation

Looking at *Spirogyra*

Requirements

Samples of *Spirogyra;* possibly include another alga for comparison, e.g. *Cladophora*; forceps; light microscope with low and high power objective lenses; two microscope slides and coverslips; mounted needle; dropping pipette; iodine; filter paper; water.

Practical skills

AMO 8, AMO 9, REC 1.

General Comments

This practical can be used to assess microscope skills (HMA 5 and HMA 6). Accurate descriptions of *Spirogyra*, including the answer to the question about the location of starch, can be assessed (AMO 10) together with diagrams (REC 1).

This exercise could be developed into an observational one comparing the similarities and differences between pond algae (testing AMO 8 and AMO 9): *Spirogyra* and *Cladophora* occur as filaments; *Cladophora* is branching, whilst *Spirogyra* is not; both have a cell wall made from cellulose; both look green because they contain chlorophyll; *Spirogyra* and *Cladophora* have large single chloroplasts; in *Spirogyra* the chloroplast is helical, while in *Cladophora* it forms a network throughout the cytoplasm.

If this is considered to be too demanding, then an aquatic angiosperm (e.g. *Lemna* or *Elodea*) could also be included. Cell sizes could be measured using micrometer eye pieces. It is important that the pupils are not hampered by a lack of appropriate vocabulary. Drawings of the specimens could accompany a written (or even spoken) report.

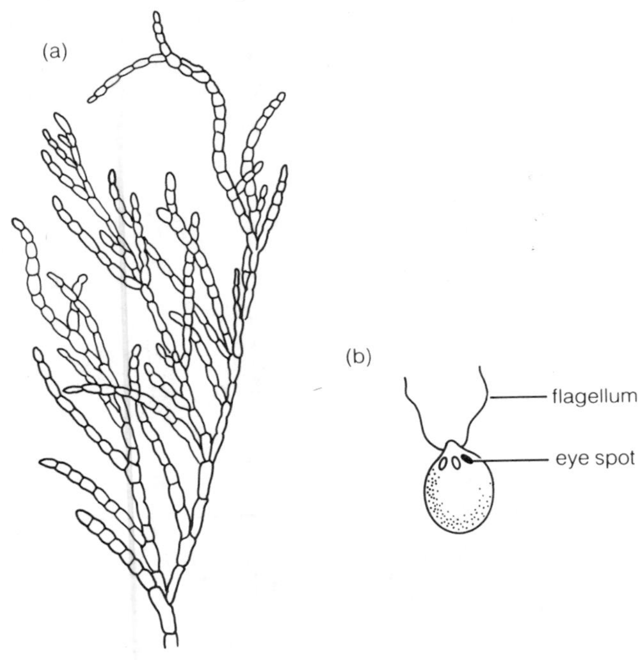

Figure 10.1 (a) *Cladophora* (× 70); (b) *Chlamydomonas* (× 2000).

—Assignments

1 (a) Chloroplasts make starch (by photosynthesis); (*1*) pyrenoids store starch. (*1*)
(b) Cell wall is made of cellulose. (*1*)
(c) Diffusion is the process by which gas exchange occurs. (*1*)
(d) *Spirogyra* reproduces (*1*) asexually (*1*) by fragmentation.

(*Total 6 marks*)

2 *There are several possible ways of doing this, some more accurate than others, e.g.:
(i) measure directly under the microscope using a micrometer eye piece;
(ii) measure the width of the microscope field of view with a transparent ruler, then estimate how many filaments could be placed side by side across the field;
(iii) estimate the average length: width ratio per cell, then count the number of cells in a measured length of filament.
Any plausible method

(*2 marks*)

3 Labelled structures in Figure 2 are:
(i) slime (mucilage); (*1*)
(ii) nucleus; (*1*)
(iii) cytoplasm; (*1*)
(iv) cellulose (or cell wall) (*1*)
(v) vacuole; (*1*)
(vi) pyrenoid; (*1*)
(vii) chloroplast; (*1*)
(viii) cytoplasmic strand. (*1*)

Model shows all the above features (*8*)
Accuracy, quality of construction, innovation, artistic merit (!) (*4*)

(*Total 12 marks*)

4 (a) Chloroplast; (*1*)
nucleus; (*1*)
cytoplasm; (*1*)
stored food. (*1*)
(*4 marks*)

(b) Shape; (*1*)
covered in slime; (*1*)
cellulose cell wall; (*1*)
large central vacuole; (*1*)
not a single cell – part of a filament; (*1*)
lacks flagellum; (*1*)
lacks pigment spot; (*1*)
lacks light sensitive swelling; (*1*)
lacks reservoir; (*1*)
lacks contractile vacuole; (*1*)
chloroplasts spiral, rather than oval. (*1*)
Any eight (*8 marks*)

(*Total 12 marks*)

—Discussion

1 To what extent is *Spirogyra* made up of 'typical plant cells'?
Note: *Spirogyra* is shown in Topic 10 Figure 2, *BFL*; a typical plant cell is in Topic 4, Figure 4.

2 *Spirogyra* actually makes quite a good plant for carrying out several biological investigations. What qualities do you think it might have in this respect?
Note: it is worth asking this question during or after a practical microscope session with *Spirogyra*. Ease of availability, handling, and seeing under microscope could all be valid answers. Providing pupils with another common filamentous alga (e.g. *Oedogonium*) for comparison with *Spirogyra* could prompt discussion. (It is difficult to see *Oedogonium*'s nucleus because it is obscured by chloroplasts. The same is true of *Elodea*.)

Topic 11
Hydra

—Investigation

Looking at *Hydra*

Requirements

Watch glass containing *Hydra*; hand lens; light microscope with low power objective lens; microscope slide; dropping pipette; mounted needle.

Practical skills

HMA 5, AMO 10, REC 1.

General Comments

This observational exercise involves the use of a hand lens and microscope (HMA 5). It could be combined with Topic 54, Investigation 1.

Good drawings of the organism, illustrating the response to touch, could be assessed (REC 1), together with a correct identification of the sting cells and the nature of the body wall (AMO 10).

—Assignments

1 Enable *Hydra* to move. (*1 mark*)

2 e.g. To 'taste' food, detect poisons. (*1 mark*)

3 Can develop (*1*) into other kinds of cell (*1*) whenever required (*1*).

(*3 marks*)

—Discussion

1 Why don't large and complex animals like ourselves have the ability to regenerate new individuals from bits cut off in the same way that *Hydra* can?
Note: refer to Topic's 90 and 91. Consider (i) the degree of complexity and (ii) the time taken to develop into a viable organism.

2 Several hundred million years ago there may have been multicellular (many-celled) animals, more advanced than *Amoeba* but less complicated than *Hydra*. What sort of design might they have been?
Note: this could be the basis for an active learning exercise. For example the class could be divided into groups of no more than four pupils, who as a team would come up with designs. These could be reported back by a spokesperson to the rest of the class, prompting discussion and criticism.

Topic 12
The Earthworm

—Investigation

Looking at the earthworm

Requirements

Live earthworm in a dish; hand lens; rough paper; smooth surface (e.g. perspex); small coin; pencil; vinegar (dilute acetic acid); dropping pipette.

Practical skills

HMA 7, AMO 10, REC 1, EXP.

General Comments

This practical can be used to assess accurate observation of the response of the earthworm to the various stimuli (AMO 10) and careful handling of the earthworm (as HMA 7).

An experiment could be devised to test the hypothesis that earthworms move more rapidly across a rough surface than across a smooth one. This could lead into an evaluation of the role of the chaetae in movement, anticipating Topic 89, Investigation 1 and developing EXP skills. The experiments designed must not harm the worm, and all worms need to be returned to the soil afterwards, which could prompt a discussion on the role of living animals in experiments.

Assignments

1 Chaetae – grip wall of burrow as worm moves along; (*1*)
clitellum – important in reproduction; (*1*)
circular muscle – enables movement. (*1*)
mucus – e.g. (i) keeps body surface moist for gas exchange, or (ii) eases movement through soil (either); (*1*)
body wall — made of muscles which enable movement (surrounds body cavity (+*1*))
(*5 marks*)

2 e.g. Streamlined; chaetae; slimy; lack of protruding structures; movement by 'bulges' moving along worm; consumes food by ingesting soil.
Any five
(*5 marks*)

3 (a) Requires blood system (*1*) (with red blood (+*1*));
(b) requires excretory organs (*1*).
(*Total 2 marks*)

Discussion

What sort of problems do you think the earthworm's small brain has to solve?
Note: consider the soil environment, and factors such as: cool, dark, moist. Physical and chemical sensations are important to it. Consider questions like: How deep does the earthworm need to burrow? How does it avoid predators? How does it find a mate? To what extent does the brain (as opposed to the nervous system in general) deal with these problems? Pupils might suggest hypotheses to answer the last question. (This might be a good opportunity to discuss the ethics of experimenting on living lower animals.)

Topic 13 Insects

Investigation 1

Looking at insects

Requirements

Dead locust and cockroach; dish; hand lens; supply of other insects: e.g. beetle, housefly, wasp, ant; drawing paper.

Practical skills

AMO 8, AMO 9, AMO 10, REC 1.

General Comments

It is important to ensure that pupils are familiar with the vocabulary in Topic 13, Figures 2 and 3 of *BFL* before the practical starts. A detailed description of one or both insects could be used to assess AMO 10 (and REC 1 if drawings are required). Alternatively, the investigation can be used as a comparison exercise – either without the hand lens (AMO 8) or in more detail (AMO 9). Suitable comparisons are:
Similarities: both have head, thorax and abdomen and the same number of wings.
Major differences: the locust has enlarged rear legs; wings extend beyond the abdomen; antennae are much longer in the cockroach. The cockroach body is shorter and fatter.
Detailed differences: the femur of the locust has ridges which it uses to make sounds; there are differences in reproductive structures.

The exercise can be extended by considering additional insects (e.g. beetle, house fly, wasp and ant), which will provide additional assessment opportunities for observational skills AMO 8 and AMO 9.

Investigation 2

Looking at live insects

Requirements

Living locusts or cockroaches in container with their usual food; large boiling tube with bung; drawing paper.

Practical skills

AMO 10, REC 1.

General Comments

The significance of the spiracles needs to be emphasised before the investigation is attempted. The brief notes and sketches can be assessed as AMO 10 and REC 1. This exercise may be combined with Topic 54, Investigation 2.

Assignments

1 (a) Ovipositor – egg tube (*1*), laying eggs (*1*);
(b) antenna – feeler – (*1*), sense organ – (*1*);
(c) tarsus – foot (*1*), walking (*1*), holding on to surfaces (*1*);
(d) spiracle – air pore (*1*), breathing (*1*).
(*Total 9 marks*)

2 Insect – differences, e.g:
(i) small:large
(ii) external skeleton:internal skeleton;
(iii) external joints:internal joints;
(iv) hard cuticle:soft skin;
(v) wings (two pairs):no wings;
(vi) tracheal system:lungs;
(vii) compound eye:'single eye';
(viii) body clearly segmented:not clearly segmented;
(ix) blood in body cavity:blood in vessels;
(x) antennae present:absent.
There are many others!
Any five – 1 mark each
(*5 marks*)

3 The cuticle supports the insect body (*1*), protects soft organs (*1*), and brings about movement (*1*), so it acts as a skeleton(*1*). Because it is outside of the muscles which work it (*1*), it is called an exoskeleton (*1*).
(*6 marks*)

Note: to get the best answers from pupils it is worth giving them cues to refer to Topics 86 ('Introducing the skeleton') and 89 ('How do other organisms move?').

4 Fly's feet:
have claws; (*1*)
and sticky pads. (*1*)
(*2 marks*)

5 *(i) light cuticle; (*1*)
(ii) efficient breathing. (*1*)

(*2 marks*)

Note: there are others. The examples given are mentioned especially in this topic. This can be followed up with a discussion.

6 *e.g. Their size made them slow and inefficient. They could not compete easily with flying reptiles and birds.
For a well-reasoned answer

(*2 marks*)

7 Good all-round vision.

(*1 mark*)

Discussion

1 If all the insects in the world disappeared overnight what would be the consequences?
Note: refer to Topic 41 'Insects, harmful and helpful'. This discussion could link the two topics.

2 What similarities are there between the design of a dragonfly and that of a helicopter? Are the similarities a coincidence, or are there functional reasons for them?
Note: pupils could draw sketches of both on paper, referring to Topic 13, Figure 1 for the dragonfly and Figure 2 for an outline of a typical insect. The question of why the helicopter has a rotor rather than beating wings will probably arise in discussion. Topic 89, Figure 7 will assist in considering this question; it shows a simplified insect wing beat, though the twist of the wing on the upstroke is omitted. Factors to discuss include the fact that it would be extremely difficult to engineer such a rapid wing beat with current technology. A rotor is more practicable since engines, unlike muscles, generally develop rotary motion.

3 Why don't insects have eyes like ours? Bear in mind that the smallest mammal is smaller than the largest insect!
Note: discuss the idea that it takes a lot longer to evolve a single complicated eye than a battery of relatively simple ones. A compound eye also has the advantage of a wide angle view with little optical distortion – consider how distorted the image is from a very wide angle ('fish-eye') camera lens. Other points to note are that insect-like eyes being developed for the next generation of industrial and military robots, and the latest space telescopes are being designed as a battery of computer-integrated small telescopes rather than a single large one.

Topic 14
Fish

Investigation

Investigating the structure of a bony fish

Requirements

Fresh herring or sprats from fishmonger or preserved material; dish; forceps; scalpel; drawing paper.

Practical skills

HMA 7, AMO 10, REC 1.

General Comments

This investigation provides an interesting opportunity to assess a pupil's ability to handle materials carefully (HMA 7), make detailed observations (AMO 10) and produce a report on the structure of the fish, incorporating the answers to the questions found in the investigation. Diagrams, if drawn, could be assessed as REC 1.

This investigation could be combined with Topic 54, Investigation 1 and Topic 89, Investigation 3. For example, the pupil could be asked to predict what effect the fins had on the movement of the fish, and then observe similar bony fish swimming in a tank.

Assignments

1 nostrils – smelling; (*1*)
gills – breathing; (*1*)
scales – skin; (*1*)
tail fin – locomotion; (*1*)
swim bladder – floating. (*1*)

(*5 marks*)

2 Plaice is flattened from side to side (*1*) since it lies on the sandy sea bed (*1*) so the eye has moved to side of head facing upwards (*1*).

(*3 marks*)

3 (a) e.g. Cold, dark, great pressure, little oxygen.
At least 3 – 1 mark each (*3 marks*)
(b) e.g. Luminescence, large eyes, giant mouth.
At least 3 – 1 mark each (*3 marks*)

(*Total 6 marks*)

4 e.g. Mud skipper differences:
(i) leg-like pectoral fins;
(ii) eyes above head;
(iii) body more 'newt-like' than 'fish-like';
(iv) other fins not clear.
At least three – 1 mark each (*3 marks*)
e.g. Sea horse differences:
(i) long mouth;
(ii) 'spiky' body;
(iii) upright posture;
(iv) other fins reduced/not visible;
(v) tapering tail;
(vi) forward-looking eyes.
At least four – 1 mark each (*4 marks*)

(*Total 7 marks*)

Discussion

Why are fish so many shapes and sizes?
Note:consider the shape of the fish as a design. A discussion could follow about structure, function and environment. Think about how many different aquatic habitats, for example running/still water, shallow/deep, different substratum, reefs with crevices, there are.
See Topic 89, Discussion Question 2, 'How do other organisms move?', p. 108 in this guide, for information about body shape, fin surfaces and how they move through water.

Topic 15
Frogs and Toads

Investigation

Looking at a frog or toad

Requirements

Preserved or living frogs and/or toads, e.g. a living *Xenopus* in tank; dish; hand lens; forceps.

Practical skills
AMO 8, AMO 9, AMO 10, REC 1, INT 1.

General Comments
Completing the investigation will allow assessment of accurate observations and appropriate conclusions (AMO 10 and INT 1).

If fish left over from the previous investigation are available, a comparison of the structure of a fish and an amphibian could be made – both similarities and differences visible without dissection (AMO 7) and internal differences (AMO 8). Alternatively a film of a frog moving and breathing could be used to provide answers to the questions in parts 2 and 4.

The movement of the frog is examined in Topic 89, Investigation 4.

Assignments

1 (i) Their skin must be kept moist (*1*) to enable them to undergo gas exchange (*1*) because they have inefficient lungs (*1*). (*3 marks*)
(ii) They mate in water. (*1*)
(iii) Tadpoles develop in water. (*1*)
((iv) They would be out-competed by more efficient reptiles and mammals in drier parts of the world.) (+ *2*)
(*Total 5 marks*)

Note: 'well adapted for swimming' is a dubious answer when applied to toads, but it might be worth a 'begrudged bonus' followed by class discussion.

2 e.g.
(i) Simple lungs;
(ii) simple thorax;
(iii) breathing movements may be temporarily suspended.
At least two – 1 mark each
(*2 marks*)

3 (a) Frog/toad skin is always kept moist (*1*) by glands in the skin (*1*) producing mucus/slime (*1*) all over body surface (*1*).
(*4 marks*)
(b) e.g. Weigh frog/toad (*1*). Put frog/toad into a bell jar (*1*). Tubes leading in and out of bell jar (*1*), and the use of a suction pump (*1*), enable air to pass through (*1*). Air leading to the bell jar (*1*) passes through water absorber (*1*) (e.g. calcium chloride) (+*1*). Air leading from the bell jar (*1*) also passes through water absorber (*1*), which was previously weighed (*1*). Air is drawn through apparatus (*1*) for a fixed time (e.g. one hour) (*1*). Re-weigh frog/toad (*1*). If the loss in mass of frog/toad (*1*) = the gain in mass by second water absorber (*1*), then the mass loss = the water loss (*1*).
The rate can be determined (*1*) by dividing the water loss by time (*1*).
(*18 marks*)
(*Total 22 marks*)

Note: the possible shortcomings of this experiment (e.g. size of the frog/toad and therefore surface area effects, speed of the air passing through system and other possible reasons why mass loss has occurred) are worth discussing.

Discussion

1 Suppose a rare species of frog from South America had a skin which secreted in its mucus a substance that cured AIDS.
Would we be justified in hunting this frog to extract the substance until no more frogs could be found?
If not, how would you set about getting large quantities of the curative substance?
Note: questions which pose dilemmas often expose the vulnerability of scientific knowledge in the real world. Hence they are highly valid. Can you 'weigh' a frog's life against a human's? Does the problem actually extend beyond that?

2 If we were intelligent amphibians instead of mammals how would this affect our way of life? Think of activities such as shopping, public transport, school, etc. What about wearing clothes?
Note: there is no reason why conceptualising shouldn't be fun!

Topic 16
Lizards

Investigation

Looking at lizards

Requirements
Vivarium with lizards; suitable food, e.g. insects; preserved lizard or video tape of lizard.

Practical skills
AMO 8, AMO 10.

General Comments
If living specimens are available, then direct comparisons of lizards with a frog or toad can be made. This can be used as a comparison of major features exercise (AMO 8) and to reinforce the major similarities between the amphibians and the reptiles. This investigation could be combined with the previous one (Topic 15).

Preserved specimens are likely to be less useful than living ones, particularly when trying to observe the smooth moist skin of the amphibian and the dry scaly skin of the reptile. Video sequences of lizards and amphibians (e.g. Life on Earth, BBC video tape – see Topic 5 of this guide), can provide an alternative source of material.

Assignments

1 e.g.
(i) To detect prey;
(ii) to detect predators;
(i.e. to find its supper and not be anyone else's!).
Both (*2 marks*)
How this is achieved:
e.g.
(i) eyes set high on head;
(ii) stretching forelegs raises head off ground;
(iii competent climbers.
At least two – 1 mark each (*2 marks*)
(*Total 4 marks*)

2 *Reptiles are cold blooded (*1*) so need to absorb environmental heat (*1*) e.g. to raise body temperature (*1*).
(*3 marks*)

Note: other ideas could be raised by asking why frogs and toads survive well in cooler parts of the world and are generally more successful in these parts than lizards. Metabolic rate, and niche availability/competition could be points raised in discussion.

3 *e.g.
(i) Skin waterproof (impervious);
(ii) tough keratin scales to protect body;
(iii) more efficient lungs;
(iv) internal fertilisation;
(v) eggs have shells, so don't dry out.
1 mark each

(*5 marks*)

Note: keratin scales important in water conservation as well as mechanical protection. Award bonus if this point is made.

—*Discussion*

1 The crocodile is the longest lasting of all large land animals. It survived when all the dinosaurs died out. Yet its brain is no bigger than a large marble. What is the secret of its success?
Note: there is no hard and fast answer, but the crocodile is obviously well adapted to its environment and has the capacity to survive change. Its ability to control its body temperature (e.g. by thermal gaping) and taking care of its young are two important factors.

2 Why do poisonous snakes bite people when they are obviously not going to eat them? Is our fear of them unreasonable?
Note: most if not all snakes end up with a reputation. This is in spite of the fact that only a small minority are poisonous and the poison is self-protective.

Topic 17
Birds

—*Investigation*

Looking at feathers

Requirements
Flight feathers of a bird; hand lens; microscope slide; coverslip; microscope; scissors; clove or olive oil; dropping pipette; water.

Practical skills
HMA 1, HMA 5, HMA 6, AMO 10.

General Comments
The sequence of operations in this investigation could be used to assess the instructions skill (HMA 1), microscopy skills (HMA 5 and HMA 6) and accurate observations of the appearance of the feather at different stages (AMO 10).

The oil will enable the barbs to be seen clearly. The hooks on the barbs mean that the barbs can separate and rejoin easily. The high oil content on the feather maintains its waterproof properties.

—*Assignments*

1 *e.g. Feathers, wings, broad tail, hollow bones, air sacs, large breast bone, well-developed flight muscles.
Any five

(*5 marks*)

2 (a) Feathers. (*1*)
(b) Air sacs/hollow bones. (*1*)
(c) Gizzard. (*1*)
(d) Colourful feathers. (*1*)
(e) Warm-blooded/flight muscles. (*1*)

(*Total 5 marks*)

3 *It is worth referring pupils to a bird spotter's guide. Examples are:
(i) night jar – diet is night flying insects;
(ii) goose – diet is grass;
(iii) stork – diet is fish;
(iv) gannet – diet is fish;
(v) vulture – diet is flesh;
(vi) woodpecker – diet is wood-boring insects;
(vii) warblers – diet is insects;
(viii) crossbill – diet is seeds from pine cones;
(ix) hummingbird – diet is nectar;
(x) skimmer – diet is food from water surface.
Note: there is such a wide variety that the limited number of examples listed above have limited value.
Marking: diet (*1*); drawing of beak (*2*); explanation (*2*).

(*5 marks*)

For two beaks

(*Total 10 marks*)

—*Discussion*

There is some evidence that the ancestors of birds were small dinosaurs which ran about on their hind legs. How do you think they started to fly?
Note: perhaps pupils could draw some dino-bird designs. Certain points apply:
(i) at each evolutionary stage the ancestor had to be efficient enough to survive;
(ii) feathers might have evolved first for warmth;
(iii) an object travelling parallel with, and close to, the ground develops additional lift called the 'ground effect'.

Topic 18
Mammals

—*Investigation*

Dissecting a mammal

Requirements
A mammal (e.g. rat, mouse or guinea pig) that has been humanely killed (e.g. with chloroform). The animal should be presented to the pupils in an undamaged state; a set of clean sharp dissecting instruments (scalpel, seeker, mounted needle, scissors, large and small forceps); paper towels; hot water; soap; a receptacle for the remains.

Practical skills
HMA 1, HMA 7.

General Comments

This practical has a value in gaining a feel for the relative sizes of the major organs of the body, and would fit well into a consideration of the organ systems of the body in Topic 43. Pupils might be allowed to perform the dissection, which is relatively simple. A careful dissection is a skilled activity and might be suited to assessing skills of following instructions (HMA 1) and handling materials (HMA 7).

The role of dissection in schools at this level is somewhat controversial and needs to be considered carefully before being undertaken. If the class are to dissect the animal (either in pairs or singly) then arrangements ought to be made for those who object to this activity to work elsewhere. Those who undertake the activity should be led through it a stage at a time. Due emphasis needs to be placed on safety techniques and hygiene. Hands should be washed immediately the practical is finished. There should be no eating in the laboratory. Adequate ventilation should be provided. The remains should be disposed of immediately, preferably by incineration. They should not be disposed of in a bag in a dustbin!

—Assignments

1 *e.g. Characteristics: hair, specialised teeth, suckle young, bear live young, parental care of young, well-developed brain.
Note: warm blooded applies to birds as well – use discretion.
Any five

(*5 marks*)

2 (i)

Function	*True for other mammals*
Alter shape of mouth	Yes
Used in speech	No
Facial gestures	Yes (some)
Kissing	Limited (chimps)
Suckling	Yes

Function 1 mark each
True for other mammals 1 mark each
At least three – notional (*6 marks*)
(ii) 'Have lips helped to make mammals successful?'
Yes – suckling in young, facial gestures (e.g. baring of teeth by (e.g.) dog for threat) are probably important to success.
For a well-reasoned, convincing argument

(*2 marks*)

(*Total 8 marks*)

3 This is very much an open question. Pupils are likely to place different emphasis on their choice depending on whether they are following 'pet enthusiasms' (e.g. horse, dog), gleaning information from encyclopaedias, guides, etc., or relying on their own natural history expertise.

Shrewd pupils might even choose the human and really go to town!

I think there is a case here for impression marking.

4 e.g.
(i) Provide milk;
(ii) Protect from predators;
(iii) teach young to feed;
(iv) young kept together in centre of social group;
(v) washing, cleaning;
(vi) provide warmth.
At least three plausible ways

(*3 marks*)

5 (a) Directs sound into ear. (*1*)
(b) e.g. Means of communication. (*1*)
(c) Taste (*1*); swallowing (*1*); speech (*1*).
(d) No function. (*1*)
(e) Keeps flies off (*1*)

(*Total 7 marks*)

—Discussion

1 Under what circumstances, if any, should mammals be used in scientific experiments?
Note: this topic could be debated. Refer to experimentation for medical research, cosmetics and defence. Note that not all animal research necessarily involves vivisection.

2 How did some small mammals outlive the dinosaurs?
Note: consider whether it is plausible that rats could survive a nuclear war. Points to think about include their subterranean life and sheer adaptability. They are known to have thrived in the uninhabitable wilderness of no-man's land in the First World War.

Topic 19
Flowering Plants

—Investigation 1

Looking at a flowering plant

Requirements

Dicotyledon plants – the choice available depends on the season in which the practical is done: in winter many indoor plants will flower in a warm room (e.g. *Impatiens*), or flowering garden plants (e.g. lupin, foxglove, tulip, sweet pea, daisy, buttercup, celandine) can be used at the appropriate time; hand lens; drawing paper.

Practical skills

AMO 10, REC 1.

General Comments

This exercise is a simple one, and could allow observation and drawing skills to be assessed. The drawing should clearly show the required features, labelled and with a scale factor.

Pupils able to observe specimens of foxglove or lupin will be able to compare the plants directly with Figure 1 in *BFL*, since these plants show the developmental sequence shown in the figure.

—Investigation 2

Comparing 'dicots' and 'monocots'

Requirements

The plants from the previous investigation plus mature grass or maize plants; a range of monocot and dicot leaves (e.g. daffodil, crocus, various grasses, wheat, barley, horse chestnut, ash, oak, dandelion, rose); hand lens.

Practical skills

AMO 8.

General Comments

This practical would make the basis of a comparison exercise (AMO 8). Comparison of mature monocot and dicot plants should enable pupils to realise the different shapes of the leaves and the pattern of leaf veins in the two types of plant. If a range of monocot and dicot leaves are available, then some idea of the relative uniformity of the monocot leaves when compared with the dicot leaves is possible.

There are other differences between the monocots and dicots. Mature plants whose roots have been washed could give an indication of the differences in root structure. Maize plants are particularly good examples of a short fibrous root system. Compare this with a carrot plant, which gives a graphic illustration of the presence of a main taproot, since it is swollen with stored food.

The idea of a cotyledon as a structure in a seed is introduced in Topic 104. Maize and broad bean seeds soaked for 24 hours in water will enable the cotyledons to be examined.

It is important to realise, however, that although there are differences between monocots and dicots there are many more similarities between them than between two plants belonging to different phyla.

—Assignments—

1 Leaves – make food (*1*)
by photosynthesis. (*1*)
Flowers – sexual (+ *1*)
reproduction. (*1*)
Roots – anchor plant; (*1*)
take up water (*1*)
and mineral salts. (*1*)
Stem – supports leaves and flowers; (*1*)
transports water and mineral salts. (*1*)
Buds – develop (*1*)
into leaves (*1*)
and flowers. (*1*)

(*11 marks*)

2 (a) Monocotyledon: seed (*1*) has one cotyledon (*1*).
Dicotyledon: seed (*1*) has two cotyledons (*1*).
(*4 marks*)
(b) Shrubs contain wood; herbs do not. (*1*)
Shrubs are larger than herbs. (*1*)
(*2 marks*)
(c) Trees are larger than shrubs. (*1*)
Trees have woody main stems or trunks. (*1*)
Shrubs are bushy. (*1*)
(*3 marks*)
(d) Deciduous trees lose leaves before winter. (*1*)
Evergreen trees lose leaves (slowly) all the time. (*1*)
(*2 marks*)

(*Total 11 marks*)

3 (i) Cutting off new branches and leaves (*1*)
does damage (*1*)
the axillary buds, (*1*)
so new growth occurs. (*1*)
(*4 marks*)
(ii) A hedge will be killed if it is cut below the lowest axillary buds. (*2*)

(*Total 6 marks*)

4 Annuals: life cycle lasts one year (then die). (*1*)
Perennials: flower year after year. (*1*)

(*2 marks*)

—Discussion—

1 In how many ways do plants affect our everyday life?
Note: consider oxygen, food, wood, paper, cotton, drugs – to give a lead into tackling this one. You could go round the class, asking for suggestions. Try to make sure that the most able pupils don't give the earliest – and easiest – answers!

2 What is a weed?
Note: 'weed' is a rather unscientific term with no clear-cut definition. It is probably best regarded as any plant which is growing in the 'wrong' place.

Topic 20 Feeding Relationships

—Investigation 1—

Building up a food web

Requirements

Large transparent container; clean sand; about 3 dm^3 pond water; floating and rooted water weeds (e.g. duckweed, *Spirogyra*); sample of animals from a pond, e.g. water beetles and larvae, dragonfly and caddis fly nymphs, mosquito larvae and pupae, shrimps, water snails and a few small fishes such as carp, minnows and sticklebacks); an aquarium aerator (possibly), identification keys; suitable reference books for the pond organisms (see Topic 4 of this guide).

Practical skills

HMA 4, AMO 7, AMO 10.

General Comments

This is an exercise in setting up the aquarium, observing the behaviour of the specimens and relating the observations to the feeding hierarchy within the aquarium. You can assess the use of identification keys (AMO 7) and useful general observations about the behaviour of the animals (AMO 10).

—Investigation 2—

A food web in a natural habitat

Requirements

Access to a suitable habitat (e.g. pond, hedgerow, grass patch, rock pool); appropriate sampling apparatus (see Topic 4 'Collecting living things' of *BFL*); reference books.

Practical skills

HMA 2, HMA 4, HMA 7, AMO 7, AMO 10.

General Comments

The value of this investigation largely depends on the enthusiasm of the teacher. Pupils can assemble various traps (HMA 4) and handle them and their contents (HMA 7). There is considerable scope for pupil initative in such an open-ended investigation (HMA 2). You can assess the use of identification keys (AMO 7), and useful general observations about the feeding behaviour of the animals (AMO 10).

—Assignments—

1 (a) Tadpoles (*1*)
(b) Water beetles; (*1*)
pike. (*1*)
(*2 marks*)
(c) Water beetles; (*1*)
pike. (*1*)
(*2 marks*)
(d) Tadpoles; (*1*)
water beetles. (*1*)
(*2 marks*)

(*Total 7 marks*)

2 (a) e.g.Sheep/cow. (*1*)
(b) e.g. Wolf. (*1*)
(c) Herring/whale (ideally a baleen/whalebone whale e.g. blue whale). (*1*)
(d) e.g. Rabbit. (*1*)
(e) e.g. Thrush. (*1*)

(*Total 5 marks*)

3 *The flower of a plant (*1*) produces a sugary liquid (*1*) called nectar (*1*), on which the bee feeds (*1*).
In the bee's stomach (*1*) the nectar is turned to honey (*1*). This is regurgitated into a wax comb (*1*) which we humans take to extract the honey (*1*) that we eat (*1*)!

(*9 marks*)

Discussion point: is plant → bee → man a typical food chain and if not, why not? (Think: do we eat bees?)

4 (i) There are eight food chains. (*1 mark*)
(ii) They are:
(1) weeds → tadpoles → pike;
(2) weeds → tadpoles → water beetles → pike;
(3) weeds → tadpoles → perch → pike;
(4) weeds → tadpoles → water beetles → perch → pike;
(5) weeds → minnows → pike;
(6) → minnows → water beetles → pike;
(7) weeds → minnows → perch → pike;
(8) weeds → minnows → water beetles → perch → pike.
One mark per chain (*8 marks*)
(iii) In food chain each consumer has only one source of food (*1*) so if the food source is destroyed/becomes scarce (*1*) so too does the consumer (*1*), and its consumers (*1*).
This results in the destruction of food chain (*1*).
In a food web, however, each consumer has more than one source of food (*1*) so if any food source is destroyed/becomes scarce (*1*) the consumer can switch to another (*1*), and the food web survives (*1*).
(*9 marks*)

Note: succinct answers might be given by the most able pupils, for example 'the survival of a food web or chain depends on the number of options available to each consumer in times of scarcity'. Use discretion in awarding marks.

(*Total 18 marks*)

5 (a) (i) e.g. Oak tree; (*1*)
blackberry bush. (*1*)
(ii) e.g. Bee/butterfly. (*1*)
(*3 marks*)
(b) e.g.Hawk (predator); (*1*)
tit (prey). (*1*)
(*2 marks*)
(c) e.g.Leaves → caterpillars → tits → hawks.
(*2*)
(d) Foods eaten:
(i) tits: insects (*1*); seeds (*1*); fruit (*1*).
(ii) blackbirds: insects (*1*); earthworms (*1*); snails (*1*); fruit (*1*).
(iii) hawks:
smaller birds (*1*); small mammals (*1*); frogs and toads (*1*); lizards (*1*).
(*11 marks*)
Food web resulting:
Assume this is based on the food source list above. A re-drawn woodland food web (see Topic 20 in *BFL*) should include the following feeding relationships:
(i) fruits and seeds → tits;
(ii) wood-boring beetles → blackbirds;
(iii) nectar-feeding insects → blackbirds;
(iv) seed-eating insects → blackbirds;
(v) woodlice and beetles → blackbirds;
(vi) woodland plants (decay) → earthworms → blackbirds;
(vii) woodland plants (leaves) → snails → blackbirds;
(viii) wood-boring beetles → frogs and toads → hawks;
(ix) nectar-feeding insects → frogs and toads → hawks;
(x) seed-eating insects → frogs and toads → hawks;
(xi) woodlice and beetles → frogs and toads → hawks;
(xii) frogs and toads → foxes;
(xiii) as (viii) to (xii) but 'lizards' instead of 'frogs and toads';
(xiv) as some small mammals can be insectivores and 'minor carnivores' (e.g. shrew):
(1) as (vi) and (vii) but with 'carnivorous small mammals' instead of 'blackbirds';
(2) as (viii) to (xii) but with 'carnivorous small mammals' instead of 'frogs and toads'.
Each feeding relationship worth one mark – twelve would be commendable (*12*)
(e) Herbivorous mammals, e.g. squirrels (*1*), because they are root eaters (*1*).
Carnivorous mammals, e.g. foxes (*1*), because root eaters form a larger part of their diet (*1*).
(*4 marks*)

Note: this answer is based on the logic of the food web in Topic 20, Figure 5. The 'real world' is much more complex and other answers to (e) might apply that are worth discussing.

(*Total 34 marks*)

6 (a) e.g. Grass → rabbits → foxes (*2*)
(b) A larger organism can easily overpower and therefore consume a smaller one. (*2*)
(c) The ideal example would get progressively smaller, e.g.: shrub → goat → parasites (*2*)
It is more common to find a food chain in which only one consumer is smaller than its food source.

(*Total 6 marks*)

7 Two reasons:
(i) Each consumer consumes only a small proportion of its food source organisms;
(ii) Much ingested material at each step of the food chain is used to release energy in respiration or passed out in faeces.
Either answer
(*2 marks*)

8 Only a small proportion of the sun's energy gets into plants (the rest is reflected) (*1*). Of the energy taken in much is released (*1*) (largely as heat) in respiration (*1*) at each step along the food chain (*1*).
(*4 marks*)

—Discussion

1 It is highly likely that in the not too distant future the whole planet Earth will be a giant ecosystem under human control. Why should this happen, and will it be a sad day when it does?
Note: discuss the increasing dominance of humans over their local ecosystem. Consider our increasing understanding of the underlying mechanism of biosphere, and our increasing need to forestall actively self-inflicted ecological catastrophes. Another question is whether humans are capable of controlling the biosphere.

2 Could the living world be seen to be one huge food web?
Note: probably the answer is yes. However, the interconnections are not always obvious, especially in the case of geographically isolated ecosystems. It is worth considering the diversity of communities making up the biosphere and trying to establish links between them, perhaps as a class game. Small groups of pupils could each be assigned a food web/community. Within a given period of time each group has to make as many links with the other groups' communities. The group that makes the most connections wins. The teacher's role is that of referee.

Topic 21 The Wheel Of Life

—Assignments

1 (a) Air rises over mountains (*1*). Water vapour condenses (*1*), forming clouds (*1*) from which there is precipitation (*1*) as either rain or snow (*1*).
(*5 marks*)
(b) Rain sinks into soil (*1*). This is called drainage (*1*). Soil water is taken up by plant roots (*1*).
(*3 marks*)
(c) Water evaporates from leaves (*1*). This is called transpiration (*1*).
(*2 marks*)
(d) Much of water in precipitation drains into sea (*1*) via rivers and ground water (*1*). It evaporates (mainly) from the sea (*1*).
(It accumulates minerals and saltiness – 1 bonus mark.)
(*3 marks*)
(*Total 13 marks*)

2 e.g. Drinking, eating, urination, defaecation, sweating, herbivorous grazing reducing transpiration.
Any four
(*4 marks*)

3 (a) (i) Photosynthesis: the process by which plants make food (*1*) from carbon dioxide and water, using sunlight (*1*) as a source of energy (*1*).
(ii) Carbon dioxide is required as a raw material (*1*).
(*4 marks*)
(b) (i) Respiration: release of energy (*1*) from food (*1*).
(ii) Carbon dioxide is released (*1*) as a waste product (*1*) from respiratory surface (e.g. lungs) (*1*).
(*5 marks*)
(c) bacteria (*1*) – even these lowly organisms respire (*1*)!
(*2 marks*)
(d) *Carbon (*1*) + oxygen (*1*) → Carbon dioxide (*1*)
(*3 marks*)
(*Total 14 marks*)

4 Roots of leguminous plants (*1*) contain nitrogen-fixing bacteria (*1*), which absorb nitrogen from the air (*1*) and build it into protein/nitrogen compounds (*1*). Ploughing puts this nitrogen back into the soil (*1*).
(*5 marks*)

5 (a)

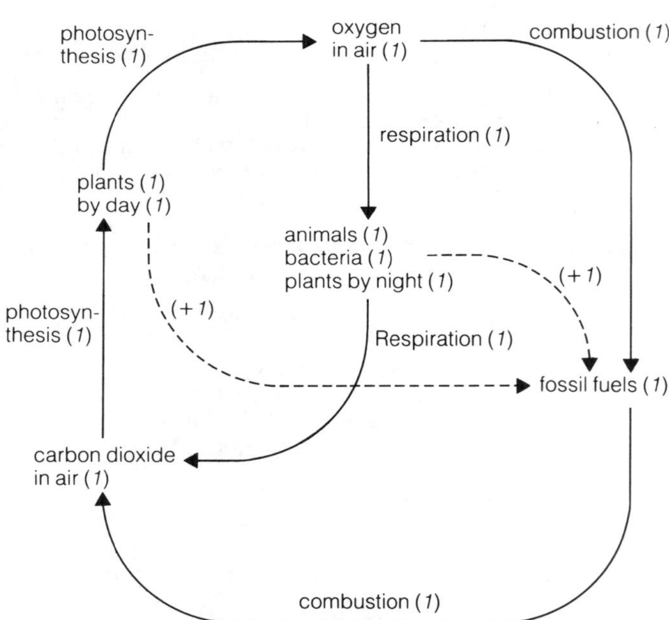

Note: award bonus marks for dotted lines.
(*14 marks*)

(b) Oxygen is needed by humans for:
(i) respiration; (*1*)
(ii) combustion. (*1*)
(*2 marks*)
(*Total 16 marks*)

Discussion

1 A tropical rain forest is always found in a place where there is a humid atmosphere. However, when the forest is cut down to make room for human activities the atmosphere turns dry. Why does this happen?
Note: consider the canopy as a barrier to evaporation, hence moisture is retained in sub-layers of rain forest. Water retention makes a reservoir, enabling water cycle to occur.

2 Perhaps burning fossil fuels is not such a bad thing from the Earth's point of view. After all it means carbon is being circulated through ecosystems rather than being uselessly buried. Do you agree?
Note: to some extent this is true, but burning fossil fuels also releases sulphur dioxide. Refer to Topic 33,'Our effects on the environment'. The removal of forest also means we are reducing the means of fixing carbon back into plant material, so carbon dioxide in atmosphere slowly (or 'geologically' rapidly!) rises.

Topic 22
The Air Around Us

Investigation 1

How do organisms affect the amount of carbon dioxide in the atmosphere?

Requirements
Eight test tubes with bungs; 250 cm^3 hydrogencarbonate indicator, equilibrated in air; four healthy leaves; a dozen woodlice; four small muslin bags with thread attached (see diagram in Topic 22 of *BFL*); a cardboard box.

Practical skills
HMA 1, HMA 4, HMA 7, AMO 10, INT 1, REC 5, EXP.

General Comments
This practical could provide an excellent opportunity to assess assembling skills (HMA 4) and manipulative skills (HMA 7). The accurate observation of the colour changes could be assessed (AMO 10) and the correct interpretation of the observations (INT 1). The practical also allows pupils the opportunity to choose the best method of presenting the results (REC 5) (e.g. coloured diagrams or written descriptions).

Alternative organisms could include *Daphnia* and small pieces of *Elodea*. This has the advantage of being slightly easier to set up as both animals and plants can be left floating in the indicator. It is possible to extend this practical by varying the relative amounts of plant and animal material in the light and dark.

Some pupils might be encouraged to design an experiment to show that the carbon dioxide released from respiration in animals can be consumed in photosynthesis. At the compensation point, all the carbon dioxide produced is being used by the plant, and there is no change in colour of the hydrogencarbonate indicator.

Assignments

1 Open the windows to keep the classroom ventilated. (*1*)
This gives plenty of oxygen. (*1*)
Carbon dioxide does not reach a harmful level. (*1*)
(*3 marks*)

2 There are more plants in summer (*1*) so more photosynthesis occurs (*1*). Carbon dioxide is taken in during photosynthesis (*1*) so its level falls (*1*).
(*4 marks*)
(Summer conditions, e.g. light, temperature, are more suitable for photosynthesis – bonus mark.)
Tropical fluctuations in carbon dioxide should be less marked than in the northern land masses, and there are local differences. However, the atmosphere is free moving and the effect of the northern winter and summer is largely global since the northern hemisphere has a disproportionately large land mass relative to the southern hemisphere.
Two points:
(i) Use your discretion in giving a mark. (*1*)
(ii) This is worth discussing with your class.
(*Total 5 marks*)

3 *No plants means no photosynthesis (*1*), so oxygen used in animal respiration (*1*) is no longer replaced (*1*). Carbon dioxide reaches harmful levels (*1*); there is no food source for animals (*1*), so life on Earth ends (*1*).
(*6 marks*)
Note: this is well worth discussing, particularly in view of the 'nuclear winter' idea. It is worth noting that the effects of carbon dioxide increase will be more immediate than those of oxygen decrease because of the 'pool' of oxygen in the atmosphere.

4 *This should be feasible, but if the verdict is 'no' consider the answer in the context of the problems described.
(*1*)
Examples of problems are:
(i) The consequences of a constant light source (e.g. uses up electricity/heating effect/natural cycles).
(ii) Ensuring the right wavelengths and light intensity for photosynthesis.
(iii) The messiness of soil/potting compost.
(iv) Plant growth in zero gravity.
(v) Condensation resulting from transpiration.
At least two problems – 2 marks each (*4 marks*)
There are many more! This is worth discussing and pooling class responses. Follow-up could involve design and problem-solving exercises. See also discussion items for Topics 30 and 93.
(*Total 5 marks*)

5 Graph:
(a) Correctly chosen and labelled axes. (*2*)
Accurately plotted (nine points, three points per mark). (*3*)
Curve/line (should go through points). (*2*)
Presentation (neatness, good use of scale). (*2*)
Note: *y*-axis need not go to zero.
(*9 marks*)
(b) Carbon dioxide reaches a maximum at midnight (*1*). In the dark there is no photosynthesis (*1*) only respiration (*1*).
Carbon dioxide reaches a minimum at midday (noon) (*1*). This is when the light is brightest (*1*) and photosynthesis is at a maximum (*1*).
(*6 marks*)

(c) Oxygen fluctuates as well (*1*) but reaches a maximum at noon (*1*) and minimum at midnight (*1*).
(*3 marks*)

(*Total 18 marks*)

—Discussion

1 Carbon dioxide is known to absorb heat. Too much carbon dioxide could result in the whole of Earth's climate warming up. The consequences of even a slight warming could be catastrophic. Why should this be so? Might the oceans act as a massive thermostat, cooling the Earth down again? If so, how?
Note: warming the Earth's climate might melt the icecaps, raising the sea level and flooding lowlands where most food is produced. However, increased evaporation from oceans increases clouds, which reflect sunlight. The exact mechanism is hardly understood at all!

2 In 1815 the Indonesian volcano Mount Tambora erupted. It was possibly the largest eruption of a volcano in human history (larger than Krakatoa). 1816 earned itself the nickname 'eighteen hundred and froze to death'. In the northern hemisphere crops failed and there was widespread death from famine. What relevance has this to the idea of a 'nuclear winter' following a nuclear war?
Note: cases such as this first suggested that the particulate matter in the atmosphere created by even a moderate nuclear exchange could have a major climatic impact, simply by cutting solar input. Even a slight fall in global temperatures could result in failed crops and starvation, creating further political turmoil.

Topic 23
Finding Out Where Organisms Live

—Investigation 1

To find out how many weeds there are in a field

Requirements

Access to a field or unkempt lawn; 1m² quadrat; identification key for weeds; clipboard.

Practical skills

HMA 1, HMA 2, HMA 4, HMA 7, AMO 6, INT 4, INT 5.

General Comments

This practical could be completed on a lawn near the school that contains a variety of different species of plant in it. Plantains or dandelions for example, might be suitable for this investigation. It could be used to assess counting and handling skills (AMO 6 and HMA 7). Instructions for deciding whether a plant should be included in the quadrat are given in the instructions of this investigation; the ability to follow these could also be assessed (HMA 1). The random selection of the quadrats could be made by throwing the quadrat (carefully!), or by some other method. The pupils could be allowed to develop some technique for ensuring that the distribution is random, which could be used to assess pupil initiative (HMA 2). The calculation of the density of the weeds could be assessed as simple calculations (INT 4).

The investigation assumes that the distribution of weeds across the field is random. Local variations in climate, soil fertility and drainage will almost certainly mean that this assumption is not justified. This conclusion, which can be produced from the questions at the end of the investigation, could also be assessed (INT 5).

—Investigation 2

Estimating the percentage area of ground occupied by grass

Requirements

A grid (1 m² quadrat divided into 100 squares); access to a piece of land that has patches of grass.

Practical skills

HMA 1, HMA 2, HMA 4, HMA 7, AMO 6, INT 4, INT 5.

General Comments

This investigation can be combined with Investigation 1. The approaches are essentially similar, and similar general comments can be made.

—Assignments

1 There are possible answers, e.g.:
(i) too rough;
(ii) open to variable interpretations;
(iii) values may differ for different organisms;
(iv) close study may contradict first impressions;
(v) confusion between numbers and cover;
(vi) difficult to define area observed.
At least four reasons – 2 marks each

(*8 marks*)

2 (a) Quadrat = square frame only (*1*), used for sampling numbers of individuals (*1*).
Grid = quadrat divided into 100 squares (*1*), used for estimating percentage cover (*1*).
(*4 marks*)
(b) Belt transect = two lines 1 metre apart (*1*), records all organisms in between (*1*).
(*4 marks*)

(*Total 8 marks*)

3 Two methods of calculating percentage cover of grass:
(i) If a grid square is half-covered or more it counts. If not it doesn't. Add up the total number of squares that count. Result: 44 ± 1%
(ii) Estimate percentage cover of each small square. Add up total. Divide by 100. Result: 45 ± 1%
Suitable method 2 marks; good working out 2 marks; correct answer 1 mark

(*5 marks*)

4 *Innovative pupils might design ingenious methods of sampling so each must be taken on its own merits. This example is based on the most straightforward method of netting.

Use net to catch minnows (*1*). Draw net along fixed distance (e.g. 2 metres) (*1*) the same number of times (e.g. 10 times) (*1*) and in the same place (*1*) in each pond (*1*). Compare the minnow catch (*1*).

(*6 marks*)

5 *There may be variations of method here. The most straightforward method is:
Set up a light-trap (*1*) (as described in *BFL* Figure 3(4)) (*1*) in each of the two locations (*1*). Leave the traps overnight (*1*). Count the moths of a particular species in each trap (*1*).

(*5 marks*)

Give bonus marks for each refinement of this fairly crude method (e.g. light-traps must be identical, sticky, trap surface, mercury vapour lamp).

6 (a) Bar chart/histogram:
correctly drawn and labelled axes; (*2*)
accurately drawn; (*2*)
x-axis numbers in intervals (i.e. below bars); (*1*)
presentation (neatness, good use of scale). (*2*)
(*7 marks*)
Note: *x*-axis need not go to zero.

(b) The assumption is that quadrats are a square metre in area.
Average no. daisies/m^2 = total no. daisies ÷ total no. of quadrats (*1*)
Total no.daisies = total of (daisies/quadrat × no. quadrats) (*1*)
$= (1 \times 4) + (2 \times 5) + (4 \times 6) + (3 \times 7) + (2 \times 8) + (1 \times 9)$ (*1*)
$= 84$ (*1*)
Total no. quadrats $= 1 + 2 + 4 + 3 + 2 + 1$ (*1*) $= 13$ (*1*)
Average no daisies/m^2 $= 84 \div 13 = 6.46$ (*1*)
(*7 marks*)

(c) Because it shows the distribution of density of daisies on the lawn (or words to this effect) (*2*)

(*Total 16 marks*)

—*Discussion*

How would you set about finding the population of Red Colobus monkeys in a Ugandan rain forest? They spend their lives in the upper tree canopy at least 30 metres above the forest floor.
Note: studies of this sort do exist using rope bridges and 'bosun's chair' arrangements for the researchers travelling between trees. This particular problem could take the form of a design exercise. Perhaps it is worth discussing the problems first of all, for example: how mobile are Red Colobus monkeys? How easy is it to climb tropical trees? How long would such a research project take?

Topic 24
What Controls Where Organisms Live?

—*Investigation 1*

To find out how blowfly larvae react to light

Requirements

Sheet of white paper (about 24 cm long); lamp; means of darkening the room; six blowfly larva in a secure container.

Practical skills

HMA 2, HMA 7, AMO 10, INT 1, EXP.

General Comments

This investigation could form the basis of an open-ended investigation of the response of blowfly larvae to light. The considerate treatment of the larvae (including returning the same number at the end of the investigation!), could be used to assess skill in handling of materials (HMA 7). The pupils should ensure that the larvae react only to the light and not to the heat from the lamp. This requires their initiative in designing a heat sheild (a beaker of water placed in front of the lamp works well enough); this could also be assessed (HMA 2).

There are a number of hypotheses that the pupils could be allowed to test, which could be used to develop and assess the experimental design skills (EXP). These include: Are larvae responsive equally to light of all colours? Are the light receptor cells located in a particular region of the larvae? Are the larvae of different ages equally responsive to light? The designs need to emphasise the standardisation of conditions. For example all larvae should be placed at the same distance from the lamp. Some compensation for the changes in light intensity when different filters are used might be considered. Satisfactory replication is also required.

—*Investigation 2*

To find out how woodlice react to humidity

Requirements

Choice chamber (e.g. diagram in Topic 24 of *BFL)* – box with perforated floor, two small glass dishes, and glass cover; anhydrous calcium chloride; water; ten woodlice.

Practical skills

HMA 1, HMA 4, HMA 7, AMO 6, REC 3, INT 1, INT 2, EXP 5, EXP 6.

General Comments

The design of the choice chamber in the diagram in *BFL* has the disadvantage of corners. Woodlice like to congregate in crevices, and may choose to move to the corners. Commercially available choice chambers are round, which (in theory anyway) should overcome this problem. In reality, however, woodlice often move round the perimeter of the circular dish, always touching the sides of the chamber. This illustrates the problem of designing this type of experiment. Woodlice are responsive to touch, light and humidity. When performing an experiment on one of these factors, it is necessary to control the others. Thus it is important to ensure that the light intensity is equal on both sides of the chamber (or preferably darkness). Similarly, if the motivation to be in the corners is stronger than the motivation to move towards the moist side, then this could bias the results obtained. Adequate replication is essential. It is also important to allow the air above the glass dishes to become affected by the water and the anhydrous calcium chloride.

Some pupils could be encouraged to consider these and other problems which arise as a consequence of counting the woodlice on each side of the chamber (AMO 6). Other assessible skills include recording and interpreting the results (REC 3, INT 1, INT 2), and manipulative skills (HMA 1, HMA 4, HMA 7).

—Investigation 3—

To see if *Euglena* is attracted towards light

Requirements

Three flat-bottomed specimen tubes with stoppers; black paper; two rubber bands; lamp; as many *Euglena* specimens as possible.

Practical skills

HMA 1, HMA 4, AMO 10, INT 1.

General Comments

Assuming that large numbers of *Euglena* can be provided, this investigation could be used to assess a number of skills: following instructions and assembling apparatus (HMA 1 and HMA 4), accurate observations (AMO 10) and drawing appropriate conclusions (INT 1).

It is important to place the tubes equal distances from the lamp,since it could also serve to heat the water. This, in turn, could affect the behaviour of the *Euglena.* It is dangerous to extrapolate from the results of such a simple investigation, but one might expect to find *Euglena* near the surface of water. Sampling techniques (e.g. Topic 4, Figure 3 (11)) could be used to investigate this hypothesis.

—Investigation 4—

An interesting project

Requirements

Suitable equipment for this open-ended investigation might include: ball of string; several disposable plastic drinking cups; small quadrat (e.g. 10 × 10 cm); compass; metre ruler; light intensity meter; measuring cylinder; light microscope with low power objective lens; microscope slide; coverslip.

Practical skills

HMA 2, EXP.

General Comments

This could make an excellent open-ended investigation, developing EXP skills and pupil initiative (HMA 2), providing that sufficient time can be found for it. Different pupils (or groups) could be given a different aspect of the problem to study, and a class presentation could be used to share the results. It allows a study of distribution to be carried out in the school grounds, if suitable trees are found.

Try to select trees that are free standing, and are not shaded by walls to any extent. Two bands of string tied around the tree 10 cm apart can serve as a random segment. The percentage cover of *Pleurococcus* can be estimated using a 10 cm square quadrat.

There could be a difference in distribution on the north- and south-facing sides, and a compass could be used to determine the aspect of the tree. Having established a difference (which is by no means easy and will require sampling several trees at different heights), it is reasonable to ask why the north side is different to the others. The amount of water running off the various surfaces of the tree could be estimated by stringing disposable plastic drinking cups together, and tying them securely to the tree. The cups need to be located high enough to prevent other pupils tampering with them. The amount of water collected in each cup could be measured with a measuring cylinder (preferably at the tree!). Once again, adequate replication is necessary. Other factors that need to be considered are light intensity, temperature and the direction of the prevalent winds.

Samples of *Pleurococcus* can be viewed under the microscope. It is clear that it is a unicellular photosynthetic organism which needs a readily available source of water.

A diagram of *Pleurococcus* is given in Topic 26 of *BFL*, together with a caption that answers the questions posed by this investigation.

—Assignments—

1 **Note:** It is worth urging pupils to use the index when attempting this question.

(a) e.g. (i) Human; (ii) water boatman; (iii) water scorpion; (iv) dragonfly nymph; (v) pond skater; (vi) great diving beetle; (vii) newt; (viii) frog; (ix) stickleback; (x) swallow.
At least six – 1 mark each (6 marks)

Notes:

(i) There are many species of mosquito.
(ii) Consider both larvae and adult forms.
(iii) Biological environment generally means host and predators. Hence that are many organisms.
(iv) More able pupils might consider mosquito-borne parasites as part of their biological environment (e.g. malaria parasite, yellow fever virus). Award marks accordingly.

(b) e.g. (i) Human; (ii) cow; (iii) pig; (iv) dog; (v) some fish.
All of these – 1 mark each (5 marks)

(c) e.g.
(i) Insect-pollinated plant, e.g. buttercup;
(ii) insect-eating bird, e.g. thrush.
At least two – 1 mark each (2 marks)

Note: it is reasonable to consider the caterpillar larvae stage so 'cabbage' for food source is acceptable. Predators, however, are likely to be similar, possible exceptions being the ichneumon wasp (caterpillar predator) and phorid fly (butterfly predator).

(d) e.g. (i) Gazelle/antelope; (ii) zebra; (iii) wildebeest.
Reasonable to expect three examples – 1 mark each (3 marks)

(e) e.g. (i) Water weed; (ii) great diving beetle/water beetle; (iii) water boatman; (iv) pike; (v) perch.
At least four examples – 1 mark each (4 marks)

Note: Topic 20, Figure 4, gives much of this answer.

(Total 20 marks)

2 (i) Two reasons:
(i) Northern side more shaded; (*1*) mosses prefer shade. (*1*)

(ii) Northern side more moist; (*1*) mosses prefer moist conditions. (*1*)
(*4 marks*)

(ii) Experiment to test reason (i):
e.g. Take two containers with moss (*1*). Put one in light, other in shade (*1*), keeping all other conditions constant (*1*). Observe over several weeks (*1*).
(*4 marks*)

Note: testing the effect of moisture involves the same basic format, but 'moist/dry' replaces 'light/shade'.
(*Total 8 marks*)

3 (i) Experimental design:
(a) Earthworm is repelled by light:
e.g.
dark container/sheet of paper; (*1*)
light source (heatless) one end; (*1*)
observe worm's movements from centre; (*1*)
repeat several times; (*1*)
expect earthworm to move away from light. (*1*)
(*5 marks*)
(b) Earthworm is attracted to the soil:
e.g.
container/choice chamber;(*1*)
evenly lit; (*1*)
moist soil at one end; (*1*)
nothing/inert substitute at other; (*1*)
observe worm's movements from centre; (*1*)
repeat several times; (*1*)
expect earthworm to move towards soil. (*1*)
(*7 marks*)

(ii) e.g.
(i) Chemical properties;
(ii) coolness;
(iii) dampness can be given if the inert substitute is dry/missing from experiment.
At least one (*2*)
(*Total 14 marks*)

—*Discussion*

Many foxes are moving into our cities. What is so attractive about an urban environment for what was until recently a countryside animal?
Note: there are other cases parrallel to this. Examples are kestrels on motorway verges and seagulls around rubbish tips.

Topic 25 Adaptation and Survival

—*Investigation 1*

Some examples of adaptation

Requirements

Living specimens (e.g. locust or gerbil); pictures of various organisms (e.g. moss, cheetah running, polar bear, giraffe, kangaroo, conifer shedding copious pollen); suitable sampling apparatus (see Topic 4, Figure 3).

Practical skills

HMA 2, HMA 7, AMO 7, AMO 10.

General Comments

The aim of this investigation is to illustrate the concept of adaptation in terms of a number of characteristics of organisms. This is somewhat artificial since organisms show a range of different adaptations to the complexities of their environment. Nevertheless, it can be useful to interpret the structure and behaviour of organisms in terms of the demands of their environments. Assignment of specimens to their appropriate classification group, can be assessed (AMO 7), accurate observations or the relevant characteristics (AMO 10), and sampling the organisms.

—*Investigation 2*

An example of homology

Requirements

Preserved specimens of locust, butterfly, beetle, housefly; hand lens.

Practical skills

AMO 9 or AMO 10.

General Comments

This is an exercise in detailed observation (AMO 9 or AMO 10); credit should be given for written (or diagrammatic) evidence of accurate observations. The wings of insects have a varied appearance, yet are homologous. This implies that they have all been derived from common evolutionary ancestors.

—*Investigation 3*

Camouflage in the peppered moth

Requirements

Portable insect trap with a UV light source and collecting funnel. Book on identifying, e.g. *A Field Guide in Colour to Insects*, by Jiří Zahradnik (Octopus Books, 1978).

Practical skills

AMO 6, INT 1.

General Comments

This is an exercise for warm evenings in the summer. It is really a demonstration, and can be used to assess counting skills (AMO 6) and interpreting the data (INT 1). The frequency of the black and white forms of *Biston* vary according to the locality. Kettlewell's survey in 1973 suggested that, even in the heavily industrialised areas of the north and midlands, the white form was still present in detectable frequencies. Indeed, there is evidence that its frequency might even be increasing, owing to the reduction in smoke pollution.

—*Assignments*

1 Criteria:
name of organism;(*1*)
type of environment;(*1*)
adaptive features and their functions.
Any five + bonus (*5 marks*)
e.g. humpback whale: oceanic (surface) waters; strong tail flukes – propulsion; blowhole on top of head – breathing; baleen – to sieve out plankton; blubber – energy reserves/buoyancy/insulation; streamline shape – pass through water easily.
(*Total 12 marks*)

2 Predators (*1*), e.g. birds (*1*), will learn not to eat it (*1*).
(*3 marks*)

3 (a) e.g. Strong claws (*1*), to climb trees (*1*).
(b) e.g. Sandy colour (*1*), for camouflage (*1*).
(c) e.g. Hooks or suckers (*1*), to hold on tight (*1*).
(d) e.g. Tough prickly leaves (*1*), hurt cows' mouths (*1*).
(e) e.g. A kidney which will adjust to widely differing salinities (*2*).
(*10 marks*)

4 Wasps have stings. (*1*)
These predators. (*1*)
Wasps have black and yellow stripes. (*1*)
These predators. (*1*)
So looking like a wasp deters predators. (*2*)
(*6 marks*)

5 (i) Owls are nocturnal (*1*) predators (*1*). White mice easier to see in the dark (*1*). So more get eaten (*1*).
(*4 marks*)
(ii) Further experiments, e.g.:
test whether a hungry owl responds more to a white mouse/model than to a black mouse/model in a darkened room;
(ii) observe whether owls are nocturnal predators and find out what sort of food they go for.
Expect two suggestions – 2 marks each (*4 marks*)
Note: the above suggestions are the most obvious, but other comparative factors between black and white mice (e.g. relative palatability/intelligence) might be suggested. These are worth discussing.
(*Total 8 marks*)

6 It seems like a birds face. (*1*)
This startles the predator. (*1*)
The moth has time to escape. (*1*)
(*3 marks*)

Further observations are, e.g.:
(i) Is it a daylight moth – is it easily seen? (*1*)
(ii) Are birds startled by the 'wing face'? (*1*)
(iii) Does the moth perch upside down on a vertical surface? (*1*)
(iv) How similar is the 'wing face' to the faces of certain predatory birds? (*1*)
Any two (*others = bonus*) (*2 marks*)
(*Total 5 marks*)

—*Discussion*

What structural adaptations have humans to their environment?
Note: the human environment is artificial. Adaptations enabling social exchange and communication probably predominate (e.g. ability to talk, use of hands). However, it could equally well be argued that we are hunter–gatherers in a new world to which we are not particularly structurally adapted, but which we adapt to suit ourselves.

Topic 26
A Look At Two Habitats

—*Investigation*

Studying a habitat

Requirements

Access to a suitable habitat; appropriate sampling apparatus (see Topic 4 of *BFL*); suitable reference books (see Topic 4, p. 13 of this guide); for each group: access to a rainfall gauge, maximum/minimum thermometer, light meter, large scale OS map, wind gauge, and local weather records of humidity and atmospheric pressure (e.g. local newspaper); long tape measure; ball of string; metal rods for line transect.

Practical skills

HMA 2, HMA 7, AMO 7, AMO 10.

General Comments

Syllabuses vary as to the relative importance of ecological field work. Detailed guidance for each habitat is beyond the scope of this guide, and advice should be sought wherever possible from local conservation groups. The examination boards should provide guidance as to the depth of study required. Naturally this is dependent upon class size, accessibility of habitat and the time available. This investigation is similar to Topic 20, Investigation 2. The two investigations can be combined successfully (the comments relevant to that topic are also relevant here). Assessment can be made of pupil initiative (HMA 2) in deciding how and where to measure various environmental factors, using apparatus (HMA 7), classification of organisms (AMO 7) and accurate observations (AMO 10).

—*Assignments*

1 Woodland plant: e.g. oak tree:
e.g.
(i) tall strong stem, raises leaves to light; (*1*)
(ii) woody branches, spread leaves out in a canopy; (*1*)
(iii) extensive root system for anchorage/absorption of water and mineral salts. (*1*)
Any three adaptations (*3 marks*)

Woodland animal: e.g. grey squirrel:
e.g.
(i) sharp hooked claws, for climbing trees. (*1*)
(ii) powerful hind legs, for running. (*1*)
(iii) bushy tail, for balance along narrow branches. (*1*)
Any three adaptations (3 marks)

(*Total 6 marks*)

2 (i) Water is more dense than air. (*1*)
(ii) Water contains mineral salts – plants can absorb direct. (*1*)
(iii) Water provides support. (*1*)
(iv) No danger of dehydration. (*1*)
(v) Less temperature variation. (*1*)
(vi) Aquatic life exists in three dimensions, life on land generally exists 'on the flat'. (*1*)
Plus any other reasonable answer.
Any four differences

(*4 marks*)

3 Most like land dweller: pond skater. (*1*)
Breathes air, not water. (*1*)
Runs along surface of water. (*1*)
(*3 marks*)
Least like : stickleback. (*1*)
Breathes water through gills. (*1*)
Spends entire life obligatorily in water. (*1*)
(*3 marks*)

(*Total 6 marks*)

4 Water lily
(i) Larger leaves.
(ii) No stomata.
(iii) Large air spaces in leaves.
(iv) Absorption occurs all over surface.
(v) Large single flower.
At least three comparisons – 2 marks each

(*6 marks*)

5 (a) e.g.
(i) Very good at picking up oxygen;
(ii) good at extracting nutrients from mud;
(iii) good burrower.
At least two adaptations – 1 mark each (2 marks)
(b) e.g.
(i) Well-adapted limbs for balance;
(ii) good agility and balance;
(iii) good vision.
At least two adaptations – 1 mark each (2 marks)

(*Total 4 marks*)

6 e.g. Woodlice.
Consequences of niche destruction:
e.g.
(i) loses water quickly and dies;
(ii) loses food supply (decaying matter);
(iii) exposed to predators.
At least two consequences – 1 mark each (2 marks)

(*Total 3 marks*)

—Discussion

Knotty Hill Wood is a local beauty spot. However, it is owned by the Rees-Williams, a long established farming family. You have read in the local newspaper that because of government subsidies for growing a new strain of EEC wonder bean the Rees-Williams intend to cut the wood down. How would you persuade the family to keep the wood?

Note: perhaps pupils could role-play this, taking the parts of farmers, conservationists, local politicians, tourist industry representatives, etc.

Topic 27
Changes Through The Year

—Investigation

Looking at horse-chestnut twigs

Requirements

This practical takes places at three times of the year.
Spring: horse-chestnut twig whose buds are still closed; jar of water; access to a warm, well-lit room; drawing paper.
Summer: horse-chestnut twig whose shoots have formed flowers; drawing paper.
Autumn: horse chestnut twig bearing fruit, drawing paper.

Practical skills

AMO10, REC 1, INT 1.

General Comments

The following can be assessed: drawing skills (REC 1), accurate observations (AMO 10), and appropriate conclusions drawn about changes in the appearance of the twig as it gets older (INT 1).

—Assignments

1 (a) Protects bud/dormant shoot. (*1*)
(b) Where leaf from previous year's growth (*1*) has fallen off (*1*)
(*2 marks*)
(c) New shoot emerges from bud (*1*). Bud scales fall off (*1*), leaving scale scar (*1*).
(*3 marks*)
(d) Pore in bark enabling gaseous exchange. (*1*)

(*Total 7 marks*)

2 (a) New shoot. (*1*)
(b) Branch. (*1*)

(*2 marks*)

3 Leaves contain yellow and orange pigments (*1*), xanthophyll (yellow) (*1*), and carotene (orange) (*1*).
They are normally hidden by chlorophyll (*1*) but in autumn chlorophyll breaks down (*1*) so can see other pigments (*1*).

(*6 marks*)

4 (i) Frost makes area of weakness (abcission layer) more brittle. (*1*)
(ii) e.g. Wind/weight of snow/raindrops. (*1*)

(*2 marks*)

5 e.g. Experiment:
Choose an animal, e.g. hamster (*1*). Carry out experiment during spring (*1*). Keep male and female pairs (*1*) in cages provided with artificial (*1*) light of different durations (*1*).
e.g.
cage 1 – no light (*1*);
cage 2 – one hour per day (*1*);

cage 25 – 24 hours lighting per day (*1*).
Relate pregnancy success (*1*) to artificial day length (*1*).
(*9 marks*)

—*Discussion*

Is the year the only cycle to which organisms have to adjust?
Note: consider circadian (24 hour) rhythms, lunar (28 day) rhythms and the presence of a 'biological clock' within all organisms.

Topic 28
Social Insects

—*Investigation 1*

Looking at the three types of bee

Requirements
Preserved specimens of a queen, worker and drone bee; hand lens; ruler; drawing paper.

Practical skills
AMO 8, AMO 10, REC 1.

General Comments
This investigation can be used as the basis of a comparison exercise (AMO 8). There are differences in size, abdomen shape, and wing shape. Similarities include the division of the body into head, thorax and abdomen, and the presence of hairs and stripes on the abdomen. Assessment can also be made of drawing skills (REC 1) and careful description of any of the insects (AMO 10).

—*Investigation 2*

To see how the worker bee is adapted to do its jobs

Requirements
Film of bees pollinating flowers; preserved specimen of a worker bee; prepared slides of the mouth parts of a worker bee; prepared slides of the front and hind legs of a worker bee; light microscope with low power objective lens.

Practical skills
HMA 5, AMO 10.

General Comments
If this investigation is completed at the appropriate season, pupils can watch bees visiting flowers for themselves. Topic 28, Figure 5 in *BFL* gives details of the adaptations shown by a worker bee. (Some teachers might like to get their more able pupils to work out what the adaptations are for themselves before studying Figure 5.) In many insects, the mandibles are for chewing food (e.g. the locust, Topic 54). Bees are liquid feeders, and the mandibles have become modified for moulding the wax combs in the bee hive, in which the new larvae develop. Accurate observations (AMO 10) and handling microscopes (HMA 5), can be assessed.

—*Assignments*

1 (i) drone: male bee (*1*) only job is to mate with queen (*1*). (*2 marks*)
(ii) royal jelly: special substance (*1*) fed to all worker larvae for the first few days (*1*); fed to queen larvae all the time (*1*). (*3 marks*)
(iii) queen substance: chemical released by queen (*1*) communicates messages around hive (*1*). (*2 marks*)
(iv) marriage flight: only surviving new queen (*1*) having murdered sisters! (+*1*) flies away from hive (*1*) pursued by drones (*1*). The first drone to catch her mates with her in mid air. (*1*) (*4 marks*)
(v) round dance: worker finds food less than 100 metres away (*1*). Dances in a circle (*1*); the closer the food, the faster is the dance (*1*). (*3 marks*)
(*Total 14 marks*)

2 Worker: sting left behind (*1*) (because it has barbs – bonus) along with part of its gut (*1*).
Drone: reproductive organs ripped out (*1*).
(*3 marks*)

3 e.g. Experiment. Main criteria are: placing food, marking a worker bee, observation.
e.g.
Transport beehive to experimental area (no flowers). (*1*)
Place food (sugar, flower) more than 100 metres away. (*1*)
Mark bee with a spot of paint. (*1*)
Observe both in (i.e. glass) and out of hive (*2*)
Bonus marks for refinements. (*5 marks*)
The correct answer is:
Top of hive represents direction of sun. (*1*) Middle of Figure 8 shows direction of flower (*1*) relative to sun (*1*). Speed of waggle indicates distance (*1*). (*4 marks*)
Note: pupil's answer can be considered to be correct if it is plausible.
(*Total 9 marks*)

4 Quite open ended, e.g.
Similarities: division of labour (*1*)
most individuals have jobs to do (!) (*1*)
similar number of individuals (*1*)
At least two – 1 mark each (*2 marks*)
Differences: three kinds of structually different individual (*1*)
rigid, inflexible behaviour (*1*)
(*2 marks*)
(*Total 4 marks*)

5 (a) Hexagon packs most cells in a given space (*1*).
(b) Poor summer means less flowers (*1*), means less nectar (*1*), so less honey (*1*). (*3 marks*)
(c) e.g. Overcrowding raises hive temperature (*1*) triggers swarming reaction (*1*).(*2 marks*)
(d) Worker bee has learned to associate flower type with nectar (*2*), but it is not clever enough to adapt to many varieties (*2*). (*4 marks*)
(e) Worker bee waiting to attend to larva's needs as they arise (*1*).
(*Total 11 marks*)

6 Whether the verdict is fair or unfair depends on pupil's reasoning:
either e.g. 'Fair comment':
lazy – contribute little to day to day running of home; (*1*)
stupid – any creature who races for the prize drones get must be stupid; (*1*)
fat – have broadest abdomen of all types of bees; (*1*)
greedy – consume what other bees produce. (*1*)
(*4 marks*)

or e.g. 'Decidedly unfair':
lazy – all bees have a particular role (*1*) and the drone's is the mating flight;
stupid – how can you establish intelligence, or lack of it, in a bee?; (*1*)
fat – a broad abdomen does not indicate fat deposits!; (*1*)
greedy – if drones 'did the decent thing' and stinted what might happen to the future of bees? (*1*)

(*4 marks*)

7 e.g. Army ants:
(i) both have queen, drones and workers;
(ii) in both the queen's role is same;
(iii) in bees all workers are structurally identical;
(iv) in ants: workers, hunters, soldiers;
(v) bees – hive; army ants – nest/bivouac/on move;
(vi) bees feed on nectar: ants – carnivores;
(vii) bees: larvae in special cells;
(viii) army ants: larvae form in nest develop rapidly;
(ix) bees fly: ants walk;
(x) bees sting: ants bite;
(xi) both swarm;
(xii) both communicate (by antennae/chemically).
At least six – 1 mark each (*6 marks*)

Note: reference for army ants: 'Life on Earth' by David Attenborough.

Biologists generally hold ants to have a more complex society, but pupil's answers are based on reasoning, and will depend on their own researched answer to the first part of this question.

e.g.
(i) Ants have many nest adaptations;
(ii) ants solve many problems while on move;
(iii) ants 'farm' fungi, aphids, etc.;
(iv) bees have 'hive architecture';
(v) bees have sophisticated dance communication.
Any reasonable explanation (*2 marks*)

(*Total 8 marks*)

8 (a) Plant flower (*1*) produces sugary liquid (*1*) called nectar (*1*) on which bee feeds (*1*). (*4 marks*)
(b) Bee collects nectar (*1*) in bee's stomach (*1*); nectar is turned to honey (*1*) regurgitated in wax comb (*1*). (*4 marks*)
(c) Humans keep bees in artificial hives (*1*) collect honeycomb (*1*); extract honey and put into pots (*1*). (*3 marks*)

(*Total 11 marks*)

—*Discussion*—

1 If a worker bee dies having used its sting, why should it defend the hive?
Note: the bee's action results from instinct (bee has no choice). The action of stinging protects the hive and the ability of queen (the only fertile female bee) to produce offspring. Warn against giving organisms human value!

2 A colony of bees, ants, wasps or termites may be called a superorganism. This is a way of saying that the whole colony seems to behave in an integrated and 'intelligent' way. Does the same apply to humans?
Note: human free will works against this concept. However, there are signs that a large body of people (e.g. a whole country) can take on an identity of its own. Because individuals do reflect their cultural and geographical backgrounds to some extent it is very important that a teacher embarks on such a discussion in both a controlled and sensitive way.

Topic 29
What Is Soil?

Soil experiments can be extremely messy! It is very important that a large bucket is available for the discarded soil and water. No soil or stones should go down the sinks, otherwise they will rapidly become blocked up. This needs to be explained very carefully before the practicals start.

—*Investigation 1*—

Separating the components of soil

Requirements
Large test tube; fresh garden soil; water; test tube rack.

Practical skills
HMA 5, HMA 6, AMO 2, INT 4.

General Comments
If the humus content of the local soil is low, it can be enriched by mixing a small amount of potting compost in with the soil sample before the lesson begins. This simple exercise in observation can be quantified by asking the pupils to measure the width of the various bands of soil, and work out the percentage of each soil component in the soil. In addition, soil particles from the different strata can be removed from the tube using a pipette, and observed using a microscope.

The additional equipment needed for these activities would be light microscope with low power objective lens; microscope slide; coverslip; mounted needle; plastic ruler. The investigation can be used to assess measuring skills (AMO 2), simple calculations (INT 4) and microscope skills (HMA 5 and HMA 6).

—*Investigation 2*—

Looking at soil crumbs

Requirements
Good garden topsoil; white paper; access to a plant that has been freshly dug up from the soil (do not remove soil from the plant).

Practical skills
AMO 10.

General Comments
Soil crumbs give the soil a texture that is very important to the growth of plants, since it allows air spaces to form between the

crumbs. Clay soil forms poor soil crumbs, and can be improved by the addition of lime or humus. The soil particles are held together by organic humus. Root hairs on the young roots of plants attach themselves to the soil crumbs, and extract the water that forms a thin film on the surface of the soil crumbs. A good description (written or oral) of the texture of soil crumbs could be used to assess AMO 10.

—Investigation 3—

To see if water moves upwards through soil

Requirements
Wide glass tube open at both ends, about 20 cm long; glass wool plug; retort stand and clamp; dry soil; mustard/cress seeds; possibly samples of dry sand, clay and loam; dish; water.

Practical skills
AMO 2, AMO 4, REC 3, REC 4.

General Comments
This practical can be performed as a demonstration with samples of sand, clay, peat and loam soil. In such cases four identical tubes will be needed, each packed with the appropriate soil type. The seeds germinate when sufficient moisture has reached the top. It might be possible to measure how far the water has travelled up each soil column at regular time intervals and use the data to plot a graph of rate of uptake of water against time, but this is not easy to do accurately without disturbing the soil (AMO 2, REC 3, and REC 4) Pupils should certainly record the time taken for the seeds to erminate (AMO 4).

—Investigation 4—

To find out how much water there is in soil

Requirements
Small crucible; fresh garden soil; access to an accurate balance and an oven at 100°C; two further soil samples – one dry and one very wet; desiccator.

Practical skills
HMA 1, HMA 3, HMA 7, AMO 5, REC 3, INT 4, INT 5.

General Comments
This practical should be linked to Investigation 5, since their procedures follow on from each other. It can be used to assess following instructions (HMA 1), handling apparatus (HMA 7), and weighing accurately (AMO 5). It is important to record the data accurately (REC 3) and to perform simple calculations on the results (INT 4).

The idea of weighing to constant mass is important and should not be neglected because of pressure of time. Soil is hygroscopic and should be placed in a desiccator when it cools down, to prevent it reabsorbing moisture, a possible source of error (INT 5).

—Investigation 5—

To find out how much humus there is in soil

Requirements
Soil from the previous investigation; crucible; tripod; gauze; bunsen burner; safety glasses; access to a desiccator and an oven at 100°C.

Practical skills
HMA 1, HMA 3, HMA 7, AMO 5, REC 3, INT 4, INT 5.

General Comments
This investigation is an extension of the previous one, and the same general skills can be assessed. Safety glasses should be worn when heating the crucible under the bunsen burner, and an assessment of working safely could be made (HMA 3).

—Investigation 6—

To find out if soil contains lime

Requirements
Test tube; concentrated hydrochloric acid; soil and, if necessary, soil enriched with lime; lime water or hydrogencarbonate indicator.

Practical skills
HMA 2, HMA 3.

General Comments
This is a simple exercise in which soil enriched with lime may need to be used if local soil conditions are inappropriate. Care needs to be taken when using hydrochloric acid, and safe working can be assessed (HMA 3). If the pupils suggest that carbon dioxide is given off, it may be appropriate to allow them to test their hypothesis by bubbling the gas through lime water or hydrogencarbonate indicator. This could be used as a test of pupil initiative (HMA 2), providing that pupils have encountered the test before.

—Investigation 7—

To find out how acidic or alkaline soil is

Requirements
A small amount of soil; test tube; distilled water; several pieces of pH paper; samples of acidic and alkaline soil (e.g. garden soil enriched with humus, and garden soil enriched with lime).

Practical skills
HMA 7, AMO 10, INT 1.

General Comments
The use of pH paper can be replaced with universal indicator solution, if that will make the estimation of a pH value any easier. Handling materials (HMA 7), accurate observations (AMO 10), and drawing correct conclusion (INT 1) can be assessed.

—Investigation 8—

To find out how much air there is in soil

Requirements
100 cm^3 measuring cylinder; 50 cm^3 garden soil; water; glass rod.

Practical skills
HMA 7, AMO 3, INT 4.

General Comments
This simple investigation could be used to measure volume (AMO 3), for handling apparatus (HMA 7), and to calculate percentages (INT 4).

—Assignments—

1 Evening is cooler (*1*). Water can sink deep into soil (*1*) from where plants can take up via roots (*1*).
But midday, being warmer (*1*) means more water evaporates (*1*) and less reaches the roots (*1*).

(*6 marks*)

2 (a) Water forms film over soil particles (*1*) so soil seems to 'soak up' water and none comes through (*1*). Soil humus also has a sponge effect (*1*). (*3 marks*)
(b) Method of watering works (*1*). Capillary action (*1*) draws water by tiny air spaces in soil (*1*).
(Blotting paper analogy (+ *1*)) (*3 marks*)

(*Total 6 marks*)

3 (a) Sandy. (*1*)
(b) Clayey. (*1*)
(c) Peaty. (*1*)
(d) Chalky. (*1*)
(e) Peaty. (*1*)

(*5 marks*)

4 e.g.
(i) Rock freshly weathered. (*1*)
(ii) Soil washed down. (*1*)
Any two well-reasoned answers

(*2 marks*)

5 (a) Put in oven at about 100°C (*1*) for at least 30 minutes (*1*). (*2 marks*)
(b) Percentage of water in soil = (mass of soil water + total mass of soil) × 100 (*1*)
mass of soil water = mass crucible + damp soil − mass crucible dried soil (*1*) = 25 − 20 =5 g (*1*)
total mass of soil = mass crucible + damp soil − mass crucible (*1*) = 25 − 10 = 15 g (*1*)
percentage of water in soils = (5 + 15) × 100
= 33% (*1*).
(*6 marks*)

(*Total 8 marks*)

6 Humus returns plant and animal material to soil (*1*). Also stores water (*1*) and prevents valuable nutrients being washed out (*1*) of soil.

(*3 marks*)

—Discussion—

1 On many occasions people in the tropics have chopped down rain forests to make room for agriculture, only to find that the rain forest soil is poor and is soon washed away. Why should such poor soil be found beneath the most fertile ecosystems?
Note: tropical rain forest soil is largely humus based with very few rock particles. The actual mixture of soil is what gives its quality. Few small plants on forest floor hold the soil together (it is too dark). Removing trees bakes the humus, which blows away easily, leaving impoverished subsoil.

2 By some strange trick of fortune you have won a thousand hectare farm. Its previous owner, however, removed most of the hedgerows so that huge combined harvesters have room to manoevre, and they also used nothing but artificial fertilisers. What will be your plans for the farm – and will the bank manager be happy?
Note: the idealists will plant hedgerows, use organic farming methods, and have to work hard to cheer up the bank manager. The pragmatists will follow the same line as the previous owner. Conservation is all about conflicts between economic and environmental interests. Ultimately the two must be reconciled – a lesson yet to be learned by the human species as a whole!

Topic 30
Life In The Soil

—Investigation 1—

Collecting organisms from the soil

Requirements
Key to soil invertebrates (see Topic 4, p. 13 of this guide).
METHOD 1. A garden fork; a bucketful of good garden soil and leaf litter (sample it from around the compost heap or other area with decaying plant material); large white plastic sheet; spoon; forceps; pooter; a supply of small plastic bags; wide-meshed kitchen sieve.
METHOD 2. 100 cm^3 25% salt solution; plastic bowl; spoon; thin paintbrush; the sample of garden soil from above.
METHOD 3. 50 cm^3 washing-up liquid in 10 litres of water; access to 1 m^2 of soil; plastic bowl for collecting worms.
METHOD 4. Tullgren funnel (see Topic 30 in *BFL*): 40 watt bulb, perforated tray with gauze bottom, plastic funnel; small beaker; water or 70% ethanol.
METHOD 5. Tullgren funnel (as above, set up as in lower diagram in Topic 30, Investigation 1 in *BFL*); cheesecloth bag; rubber tubing; metal clip; 250 cm^3 beaker; light microscope with low and high power objective lenses; microscope slide; coverslip; mounted needle; pipette.

Practical skills
HMA1, HMA 4, HMA 5, HMA 6, HMA 7, AMO 7.

General Comments

A variety of methods can be tried, and the organisms collected identified using a suitable key to invertebrates. Handling materials and apparatus (HMA 7), microscopic skills (HMA 5 and 6) and the use of keys (AMO 7) can be assessed.

—Investigation 2

To find the effect of eathworms on the soil

Requirements

Wormery as shown in diagram of Topic 30, Investigation 2 of *BFL*; box with two glass panels; hardboard lid; bucketful of good garden soil; mixture of chalk and sand; dead leaves; supply of worms (see Method 3, Investigation 1 of this topic).

Practical skills

HMA 1, AMO 10.

General Comments

Following instructions to successfully construct the wormery could be assessed as HMA 1. A description of the changes made to the soil composition by the worms could be assessed as AMO 10.

—Assignments

1 e.g. Helpful soil animals:
   (i) Earthworm turns over soil (*1*), fertilises (*1*), makes soil finer (*1*). (*4 marks*)
   (ii) Mole (*1*) eats soil pests (*1*); burrows act as irrigation channels (*1*). (*3 marks*)

   e.g. Harmful soil animals:
   (i) Wireworms (*1*) (larvae of certain beetles) eat plant roots (*1*). (*2 marks*)
   (ii) Leather jackets (*1*) (daddy long leg larvae) eat plant roots (*1*). (*2 marks*)

(*Total 11 marks*)

2 (a) Microbes in soil are respiring. (*1*)
   They produce carbon dioxide. (*1*)
   This is absorbed by potassium hydroxide solution. (*1*)
   It uses oxygen. (*1*)
   Results in water rising up left-hand arm of U-tube. (*1*) (*5 marks*)
   (b) Same apparatus; (*1*) but baked sterilised soil. (*1*) (*2 marks*)

(*Total 7 marks*)

3 e.g. Soil in one part of the garden too heavy or compact (clay) for worms to burrow through. (*2*)
   (Other reasons might include unsuitable pH, presence of predators, dryness. (*2*))
   e.g. Experiment to test effect of soil compactness.
   Remove compact section of soil. (*1*)
   Keep intact. (*1*)
   Transfer to wormery. (*1*)
   Place worms on top of soil. (*1*)
   Observe degree of burrowing. (*1*)
   Repeat with soil from other part of garden. (*1*) (*6 marks*)

(*Total 8 marks*)

4 e.g. Experiment to show earthworms prefer beech leaves to oak leaves:
   Set up wormery (*1*). On top of soil (*1*) put beech leaves on one side and oak leaves the other (*1*). Preferred leaves are dragged down into soil (*1*).

(*4 marks*)

5 (a) e.g.
   (i) Prevents dehydration of soil organisms;
   (ii) moist respiratory surface;
   (iii) needed by plant roots.
   At least two reasons – 1 mark each (*2 marks*)
   (b) Required for (aerobic (+*1*)) respiration. (*1*)

(*Total 3 marks*)

6 Dead leaves (*1*): plant material useful food source (*1*). Humus (decayed plants and animals) in soil itself (*1*). Valuable source of nutrients (*1*).

(*4 marks*)

Note: mineral particles, e.g. chalk/limestone, probably play a part in maintaining worm's gut pH.

—Discussion

A combination of government subsidies and improvements in tractor technology has resulted in crop farming in upland (hilly) areas. Until recently such areas were limited to sheep farming. Could there be consequences for the soil and, in the long run, for the farmer's business?

Note: I've seen erosion occur for this reason in North Wales over as little as three years. What a new tractor is capable of doing can so appeal to a farmer that it can overshadow the consequences of such actions. Technology can be too clever for its own good!

Topic 31
Decay

—Investigation 1

Looking at organisms which bring about decay

Requirements

Mould on stale bread; forceps; decaying earthworm; light microscope with low and high power objective lenses; two microscope slides; two coverslips; mounted needle; water.

Practical skills

HMA 5, HMA 6, HMA 7, AMO 10.

General Comments

The study of bread mould extends the work of Topic 9. Assessment can be made of the hygienic handling of materials (HMA 7), microscopy skills (HMA 5 and HMA 6) and accurate descriptions of the decay of the objects (AMO 10).

—Investigation 2—

To find out how quickly different things decay

Requirements

Plant pot filled with damp soil; dead earthworm and insect; small pieces of leaf, stick and bone; polythene bag big enough to cover the pot; elastic band or thread for tying bag to pot.

Practical skills

AMO 10, INT 1.

General Comments

It is important to cover the pot with a bag since the earthworm will decay rapidly only in humid conditions. Accurate descriptions of the decay of the objects can be assessed (AMO 10), and interpretations of why some structures should decay faster than others (INT 1).

—Assignments—

1 (i) Self-digestion by own enzymes. (*1*)
(ii) Birds. (*1*)
(iii) Worms. (*1*)
(iv) Rain. (*1*)
(v) Freezing and thawing. (*1*)

(*5 marks*)

2 (i) Too dry. (*1*)
So bacterial spores cannot germinate. (*1*)
As a result bacteria do not decay body. (*1*)
(ii) No scavengers. (*1*)

(*4 marks*)

3 (a) Ventilates compost heap (*1*) ensuring a good supply of oxygen (*1*) for 'compost bacteria' (*1*). (*3 marks*)
(b) Increase surface area for bacteria to act on (*1*), and fractures the plant tissue (*1*) enabling bacteria to penetrate deep into stalks (*1*). (*3 marks*)
(c) Grass cuttings expose a large surface area of readily rottable plant material (*1*).
As a result they rot quickly (*1*) enabling bacteria to multiply to large enough numbers (*1*) to speedily rot bulkier items (*1*). (*4 marks*)
(d) (i) Moist: prevents bacteria from dehydrating (*1*).
All biochemical reactions, including those of decay, occur in an aqueous medium (+*1*).
(ii) Not saturated: if waterlogged there would be no oxygen (*1*). Lactic acid would be formed (*1*) and decay would stop (*1*). Silage rather than compost would result (*1*). (*4 marks*)
(e) Mixes rich supply of bacteria (*1*) (nurtured in the compost heap (+*1*)) with a rich supply of fresh food material (*1*) accelerating decay within the compost heap (*1*). (*3 marks*)

(*Total 17 marks*)

4 (i) Temperature rises:
Increase in bacterial numbers (*1*) increases respiratory activity (*1*). Some of the energy released as heat (*1*) results in a rise in temperature (*1*). (*4 marks*)
(ii) Temperature falls:
The increase in bacterial numbers leads to depletion of food supply (*1*), and rise in toxic waste (*1*).
Also the respiratory energy released as heat (*1*) raises the temperature to above the normal working temperature for enzymes (*1*), which become destroyed/denatured (*1*). Without enzymes life processes, e.g. respiration, stop functioning (*1*).
Bacterial population falls as they die (*1*).
Less bacteria release less heat (in respiration) so the temperature falls (*1*). (*8 marks*)

(*Total 12 marks*)

Note: this whole question is well worth discussing with a class. Apart from the self-destructive effects of uncontrolled population rise (refer to Topic 32 and Topic 33), aspects of respiration may be discussed (refer to Topic 50), and the open question, 'Why do some bacteria survive?'.

—Discussion—

1 It would be profitable to genetically engineer strains of bacteria capable of accelerating decay. Having ploughed wheat stubble back into the soil would it be reasonable for a farmer to spray a culture of one of these strains over the farm's wheat field? What advantages would this have over present practice and what misgivings would you have?
Note: it would avoid burning stubble with consequent pollution, and enable higher humus content of soil. However, the consequences of artificially created bacteria functioning in natural cycles have to be considered most carefully.

2 If space stations are to be self-sufficient one day, then 'gardens in space' are almost certainly going to become a reality. If soil is used, decay bacteria and moulds are bound to be present. What problems might this pose and what are the possible solutions?
Note: transfer of fungi and bacteria inadvertently to all parts of space station may expose many other things to the process of decay. Hydroponics could be one solution; treated 'soil medium' could be another. Also see Discussion for Topic 93, 'Growth responses in plants', and Assignment 4, Topic 22, 'The air around us'.

Topic 32
Populations

—Assignments—

1 e.g.
(i) Population growth is exponential (grows by multiplication). (*1*)

(ii) At the beginning there are very few reproducing individuals: (*1*) multiplication takes time to build up numbers. (*1*)

(*3 marks*)

2 e.g. Predators (*1*), disease (*1*), shortage of food (*1*).

(*3 marks*)

3 (a) We know population grows exponentially; (*1*) so can work backwards (extrapolate) from figures we know (*1*). (*2 marks*)

(b) e.g.
Development of agriculture, improvements in housing, improvement of the climate, boiling food in clay pots.
Any one (*1*)

(c) Black death. (*1*)

(d) e.g.
Major improvements in agriculture, housing, medicine, environmental health.
At least three – 1 mark each (*3 marks*)

(e) Birth control (*1*), economic restraints (*1*). (*2 marks*)

(*Total 9 marks*)

4 UK: 1.71 – 1.19 (*1*) = 0.52% (*1*).
USA: 1.76 – 0.96 (*1*) = 0.8% (*1*)
China: 2.9 – 1.3 (*1*) = 1.6% (*1*).
India: 4.2.– 1.7 (*1*) = 2.5% (*1*).
(*8 marks*)

Reasons:
UK – birth control effective (*1*), reasonably good living conditions (*1*).
USA – birth control effective (*1*), very good living conditions (*1*).
China – birth control introduced (*1*), improvement in living conditions (*1*).
India – ineffective birth control (*1*), relatively poor living conditions (*1*).
(**Note:** living conditions includes medical care and environmental health) (*8 marks*)

(*Total 16 marks*)

5 (a) 30–34 year olds. (*1*)

(b) At the end of war husbands and wives reunited, lovers married and had families (*2 marks if well explained*). (*2*)

(c) Offspring of the post-war bulge. (*1*)

(d) These are likely to be children of the age group after the bulge. (*1*)

(*Total 5 marks*)

6 Look for the following indicators for 'pyramid 2000':

(i) still more females than males (*1*) (maybe not markedly so – bonus);
(ii) 80–84 age group: males increase (e.g. 2%); (*1*) females increase (e.g. 4%); (*1*)
(iii) 75–79 age group: very slight bulge; (*1*)
(iv) 50–54 age group: noticeable bulge (post-war bulge); (*1*)
(v) 35–39 age group: noticeable bulge (even if slight); (*1*)
(vii) 0–5 age group: reduction in birth rate (both sexes) to about 5%. (*1*)
Indicators (*7 marks*)

Reasons (numbers relate to indicators):

(i) females were more likely to live longer; (*1*)
(ii) general increase in life span; (*1*)
(iii) follow on from 1980, 55–59 bulge; (*1*)
(iv) post-war bulge; (*1*)
(v) children of post-war bulge; (*1*)
(vi) grandchildren of post-war bulge; (*1*)
(vii) increase in birth control. (*1*)
Reasons (*7 marks*)

Note: this is only one interpretation and there are others, e.g. 1980 10–14 age group might be affected by an AIDS epidemic with consequent results for the under 10s in 2000.
Drawing pyramid (*3*)

(*Total 17 marks*)

Discussion

The human population won't go up for ever. What do you think will check it?
Note: famine, disease, war are the catastrophic ways, but human behaviour, e.g. contraception, will in the longer term hopefully prevail. In the west economics is a key factor in limiting the size of families.

Topic 33
Our Effects On The Environment

Investigation 1

To find out how much dust is deposited on outside walls

Practical skills

HMA 2, AMO 10, INT 6.

General Comments

It is interesting to compare the distribution of dust particles with the prevailing wind direction. Accurate observations (AMO 10) and recognition of patterns in data (INT 6) can be assessed. The pupils need to devise some sort of semi-quantitative 'index of dirtiness' with which they can assess different strips of sellotape; their initiative in doing this can also be assessed (HMA 2).

Investigation 2

To find out how much dust there is in the atmosphere

Requirements

Six microscope slides that have been coated in a thin layer of agar (technique: (i) pour a thin layer of liquid agar into a dish and insert several microscope slides; (ii) pour a further layer of agar on top of the slides; (iii) allow to set before cutting the slides out); light microscope with low power objective lens.

Practical skills
HMA 2, AMO 10, INT 6.

General Comments
The comments of the previous investigation are also relevant here.

—*Investigation 3*—

Estimating the amount of pollution in rainwater

Requirements
Gas jar; filter funnel; filter paper; universal indicator solution or paper.

Practical skills
AMO 10.

General Comments
This simple investigation could be used to show that acid rain is a real phenomenon. AMO 10 assesses accurate observations.

—*Investigation 4*—

Finding the effect of chemical pollutants on organisms

Requirements
Two (or more) jars; 100 cm^3 measuring cylinder; supply of tadpoles, *Daphnia,* or insect larvae; pollutants (e.g. oils, detergent, paraffin, dilute acid); distilled water.

Practical skills
HMA 5, AMO 10, EXP.

General Comments
It is necessary to choose the same species of organism for each tube *Daphnia* might be a more appropriate choice of organism than tadpoles, since it is an invertebrate. If it is necessary to observe organisms over a period of days, then the tubes should be aerated. The heart rate of *Daphnia* can be measured under the microscope (HMA 5).

The experimental design problem could be set as a written exercise, and used to assess the EXP skills.

—*Investigation 5*—

Measuring the noise level in different places

Requirements
Access to a sound meter.

Practical skills
HMA 7, REC 3, INT 4.

General Comments
The average sound level can be estimated by averaging the loudest and quietest reading in a single locality. Assess handling apparatus (HMA 7), accurate recording (REC 3) and simple calculations (INT 4).

—*Assignments*—

1 Smog = smoke (*1*) + fog (*1*). (*2 marks*)
Temperature inversion (*1*): layer of cold air trapped under layer of warm (*1*) holding with it smoke, motor vehicle exhaust fumes, etc., from city (*1*). (*3 marks*)
(*Total 5 marks*)

2 (a) Bacteria act on sewage. (*1*)
Reproduce rapidly. (*1*)
Use up all oxygen. (*1*)
Fish die through lack of oxygen. (*1*) (*4 marks*)
(b) Sunlight acts on motor vehicle exhaust; (*1*)
This makes photochemical smog. (*1*) (*2 marks*)
(c) DDT enters food chains (*1*) and becomes more concentrated (*1*) in each consumer along the chain (*1*) causing damage to living tissues (*1*) and possibly eventually harmful to humans (*1*). (*5 marks*)
(*Total 11 marks*)

3 $2SO_2$ (*1*) + $2H_2O$ (*1*) + O_2 (*1*) $\rightarrow$ $2H_2SO_4$ (*1*) but use individual discretion in accepting:
sulphur dioxide (*1*) + water (*1*) + oxygen (*1*) $\rightarrow$ sulphuric acid (*1*) (*4 marks*)

Note: GCSE syllabi generally require only word equations for photosynthesis and respiration. For this question it is worth advising pupils whether you want them to research a chemical equation or to apply their knowledge in producing a word equation. Pupils with some knowledge of chemistry should, however, be encouraged to attempt the chemical equation.

e.g. Dissolves buildings, kills fish in rivers, damages crop growth, destroys trees/forests, causes respiratory disorders, e.g. bronchitis (acid mist).
Any two (*2 marks*)
(*Total 6 marks*)

4 More sulphur dioxide produced in industrial areas (*1*) damages the particularly sensitive lichens (*1*).
e.g. experiment:
e.g. Take two 'country lichens' (*1*); put one in chamber containing sulphur dioxide (*1*) at similar concentration to industrially polluted atmosphere (*1*), other in chamber containing clean air (*1*).
Observe over a period of time(*1*). (*5 marks*)
(*Total 7 marks*)

5 Mercury remains in tissue (*1*) so accumulates along food chain (*1*). Even a tiny concentration of mercury in seawater (*1*) can prove deadly to top carnivores (including humans) (*1*).
(*4 marks*)

6 (a) Artificial fertilisers (*1*) draining into reservoirs (*1*). (*2 marks*)
(b) Analysis of data about stomach cancer victims and nitrate levels in drinking water (correlation). (*2*)
(c) Use of organic/natural fertilisers, advanced water treatment, developments in nitrogen fixation, better drainage.
At least three – 1 mark each (*3 marks*)
(*Total 7 marks*)

Discussion

1 Why might a healthier environment result in a lower standard of living? If it did, would you accept the choice?
Note: does having a healthier environment mean we will change our perception of what we mean by 'standard of living'?

2 Should countries be liable for the air pollution they inflict on others? Should Russia compensate British sheep farmers whose livestock had to be destroyed following contamination by radioactive fallout (in rain) from the Chernobyl nuclear power station? If so, should Britain compensate Norway for serious environmental damage caused by acid rain resulting from sulphur dioxide released from our coal-fired power stations?
Note: the public/press are always much more aware of the short-term acute environmental disaster, rather than the longer-term, chronic 'environmental sickness' such as that caused by sulphur dioxide.

3 Congratulations! Your class has been given the task of organising the conversion of Ghastly Grimes gravel pits to a scene of local beauty and recreation. Now all you've got to do is produce the plans. Good luck.
Note: it is probably worth providing pupils with a sketch map of the gravel pits. Opportunities for group work exist.

Topic 34
Organisms As Food For Humans

Assignments

1 Needs:
(i) supply of wheat seeds;
(ii) chemical fertiliser;
(iii) selective weedkiller;
(iv) pesticide;
(v) combine harvester;
(vi) other agricultural machinery (e.g. tractors, ploughs etc.).
At least four (*4 marks*)

Problems:
(i) late summer;
(ii) insufficient rain during growing season;
(iii) too much rain at harvest time;
(iv) resistant weeds;
(v) resistant insects;
(vi) wheat surplus – poor prices.
At least four (4 marks)

Solutions to problems above:
(i),(ii) and (iii): partly solved by selecting the right strain of wheat, but 'no real solution' is fair comment;
(iv) change weedkiller;
(v) change crop/sell land to megastore chain for giant car park!
One mark per solution or realisation of the problem (*4 marks*)

(*Total 12 marks*)

2 e.g. Reasons:
(i) perch is cold-blooded (less energy is needed to produce metabolic heat (+ *1*));
(ii) perch spends less energy getting nutrients from food;
(iii) perch is a carnivore; food has higher energy content than grass per unit mass;
At least three reasons – 2 marks per reason

(*6 marks*)

3 Of the energy that reaches the leaf only 9% is turned into (chemical energy in (+ *1*)) sugar (*1*) of which only 5% is stored (*1*). Only the stored energy is of any use to the cow (*1*); of this only 4% gets into cow's tissues (*1*).
So of the original energy in sunlight: only 5% × 4% (i.e. 0.05 × 0.04) (*1*) = 0.2% (0.002) (*1*) gets into the cow's tissues.

(*6 marks*)

4 If the animals are reared they convert very little of the energy in the plants they feed on into edible body tissues (*1*). More people can therefore be fed using plant crops (*1*).

(*2 marks*)

Discussion

1 Some parts of the world produce more food than they need. Other parts are plagued by famine. It seems a crazy situation, so why is it such a difficult one to resolve?
Note: discuss EEC food mountains, cost of transportation, nation states and political self-interest, and world economic systems. The real solutions seem to lie in developing and supporting self-help in Third World countries. Cheap imports of surpluses from elsewhere can undercut local farm production – lost profits result in a descending agri-economic spiral. Appreciation that there are no easy solutions to existing problems is valuable in itself.

2 Should land be given over to growing cash crops to produce fuel for cars, for example growing sugar to make alcohol?
Note: this happens in Brazil. There is the problem of cash crop versus food crop in countries where hunger might exist. Consider the suitability of crop-derived fuels such as alcohol and methane, and the inevitable exhaustion of fossil fuels. The overriding demand for fuel can precipitate international problems (e.g. the extent to which oil tanker convoys have been protected in the Persian Gulf).

Topic 35
Useful Microbes

Assignments

1 Note:product – e.g. use.
Bacterially produced chemicals:

acetic acid – vinegar (condiment);
acetone – nail varnish;
butanol – industrial raw material;
polysaccharides – drug manufacture;
protein – animal feed;
enzymes (proteases) – washing powders;
antibiotics (e.g. gramicidin) – antibacterial drugs;
steroids – drugs;
insulin – treats diabetes;
growth hormone – treats growth deficiencies;
interferon – treats cancer;
bioinsecticides – destroy insect pests;
vitamins – good health;
methane – fuel (biogas).

Fungus-produced chemicals:
alcohol – drink, cleaning agent, fuel;
citric acid – food additive (for 'sharp' flavours);
enzymes – industrial processes (e.g. rennet – making cheese);
penicillin – antibacterial drug;
steroids – drugs;
carotene – food colouring.
Three bacterial chemicals; one fungal chemical – for each: 1 mark for chemical; 1 mark for use
(*8 marks*)

Note: the list is longer than can be derived from the textbook, this is in the hope that it can lead to further discussion.

2 (i) Getting rid of sewage:
Sewage pumped into a large tank (*1*); the solid matter sinks, forming sludge (*1*). It is broken down by bacteria

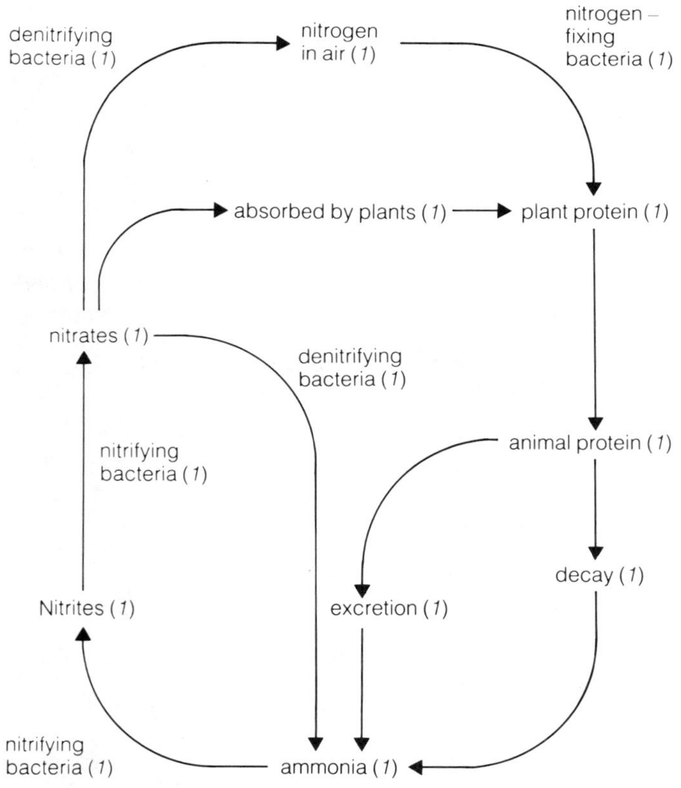

Note: the cycle best covers any explanation.

(*1*). Methane produced acts as fuel (*1*). Dried sludge is used as fertiliser (*1*).

Liquid part sprinkled on to filter bed (*1*) of stones coated with aerobic bacterial (*1*) which break up organic matter into simple substances (*1*) such as carbon dioxide and nitrogen salts (*1*). Resulting liquid is treated with chlorine to kill bacteria (*1*) and can then be discharged into nearby river.
(*10 marks*)

(ii) Nitrogen cycle (*1*).

(iii) Making yoghurt: (*1*)
certain bacteria make milk go sour (*1*) and convert milk sugar/lactose (*1*) to lactic acid (*1*) which makes milk curdle and go lumpy (*1*).
Yoghurt dessert – add flavouring to solidified milk (*1*).
(*5 marks*)

Note: yoghurt need not be flavoured. Making butter is similar, involving churning sour cream.

(iv) Making cheese: (*1*)
certain sour milk bacteria (*1*) convert milk/sugar lactose (*1*) to lactic acid (*1*) which makes milk curdle and go lumpy (*1*).
The solid part is separated from the liquid part (whey) (*1*) perhaps by squeezing through muslin (*1*). The resulting solid is cheese (*1*). Cheese is ripened by decay microbes (*1*). They break cheese down (*1*) and give it characteristic smell and flavour (*1*). (*10 marks*)

Note: award bonus marks for additional information about cheesemaking.

(v) Making linen: (*1*)
fibres are extracted (*1*) from stem of flax plant (*1*) by letting rest of stem rot (*1*). The process is called retting (*1*). It is carried out in water (*1*) and takes as little as three days (*1*). (*6 marks*)

Note: there is no parity of marks between (i), (ii), (ii), (iv) and (v), although (i) and (iv) carry the same number of marks.

Two options are open in tackling this problem:
1 Giving each pupil their own total (and converting it to, say, a mark out of ten for the records).
2 Converting each description to a mark out of five. Note that each named process has been awarded a mark separately, so that naming each process carries equal weight if this second method is used.

3 e.g.
Dear Editor,
Why does the junior health minister make such senseless remarks? You would think that those running the country would have a bit more intelligence. Or then again, maybe not!
Bacteria are so useful in decaying dead plants and animals (*1*) and circulating matter in nature (*1*). If bacteria did not help to recycle nitrogen (*1*), for example, no plants would grow (*1*) and since all animals, including ourselves, depend on plants (*1*) where would we be then?
Moreover, bacteria are useful in our everyday lives (*1*). Without bacteria none of the following would be possible: getting rid of sewage (*1*), making butter (*1*), yoghurt (*1*), cheese (*1*), linen (*1*), vinegar (*1*), enzymes (*1*) (as in washing powders (+ *1*)), proteins (*1*), drugs (*1*), and with genetic engineering (*1*) in the future creates the possibility of using bacteria to make all sorts of useful chemicals (*1*). Even the meat the minister doubtlessly eats was made with the help of grass-digesting bacteria (*1*).
Why not concentrate on viruses (*1*)? We haven't a cure for the common cold and AIDS is proving very difficult to control

(*1*). This would be a much more useful way for scientists to spend their time.

Yours sincerely,
Mike Robe

(*Notional 20 marks*)

Note: award 1 mark per relevant point made and up to 4 discretionary marks for other qualities such as presentation, clarity and humour. My marks exceed 20 for the sample – it's okay, I *can* count! The total is notional.

—Discussion—

1 How would you process and market bacterial protein for human consumption?
Note: ICI 'protein' is used for animal feed. Bacterial protein is just as adaptable as soya protein so it can be powder, pellets, even reconstituted 'meaty chunks'.

2 How important do you think biotechnology will be in the future?
Note: current products include alcohol, antibiotics, many industrial 'raw materials' (i.e. chemicals which can be processed into others) and pharmaceutical products. Bacteria are used in extracting copper from low grade ores (see marking scheme to question 1).

Topic 36
Food Spoilage And Its Prevention

—Investigation 1—

To find out what makes food go bad

Requirements

Single tablet of nutrient broth; test tube; 10 cm^3 distilled water; sterile glass tube; s-shaped glass tube; cotton wool; access to autoclave or pressure cooker (alternatively bunsen burner, tongs); microscope with low and high power lenses; microscope slide; coverslip.

Practical skills

HMA 3, HMA 4, HMA 5, HMA 6, HMA 7, AMO 10, EXP 5.

General Comments

If pupils are to have access to the autoclave, then it is essential that they are closely supervised at all times, particularly when it is hot. This investigation could have an additional control, namely broth in an open tube, since microbial contamination may be reduced in the tube with the open straight tube. This is because the narrow tube effectively reduces the surface area of the broth in contact with the air. Pupils could be asked to design a more suitable control, which could be used to develop skills. This practical could also be used to assess assembling apparatus (HMA 4), handling it correctly (HMA 7), accurate observations of the contamination (AMO 10) and microscopy skills at step 5 (HMA 5 and HMA 6).

—Investigation 2—

Finding ways of stopping food going bad

Requirements

Piece of fresh meat about 6 cm square; six large test tubes; sharp knife; plate; cotton wool; few crystals of silica gel; 20 cm^3 vinegar; 5 g salt; access to refrigerator; hair drier; autoclave or pressure cooker; soap; hot water; towels; other materials at the suggestion of the class.

Practical skills

HMA 2, HMA 7, AMO 10, EXP.

General Comments

Spoiled meat has a characteristic odour and a slimy texture. Hygiene is important in this practical, and it is essential that pupils handling the spoiled meat should wash their hands afterwards. Tubes B, E and F are traditional methods of slowing down the spoilage of food. This practical can be used to assess handling skills (HMA 7), accurate observations (AMO 10), and also pupil initiative (HMA 2) in the responses to the suggestions in question 4. It is possible to develop ideas in this practical as experimental design exercises (EXP); suitable hypotheses might include: Design an experiment to discover how long meat can stay 'fresh' in a refrigerator. Will meat spoil faster if it has been completely cooked, partly cooked or raw? Will vegetables (e.g. onions) spoil faster than meat? Will meat that has been frozen and then thawed spoil faster than a comparable piece of fresh meat?

—Assignments—

1 e.g.
(i) Any fresh vegetable (onions and potatoes keep quite well outside the fridge);
(ii) any fruit;
(iii) fresh meat;
(iv) milk;
(v) eggs;
(vi) bread – usually eaten quickly anyway.
Any five examples – 1 mark each

(*5 marks*)

Note: individual items e.g. 'cabbage' count as much as groups, e.g. 'vegetables'.

2 Bread contains enough moisture for moulds to grow. (*1*)
Biscuits are too dry. (*1*)
Pickled onions – vinegar kills bacteria. (*1*)

(*3 marks*)

3 (a) Extreme cold (*1*) did not kill microbes (*1*) but stopped them from multiplying (*1*) and slowed down their action (to a virtual standstill) (*1*). (*4 marks*)
(b) Not all bacteria are destroyed in canning (*1*). Those surviving multiply (*1*) and respire (anaerobically) (*1*) producing carbon dioxide which makes the can swell (*1*). (*4 marks*)
(c) Pasteurising milk heats milk long enough only to kill the dangerous bacteria (*1*), so the flavour of milk is not affected (*1*). Some non-disease causing bacteria survive this treatment (*1*). These will eventually break down milk, so it goes bad (*1*). (*4 marks*)

(*Total 12 marks*)

4 (a) To prevent microbes in the air from affecting food (*1*), and those already on the food from multiplying (*1*) along with slowing down their activity (*1*). (*3 marks*)
(b) To prevent microbes on skin (*1*) being transferred to food (*1*). (*2 marks*)
(c) The colder the freezer (*1*) the faster the food will freeze (*1*) and the less effect microbes will have (*1*). (*3 marks*)
(d) Ice crystals (*1*) break open cells of food (*1*) so bacteria can act on it more easily (*1*). (*3 marks*)

(*Total 11 marks*)

5 e.g. Take two test tubes (*1*). Into one put some dried milk powder (*1*); into the other put some dried milk power made up in water (*1*). Leave the test tubes in identical conditions for several days (*1*) observing daily (*1*).
(*5 marks*)

6 (a) Percentage = (mass of protein + mass of fresh fish) × 100 (*1*)
= (22 + 120) × 100 (*1*)
= 18 (*1*) % (*1*) (18.3%) (*4 marks*)
(b) Percentage = (mass of protein + mass of dried fish) × 100 (*1*)
= (22 + 31.5) × 100 (*1*)
= 70 (*1*) % (*1*) (69.8%) (*4 marks*)
(c) Much of the fresh fish's mass (74% (+ *1*)) is water. (*1 mark*)
(d) Dried foods
(i) are compact and light therefore easy to transport;
(ii) have high food value for bulk consumed;
(iii) are preserved – none is lost by going bad.
Any two reasons – 2 marks each (*4 marks*)
(*Total 13 marks*)

—*Discussion*—

1 A nutritionist commented recently that preventing food from going bad spoils it in other ways. Do you agree, and are some methods of preserving worse for the quality and nutritional value of the food than others?
Note: refer to *E for Additives,* by Maurice Hanssen, published by Thorsons, easily available from most bookshops. Not only preservatives, but also emulsifiers, stabilisers and antioxidants, might be added. Dried foods to be reconstituted are usually the most suspect in terms of nutritional value although there are exceptions (e.g. vegetarian dried foods). Frozen vegetables often have no additives at all (unless pre-prepared). Some frozen meats (e.g. chicken) contain polyphosphates to increase weight (increased water content!).

2 Which methods of preserving food are truly modern?
Note: canning developed in 1800 for Napoleon's army. Most other methods appear to have examples of long-established use, for example drying (see Topic 36, Figure 7, in *BFL*) and freezing a traditional practice among Eskimos/Inuits and Scandinavians. One horrible way is to bury the food in acid soil/peat, which is practised traditionally in parts of Norway. The only truly modern method is radiation treatment, which because of fears of health hazards is still not accepted.

Topic 37
Microbes And Disease

—*Investigation*—

Preventing the growth of bacteria

Requirements

Soap; hot water; towels; four sterile petri dishes containing nutrient agar; spirit marker pen; culture of *Bacillus subtilis* or other harmless bacterium (microbial suspensions from Topic 36, Investigation 1 might be appropriate); bunsen burner; sterilising wire loop; piece of filter paper 4 cm square; scissors; 5 cm^3 of each of the following solutions: Dettol, iodine, penicillin, distilled water; sellotape; access to an incubator at 37 or 25°C.

Practical skills

HMA 3, HMA 7, AMO 10.

General Comments

This investigation is a development of the one in Topic 7. The sterile techniques used there should be reviewed before the practical starts, as they will be needed here. Step 3 of the investigation requires that the wire loops are flamed first. Assessments can be made of working safely (HMA 3), handling materials (HMA 7), and accurate observations of the distribution of the bacterial colonies on the plates (AMO 10).

A pure culture of harmless microbes should be used (e.g. *Bacillus subtilis*). It is probably not necessary (or even desirable) to incubate the plates at 37°C. Incubation can be successful at 25°C. Under no circumstances should the pupils be allowed to open the plates after they have incubated. The pupils should let the chemicals soak into the agar jelly before turning them upside down for the incubator. Leaving them to stand for ten minutes should ensure this.

—*Assignments*—

1 Note: the order is: disease, organism causing it, how it spreads, and how it is controlled.
(i) Cholera (*1*); bacteria (*1*); sewage in food or drinking water (*1*); sewage treatment/clean water supplies (*1*). (*4 marks*)
(ii) Tuberculosis/TB (*1*); bacteria (*1*); coughing/damp living conditions (*1*); vaccination/improved living conditions/isolation (*1*). (*4 marks*)
(iii) Cold/common cold (*1*); virus (*1*); coughing/sneezing (*1*) difficult if not impossible to control (*1*) (some vaccines have limited success (+*1*)). (*4 marks*)
(iv) Flu/influenza (*1*); virus (*1*); coughing/sneezing (*1*); difficult if not impossible to control (*1*) (some vaccines have limited success (+*1*)). (*4 marks*)
(v) Diptheria (*1*); bacteria (*1*); dust (*1*); vaccination (*1*). (*4 marks*)
(vi) Scarlet fever (*1*); bacteria (*1*); dust/coughing/contaminated food (*1*); difficult to control but measures such as better living conditions/isolation/food hygiene help (*1*). (*4 marks*)
(vii) Impetigo (*1*); bacteria (*1*); touching/contact with clothes and personal effects (*1*); isolation (*1*). (*4 marks*)
(viii) Athlete's foot (*1*); fungus (*1*); contact between feet and changing room floors (*1*); walk through a foot bath before and after using a swimming pool (but athlete's foot is actually quite difficult to control fully since it depends so much on personal hygiene) (*1*). (*4 marks*)
(ix) Typhoid (*1*); bacteria (*1*); sewage in food or drinking water (*1*); sewage treatment/clean water supplies (*1*). (*4 marks*)
(x) Malaria (*1*); malarial parasite/protist (*1*); mosquito (*1*) (vector (+*1*)); anti-malarial tablets/draining land/using insecticides (*1*) (limited success (+*1*)). (*4 marks*)
(xi) Yellow fever (*1*); virus (*1*); mosquito (*1*) (vector (+*1*)); vaccination/draining land/using insecticides (*1*) (limited success (+*1*)). (*4 marks*)

(xii) Plague (*1*); bacteria (*1*); fleas on rats (*1*); good sanitation/clean living conditions (*1*). (*4 marks*)
(xiii) Rabies (*1*); virus (*1*); bitten by dogs/cats/wildlife (*1*); quarantine/destruction of diseased animals/strict legislation/isolation as an island (*1*). (*4 marks*)
(xiv) Hepatitis (*1*); viral (*1*); blood or objects which have been in contact with blood (*1*); high level of hygiene in hospitals, doctors' surgeries, etc. (*1*). (*4 marks*)
(xv) AIDS (*1*); virus (*1*); blood transfusions/sexual intercourse/any activity which involves any body fluids to mix (*1*); health education/condoms/blood screening (*1*). (*4 marks*)
(xvi) Smallpox (*1*); virus (*1*); contact/droplets in exhaled air (*1*); vaccination (*1*). (*4 marks*)
Note: smallpox is claimed to have been eradicated worldwide by vaccination programmes. The occasional isolated outbreak may still occur.
(xvii) Foot and mouth disease (*1*); virus (*1*); virus picked up by feet and mouths of farm animals (*1*); disinfecting boots and tyres (*1*); destroying farm animals and burning them/burying them in quick lime (*1*). (*5 marks*)
(xviii) Gangrene (*1*); bacteria (*1*); dirt/infection in open wounds (*1*); high level of hygiene in hospitals, doctors' surgeries' etc. (*1*). (*4 marks*)
(xix) Cowpox (*1*); virus (*1*); contact/exhaled air/contaminated bedding (*1*); vaccination (*1*). (*4 marks*)
(xx) Polio (*1*); virus (*1*); sewage in food and drinking water (*1*); isolation/closure of schools, swimming pools, etc./good sanitation/vaccination. (*4 marks*)
(xxi) German measles/rubella (*1*); virus (*1*); exhaled air (*1*); vaccination (*1*). (*4 marks*)
(xxii) Tetanus (*1*); bacteria (*1*); dirt in open wound (*1*); vaccination/antiseptic treatment of wounds (*1*). (*4 marks*)
(xxiii) Syphilis (*1*); bacteria (*1*); sexual intercourse (*1*); effective treatment with antibiotics/health education/condoms (*1*). (*4 marks*)
(xxiv) Gonorrhoea (*1*); bacteria (*1*); sexual intercourse (*1*); effective treatment with antibiotics/health education/condoms (*1*). (*4 marks*)

(*Total 97 marks*)

Notes:
1. Be warned – this question is very demanding and time consuming. On its own it would suffice as a very respectable homework.
2. The organisms causing all diseases except foot and mouth can be traced in the textbook. The way in which the disease is spread is covered in all diseases except smallpox, cowpox, polio and rubella. Control measures are covered in all diseases except scarlet fever, impetigo, athletes foot (these can all be worked out).
3. 'Sewage' can be taken to mean human faecal contamination.

2 e.g.
(i) Schools; (ii) buses/trains; (iii) shops; (iv) cinemas/theatres; (v) doctors' waiting rooms. *One mark each*

(*5 marks*)

3 (a) Flies are not choosy about where they eat (*1*) so their legs may be covered with germs (*1*). When feeding they also put saliva on to food (*1*). (*3 marks*)
(b) Plague bacteria (*1*) carried by fleas (*1*) living on rats (*1*). (*3 marks*)
(c) Mosquitos suck blood (*1*) and can so transfer diseases (*1*) such as malaria (*1*) and yellow fever (*1*). (*4 marks*)
(d) If the same needle is used by two people (*1*) (without being sterilised (+ *1*)) AIDS/viral hepatitis can be passed on (*1*). (*2 marks*)

Note: most hypodermic needles these days are disposable.

(e) Because air travel is so fast (*1*) an infected person can travel from one country to another (*1*) before he/she feels ill (*1*) during which time many people may become infected (*1*). (*4 marks*)

(*Total 16 marks*)

4 (a) To make sure it doesn't bring in rabies. (*1*)
(b) To prevent infection getting established. (*1*)
(c) To prevent droplets in his exhaled air (*1*) contaminating patient's body (*1*). (*2 marks*)
(d) To prevent contamination(*1*) by microbes on customers' hands or in the air (*1*). (*2 marks*)
(e) To kill any bacteria which might be present. (*1*)

(*Total 7 marks*)

5 (a) From his faeces. (*1*)
(b) e.g.
(i) Sewage leaks into drinking water supply; (*1*)
(ii) natural disaster, e.g. earthquake or flood. (*1*)
(*2 marks*)
(c) e.g.
(i) Close hamburger/butcher's shop;
(ii) destroy any remaining food in Mr. X's shop;
(iii) isolate all typhoid sufferers;
(iv) check drinking water supplies;
(v) check effectiveness/consequences of sewage treatment;
(vi) notify and advise public (via radio, TV, local news);
(vii) check for other carriers in food outlets.
At least four – 1 mark each (*4 marks*)

(*Total 7 marks*)

6 Some moulds contain antibiotics/penicillin (*1*) which will treat bacterial infection of wounds (*1*).

(*2 marks*)

7 (a) Operations involved cutting people open (*1*) which makes them especially vulnerable to infection (*1*). (*2 marks*)
(b) Many diseases are caused by bacteria in faeces. (*1*)
(c) Microbes on food can lead to infecting many customers. (*1*)
(d) Many people use pools and it is easy to swallow a little (potentially infected (+ *1*)) water. (*1*)
(e) Many people with diseases use doctors' surgeries; risk of cross infection must be minimised. (*1*)

(*Total 6 marks*)

8 (a) No cure for many infectious diseases (*1*) so patients isolated to prevent infection spreading (*1*). (*2 marks*)
(b) Immunisation/vaccination. (*1*)
Antibiotics. (*1*) (*2 marks*)
(c) e.g.
(i) Very hard to isolate hospital staff;
(ii) low morale of patients (if disease fatal);
(iii) are visitors allowed (risky) or are patients 'prisoners' (demoralising)?;
(iv) lack of effective medication;
(v) safe removal of infected dead bodies.
Any three – 2 marks each (*6 marks*)

(*Total 10 marks*)

9 e.g.
(i) Mask does not cover mouth;
(ii) impractical to carry around 24 hours a day;

(iii) viruses are impossible to filter.
Any reason (*1 mark*)

—*Discussion*

1 When Edward Jenner gave the young boy serum from a girl suffering from cowpox he knew that the girl was a milkmaid, and that milkmaids rarely, if ever, suffered from smallpox. What investigations do you think Jenner had carried out before giving the vaccination – a very risky thing to do if he was wrong!
Note: he may have examined medical records to establish whether any milkmaids had contracted smallpox – but this would have been difficult in those days. More likely he had relied on anecdotal evidence from farming communities, backed up by questioning milkmaids about whether they have ever contracted smallpox.

2 Suppose a form of deadly virus (as lethal as AIDS is at the time of publication) suddenly appeared that spread like the common cold. What steps do you think governments and health organisations ought to take?
Note: the photograph in Topic 37 of *BFL* suggests one control method that was previously used (not effectively!). Others are more likely: isolation, publicity, legislation (notifiable illness) and intense research to develop a vaccine and methods of treatment.

3 A friend holds the opinion that people in countries with rapidly expanding populations should neither be vaccinated against diseases nor treated for them once infected so that 'nature can take its toll'. Do you agree?
Note: I find such sentiments more than unsavoury! Population control through birth rate rather than death rate is more humanitarian.
Countries with rapidly rising populations are usually poor, so medical facilities are scant anyway. Diseases are unlikely to check the population fully. High mortality in peasant communities is usually an underlying reason for large families! 'Social Darwinism' is often used as excuse for unsound, repugnant political actions (e.g. in Nazi Germany).

Topic 38
Harmful Protists

—*Investigation 1*

Looking at the malarial parasite

Requirements
Light microscope with low and high power objective lenses; prepared microscope slides of normal blood and malarial blood.

Practical skills
HMA 5, AMO 10, REC 1.

General Comments
Assessment can be made of the use of the microscope (HMA 5), accurate observation of the parasites correctly distinguished from red blood cells (AMO 10) and, if diagrams are required, REC 1.

—*Investigation 2*

Looking at the sleeping sickness parasite

Requirements
Light microscope with low and high power objective lenses; prepared microscope slides of blood of sleeping sickness patient; drawing paper.

Practical skills
HMA 5, AMO 10, REC 1.

General Comments
The use of the microscope (HMA 5), accurate observation (AMO 10) and drawing skills (REC 1) can be assessed.

—*Investigation 3*

Looking at live parasitic protists

Requirements
Watch glass containing the contents of the rectum of a frog or toad, mixed with 1% salt solution; dropping pipette; light microscope with low power objective lens; microscope slide; coverslip; mounted needle; soap, hot water and towels.

Practical skills
HMA 5, HMA 6, AMO 10, REC 1.

General Comments
Microscopy skills (HMA 5 and 6), and accurate observations (AMO 10), which can be recorded in drawings (REC 1) or prose, can be assessed. Hands should be washed after this practical.

Opalina (below) is a parasitic protist that lives inside the rectum of amphibians.

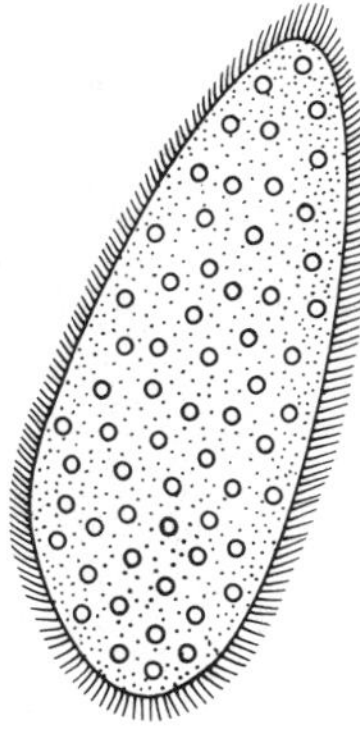

(magnification × 100)

—Assignments

1 (i) Parasite – an organism which feeds on another living (*1*) organism (*1*). (*2 marks*)
(ii) Fever – high temperature; (*1*)
sweating; (*1*)
shivering; (*1*)
delirious; (*1*). (*4 marks*)
(iii) Delirious – in a confused state due to being ill. (*1*)
(iv) Life cycle – series of events which take place (*1*) between when an organism reproduces and its offspring reproduce (*1*). (*2 marks*)
(v) Fission – asexual (*1*) reproduction (*1*); the organism divides in two (*1*). (*3 marks*)

(*Total 12 marks*)

2 Malaria occurs when *Anopheles* (*1*) mosquito is found (*1*) which is in hot countries (*1*). (*3 marks*)
Malaria sufferer caught disease in hot climate (*1*); since the disease recurs (*1*) it could appear after returning to Britain (*1*). (*3 marks*)

(*Total 6 marks*)

3 There is more metabolic activity (*1*) when parasite attacks red blood cells/liver/body (*1*) in large numbers (*1*) so the temperature rises.

(*3 marks*)

4 Malaria parasite – red blood cells, (*1*)
liver cells; (*1*)
sleeping sickness parasite – food substances, (*1*)
in plasma; (*1*)
dysentery amoeba – lining of large intestine, (*1*)
red blood cells (in bleeding lining). (*1*)

(*6 marks*)

5 Anti-malaria tablets, (*1*)
mosquito netting (*1*).

(*2 marks*)

6 Sometimes the parasite is benign and the host is well (*1*); at other times the parasite is virulent and the host is feverish (*1*).

(*2 marks*)

Note: award bonus marks for mentioning the terms 'dormant' and 'active' since, although they do appear elsewhere in the textbook, they are not emphasised in this topic.

7 Parasite reproducing in (*1*), and released from (*1*), red blood cells so maximum damage is being caused to patient (*1*), resulting in height of fever (*1*). (*4 marks*)
Large numbers of parasite (*1*) are following their life cycle (*1*) simultaneously (*1*). (*3 marks*)

(*Total 7 marks*)

—Discussion

How would you set about controlling malaria? What practical problems might you face?

Note: consider breaking the cycle: e.g. draining marshes so larvae cannot develop; this is expensive and has ecological consequences. Spraying with DDT was used, but now we have DDT-resistant mosquito and toxins accumulating in food chains! Communities may be moved away from wetlands – this is not always easy (e.g. in case of a fishing community). Giving anti-malarial tablets is both expensive, since it is not a 'one-off' prevention (such as vaccination) and difficult to guarantee that everyone will take them. Mosquito netting is effective by night but you can get bitten during the day!

Topic 39
Parasitic Worms

—Investigation 1

The front and back of a tapeworm

Requirements
Light microscope with low and high power objective lenses; prepared microscope slides of the head of a tapeworm and the mature segment of the posterior of the tapeworm; drawing paper.

Practical skills
HMA 5, REC 1, INT 1.

General Comments
You can assess the use of the microscope (HMA 5), drawing skills (REC 1), and the answer to the question in step 3 (INT 1).

—Investigation 2

Liver flukes and roundworms

Requirements
The dissected lungs of a frog; watch glass; 20 cm^3 1% saline solution; two mounted needles; dropping pipette; light microscope with high and low power objective lenses; microscope slide; coverslip.

Practical skills
HMA 5, HMA 6, INT 1.

General Comments
Microscopy skills can be assessed (HMA 5 and 6), and the interpretation question following step 6 (INT 1).

—*Assignments*—

1 e.g.
(i) Surrounded by digestive enzymes;
(ii) churning movements of intestine;
(iii) intestine wall might ulcerate so become detached;
(iv) human might take anti-tapeworm medicines,
At least three – 1 mark each
(*3 marks*)

2 No gut:
nutrients are already digested (*1*) so can be absorbed through body surface (*1*).
No senses: tapeworm doesn't need to find its food (*1*) and it cannot be threatened by being eaten (*1*).
(*4 marks*)

3 (a) e.g.
(i) Go to a reputable butcher's;
(ii) closely inspect meat;
(iii) cook meat very thoroughly;
(iv) clean hands before cooking/eating.
At least three – 1 mark each (*3 marks*)
(b) e.g.
(i) Don't paddle in freshwater when you next go on safari/rice harvesting;
(ii) unless you've brought your wellies with you;
(iii) be especially careful if you suspect human sewage/ faeces has entered the water.
At least two – 1 mark each (*2 marks*)
(*Total 5 marks*)

4 Eggs rely on chance (*1*) to be transferred from one host to another (*1*). For each egg the chance of successful transfer is low (*1*) so many eggs are produced to compensate for this (*1*).
(*4 marks*)

5 e.g. Tapeworm:
(i) head with hooks or suckers;
(ii) can release many segments – asexual reproduction;
(iii) can produce millions of eggs;
(iv) resistant to digestive enzymes;
(v) intermediate host;
(vi) soaks up/absorbs pre-digested food;
(vii) large body surface area.
At least four – 1 mark each (*4 marks*)

e.g. Blood fluke:
(i) slender shape to live in host's blood vessels;
(ii) very large number of eggs;
(iii) intermediate host;
(iv) sucker – attaches fluke to blood vessels;
(v) can bore into feet;
(vi) sucks blood.
At least four – 1 mark each (*4 marks*)
(*Total 8 marks*)

6 e.g.
(i) Too cold for ciliated larva;
(ii) too cold for snails;
(iii) running water;
(iv) not many people.
At least two – 1 mark each
(*2 marks*)

—*Discussion*—

An entrepreneur decides to market a certain type of tapeworm as a slimming aid, selling 'bladders' coated in sugar and coloured with a non-toxic dye (for appeal!). Is this an acceptable way to make money?
Note: are ingenuity and free enterprise not always virtues? This *did* happen in the USA. Problems could include a tenacious individual tapeworm which might prove difficult to dislodge, cause ulceration of the gut and put slimmers in hospital.

Topic 40
Parasitic Fungi

—*Investigation*—

Looking at a fungal disease

Requirements
Light microscope with low and high power objective lenses; microscope slide; coverslip; two mounted needles; lactophenol stain; hand lens; a binocular microscope; small piece of filter paper; prepared slide of a leaf infected with a fungus; leaves of a plant (e.g. wallflower or shepherds purse) that are infected with mildew; 5 cm^3 distilled water.

Practical skills
HMA 5, HMA 6, AMO 10, INT 1.

General Comments
Assessment can be made of microscope skills (HMA 5 and HMA 6), accurate observations of hyphae and, if present, reproductive structures (AMO 10) and how the observations relate to the understanding of the fungal mode of life (INT 1).

—*Assignments*—

1 Spores produced by the fungus (*1*) can be carried by the wind to other plants (*1*). (Even spores landing on soil can infect tubers (+*1*)). (*2 marks*)
Means of controlling include:
(i) spray potato plants with fungicide (*1*) (e.g. copper sulphate) (+*1*).
(ii) avoid planting in warm humid areas; (*1*)
(iii) avoid planting down prevailing wind; (*1*)
(iv) avoid planting (potentially) infected tubers; (*1*)
(v) develop fungus-resistant strains of potato. (*5 marks*)
(*Total 7 marks*)

2 e.g.
(i) Both 1845 and 1846 were damp years.
(ii) Little understanding of how potato blight worked led to a repeat of the famine.
(iii) Infected tubers were planted.
At least two – 1 mark each
(*2 marks*)

3 (a) Spore forming body/fruiting body/bracket. (*1*)
(b) Under bark of tree (*1*); looks like cotton wool (*1*). (*2 marks*)
(c) The fungus would be parasite (*1*) if it had absorbed nutrients from the tree (*1*) (radioactive tracers could be used to show this (+ *1*)) and the tree was living (*1*). The fungus could be either a saprophyte or an epiphyte (*either 1*). (*4 marks*)

Note: it is difficult to tell how this fungus could be an epiphyte, but is worth a qualified mark.

(*Total 7 marks*)

4 e.g. Take samples of wood from infected dead tree (*1*). Using a microscope (*1*) check for evidence of Dutch elm disease fungus (*1*) and disease fungus carrying beetle (*1*).

(*4 marks*)

Discussion

1 Why did potato blight have such a devastating effect on the people of Ireland? After all, it was only one crop.
Note: for most of the peasants in nineteenth-century Ireland it was their *only* source of food! The Irish potato famines were as much the consequence of poverty and social inequalities as the blight itself. The recent famines in Ethiopia, Sudan and Mozambique also have underlying human causes rather than simply natural/biological ones.

2 Why are some people more prone to athlete's foot than others?
Note: resistance by the body itself, toughness of skin on soles of feet and between toes and personal cleanliness all play a part.

Topic 41
Insects, Harmful And Helpful

Investigation 1

Getting rid of mosquitoes

Requirements
Dish containing several mosquito larvae or pupae; 5 cm^3 liquid paraffin or vegetable oil; preserved adult mosquito; white paper; ruler.

Practical skills
AMO 2, AMO 10.

General Comments
Floating oil on the surface of still water is a method employed to control the spread of the mosquito. It works by reducing the surface tension of the water, causing the larvae and pupae to sink. The main disadvantage is that it prevents oxygen penetrating the water surface, killing other organisms in the water. AMO 10 assesses accurate observation of the behaviour of the larvae, and AMO 2 the measurement of the length of the female adult fly.

Investigation 2

A look at some harmful insects

Requirements
Light microscope with low and high power objective lenses; microscope slide; coverslip; mounted needle; preserved specimen of female mosquito, louse and cabbage white butterfly.

Practical skills
HMA 5, INT 1.

General Comments
HMA 5 assesses the use of the microscope, and INT 1 the ability of the pupils to relate the structure of the organism to its mode of life.

Assignments

1 (i) Locust – eats crops (*1*) in large numbers (*1*). (*2 marks*)
(ii) Mosquito – disease carrier (*1*) of e.g. malaria, yellow fever (*1*). (*2 marks*)
(iii) Head louse – sucks blood (*1*), can carry disease (*1*), irritates (*1*). (*3 marks*)

Note: typhus is carried by body lice but I'd be tempted to give a qualified mark.

(iv) Cabbage white butterfly – caterpillar (*1*) eats crops (*1*). (*2 marks*)
(v) Housefly – carry disease germs to food (*1*), lays eggs on food (especially meat) (*1*). (*2 marks*)

(*Total 11 marks*)

2 From an aircraft (*1*): insecticide is sprayed over wider area (*1*) killing more locusts (*1*).

(*3 marks*)

3 e.g.
(i) The greater the number, the sooner food runs out, so they get agitated sooner.
(ii) A hopper's activity depends on the activity it observes. Large numbers cause a 'chain reaction'.
(iii) Hoppers release a substance (pheromone) which stimulates others. More hoppers = more substance around.
At least three – 2 marks each (*6 marks*)

e.g. Investigations for (i)–(iv) above:
(i) measure hopper activity and vary food availability;
(ii) measure hopper activity while surrounded by a model crowd;
(iii) measure hopper activity while surrounded by moving models;
(iv) put hoppers in chamber. Transfer air to second chamber with other hoppers in and measure activity.
2 marks for any reasonable investigation. Assuming three reasons originally given (*6 marks*)

(*Total 12 marks*)

4 (i) Locust – swarms.
(ii) Death watch beetle – furniture.
(iii) Ladybirds – greenflies.
(iv) Bees – pollination.

(v) DDT – insecticide.
1 mark each

(*5 marks*)

5 e.g. The cold makes it more likely for people to (*1*) huddle close (and makes it easier for lice to detect body warmth (+*1*)); this gives lice more chance to spread (*1*).

(*2 marks*)

6 (i) Spraying:
e.g.argument for spraying – quick and convenient; (*1*)
e.g.argument against spraying – insecticides can get into food chains and may destroy useful insects as well as pests. (*1*)

(ii) Predator:
e.g.argument for predator – only destroys pests; (*1*)
e.g.argument against predator – keeps pests numbers low but doesn't eradicate it and may upset ecosystem. (*1*)

(*4 marks*)

7 (a) Chad, Djibouti, Ethiopia, Guinea, Guinea Bissau, Kenya, Mali, Mauritania, Morocco, Niger, Nigeria, Saudi Arabia, Senegal, Somalia, Sudan, Tanzania, Uganda, Upper Volta, Yemen.
Notional: 1 mark each (*12 marks*)

(b) These countries are hot and dry; (*1*)
overfeeding is likely to quickly lead to scarcity; (*1*)
resulting in swarming behaviour (*1*). (*3 marks*)

(c) e.g.
(i) United Nations enables forecasting across several countries.
(ii) Many of these countries are now totally arid – not even fit for locusts!
Any reason (*2 marks*)

(*Total 17 marks*)

—Discussion

1 Why has it been so hard to eradicate any insect pest?
Note: the high reproductive rate, sheet resilience, small size and adaptability seem to keep the insects one step ahead.

2 In balance, are insects more helpful than harmful?
Note: most likely, the answer is yes. The tendency is to judge the class insecta by the few rogues. Most insects quietly participate in natural cycles (e.g. pollinating, breaking down leaf litter, food chains).

Topic 42
Cells, The Bricks Of The Body

—Investigation 1

Looking at cheek cells

Note: the DES statement on safety recommends that this practical be discontinued (see p. 6).

An alternative source of epithelial cells, which avoids the possible health hazards associated with the use of human cheek cells, is the common frog or African clawed toad (*Xenopus*). In the case of the frog, scrape off a small piece of epithelium from the surface of the skin with a blunt scalpel blade, mount the tissue in water on a slide and irrigate with methylene blue. The cells are small but can be clearly seen under high power.

For *Xenopus*, the sloughed-off skin can be lifted out of the water in which the animals are kept. This has the advantage that the animals do not have to be handled, and if the pieces of epithelium are lifted with a spatula they can be laid out flat on the slide and the way the cells fit together can be seen. As with the frog, the tissue should be mounted in water and irrigated with methylene blue. Skin cells can be found in the water, but there might be more debris.

Requirements

Light microscope with low and high power objective lenses; microscope slide; coverslip; clean blunt spatula; blunt scalpel blade; methylene blue stain; mounted needle; dropping pipette; pieces of filter or blotting paper.

Practical skills

HMA 5, HMA 6, REC 1.

General Comments

This could provide a useful opportunity to assess the use of the compound microscope (HMA 5), and teach the correct way to stain cells. The coverslip needs to be lowered on to the slide carefully so that the slide is bubble free. The stain needs to be applied evenly. Uneven distribution of stain can be corrected by placing a small piece of filter or blotting paper on the opposite side of the slide, and drawing the stain towards the paper. This skill is assessed as HMA 6, and the drawing of the cells, complete with scale factor, as REC 1.

—Investigation 2

Looking at plant cells

Requirements

Light microscope with low and high power objective lenses; microscope slide; coverslip; onion; *Elodea*; any moss; forceps; scissors; dilute iodine dissolved in potassium iodide solution (for recipe see Topic 47, p. 58 of this guide); scalpel.

Practical skills

HMA 5, HMA 6, HMA 7, REC 1.

General Comments

This investigation accompanies Investigation 1, and the same general comments apply.

—Assignments

1 20 µm = $\frac{1}{50}$ mm; (*1*)
line 2 = 7 mm (as far as the full stop); (*1*)
no. of cells = 7 × 50 (*1*)
= 350 cells. (*1*)

(*4 marks*)

2 Glycogen – storage; (*1*)
chloroplast – sunlight; (*1*)
mitochondrion – energy; (*1*)

chromosomes – inheritance; (*1*)
cellulose – elastic. (*1*)

(*5 marks*)

3 (a) Glycogen granules. (*1*)
(b) Chloroplasts; (*1*)
starch grains; (*1*)
cell wall. (*1*) (*3 marks*)
(c) Cytoplasm; (*1*)
nucleus; (*1*)
vacuole; (*1*)
chromosomes; (*1*)
cell membrane; (*1*)
mitochondria. (*1*) (*6 marks*)

(*Total 10 marks*)

4 Light microscope:
nucleus; (*1*)
chromosomes; (*1*)
chloroplasts. (*1*)
Electron microscope only:
endoplasmic reticulum; (*1*)
ribosomes. (*1*)

(*5 marks*)

5 Because the nucleus only occupies a small part of the cell. (*1*)
So the microtome slice can miss it out altogether. (*1*)

(*2 marks*)

Discussion

1 What advantages are there in an organism being made up of separate cells?
Note: it enables ease of regeneration relatively easy, removal of defective cells, division of labour, and allows same type of tissue to develop in different parts of body (e.g. epithelium connective tissue).

2 'An organism is made up of cells in the same way as a house is made of bricks.' Can you think of any ways in which this comparison is *not* a good one?
Note: cells are functional as well as structural, and come in variety of shapes and sizes. Some are mobile; some change shape.

Topic 43 Tissues, Organs And Organisation

Investigation 1

Looking at epithelium

Requirements

Light microscope with low and high power objective lenses; microscope slide; coverslip; frog skin; methylene blue stain.

Pratical skills

HMA 5, HMA 6.

General Comments

This activity provides an opportunity to use and assess the microscope techniques already learnt (HMA 5 and HMA 6). The epithelium of a frog has a major role in gaseous exchange. The need for a thin, tough, epithelium, can be developed. Gaseous exchange in the frog is developed further in Topic 57.

Investigation 2

Looking at plant packing tissue

Requirements

Tomato; dish; knife; light microscope with low and high power objective lenses; microscope slide; coverslip; pointed needle; dropping pipette; water.

Practical skills

HMA 5, HMA 6, AMO 8, AMO 9.

General Comments

This activity, when combined with the previous one, allows similarities and differences in cell structure and in the structure and function of the two tissues to be reviewed. The relative strengths of the two tissues, and their thicknesses ought to be noted. This could form the basis of a class report on the two tissues, and assessment for AMO 8 and AMO 9.

For AMO 8, obvious similarities and differences without close inspection, both tissues are comparatively extensive macroscopic structures, and the cells are joined together to form a tissue. The cells of the epithelium are one layer thick, forming a thin sheet of tissue; the parenchyma cells are joined to form a mass of tissue. There are also differences in texture, strength and colour between the two tissues, which can be related to their function within the organism.

For AMO 9, both tissues consist of a large number of cells, probably of only one type. Both cell types have a cytoplasm and a nucleus, but the parenchyma cells also have a cellulose cell wall.

It might be appropriate to link the next two activities with the mammalian dissection in Topic 18.

Investigation 3

Looking at organs

Requirements

Some or all of the following: lungs, stomach, intestine, tongue, liver, pancreas, heart, kidney, muscle, brain and eye; plates; sharp knives.

Practical skills

AMO 10.

General Comments

This activity enables pupils to observe a number of different mammalian organs. It can be as open ended as the teacher wishes, but emphasise that the pupils will have the opportunity to handle all of these organs again in more detail later in the course. It may be better to leave some of the organs (e.g. the eye) until later, thus retaining the element of curiosity. Examination of one or two organs (e.g. tongue or pancreas) would provide pupils with the opportunity of examining an organ in the light of Topic 43, Table 2, in *BFL*, and assessing their reports (AMO 10).

—*Investigation 4*—

Examining the inside of an organ

Requirements

Light microscope with low and high power objective lenses; prepared microscope slide of TS through appropriate mammalian organ.

Practical skills

AMO 10.

General Comments

This investigation accompanies the previous one, and could allow those organs to be studied at the microscopic level. The number of different types of tissue in the slide can be estimated (AMO 10), with an indication of their function. This could prove difficult, however, unless the class were given some help as to the function of the organ studied and the sort of tissues that they might be expected to find.

—*Assignments*—

1 (i) Tissue – large numbers (*1*) of similar cells (*1*) massed together (*1*). (*3 marks*)
(ii) Organ – different tissues (*1*) combined together (*1*) to carry out one or more jobs(*1*). (*3 marks*)
(iii) Muscle – organ (*1*) which brings about movement (*1*). (*2 marks*).
Note: more elaborate explanations of muscle are likely/possible, e.g. 'made of muscle tissue', 'smooth and striped/striated'. Award additional marks as appropriate.
(iv) Epithelium – one of the simplest tissues (*1*) consisting of a single sheet (*1*) of cells, it lines spaces and tubes of body (*1*). (*3 marks*)
(v) Multicellular – body made of (*1*) many cells (*1*). (*2 marks*)
(*Total 13 marks*)

2 Photosynthetic tissue – feeding; (*1*)
epithelial tissue – protection; (*1*)
connective tissue – strength; (*1*)
blood tissue – transport; (*1*)
nervous tissue – messages. (*1*)
(*5 marks*)

3 (a) Packing tissue. (*1*)
(b) Blood tissue. (*1*)
(c) Muscle tissue. (*1*)
(d) Photosynthetic tissue. (*1*)
(e) Vascular (conducting tissue). (*1*)
(f) Skeletal tissue. (*1*)
(g) Epidermal tissue. (*1*)
(h) Nerve tissue. (*1*)
(i) Connective tissue.(*1*)
(j) Epithelial tissue. (*1*)
(*10 marks*)

4 By doing their own jobs well (*1*) and working in harmony (*1*) it makes it possible for a complex animal to run smoothly (*1*).
(*3 marks*)

5 Animals do not feed by photosynthesis. (*1*)
Plants do not move around. (*1*)
(*2 marks*)
Note: watch out for exceptions. Some animals, e.g. green hydra *do* feed by photosynthesis but this is the result of a relationship with photosynthetic protists. Some varieties of plant, e.g. Venus fly trap, sensitive plant (mimosa), do move quickly but the exact mechanism is unclear. It is, however, non-muscular.

6 e.g. Paired organs: ears, eyes, salivary glands, lungs, kidneys, adrenal glands, ovaries, seminal vesicles, testes, muscles, mammary glands.
Any two – 1 mark each (*2 marks*)
e.g. Single organs: brain, pituitary gland, nose, mouth, tongue, larynx/voice box, heart, thyroid gland, thymus gland, diaphragm, liver, gall bladder, stomach, pancreas, small intestine, large intestine, bladder, uterus, vagina, prostate gland, penis, appendix.
Any one – 1 mark each (*2 marks*)
e.g. Advantages of paired organs:
(i) reduces the 'load' for each organ;
(ii) if one breaks down, the other works.
(**Note:** people who have had e.g. one lung or one kidney surgically removed.)
Any one advantage (*2 marks*)
(*Total 6 marks*)

7 e.g.
Functions of head:
(i) thinking;
(ii) co-ordinating/controlling;
(iii) seeing;
(iv) hearing;
(v) smelling;
(vi) tasting;
(vii) eating (and drinking);
(viii) taking in air during breathing;
(ix) talking;
(x) making facial gestures.
At least eight – 1 mark each (*8 marks*)
e.g. Why head is at anterior end:
most animals move forward (*1*); important that animal is equipped with (*1*) structures to encounter (*1*) the world in its way at the front (*1*).
(It's better to see where you're going than where you have been!)
Good answer (*4 marks*)
(*Total 12 marks*)

8 (i) Bilateral symmetry – structures on one side mirror images of other. (*1*)
Radial symmetry – structures arranged evenly about a central point. (*1*) (*2 marks*)
(ii) e.g. Bilateral : human. (*1*)
e.g. Radial: jellyfish. (*1*) (*2 marks*)
(iii) No. (*1*)
Some internal organs (*1*) (e.g. liver, stomach (+*1*)) are not symmetrically placed/show no symmetry (*1*).
(*3 marks*)
(*Total 7 marks*)

—Discussion

1 Are humans the most complex of animals?
Note: humans are structurally unexceptional as mammals; even complex brains can be found in other mammals (e.g. dolphins, primates). We tend to set ourselves aside because of our particular kind of intelligence.

2 Are plants simpler in structure than animals, and if so, why?
Note: plants are static structures; animals are generally dynamic. Dynamic structures are usually more complex.

Topic 44
Molecules In Motion

—Investigation 1

Watching osmosis

Requirements
Scissors; length of visking tubing (about 8 cm); length of strong thread (about 10 cm); 50 cm^3 of 20% sucrose solution; thin bore capillary tube (about 30 cm long); a retort stand and clamp; a 250 cm^3 beaker; a plastic ruler measure in millimetres; clock; graph paper; access to sink; water.

Practical skills
HMA 1, HMA 2, HMA 4, HMA 7, AMO 2, AMO 4, REC 2, REC 3, REC 4, INT 1, INT 3.

General Comments
This experiment requires pupils to manipulate the apparatus carefully if they are to achieve accurate results. The bag must not be moved during the experiment, for this will alter the level of liquid in the capillary tube. It is necessary to see the level of liquid in the capillary tube and to record its height from a set point. This will enable following instructions (HMA 1), manipulative skills (HMA 7), assembling apparatus (HMA 4), use of initiative (HMA 2), and measuring skills (AMO 2), to be assessed. The results will be taken at set time intervals (AMO 4) and the results recorded in a table (REC 2, REC 3). From this, a graph will be plotted (REC 4). The question at the end of the investigation will provide a way of assessing the ability to draw the correct conclusion (INT 1).

—Investigation 2

Osmosis in a potato

Requirements
Potato; potato peeler; knife; dish of water big enough to contain half of the potato; strong sucrose solution (20%); pin; clock.

Practical skills
AMO 2, INT 1, EXP.

General Comments
In this demonstration the level of the solution relative to the pinhead below the top of the potato is observed. Water is drawn from the cells surrounding the sugar solution by osmosis. These draw water from the cells that surround them, and so on. In this way water is drawn from the dish into the potato. The rate of water uptake can be measured as the level the solution rises in the potato (AMO 2). The answer to the question at the end of the investigation can be used to assess INT 1.

It is possible to extend this practical to develop EXP skills by altering the variables in the experiment. Suggested questions include: 'To what extent does the epidermis of the potato act as a barrier to water uptake?'; 'What is the effect of replacing the sugar solution with sugar crystals or salt?'; 'What effect does boiling the potatoes for a short time (parboiling) have on the uptake of water into the potato?'.

—Investigation 3

The effect of osmosis on a plant cell

Requirements
Light microscope with low and high power objective lenses; microscope slide; coverslip; small section of rhubarb epidermis (about 3 cm long), or a 3 cm length of *Cladophora*; forceps; scissors; distilled water; 5 cm^3 50% sucrose solution; filter paper.

Practical skills
HMA 5, HMA 6, REC 1, INT 1.

General Comments
One of the major problems of this practical is peeling off a piece of epidermis that is thin enough to see one or two cells clearly enough to watch plasmolysis occurring. This problem may be overcome by observing osmosis in *Cladophora*, which is a filamentous alga that is already only one cell thick.

Assessment can be made of using the microscope (HMA 5 and HMA 6), drawings of the appearance of the cells before and after plasmolysis (REC 1) and the explanation of the effect (INT 1).

Osmosis in animal blood cells is studied in Topic 59, Investigation 4. Teachers might like to do both of these practicals at the same time.

—Assignments

1 (a) Lettuce gets floppy when its cells have (*1*) lost water. Put in cold water and cells take up (*1*) by osmosis (endosmosis) (*1*). (*3 marks*)
(b) Sugar dissolves (slightly) (*1*) to form a strong solution on the strawberry's surface (*1*). This draws water out of the strawberry's cell (*1*) by osmosis (*1*) (exosmosis (+*1*)). (*4 marks*)

Note: endosmosis and exosmosis might be worth extra marks if mentioned in addition, rather than as an alternative, to just osmosis.

(*Total 7 marks*)

2 (a) Sugar solution is stronger than cell contents (*1*). Water is drawn out (*1*) by osmosis (*1*) (exosmosis), so the piece of potato shrinks. (*3 marks*)

(b) A piece of potato in sucrose solution the same strength as its cell sap;
or in a solution of its own sap;
or just water;
or air saturated with water vapour. (*2 marks*)

Note: what the control ought to be is well worth discussing.

(*Total 5 marks*)

—*Discussion*

1 What is the largest animal you can think of which has no special respiratory organs? How does it manage without them?
Note: my guess is a Portugese Man o' War. Tissues are all superficial, the bulk of the organism being non-cellular mesogloea.

2 When is osmosis important in modern medicine?
Note: consider kidney dialysis, saline drip, poultices and salt baths to reduce swelling.

Topic 45
The Chemistry Of Life

—*Investigation 1*

What are you made of and how much are you worth

Requirements

Weighing scales in kilograms; the current supermarket price for 1 kg of sugar, 1 kg of stewing steak, and 1 kg of salt.

Practical skills

INT 4.

General Comments

Interpreting proportions and percentages is a concept that many pupils find difficult. This activity enables percentages to be interpreted in terms of actual masses, and is a useful way of either developing the skills for, or assessing, INT 4. It will lead on to an interesting philosophical discussion on the dangers of adopting a too literal reductionist viewpoint! Another interesting question would be 'Are there any circumstances when this is a valid way of expressing the value of a person?'.

—*Investigation 2*

Some biologically important chemicals and their properties

Requirements

1 g of each of the following substances: glucose, sucrose, starch, vegetable oil, lard, albumen; one human hair; distilled water; six standard test tubes; 5 cm^3 syringe; glass rod.

Pratical skills

AMO 10, INT 1.

General Comments

The pupil should place 5 cm^3 of water in each test tube, and should add one of the substances to each of the tubes, stirring each one to the same extent.
Given the statement that small molecules dissolve more easily than larger ones, it would to be possible for pupils to deduce that glucose, sucrose and starch can be arranged in an ascending order of molecule size; this then leads into the question in step 3 of the investigation, which can be assessed as AMO 10 and INT 1. The immiscibility of fats and water can lead to an appreciation of the waterproofing properties of fats. It would also be pointless to have membranes that were soluble in water! Globular proteins (e.g. albumen) have a folded shape and form colloidal suspensions more easily than insoluble fibrous proteins (e.g. keratin, the protein in hair).

—*Assignments*

1 Carbohydrate:
energy source (glucose); (*1*)
energy storage (glycogen). (*1*)
Fat:
energy storage; (*1*)
insulation. (*1*)
Protein:
structures; (*1*)
enzymes. (*1*)
Water:
e.g. dissolving substances; (*1*)
transporting substances. (*1*)

(*8 marks*)

2 Condensation:
joining small (e.g. glucose) molecules (*1*) to form a larger (e.g. starch) molecule (*1*) by removing water (*1*). (*3 marks*)
Hydrolysis:
breaking down a larger (e.g. starch) (*1*) molecule into smaller (e.g. glucose) molecules (*1*) by adding water (*1*). (*3 marks*)
Importance of:
(i) condensation – in building up the large molecules organisms are made of; (*2*)
(ii) hydrolysis – in breaking down large molecules taken in as food. (*2*)

(*Total 10 marks*)

3 The shape (*1*) of the glucose chain differs between (*1*) starch, cellulose and glycogen.
(Pupils hypotheses that the *type* of glucose may differ deserve a bonus mark).
(*2 marks*)

4 In a straight strand (*1*) because hair is strand-like (*1*).
(*2 marks*)

Note: keratin actually consists of triple collagen-like alpha helix. Many pupils are likely to find such an explanation complicated and difficult to understand. However, able pupils are likely to suggest a helical structure 'because hair is springy'. 'Why should hair be springy?' is a question which could lead to both discussion and design, the teacher providing cues.

5 Metabolism – the reactions occurring inside our cells
Importance:
(i) to build things up (*1*)
e.g. for storage and body-building; (*1*)
(ii) to break things down (*1*)
e.g. to release energy. (*1*)
(*4 marks*)

—*Discussion*

1 Look at Topic 45, Figure 1 in *BFL*. Can this pie chart vary? If so, how?
Note: consider fat/thin people, muscular/non-muscular people, and variation in water content both over time and between individuals (e.g. women have a slightly higher water content than men).

Topic 46 Enzymes

—*Investigation*

Watching an enzyme in action

Requirements

Three test tubes; 50 cm^3 hydrogen peroxide solution; 3 g fresh liver; distilled water; water bath at 60°C; alternatively a beaker of water on a tripod and gauze over a bunsen burner will suffice; safety goggles.

Practical skills

HMA 1, HMA 3, HMA 7, AMO 10, EXP.

General Comments

Hydrogen peroxide is an oxidising agent, and needs to be handled with care. Safety goggles need to be worn and any spillage on skin or clothes should be reported and removed immediately by washing with cold water. Working safely can be assessed (HMA 3), also following instructions (HMA 1), handling the materials and apparatus (HMA 7) and the observations (AMO 10).

In step 3 it is safer to use an electrical water bath set to 60°C than to boil a beaker of water on a tripod and gauze over a bunsen burner. Frozen liver does not work effectively in this practical.

Step 5 will allow a number of further experiments to develop which can be used to develop and assess the EXP skills. Additional experiments might be to investigate the effect of freezing on the enzyme catalase, or to study the volume of oxygen released per minute when different amounts of fresh liver are used with the same amount of hydrogen peroxide. It ought to be possible to devise a way of quantifying the oxygen released by the liver (e.g. the quantity of gas produced per minute?). An alternative experiment to add different volumes of hydrogen peroxide to fixed quantity of hydrogen peroxide and to time the duration of the bubble formation. Presumably bubbles will be given off until all of the hydrogen peroxide molecules are broken down, and this will depend on the volume of hydrogen peroxide added.

—*Assignments*

1 e.g.
Advice to public on biological washing powders:
(i) Do not use in very hot water – enzymes destroyed by heat.
(ii) Best used in a pre-wash soak – give enzymes time to digest.
(iii) Best used for 'natural' stains – enzymes are proteases.
(iv) Never soak silk or leather – these materials are protein-based and might be part-digested.
Any three: 1 mark for advice, 1 mark for reason
(*6 marks*)

2 e.g. Take thirty or so test/boiling tubes (*1*). Fill each with trypsin solution (*1*). Keep the first tube at room temperature (say 20°C) (*1*). Heat the second to 21°, the third 22° and the others at 1°C steps to 50° (*2*).
Allow all tubes to cool to room temperature (*1*). Put an identical piece of egg white in all tubes (*1*). Leave for several hours (*1*) and observe results (*1*). Temperature at which trypsin is destroyed will be lowest temperature at which egg white is not digested (*1*).
(*10 marks*)

3 At a low temperature (e.g. 5°C) the reaction is (*1*) slow. It increases rapidly with temperature (*1*) up to above 40°C (*1*). At about 45°C the reaction stops working (*1*) (because the enzyme is destroyed by heat (+*1*)).
(*4 marks*)

—*Discussion*

1 What problems might a large scale industry have in using enzymes?
Note: discuss replacing enzymes which have been e.g. washed out of reaction vessel, health and safety, finding the right enzyme to do the job.

2 How many different types of enzyme might be found in our bodies? Why are there so many?
Note: there are a very large number probably over a thousand. Reactions in the body go step by step, each step being catalysed by a different enzyme. Many biochemical pathways make up metabolism; there are at least a thousand individual reactions in a single cell.

Topic 47 Food And Diet

—*Investigation 1*

To find out what substances are present in various foods

Requirements

Food substances 5 g of the following foods: orange juice; banana; bread; milk; egg white; butter; margarine; a breakfast cereal (e.g. cornflakes); a tinned baby food (e.g. a beef dinner).

Reagents about 50 cm^3 of each of the following substances: Benedict's/Fehlings reagent; iodine dissolved in KI solution; absolute ethanol (alcohol); distilled water; sodium or potassium hydroxide; dilute copper sulphate solution.
Apparatus access to waterbath at 40°C, or bunsen burner; tripod; gauze; 250 cm^3 pyrex beaker; six test tubes; white tile; pestle and mortar; pipette; thin paper.

Recipes for certain reagents

Benedict's reagent This can be made by dissolving 173 g hydrated sodium citrate and 100 g hydrated sodium carbonate in 800 cm^3 warm distilled water. Filter the solution, and make up the filtrate to 850 cm^3 by adding more warm distilled water. Dissolve 17.3 g hydrated copper (II) sulphate in 100 cm^3 cold distilled water. Mix the copper sulphate solution and the citrate-carbonate mixture together. Make up the volume to 1000 cm^3 with cold distilled water.
Iodine in KI solution 6 g potassium iodide in 200 cm^3 of water. Add 3 g iodine crystals and make up to 1 dm^3 with distilled water. Leave for 24 hours before use, whilst the iodine dissolves.

Practical skills

HMA 1, HMA 3, HMA 7, AMO 10.

General Comments

It is essential that pupils be able to carry out food tests reliably. It might be worth demonstrating the tests using pure chemicals, e.g. glucose, sucrose, starch, vegetable oil and albumen, so that the pupils can see unambiguous results before they test the food substances.

The tests require that the pupils follow instructions (HMA 1) and work with practical dexterity (HMA 7) and safely (HMA 3). Observing and noting the correct colour changes could be assessed (AMO 10).

—*Investigation 2*—

Testing food for vitamin C

Requirements

25 cm^3 of each of these solutions: fresh lemon juice or PLJ; 1% and 0.1% solutions of ascorbic acid; 50 cm^3 of DCPIP solution; white tile; 5 cm^3 syringe; mounted needle; bunsen burner; pyrex test tube; test tube holder; safety goggles; pipette.
DCPIP. A 0.1% solution of phenol-indo-2:6-dichlorophenol. The solution is easily oxidised by the air, and should be freshly prepared each time it is used. The bottle should be stoppered, and preferably made of dark glass.

Practical skills

HMA 1, HMA 2, HMA 3, HMA 7, REC 2, REC 3, REC 4, INT 1, INT 3, INT 4, EXP 5, EXP 6.

General Comments

The reliability of this experiment depends upon the accurate determination of the point at which the dye becomes discoloured. Teachers and pupils will need to practise this before performing the experiment properly.

The experiment can be performed using fresh, bottled and boiled lemon juice. It is important to obtain repeat measurements of each sample in order to obtain an average result. This will enable EXP 6 to be discussed and assessed. Accurate records will need to be taken (REC 3) preferably in table form (REC 2). The calculation of the average number of drops (INT 4) and the need for a control (distilled water rather than the lemon juice, also can be discussed and assessed as EXP 5).

The technique can be developed further by obtaining results using 0.0%, 0.1% and 1.0% solutions of ascorbic acid. The 0.0% solution being distilled water! This will enable a graph of 'number of drops of ascorbic acid solution needed to decolorise 1 drop of DCPIP' to be plotted against the concentration of DCPIP. This simple calibration curve will enable the pupils to estimate the ascorbic acid in the samples of lemon juice. The use of the calibration curve will enable REC 4, INT 1 and INT 3 to be assessed.

—*Assignments*—

1 e.g.
(i) Fuel for providing energy; (*1*)
(ii) growth and repair; (*1*)
(iii) provides us with important substances for metabolism; (*1*)
(iv) helps to fight disease. (*1*)
Note: these are the 'best' reasons. There may well be others.
(*4 marks*)

2 All are examples:
(a) milk; (*1*)
(b) cane sugar (= 'sugar'/sweets); (*1*)
(c) wholemeal bread/bran-based cereal; (*1*)
(d) sunflower margarine/cooking oil; (*1*)
(e) egg white/milk. (*1*)
(*5 marks*)

3 (a) Starch grains swell and burst. (*1*)
(b) Cellulose softens. (*1*)
(c) Butter melts. (*1*)
(d) No real change (smokes when really hot). (*1*)
(e) Coagulates. (*1*)
(*5 marks*)

4 (a) Proteins are needed for growth and bodybuilding. (*1*)
(b) Eggs contain a higher proportion of protein. (*1*)
(*2 marks*)

5 (a) Dried fish. (*1*)
(b) Maize. (*1*)
(c) Cabbage. (*1*)
(d) Dried fish. (*1*)
Most protein. (*1*)
(e) Soya beans. (*1*)
Plant food with most protein (wide variety of nutrients). (*1*)
(*7 marks*)
Note: some pupils might choose 'other beans' due to relatively high protein but low fat.

6 Wholemeal bread : roughage. (*1*)
Sugar : energy. (*1*)
Butter : insulation. (*1*)
Eggs : protein. (*1*)
Soya beans : artificial meat. (*1*)
Note: roughage and soya beans match quite well.
(*5 marks*)

7 Proteins are made up of amino acids (*1*). For bodybuilding to occur. Certain essential amino acids (*1*) need to be found in that protein (*1*).
(*3 marks*)

8 Vegetable proteins are short (*1*) in certain essential amino acids (*1*). The diet needs to be varied to ensure we get all the essential amino acids (*1*).
(*3 marks*)

9 Night blindness : vitamin A. (*1*)
Rickets : vitamin D; (*1*)
calcium. (*1*)
Anaemia : iron. (*1*)
Goitre : iodine. (*1*)
Xerophthalmia : vitamin A. (*1*)
(*6 marks*)

10 (a) Carrots rich in vitamin A (*1*)
(b) Salt lost through sweating (*1*), replaced by taking tablet (*1*). (*2 marks*)
(c) Orange juice is rich in vitamin C. (*1*)
(d) Too poor to afford (*1*) (and/or too infirm to go and buy) (in the cold) (+ *1*) fresh fruit and vegetables (*1*) leads to lack of vitamin C and therefore scurvy (*1*). (*3 marks*)
(*Total 7 marks*)

11 (a) No (*1*). It might have been caused by a germ (bacterium or virus) (*1*) to which Goldberger was immune (*1*). (*3 marks*)
(b) e.g. By repeating the investigations he carried out on himself (*1*) with several people (*1*). (*2 marks*)
Note: it is said that he persuaded his wife to participate!
(*Total 5 marks*)

12 e.g. Take 20 rats. (*1*)
Split into two groups of 10. (*1*)
Feed one group on rice seed with husks. (*1*)
Feed other with husk-less rice. (*1*)
Observe each group. (*1*)
Watch for symptoms of beri-beri. (*1*)
(*6 marks*)

13 (a) Correctly chosen and labelled axes. (*2*)
Accurate plotting (*½ mark per point*). (*3*)
Curve well drawn. (*2*)
Presentation. (*2*) (*9 marks*)
(b) e.g.
(i) Vitamin C destroyed by boiling.
(ii) Vitamin C leaves cabbage into the surrounding water.
(iii) Cabbage swells in boiling water. This means that water enters the cabbage diluting any vitamin C present.
At least two reasons – 2 marks each (*notional*) (*4 marks*)
(c) (i) Take a small sample of vitamin C in a test tube. Place in a beaker of boiling water.
Test for vitamin C, using DCPIP solution from 0 to 10 minutes
(ii) Test the water surrounding the cabbage for vitamin C, using DCPIP solution at intervals from 0 to 10 minutes.
(iii) When testing the cabbage at intervals for vitamin C, using DCPIP solution, dry off any surface water, squeeze the joice out of the cabbage and note *both* the volume of extract and estimated percentage of vitamin C.
One experiment for each answer to 13(b) – 3 marks per experiment (notional) (6 marks)
Note: getting the right idea of the experiment is more important than the 'working details'.
(d) Boil for the minimum amount of time necessary to make cabbage edible. (*1*)
(*Total 20 marks*)

14 (a) Kwashiorkor (*1*) – lack of protein (*1*) led to restricted growth (*1*) (*3 marks*)
(b) (i) Insufficient protein in diet. (*1*)
(ii) e.g. Sarah is incapable of digesting clinic's protein diet efficiently.
or Sarah was taken to clinic because of an acute illness resulting from Kwashiorkor, not the syndrome itself. This illness used up some of Sarah's protein reserves, causing a loss in body mass.
A well-reasoned answer (*2*)
(iii) A normal protein diet (*1*) returned Sarah to a normal growth pattern (*1*). (*2 marks*)
Note: Sarah's protein deficiency might have resulted from many factors – e.g. insufficient protein in mother's milk, mother diluting powdered milk to make it go further, etc. Scenes of crowds around clinics in Africa might elicit answers to (ii) such as 'Sarah had to wait a long time at the clinic before she was treated'. Be open minded.
(*Total 8 marks*)

—Discussion

1 Suppose you were a journalist who had been asked to investigate hunger in Great Britain today. What would your definition of hunger be? Would it be the same as hunger elsewhere in the world?
Note: it is probably fair to describe hunger in Britain as being an inadequate diet. Hunger at its most extreme means starving to death.

2 With all that stodge and greasiness in the chippie's food why do so many of us (including biology teachers!) occasionally get our food there?
Note: filling, salty, greasy foods give feeling of having had a good meal and a sense of well-being. This does not mean that the food has been especially good for you! The frequency of eating high fat food matters more than the odd occasion on which you yield to temptation. Regular meals from the chippie are not to be advised even though they may be tasty, convenient and filling.

3 If you were put in charge of the family's weekly shopping, what changes would you make? What restrictions would you make on the diet you would ideally like to have?
Note: this is best done upon completion of the topic. Once done, pupils can take their suggestions home to parents, who can then feed back their own comments. This is a very worthwhile exercise, and health education in its broadest sense. Pupils might discover the consequences of limited family budgets and on what can be purchased. This can tie in with Discussion Question 2, Topic 61, 'How does blood move round the body?', p. 80 in this guide.

Topic 48
How Are Substances Stored?

—Investigation 1

To see if potato juice will turn glucose into starch

Requirements

Potato; knife; plate; pestle and mortar; pinch of washed sand; muslin cloth and centrifuge or filter paper and funnel; water; white tile; iodine solution (see Topic 47); 0.5% glucose 1-phosphate solution (6 drops); test tube.

Practical skills

HMA 1, HMA 4, HMA 7, AMO 4, AMO 10, INT 1, EXP 5.

General Comments

The potato pulp can be squeezed through a sheet of muslin and then centrifuged or filtered through coarse grain filter paper (e.g. number 71 paper). It is essential that the extract containing the enzyme is starch free, and the importance of step 4 must be emphasised. The successful completion of the experiment reveals a competent use of materials and apparatus (HMA 7), an ability to follow instructions (HMA 1), successful timings (AMO 4) and accurate observations (AMO 10). The questions at the end can be used to assess the correct interpretation of the data (INT 1) and develop the idea of controls (EXP 5).

—Investigation 2—

To see if a leaf will turn glucose into starch

Requirements

A potted plant that has been destarched by being kept in a dark place for at least three days, and preferably longer; iodine solution (see Topic 47); two 100 cm^3 beakers; 50 cm^3 5% glucose solution; 50 cm^3 water; two sticky labels, access to a dark place; beaker of boiling water; bunsen burner; tripod; gauze; test tube; 25 cm^3 50% ethanol; forceps; iodine solution (see Topic 47); petri dish; dropping pipette.

Practical skills

HMA 1, HMA 3, HMA 7, INT 1.

General Comments

This experiment will work successfully if the plant is completely destarched at the start of the experiment. It is well worth checking this *before* starting the practical! Safety precautions must be enforced rigorously when testing the leaves. All bunsen burners must be extinguished before the tubes containing ethanol are placed in the boiling water bath. Safety glasses should be worn. If thermostatically controlled waterbaths are available, these can make a safer substitute for the beakers of boiling water.

—Investigation 3—

Looking at starch in a potato

Requirements

Potato; knife; plate; light microscope with low and high power objective lenses; microscope slide; coverslip; iodine solution.

Practical skills

HMA 5, HMA 6.

General Comments

The preparation of a microscope slide, correctly stained can be assessed (HMA 6), and the correct use of a microscope (HMA 5).

—Assignments—

1 (a) Liver (*1*) as glycogen (*1*) beneath skin (*1*) and around some organs (*1*) (e.g. heart, kidney (+*1*)) as fat (*1*). (*5 marks*)

(b) Swollen (*1*) underground (*1*) stem (*1*) as starch (*1*). (*4 marks*)

(c) In seeds (*1*) as starch (*1*). (*2 marks*)

(d) Thick (*1*) stem (*1*) as sucrose (*1*). (*3 marks*)

(e) Swollen (*1*) root (*1*) as sucrose (*1*). (*3 marks*)

(*Total 17 marks*)

2 e.g.

(i) To survive a period of food shortage. (*1*)

(ii) To pass on food reserves to developing offspring (e.g. seed, egg) (*1*).

(*2 marks*)

3 Grain. (*1*)

e.g. reasons:

(i) seeds are drier so stored food is in more concentrated form;

(ii) grain can grow in a wider range of climates than storage organs;

(iii) grain is easier to harvest and store on a large scale.

At least two reasons – 3 marks per person

(*6 marks*)

4 (a) Starch is solid and does not dissolve in water. (*1*) Glucose does dissolve. (*1*) So it can be transported. (*1*) (*3 marks*)

(b) Enzyme(s). (*1*)

(*Total 4 marks*)

5 Grind up plant stem with pestle and mortar (*1*). Filter the extract (*1*). Test filtered extract for starch (*1*) using iodine solution (*1*). Put six drops of 0.5% glucose 1-phosphate on to white tile (*1*). To each add a drop of plant juice (*1*). To each drop of the mixture add a drop of iodine solution (*1*) at two minute intervals (*1*). If the stem can turn glucose to starch a blue–black colour will appear after a few minutes (*1*).

(*9 marks*)

6 Towards the end of the growing season carbohydrate in the leaves is changed from starch to glucose (*1*) and transported to the roots (*1*) where it is re-built into starch (*1*).

(*3 marks*)

7 (a) To be a food source for disperser-animals. (*1*) (Tomato seeds – food reserves for offspring plant (+*1*).)

(b) As a food supply for the developing embryo. (*1*)

(c) As a food supply for the developing bean seedling. (*1*)

(d) As a food supply for the developing coconut tree seedling. (*1*)

(e) As food reserves to survive the winter. (*1*)

(*Total 5 marks*)

—Discussion—

1 Do potatoes, onions and carrots store food to make sure that *we* guarantee their survival?
Note: we have selected for size to suit our own purposes over a long period of time. Wild ancestral storage organs, though small, did exist.

2 If glycogen is 'animal starch' and it is stored especially in the liver, why isn't liver stodgy like potatoes?
Note: stodginess results from a high concentration of starch in starch grains. Glycogen storage in liver cells is much more diffuse.

Topic 49
Getting Energy from Food

—Investigation—

A simple way to find out how much energy a piece of food contains

Requirements

Measuring cylinder or syringe to measure out 20 cm^3 of water; large test tube; retort stand and clamp; long stem thermometer;

accurate weighing balance; mounted needle; bunsen burner; ground nuts.

Practical skills

AMO 1, AMO 3, AMO 5, AMO 10, INT 4, INT 5, EXP 3, EXP 4.

General Comments

This practical allows a number of measuring skills to be assessed, including volume (of water, AMO 3), temperature (AMO 1), and mass (AMO 5), also accurate observations of the changes to the peanut (AMO 10) and simple calculations of energy content (INT 4). It is important to stir the water before measuring the temperature. The mass of the water is 20 g.

This exercise will produce great variation in results, which can lead to an evaluation of the significance of the data, and of the major sources of error (INT 5). It is possible to ask pupils to design an improved apparatus (EXP 3 and EXP 4).

Assignments

1 Mass of groundnuts required
= daily energy requirement ÷ energy per gram of groundnuts (*1*)
= 15 000 ÷ 24.5 (*1*)
= 612 grams. (*1*)

(*3 marks*)

2 Notes:
(i) It might be a good idea to evaluate along given criteria (rather than 'point mark'). A suggested list of criteria are:
(a) organisation of work into a table/clear signs of methodical working;
(b) accurate reading and transcription of energy values;
(c) good estimates of quantities eaten;
(d) correct calculation;
(e) presentation.
(ii) Selecting criteria presents two options in marking:
(a) as a guideline to an impression mark;
(b) using a 0, 1, 2 mark scale for each criterion

(*10 marks*)

(iii) For estimating:
(a) 1 teaspoon ≈ 10 grams food
i.e. 100 grams ≈ 10 teaspoonfuls.
(b) 1 fork ≈ 25 grams food
i.e. 100 grams ≈ 4 forkloads.
(c) 1 dessertspoon ≈ 33 grams food
i.e. 100 grams ≈ 3 dessertspoonfuls
It is assumed no one eats off the knife!
(iv) A more comprehensive table of energy values of foods along with their composition can be found in '*Biology, A Functional Approach - Student's Manual*' by M.B.V. Roberts, 1st edition, Appendix 3, page 417.
(v) Girls shouldn't exceed 9500 kJ/day, boys 12000 kJ/day.

3 **Note:** Pupils with arithmetic difficulties might well be advised to consider a 100 g sample of each and then to use the energy values for carbohydrate, fat and protein in Topic 49, Table 1.
Working:
(i) plain chocolate = (59 × 17) + (33 × 39) + (4 × 18) (*1*)
= 2362 (*1*) kJ/100 g (*1*)
(ii) milk chocolate = (54 × 17) + (36 × 39) + (8 × 18) (*1*)
= 2466 (*1*) kJ/100 g (*1*)
(iii) cocoa powder = (36 × 17) + (26 × 39) + (19 × 18) (*1*)
= 1968 (*1*) kJ/100 g (*1*)

Note: more able pupils will easily convert percentages to decimal values.
Working:
(i) plain chocolate = (0.59 × 17) + (0.33 × 39) + (0.04 × 18) (*1*)
= 23.62 (*1*) kJ/g (*1*)
(ii) milk chocolate = (0.54 × 17) + (0.36 × 39) + (0.08 × 18) (*1*)
= 24.66 (*1*) kJ/g (*1*)
(iii) cocoa powder = (0.36 × 17) + (0.26 × 39) + (0.19 × 18) (*1*)
= 19.68 (*1*) kJ/g (*1*)

Milk chocolate contains the most energy. (*1*)
Cocoa powder contains the least (*1*)

(*Total 11 marks*)

4 e.g.
(i) Some energy is lost in the process of breaking the food down.
(ii) Not all food taken in is absorbed.
(iii) Not all foods (including carbohydrates – e.g. in forming glycoproteins) are broken down
At least two plausible explanations – 2 marks per explanation

(*4 marks*)

5 (a) From medical records (*1*) especially weight (body mass) at death (*1*) and age at which death occurred (*1*). (*3 marks*)
Note: the death rate at each age could then be calculated and a weight–death profile at each age could then be assembled.
(b) The chance of any client dying (*1*) has to be calculated (*1*) in order for the company to determine premiums and ensure that they don't lose money (*1*).
(*3 marks*)

(*Total 6 marks*)

6 (a) e.g. Chocolates, raisins, peanuts (preferably unsalted).
At least any three energy-rich foods (*3*)
(b) e.g. Cabbage, lettuce, skimmed milk.
At least any three energy-poor foods (*3*)
Note: even boiled potatoes would do!

(*Total 6 marks*)

7 (a) As in question 2 a criterion-based method of marking could be used.
Criteria:
(i) organisation of work into a table/clear signs of methodical working;
(ii) correct transcription of energy use in each activity;
(iii) plausible estimates of activity times;
(iv) correct calculation;
(v) presentation.
Either use as a guide, or as the basis for a 0,1,2 mark scale for each criterion. (*10*)
(b) As question 2. Award two extra marks for balancing energy income and expenditure. (*12*)
(c) Insufficient vitamins/minerals/fibre/possibly water.
Any reasonable explanation (*2*)

(*Total 24 marks*)

8 (a) Correctly chosen and labelled axes. (*2*)
Accurate plotting (*½ mark per point*). (*3*)

Curve well drawn. (*2*)
Presentation. (*2*)
(*9 marks*)

(b) (i) Energy requirements increase most rapidly from birth to 2 years (*1*)
Because maximum growth occurs (*1*)
(ii) Steady though less marked increase from 2–12 years. (*1*)
Growth continues though less pronounced (*1*)
(iii) Energy requirements increase faster from 12 to 18 years than from 2 to 12 years. (*1*)
Growth and development accelerate during adolescence. (*1*)
(*6 marks*)

(c) e.g. Assumptions:
(i) energy requirements same for both sexes;
(ii) person is of average physical size;
(iii) person has average physical rate of activity.
Any two – 1 mark each (*2 marks*)

(d) Should level out/be dependent on person's activity rather than growth. (*1*)

(*Total 18 marks*)

—Discussion

1 One reasonably large peanut contains enough energy to lift a family saloon car to a height of two metres. If we are taking all this energy in are we really using it?
Note: energy is used in metabolism, maintaining warmth (we need more 'energy foods' in winter) and activity. Excess energy is stored as fat, so if slimming avoid peanuts at all costs!

2 Why is eating less a more effective way of slimming than exercising more. Why then is exercising such an important part of any slimming plan?
Note: get a pupil to lift a single copy of *BFL* (mass about one kilogram) from bench level to above head (distance about one metre) to show one joule's worth of work. One kilojoule is equivalent to a thousand lifts! Look at the values in Topic 49, Table 1. Exercise combines losing weight with improved muscle tone, physical fitness and general well-being. An obsession simply with losing body mass is far from healthy and can lead to anorexia.

Topic 50
How is Energy Released?

—Investigation 1

To find out if burning food produces carbon dioxide

Requirements

One level teaspoonful of sucrose; large boiling tube; retort stand and clamp; bunsen burner; delivery tube; two bungs with holes; test tube; lime water.

Practical skills

HMA 1, HMA 4, HMA 7, AMO 10.

General Comments

This practical provides an excellent opportunity to assess the following instructions, assembling and handling apparatus skills (HMA 1, HMA 4, HMA 7). The pupils should report all of the changes occurring in the tube (AMO 10). Accurate reports will include a reliable description of the colour of the lime water at the start and finish of the experiments, and the changes in the colour and smell of the sugar.

—Investigation 2

To find out if germinating peas give out heat

Requirements

Moist cotton wool; two thermos flasks; two equal volumes of pea seeds, soaked in water for 24 hours before the experiment (one half of the peas have been boiled for five minutes to kill them); two long-stem thermometers.

Practical skills

HMA1, HMA 4, HMA 7, AMO 1, INT 4, INT 5, EXP 5.

General Comments

This experiment is useful for evaluating the need for appropriate controls (EXP 5), and for the likely sources of error in the experiment (INT 5). Microbial growth on the surface of the peas can contribute to the heat rise. This can be minimised by washing the surfaces of the peas with 1% formalin solution or 5% sodium hypochlorite solution before placing them in the thermos flasks. Measuring the changes in temperature can be assessed (AMO 1). After 24–48 hours a significant rise in temperature can be recorded in the flask containing living peas. Comparison of the initial and final temperatures can enable the percentage increase in temperature to be recorded (INT 4)

—Investigation 3

To find out if a person breathes out carbon dioxide

Requirements

Two tubes; two bungs with two holes per bung; two long straight glass tubes; two short straight glass tubes; mouthpiece attachment; one T-shaped glass tube; short lengths of connecting rubber tubing; antiseptic to clean mouth tube; lime water; assemble apparatus according to the diagram in *BFL*.

Practical skills

HMA 1, HMA 7, AMO 10, INT 1.

General Comments

It can be dangerous for pupils to try to insert glass tubing into rubber bungs. For this reason it might be best if the pupils received the glass tubing arrangement already assembled. Correct handling of the apparatus should include not blowing or sucking too hard.

Accurate observations (AMO 10) will include a reliable description of the appearance of the lime water in both tubes at the start and finish of the experiment. The significance of these changes is important (INT 1).

Replacing hydrogen carbonate indicator with lime water can introduce ideas of sensitivity and specificity. Lime water is a *specific* test for carbon dioxide, but is less sensitive than hydrogencarbonate indicator. The latter works because carbon dioxide dissolves in water to form a dilute acid, and the indicator responds to acidity.

—Investigation 4—

To find out if a small mammal gives out carbon dioxide

Requirements

Bell jar; soda lime; lime water; two wash bottles; connecting glass tube; mouse; suction pump; glass plate; vaseline.

Practical skills

EXP 3, EXP 4, EXP 5.

General Comments

This demonstration shows that small mammals give out carbon dioxide and may be used in conjunction with the theoretical account of the radioactive glucose experiment (see Topic 50 in *BFL).* The experiment has a historical importance, and pupils can be encouraged to modify the experimental design (EXP 3, EXP 4) to develop a suitable control (EXP 5).

The use of mammal in this experiment must be carefully supervised, and the animal removed if it begins to show signs of distress.

—Investigation 5—

To find out if small animals and plants give out carbon dioxide

Requirements

Three boiling tubes with rubber bungs; hydrogencarbonate indicator; muslin bag with attached cotton; several woodlice; healthy photosynthetic leaf; cardboard box.

Practical skills

HMA 1, HMA 4, HMA 7, AMO 10, EXP.

General Comments

There are a number of similarities between this investigation and that of Investigation 1 in Topic 22. This is a demonstration that the pupils can set up themselves, which can be used to assess the handling skills (HMA 1, HMA 4, HMA 7). It is possible for this to be given to the pupils as an experimental design exercise, if the pupils are familiar with the function of the CO_2 indicator. If the pupils design their own experiment, including appropriate controls, the EXP skills could be tested. Interpreting the colour changes accurately (AMO 10) is important.

—Investigation 6—

To find out if small animals take up oxygen

Requirements

Boiling tube; bung with two holes; muslin bag with cotton attached; soda lime; short length of glass tubing; short length of rubber tubing; screw clip; U-shaped capillary tube; small beaker; coloured water; measuring scale; small animals, e.g. woodlice.

Practical skills

HMA 1, HMA 4, HMA 7, AMO 2, AMO 4, INT 1, INT 4, INT 5, EXP.

General Comments

This practical will allow the handling skills to be assessed (HMA 1, HMA 4, HMA 7). Measurement of the change in the level of coloured liquid in the capillary tube (AMO 2), and the time taken for the change to occur (AMO 4) can be used to obtain an estimate of the rate of oxygen consumption (INT 4). This practical would also enable the value of controls to be considered (EXP 5), and likely sources of error (INT 5). Pupils might be encouraged to improve the design of the apparatus so that it produces more reliable results.

Open-ended investigations on the effect of temperature on the rate of respiration in poikilotherms can be made using water baths at different temperatures (EXP).

—Assignments—

1 (a) Oxygen is needed for any material to burn. (*1*)
(b) Carbon dioxide is produced when food is burned.(*1*)
(*2 marks*)

2 e.g. Put food into a container/holder (*1*). Set fire to it (*1*). Draw air from the burning food through a test tube (*1*) surrounded by a beaker of cold water (*1*). Test the condensed liquid in test tube (*1*) with cobalt chloride paper (*1*); if it turns from blue to pink water has been produced (*1*).
(*7 marks*)

3 There is no control. (*1 mark*)

4 e.g. Dear Uncle Boris,
I have a wonderful biology teacher who has told me exactly how the air we breathe out contains carbon atoms we have eaten.
First you take two rats (*1*). One is fed on glucose containing radioactive carbon (*1*) (carbon-14(+*1*)).
The other (control (+*1*) is fed on glucose containing ordinary carbon (*1*) (carbon-12 (+*1*)).
The air breathed out from each rat is passed through limewater (*1*). Then each sample of limewater (*1*) is tested for radioactivity (*1*) using a geiger counter (*1*). The lime water sample which had absorbed carbon dioxide breathed out by the rat fed on radioactive glucose (*1*) was much more radioactive (*1*) than the lime water sample which had absorbed carbon dioxide breathed out by the rat fed on 'ordinary glucose' (*1*).

If only you hadn't truanted from your science lessons!
All my love,
Little Smudge.
Content 10 marks, style 3 marks

(*13 marks*)

5 e.g.

	food burned	*energy released in cells*
(i)	hot	cooler/warm
(ii)	uncontrolled	controlled
(iii)	only heat and light energy released	some of the energy is released in biologically useful forms
(iv)	very rapid energy release	much slower energy release
(v)	carbon residue	no carbon residue

Any two comparisons – 2 marks each

(*4 marks*)

6 *(a) Respirometer. (*1*)
(b) e.g.
(i) Up to 44°C the rate of respiration increases rapidly.
(ii) From 10°C to 40°C the rate of respiration doubles for each 10°C rise in temperature (this relationship implies that chemical reactions are involved (+*1*)).
(iii) The maximum rate of respiration is at 44°C
(iv) The rapid decrease in respiration rate above 44°C (due to enzyme denaturation (+*1*)) shows that respiration is controlled by enzymes.
At least two conclusions – 2 marks each (*4 marks*)

(*Total 5 marks*)

Discussion

1 Discuss the statement: 'All flesh is grass'.
Note: as well as this topic, Topic 65 'Photosynthesis', and Topic 20 'Feeding relationships' will help. Essentially this discussion question is about the First Law of Thermodynamics (i.e. energy cannot be created or destroyed, but only changed from one form to another). I have found it worthwhile pointing out to classes that when a thought goes through their minds the energy creating the nervous impulses in their brains is derived from the sun.

Topic 51
How do we Digest our Food?

The five investigations in this topic can be used to develop and assess the Handling Materials and Apparatus skills (HMA 1–4 and 7).

There is a very slight possibility that the AIDS virus can be transmitted through saliva, and some teachers may prefer to omit Investigations 1 and 2. Some examination boards have recommended that investigations involving the use of body fluids, such as saliva, should be discontinued (see p. 6). If teachers wish to use these practicals, care needs to be taken when completing them. It is important that the saliva is washed away at the end of the practical with plenty of water, and that it is not allowed to splash into people's faces or onto cuts or abrasions. With those precautions the practicals are safe for class use. An alternative is to purchase amylase extracted from barley.

Investigation 1

To find out if saliva breaks down starch

Requirements
Rubber band; two test tubes; 4% starch solution; few drops of iodine dissolved in KI solution; dropping pipette; white tile; glass rod; clock or stop watch.

Practical skills
HMA 1, HMA 2, HMA 3, HMA 4, HMA 7, AMO 10, INT 6, EXP.

General Comments
This simple demonstration can be used to assess accurate observation of the colour changes observed (AMO 10); relating the activity of saliva to the disappearance of starch is recognising patterns in data (INT 6). It can also be developed into open-ended investigations to test a number of interesting hypotheses: Does cigarette smoke or salt affect the activity of saliva? Does the reaction occur more rapidly at higher temperatures? Does boiled saliva break down starch? Does saliva work in an acid environment at 37°C? This last investigation requires the use of an appropriate control (EXP 5), because starch can be hydrolysed to reducing sugars by acids at higher temperatures. These investigations could profitably be used to develop the EXP skills.

Investigation 2

To compare the actions of saliva and pepsin

Requirements
Four large test tubes; 50 cm^3 acidified pepsin (three drops of 10% hydrochloric acid in 1 cm^3 of 1% pepsin); hard-boiled egg white; white bread; small test tube; incubator at 37°C.

Practical skills
HMA 1, HMA 3, HMA 4, HMA 7, AMO 10, INT 1, INT 4, INT 6.

General Comments
This experiment can be used to teach the principles of balanced experimental design. If the pepsin is given to the pupil in an acidified form then the only variables present are the effects of the two enzymes of the two substrates. This develops the idea of enzyme specificity (Topic 46). The experiment can be used to assess accurate observation (AMO 10) and drawing appropriate conclusions (INT 1). Relating the pattern of activity of pepsin to the substrate is INT 6.

If the masses of the substrates are known before and after the experiment, a quantitative assessment of the actions of the two enzymes can be obtained. Simple calculations, (e.g. percentage change in mass), can be made from the data (INT 4).

—Investigation 3—

To find out if pepsin works best in acid conditions

Requirements

Four large test tubes; hard-boiled egg white; 50 cm^3 1% pepsin; a few drops of 10% hydrochloric acid and 10% sodium hydroxide; distilled water; incubator at 37°C.

Practical skills

HMA1, HMA 3, HMA 4, HMA 7, AMO 10, INT 6, EXP 5.

General Comments

Pepsin is suspended in distilled water, and tubes C and D are controls that show that the water/acid and the water/alkali mixtures are not able to break down the egg white. Pupils must realise this, and it can be used to develop the skill of controlling variables (EXP 5). Pupils should see a reduction in size of the egg white solid, and an increase in the level of the liquid in the tube when pepsin plus acid is used (AMO 10). Relating the activity of pepsin to the acidity of the conditions is INT 6.

—Investigation 4—

Observing emulsification

Requirements

Five test tubes; sticky labels; 20 cm^3 corn oil; few drops of distilled water; 1 g powdered bile salts; few drops of washing-up liquid; small piece of solid fat (e.g. lard).

Practical skills

HMA 1, HMA 3, HMA 4, HMA 7, AMO 10.

General Comments

Bile salts may have an unpleasant smell, and need to be used only sparingly in this practical. Adequate ventilation in the room may be needed, and it may not be wise to attempt this exercise immediately before lunch!

Bile is an emulsifying agent, not an enzyme, and this point needs to be stressed, particularly if the pupils observe the solid fat break up in a comparable way to the egg white in the previous investigation. Pepsin breaks down proteins into simpler peptide molecules; bile breaks down fat into smaller droplets, but the composition of each fat molecule remains unchanged. The value of the bile salts in digestion is partly to neutralise the acidity of the stomach contents when they enter the small intestine, and partly to break the fat into many small droplets, thus increasing the surface area of the fat exposed to the enzyme.

—Investigation 5—

To find out if trypsin works best in alkaline conditions

Requirements

Four large test tubes; hard-boiled egg white; 50 cm^3 1% pepsin; a few drops of 10% hydrochloric acid and 10% sodium hydroxide; distilled water; incubator at 37°C.

Practical skills

HMA 1, HMA 3, HMA 4, HMA 7, AMO 10, INT 6, EXP 5.

General Comments

Trypsin is an enzyme of the small intestine, and works most effectively at alkaline pH values. It thus contrasts with pepsin, which requires the acidic conditions found in the stomach.
The parallels between this investigation and Investigation 3 are great; it might even be possible to combine them into a single investigation with a more able group.

—Assignments—

1 (a) Colon (large intestine). (*1*)
(b) Duodenum (small intestine). (*1*)
Note: names in brackets might be accepted under some circumstances but not others – most likely ability-related.
(c) Stomach. (*1*)
(d) Stomach. (*1*)

(*4 marks*)

2 (a) Chewing breaks food into small pieces (*1*) which increases the surface area over which enzymes act (*1*).
(*2 marks*)
(b) Roughage adds to bulk of food (*1*) stretching intestine wall (*1*) stimulating muscles of intestine wall (*1*) to push the food along (*1*).
(*4 marks*)

(*Total 6 marks*)

3 (a) Lubricates food (*1*) so it is easy to swallow (*1*).
(*2 marks*)
(b) Coats stomach lining (*1*) preventing attack (*1*) by hydrochloric acid (*1*) (and pepsin/protease (+*1*)) in gastric juice (*1*).
(*4 marks*)
(c) Lubricates faeces (*1*), easing their passage (*1*).
(*2 marks*)

(*Total 8 marks*)

4 Loss of villi reduces surface area (*1*) over which absorption (*1*) of useful nutrients occurs (*1*).

(*3 marks*)

5 (i) Collect samples (2 cm depth in test tube) (*1*) of saliva produced before and during meal (*1*).
(ii) With each sample carry out the following:
(a) Half fill another test tube with (4%) starch solution.
(b) Pipette several (fifteen) drops of iodine solution on a white tile.
(c) Test the starch solution by adding one drop to the iodine solution with a glass rod.
(d) Mix saliva and starch solution.
(e) Immediately test the mixture as in step (c).
(f) Repeat step (e) at half-minute intervals.
(g) Do this until blue–black colour does not appear.
(h) Compare results for each saliva sample.
One mark per step

(*10 marks*)

Note: it is likely that some pupils will copy Investigation 1. What is most crucial is that the two samples of saliva are compared.

6 (a) Test the water surrounding the bag (*1*) with Benedict's solution (*1*) and iodine solution (*1*) at the beginning (*1*) and end (*1*) of the experiment. At the beginning both tests are negative (*1*). At the end the starch test is negative (*1*) but Benedict's test is positive (*1*).
(*8 marks*)

(b) The starch molecules are too large (*1*) to pass easily through the pores in the visking tubing bag (*1*) but the glucose molecules are small enough (*1*).
(3 marks)

(c) It is similar in the sense that only small molecules can pass through (*1*) but differs because the human gut wall is living whereas the visking tubing bag is not (*1*).
(2 marks)

(Total 13 marks)

—Discussion

1 Why do diarrhoea-causing diseases, e.g. cholera, typhoid, amoebic dysentery, often lead very quickly to death?
Note: secretion of digestive juices involves large volume of water which must be reabsorbed. Colon failure can lead to rapid dehydration; 20 per cent dehydration is fatal. Diarrhoea-related dehydration is the commonest cause of death worldwide, but can be largely treated with a pinch of salt, a spoonful of sugar (glucose) and a cup of water.

2 Now we are learning to take care of our heart, lungs and muscles, do you think we're still careless when it comes to our digestive system?
Note: digestive tract troubles can be caused by many ingredients of foods we eat, e.g. hot spices (in curry, chilli), phosphoric acid (in cola), benzoic acid (in jams), the azo-dye E102 'sunset yellow' (in many yellow- and orange-coloured foods and drinks), preservatives sodium nitrite and saltpetre (in sausages and cold meats), antioxidants propyl of gallate (in vegetable oils and products) and tartaric acid (in jams). Do our eating habits take into consideration our digestive well-being?

Topic 52
Teeth

—Investigation 1

Looking at human teeth

Requirements

Mirror; a human skull and lower jaw; teeth extracted by dentist.

Practical skills

AMO 10.

General Comments

This is a simple demonstration which aims to allow pupils to interpret Topic 52, Figure 1 (in *BFL*), in terms of their own teeth. When combined with Investigation 2 of this section it can be used as a basis for a lesson on dental hygiene.

The fulcrum of the lower jaw is a projection of bone which fits into the skull. There are two sets of muscles which close the mouth: the masseter and the temporal muscles. The temporal muscle runs from the side of the skull to the jaw (the top muscle in Figure 1); the masseter muscle runs from the cheek of the skull to the jaw (the lower muscle of Figure 1). The masseter muscle closes the jaw when it contacts, with the jaw pivoting on the fulcrum. The temporal muscle also closes the jaw, but in doing so pulls the jaw forward slightly.

—Investigation 2

To see the plaque on you teeth

Requirements

It is essential that the pupils are informed in advance of the need to bring a toothbrush and toothpaste into the lesson. Pupils should not be allowed to use each other's toothbrushes or cup, since this is unhygienic.
Disclosing tablet from a pharmacy; dental floss; spare toothpaste; mirror; clean cup; drinking water.

Practical skills

AMO 10.

General Comments

Sufficient time needs to be given to allow the pupils to remove all traces of coloured plaque from their teeth. The relationship between plaque and decay needs to be emphasised, as does the correct procedure for using a toothbrush. Leaflets from a dentist can be used to make this point clearly. Dental floss is good at removing plaque from crevices inaccessible to a toothbrush. This exercise can be linked with Assignment 2 of this topic.

—Assignments

1 Enamel – hard.
Pulp – sensitive.
Tooth fibres – pyorrhoea.
Canine – sharp.
Molar – crushing.
One mark each

(5 marks)

2 Points to look for:
(i) use a good toothbrush;
(ii) use an anti-plaque toothpaste (with fluoride?);
(iii) brush teeth regularly three times daily, after meals;
(iv) up and down movement;
(v) front, top and back of teeth;
(vi) where brush cannot reach use a smaller interdent brush or dental floss.
(vii) if plaque hardens to form tartar get the dentist to clean it off.
(viii) crisp vegetables, e.g. celery, carrot, will naturally clean teeth.

Note: some anti-plaque toothpastes contain formaldehyde which can help to precipitate mouth ulcers.
Marking: Consider the number of points raised, clarity of the writing and overall presentation in evaluating the piece of work. Comments are probably more valid than a mark *per se.*
Notional

(10 marks)

3 e.g.
Select areas naturally rich and poor in drinking water fluoride (*1*) and match fluoride concentration with level of tooth decay (*1*).

(2 marks)

4 (a) Will vary, but few should have a full set of molars. (*2*)
(b) Will vary, should usually include wisdom teeth (not emerged). Other teeth might have been removed (to prevent overcrowding, severe decay or accidentally knocked out). (*2*)
(c) i 2/2 c 1/1 pm 2/2. (*1*)
(d) Milk teeth replaced by permanent teeth (*1*); new teeth in dentition are molars (*1*).
(*2 marks*)

(*Total 7 marks*)

Discussion

1 Do you take your teeth for granted until you need to go to the dentist?
Note: I think people tend to. How many pupils are rigorous in cleaning teeth?

2 Our dentition is as unique as our fingerprints. What clues will a forensic dentist look for in either a dead person's mouth or a bite mark?
Note: everybody's mouth differs, for instance in the shape of jaw, number of teeth, angle of teeth, condition of teeth (i.e. fillings), etc. It is possible to have a good idea of the shape of the face from the shape of jaw!

Topic 53 Feeding in Other Mammals

Investigation

Comparing the teeth of different animals

Requirements

A skull of a carnivore (e.g. dog or cat), a herbivore (e.g. a sheep) and an omnivore (e.g. human); drawing paper; film of animals feeding.

Practical skills

AMO 8, AMO 10, REC 1.

General Comments

The pupil can be asked to prepare a report comparing the similarities and differences between the dentition of the skulls, which can be assessed as AMO 8. The pupil can be told which type of food was eaten by each animal. The function of each type of tooth and the way that the animal feeds can also be discussed. Alternatively, a description of the dentition of one of the skulls can be assessed (AMO 10 and REC 1). A film loop showing animals feeding can also be shown. This can be used to illustrate the role of the carnassials and the diastema in the feeding of the carnivore and the herbivore, respectively.

Assignments

1 (a) Humans lack cellulase-secreting microbes. (*1*)
(b) Digestion is particularly slow in herbivores. (*1*)
(c) So enamel ridges on cheek teeth can grind the grass. (*1*)
(d) Incisors from lower jaw meet hard pad to grip and pull grass. (*1*)

(*4 marks*)

2 (a) Grass is hard to break down in its 'raw state' (*1*). When swallowed whole it goes to the rumen (*1*) where it is stored (*1*) and partly broken down by microbes(*1*). When regurgitated – chewing the cud – the part-digested grass is easier to chew (*1*).
(*5 marks*)
(b) Grinding breaks the grass up (*1*), increasing the surface area (*1*) for microbes to act upon (*1*).
(*3 marks*)

(*Total 8 marks*)

3 (a) Large. (*1*)
Dagger-like. (*1*)
(*2 marks*)
(b) Large. (*1*)
Sharp-edged. (*1*)
Slide past each other. (*1*)
(Scissor-like (+*1*).)
(*3 marks*)
(c) Have cusps (*1*) which fit closely together (*1*).
(*2 marks*)
(d) Always growing (*1*) (open root (+*1*)) and wear away (*1*). Hard enamel wears less than soft dentine and cement (*1*) so forms grinding ridges (*1*).
(*4 marks*)

(*Total 11 marks*)

4 e.g.
(i) Don't eat sugary food.
(ii) Mouth bacteria different.
(iii) Food rarely soft – stimulates enamel production.
At least two answers – 2 marks each

(*4 marks*)

5 e.g.
(i) Cat – carrying kittens.
(ii) Beaver – cutting wood.
(iii) Dog – grooming (flea-gnashing!).
(iv) Elephant – tusk: display, defence.
Any two: name of animal 1 mark, use of teeth 1 mark

(*4 marks*)

6 (a) Although very different, both these constitute plausible answers.
(i) Dolphin; (ii) Solenodon/Tenrec } long thin snout.
(*2*)
(b) (i) Fish; (ii) Insects } small pointed teeth.
(*2*)
(c) Gripping prey (*1*); one type (*1*), not specialised (*1*), small and pointed (*1*).
(*4 marks*)

(*Total 8 marks*)

Discussion

Other than those mentioned in this topic, how many other mammals' diets can you think of ? What sort of feeding adaptations might such diets necessitate?

Note: the terms 'herbivore' and 'carnivore' apply to the bulk part of diet, but in fact other foods may be eaten, e.g. dogs and cats eat grass to assist digestion, many rodents eat grubs, insects and other small invertebrates. Other herbivores include browsers (e.g. goats, giraffes), and eaters of fruit and seeds (e.g. mice, voles), bark eaters (e.g. beaver), roots (e.g. mole-rat), flowers (e.g. sugar glider – gliding small marsupial) and nectar (e.g. nectar-feeding bats). Other carnivores include eaters of fish (e.g. otter, dolphin), insects (e.g. shrew, hedgehog), blood (e.g. vampire bats) and krill (e.g. blue whale).

Topic 54
How Do Other Organisms Feed?

—Investigation 1

Watching *Hydra* feeding

Requirements
Watch glass containing a hydra that has been starved for several days; several *Daphnia*; dropping pipette; hand lens.

Practical skills
AMO 10, REC 1.

—Investigation 2

Examining the mouth parts of insects

General Comments
The feeding behaviour of *Hydra* is described in Topic 54 of *BFL*. *Hydra* swallows its prey whole and so, presumably might suffer from indigestion, particularly as *Daphnia* has a rather indigestible exoskeleton!

A drawn account of the feeding behaviour of *Hydra* could be assessed (REC 1).

Requirements
Preserved locust, grasshopper or cockroach; mounted needle; mouthparts of housefly, butterfly or mosquito; light microscope; microscope slides; coverslips; distilled water; strips of filter paper.

Practical skills
HMA 5, HMA 6, AMO 9, AMO 10.

General Comments
Living specimens of locusts and blowflies (obtained from fishermen's maggots) in separate closed tubes containing, respectively, grass and cotton wool soaked in sucrose, can be used to observe the actual feeding behaviour of living insects. This is more informative than merely looking at the preserved mouthparts. Comparison of the feeding strategies of the two insects could be assessed (AMO 9), or a description of one of the insects (AMO 10) or the preparation of microscope slides containing other insect mouthparts (HMA 6).

—Investigation 3

Examining the gut of a fish

Requirements
Ungutted bony fish (e.g. herring, or mackerel); plate; dissection kit (scalpel, large scissors, mounted needle); access to soap and hot water.

Practical skills
HMA 1, HMA 3, HMA 7, AMO 10.

General Comments
Proper hygienic precautions need to be taken when investigating the intestinal contents of the fish. A number of intestinal parasites may also be seen.

The general plan of the digestive system of a fish is similar to that of a mammal; both possess a stomach leading to an intestine, which eventually opens to the outside through a pore. There are, however, a number of differences. The oesophagus in the fish is short and is not really separated from the rest of the pharynx. The stomach is a U-shaped tube which leads into the intestine. The intestine is much shorter in the fish than in the mammal and is much less coiled. The intestine opens into a short narrow rectum which opens to the outside on the ventral side just behind the pelvic fins. Immediately behind the anus is the opening of the urinary and genital systems.

—Assignments

1 Surrounds prey with its cytoplasm (*1*) to form a cup (*1*). Cytoplasm eventually surrounds cup (*1*) and a food vacuole is formed (*1*).
Prey is killed and digested (*1*). Soluble products are absorbed into cytoplasm (*1*). Indigestible material is got rid of across cell membrane (*1*).
(*7 marks*)

2 *Euglena.* (*1*)
e.g. Can adapt to a wide range of environments. (*1*)
(*2 marks*)

3 (a) Digestive enzymes produced (*1*) to break down solid food into soluble substances (*1*) which are absorbed (*1*).
(*3 marks*)
(b) Bread mould digests food outside its body (*1*). Mammals digest food (in special cavities (+ *1*)) inside theirs (*1*).
(*2 marks*)
(*Total 5 marks*)

4 (a) Slender bars called rakers (*1*) stick out from the base of each gill (*1*).
(*2 marks*)
(b) A drop of saliva (*1*) flows down the proboscis (*1*) and liquifies the food.
(*2 marks*)
(c) A drop of saliva (*1*) is injected into the wound (*1*), which stops the blood clotting when it is sucked up (*1*).
(*3 marks*)
(d) First senses movements in water (*1*) then as it moves closer sense of smell takes over (*1*). As it closes in it depends on its eyes (*1*). When very close it closes the eyes and depends on a radar-like electrical sense (*1*). Pressure of prey on shark teeth causes jaws to snap shut (*1*).
(*5 marks*)
(*Total 12 marks*)

5 *e.g. Put sea anemone(s) in a tank (*1*) along with a number (say 20) of shrimps (*1*), and an equal number of small fish (*1*). Count the number of fish and shrimps (*1*) daily (*1*).
(*5 marks*)
Note: How could you show that chance alone hasn't produced the results? This is worth discussing.

6 e.g. Explanations:
(i) sting cells respond to moving objects;
(ii) sting cells respond to contact with living cells;
(iii) sting cells respond to chemicals released by the water flea;
(iv) sting cells respond only to sudden movements e.g. a 'bump' but not when the *Hydra* they belong to makes gentle contact;
(v) sting cells don't work when *Hydra* moves.
At least three – 2 marks each
(*6 marks*)
Note: hypotheses are more important than factual explanations.

—Discussion

1 In the Pacific and Indian Oceans the clownfish lives among the tentacles of sea anemones but never gets stung. Other fish are not so lucky, so how does the clownfish get away with it?
Note: this is about hypothesis formation. Hypotheses include; clownfish is immune to sea anemone sting, clownfish secretes a protective substance (it does have a thick mucous coating), clownfish only co-exist with non-stinging anemones, sea anemone secretes substances inhibiting response of its stinging cells which clownfish accumulates, and the presence of clownfish alters the sea anemone's behaviour, suppressing stinging response. It turns out that the mucous coating is chemically neutral; sea anemone cannot recognise it as foreign protein. It is as if the clownfish isn't there! Refer to Topic 54, for a bitter alternative!

2 How many different ways of feeding other than those in this topic can you think of?
Note: other feeding methods include rasping (e.g. snail), filter feeding (e.g. mussel, fanworm), grasping prey with telescopic jaws (e.g. ragworm, dragonfly larva (refer to Topic 20, Figure 1, p. 26) and pike), mud swallowing (e.g. earthworm), sucking up food like a vacuum cleaner (e.g. flatworm *Planaria*), parrot-like beak (e.g. octopus, parrots!), beaks in general (refer to Topic 17, p. 24) and blood sucking (e.g. lamprey, leech). For parasitic feeding adaptations refer to Topic 39, 'Parasitic worms'.

Topic 55
How do we Breathe?

—Investigation 1

Looking at the lungs of a mammal

Requirements

Fresh lungs with attached trachea, from sheep or pig (obtainable from local abattoir or butcher); scalpel; bellows; bowl of water; hot water, soap and towel; prepared microscope slides of lung section; microscope.

Practical skills

HMA 5, REC 1.

General Comments

This investigation is best done as a demonstration, although all pupils should be given the opportunity to handle the material. Encouragement to overcome natural squeamishness may be needed! Hands should be washed immediately afterwards. The important feature of the investigation is that pupils should appreciate the spongy nature of the alveoli, and the hard cartilaginous trachea and bronchi. The distribution of these and other tissues through the lungs can be investigated using prepared slides. The C-shaped rings of cartilage around the trachea (Topic 55, Figure 4) should also be pointed out. The spongy nature of the lung tissue can be shown by removing a small portion and floating it on a bowl of water. If the lungs have not been damaged at the abattoir, they can be inflated by inserting a tube into the trachea, and blowing air into them.

—Investigation 2

A working model of the chest

Requirements

Bell jar model (make sure that the string around the rubber diaphragm is intact, and that no rubber parts have perished).

Practical skills

AMO 8, AMO 10.

General Comments

This model shows that when the volume inside the jar increases, the pressure falls, and air is drawn into the balloons. It is a crude, but effective, model of the human chest. The similarities and differences between the model and the human chest could be assessed (AMO 8) if pupils are already familiar with Figure 3. The major differences are that only trachea, bronchi, lungs, thoracic wall and diaphragm are shown in the model; movable ribs, heart, bronchial tree, and pleural membranes are omitted. The pleural cavity is very large relative to the 'lungs', and the diaphragm is the wrong shape. In mammalian thorax, the movement of the ribs (the jar) *and* the diaphragm cause inspiration and expiration.

—Investigation 3

Comparing the composition of inhaled and exhaled air

Requirements

J-tube, cleaned thoroughly with detergent so that it is free from grease; 10 cm^3 syringe; bowl of water; two small bottles containing about 50 cm^3 of concentrated potassium hydroxide solution and potassium pyrogallol solution; clocks; test tube for collecting exhaled air; delivery tube.

Practical skills

HMA 1, HMA 3, HMA 4, HMA 7, AMO 1, AMO 2, AMO 4, REC 2, REC 3, REC 5, INT 1, INT 4, INT 5.

General Comments

This is a major investigation which could be used to assess a range of experimental skills. It is also a complex experiment that is fraught with technical problems. Pupils need time to get used to handling the apparatus, and a preliminary lesson should be devoted to this purpose. At this stage no assessment should be made. The experiment itself should occupy a double period, and involves the repeated analysis of laboratory air and exhaled air. Windows should be open in the laboratory to let fresh air in. The practical can be used to assess the handling apparatus skills (HMA 1, HMA 4, HMA 7).

The chemicals need careful handling because they are caustic, and safe working can be assessed (HMA 3). Careless handling or dirty J-tubes can cause the bubble to break up. If this occurs, it is best to start again, unless one of the fragments of bubble is large enough to work with. It is important that the potassium hydroxide is added before introducing the pyrogallol – see note below.

The length of the bubble depends upon the temperature of the water, and it is important that the temperature is monitored throughout (AMO 1). The calculation of percentages (INT 4), can cause problems for some pupils; the more able can calculate the actual volumes of the gas used, providing that they measure the diameter of their J-tube accurately.

The pupils will need to select the most appropriate method of presenting their results (REC 5), which may include designing tables (REC 2). The limitations of the procedure and the sources of error should be considered (INT 5).

Note: it is conventional in gas analysis to use previously prepared potassium pyrogallate (alkaline pyrogallol) for absorbing oxygen. Potassium pyrogallate is unstable and must be made up immediately before the practical session by mixing equal quantities of pyrogallol (pyrogallic acid) and potassium hydroxide. The potassium pyrogallate thus formed must then be covered with liquid paraffin to prevent it taking up oxygen. When the experiment is performed, the end of the J-tube has to be inserted through the liquid paraffin before the potassium pyrogallate is sucked up. This is messy and can be avoided by sucking up pyrogallol instead of potassium pyrogallate and allowing it to react with potassium hydroxide still in the J-tube following carbon dioxide absorption, as described in the instructions for this experiment.

Assignments

1 (a) Closes opening to trachea/larynx (i.e. glottis) (*1*) while swallowing (*1*).
(*2 marks*)

(b) When they contract (*1*) they move ribs upwards and outwards (*1*).
(*2 marks*)

(c) Flattens/moves downwards (*1*) to increase size of thorax (*1*) to enable inhalation (*1*).
(*3 marks*)
(Also: 'separates thorax from abdomen' might be worth bonus mark but is a structural rather than functional feature.)

(d) Lubricant (*1*), allows pleural membranes to slide over each other (*1*) during breathing (*1*).
(*3 marks*)

(*Total 10 marks*)

2 (a) The nose warms (*1*), moistens (*1*), cleans (*1*) (thus preventing lung infection (+*1*)) and tests air we breathe (*1*).
(*4 marks*)

(b) When talking – epiglottis is open (*1*)
Stop talking – epiglottis is closed (*1*)
So food doesn't enter larynx/trachea. (*1*)
(*3 marks*)

(c) Ensures fresh air drawn into lungs as far as possible (*1*).
So more oxygen reaches blood. (*1*)
(*2 marks*)

(d) Preferable for air to enter through nose. (*1*) Blowing clears the nose for breathing. (*1*)
(*2 marks*)

(*Total 11 marks*)

3 Oxygen diffuses (*1*) from lung alveolus (*1*) into blood (*1*) (red blood cells (+*1*)).
Carbon dioxide diffuses (*1*) from blood (*1*) (red blood cells (+*1*)/plasma (+*1*)) into lung alveolus (*1*).
No significant change in nitrogen (+*1*) – not used by body (+*1*).

(*6 marks*)

Note: Topic 55, Figure 7 shows carbon dioxide being released from a red blood cell. It is explained in the text that 30% of carbon dioxide is carried in red blood cells, and 70% in plasma.

4 (i) Cough: sharp/rapid (*1*) exhalation (*1*).
(*2 marks*)

(ii) Gasp: sharp/rapid (*1*) inhalation (*1*).
(*2 marks*)

(iii) Sneeze: long inhalation (*1*) sharp exhalation (*1*), especially via nose (*1*).
(*3 marks*)

(iv) Sigh: long (*1*) exhalation (*1*).
(*2 marks*)

(v) Laugh: series (*1*) of shallow (*1*) exhalations (*1*).
(*3 marks*)

(*Total 12 marks*)

5 (a) Volume breathed in per minute (resting)
= 450 × 20 (*1*)
= 9 000 (*1*) cm^3 (*1*)
Volume breathed in per minute (after running)
= 1 000 × 38 (*1*)
= 38 000 (*1*) cm^3 (*1*)
(*6 marks*)

(b) Percentage of oxygen entering blood
= percentage of oxygen (inhaled air)
– percentage of oxygen (exhaled air) (*1*)
= 20 – 16
= 4% (*1*)
Volume of oxygen entering blood per minute (resting)
= 9 000 × 0.04 (i.e. 9 000 × 4%) (*1*)
= 360 (*1*) cm^3 (*1*)
Volume of oxygen entering blood per minute (after running)
= 38 000 × 0.04 (*1*)
= 1 520 (*1*) cm^3 (*1*)
(*8 marks*)

(c) Muscles have been doing more work (*1*) so they need more oxygen (*1*). **or** Fast breathing continues (*1*) so more oxygen enters blood (*1*).
(*2 marks*)

(d) Brain reflex (*1*) responding to carbon dioxide levels (*1*).
(*2 marks*)

(*Total 18 marks*)

6 e.g.
(i) Results in deeper breathing.

(ii) Lungs become more efficient at absorbing oxygen into blood.
(iii) Strengthens intercostal muscles (and those of diaphragm).
(iv) Slows down rate of breathing, i.e. frequency of inhalation (so lungs/chest do not have to work as hard).
Any three reasons – 2 marks per reason + bonus for others

(*6 marks*)

Discussion

1 Several well-known pop singers (e.g. Elton John, Annie Lennox of 'Eurythmics', Freddie Mercury of 'Queen') have suffered from throat nodules – growths in the larynx. This condition, which can sometimes develop into cancer of the throat, is much less common in opera singers, although both sing loudly. Why should this be?
Note: opera singers have trained voices and tend to produce 'purer' sound. This strains the vocal cords significantly less than simply singing loudly. There are links between cancer and tissue damage. Nodules are benign (i.e. non-malignant) growths.

2 If you were to ask someone who practises yoga, 'How can I improve my life?' it is likely that you will be given the advice, 'Learn how to breathe properly', since from breathing deeply and slowly all other improvements follow. Is breathing properly really so far reaching in its effects?
Note: deeper breathing means more oxygen enters blood and reaches tissues. Carbon dioxide more effectively carried away. Consequently cells function more efficiently and greater well-being results.

Topic 56
Breathing and Health

Assignments

1 (i) Bronchitis:
cause: e.g. smoking/germs/pollution; (*1*)
symptoms: severe coughing. (*1*)
(*2 marks*)
(ii) Pleurisy:
cause: infection of pleural membrane; (*1*)
symptom: painful breathing. (*1*)
(*2 marks*)
(iii) Tuberculosis:
cause: bacterial (*1*) infection of lung tissue (*1*);
symptom: short of breath. (*1*)
(*3 marks*)
(iv) Emphysema:
cause : smoking/severe coughing; (*1*)
symptom: very (*1*) short of breath (*1*).
(*3 marks*)
(v) Asthma:
cause: something to which sufferer is allergic; (*1*)
e.g. pollen/dust/food. (*1*)
symptoms: difficulty in breathing; (*1*)
wheezing. (*1*)
(*4 marks*)

(*Total 14 marks*)

2 *(i) Mouth to mouth resuscitation is used to restart breathing (*1*) in an unconscious person (*1*) by breathing out into his/her mouth (*1*) and forcing your own exhaled air (*1*) into his/her lungs (*1*).
(*5 marks*)
(ii) Impossible circumstances, e.g.
(i) blocked throat;
(ii) if the subject was an AIDS sufferer/carrier (although at time of writing this is in dispute).
Any suitable answer (*1*)
Note: there are now mouth-to-mouth tubes which ambulance crews use. Is it unnecessary hysteria? – Worth discussing.

(*Total 6 marks*)

3 (a) Not all heavy smokers get lung cancer. (*1*)
(Even though they are much more likely to (+*1*)!)
(b) Smoking is not the only cause of lung cancer (*1*)

(*Total 2 marks*)

4 *(a) Whether smokers (especially heavy smokers (+*1*)) are particularly likely (*1*) to develop lung cancer (*1*).
(*2 marks*)
(b) To demonstrate that susceptibility to lung cancer (*1*) is notably different (*1*) from susceptibility to other diseases (*1*).
(*3 marks*)
(c) The susceptibility of smokers to lung cancer (*1*) is more pronounced (*1*) than their susceptibility to other diseases (*1*).
(*3 marks*)
Note: without access to data it cannot be concluded that smokers are also more susceptible to disease in general. In 1952 smoking was fashionable and so a low number of non-smokers by today's standards might be expected. However, for a present day pupil to note the low incidence of non-smokers in both groups (especially notable in Group A) displays a skill in closely interpreting data and is therefore worth rewarding.
(d) e.g. suggestions:
(i) connection between number of cigarettes smoked daily and lung cancer incidence;
(ii) to consider smokers and non-smokers as the two groups;
(iii) to investigate different age groups/over a wider age range.
Any plausible suggestion (*2 marks*)

(*Total 10 marks*)

5 *Investigations would have to question the premises:
(i) that a particular kind of person needs to smoke;
(ii) that a particular kind of person gets cancer.
Causal connection (correlations) would then have to be investigated between people, smoking and cancer. Criteria which could be used might include:
(i) personality;
(ii) activities;
(iii) occupation;
(iv) social environment;
(v) income;
(vi) daily cycle – getting up, going to bed, etc.

Three criteria would constitute a good answer.
Marking:
Identifying the two premises – 4 marks
Selecting criteria – 3 marks
Other points: e.g. describing the investigations, clarity of response – 3 marks

(*10 marks*)

Note: this is an open question and can be marked in other ways, e.g. on a 'can do' or simply 'subjective response'. The total is therefore a suggested one.
The question might also be tackled totally in the form of a class discussion exercise.

Discussion

1 Why is the human respiratory system so vulnerable to diseases?
Note: consider airborne viruses, bacteria and bacterial spores. Discuss also the delicate lining of alveoli and air being constantly drawn into lungs.

2 Should smoking be made illegal? If so how could such a law be enforced (what would you do with the 'smokers'?).
Note: might there be the death penalty for tobacco smugglers?

Topic 57 How do Other Organisms Breathe?

Investigation 1

Looking at gills

Requirements
Preserved bony fish; plate; scissors; piece of thread.

Practical skills
HMA 7, AMO 10, INT 1.

General Comments
This simple exercise could be used to assess handling materials (HMA 7) and accurate observations (AMO 10). Relating the structure of the gills and operculum to their function could be used to assess INT 1.

Investigation 2

Examining the tracheal system

Requirements
Dead cockroach; forceps; scalpel; plate; light microscope with low and high power objective lenses; microscope slide; coverslip; mounted needle; water.

Practical skills
HMA 5, HMA 6, HMA 7.

General Comments
The dissection of the cockroach could be used to assess handling skills (HMA 7), and preparation of the microscope slide can also be assessed (HMA 6). The air in the tracheal system becomes visible if the opened body of the cockroach is placed under water. The air-filled tubes become visible as silver threads. Muscle fibres with cross-striations may also be seen if the illumination is not too great.

Assignments

1 *As an organism increases in size (*1*) the amount of surface area (*1*) relative to volume (*1*) gets smaller (*1*).

(*4 marks*)

(**Note:** refer to Topic 44.)

2 (i) Large surface area: so that enough oxygen diffuses into the animal (*1*) and enough carbon dioxide diffuses out (*1*).
(2 marks)
(ii) Be permanently moist: oxygen must dissolve in water (*1*) before it can diffuse across the surface (*1*).
(2 marks)
(iii) Have a good blood supply: to carry the oxygen (taken up by the respiratory surface (+*1*)) to all parts of the animal (*1*), and to carry all the carbon dioxide back to the respiratory surface (*1*).
(2 marks)

(*Total 6 marks*)

3 e.g.
(i) Control amount of air (*1*) entering tracheal system (*1*).
(ii) Co-ordinate gas exchange (*1*) with body movements (*1*).
(iii) Prevent excessive water loss (*1*) especially when insect is inactive (*1*).
2 marks per well-explained reason

(*6 marks*)

4 The tracheal system (*1*) penetrates all tissues of insect body (*1*) so oxygen-carrying red blood pigment (*1*) is not necessary (*1*).

(*4 marks*)

5 e.g.
Put locust in a glass tube (*1*) (about 25 mm diameter (+*1*)) open at both ends (*1*). Partition glass tube between locust thorax and abdomen (*1*) (so air can only pass through the tube via the locust (+*1*)). Attach bung either end (*1*) with tube leading from each bung (*1*) to a manometer/capillary tube with 'marker' (*1*).
Expected result: liquid in manometer in front of locust moves towards locust (*1*). Liquid in manometer behind locust moves away from locust (*1*).

(*8 marks*)

Other designs might involve radioactive oxygen, smoke or ways of measuring airflow.
A good design should use standard apparatus and should be feasible.

—Discussion

1 Does an insect's tracheal system limit how large it can grow?
Note: the larger the insect the greater is the body volume (refer to surface area/volume ratio, Topic 44) and the less effective the tracheal system becomes in carrying oxygen to all parts of the body. Largeness demands a circulatory system but the tracheal system works independently of circulation.

2 Why are gills so suitable for water and lungs so suitable for air?
Note: water is 750 times more dense than air. A through-flow system is here more efficient than a 'to and fro' system and there is no residual water. A ventilating system works easily in air which can be held in lungs for a period of time to increase gas exchange. Lungs have been known to work in oxygen-enriched water.

Topic 58
Living Without Oxygen

—Investigation 1

Can seeds respire without oxygen?

Requirements

Two dishes; two large boiling tubes; two identical samples of five peas or beans: one sample placed in boiling water for two minutes, then both samples soaked in water for 24 hours prior to practical; 20 cm^3 potassium hydroxide solution (prepared by dissolving 200 g potassium hydroxide pellets in 1 dm^3 distilled water); 500 cm^3 oil; pipettes.

Practical skills

AMO 10, INT 1, EXP 5.

General Comments

This investigation could be used to assess accurate observations (AMO 10) and drawing the appropriate conclusions (INT 1). This practical has the potential to become extremely messy, and is probably best left to the teacher to perform as a demonstration. It is essential that no air surrounds the peas before the practical starts. Anaerobically respiring peas will produce carbon dioxide which will be trapped by the oil.

BFL mentions the need for a control, and it would be useful to establish exactly why a control is needed in this example. There is a possibility that microbes growing on the surface of the soaking peas might be respiring in both tubes, and the existence of the control could be used to check for this, assuming that both sets of peas were allowed to soak in water for identical lengths of time.

Investigation 3 of Topic 55 introduced potassium hydroxide as a carbon dioxide absorbing agent, and its use here will enable the gas to be identified as carbon dioxide. Anaerobic respiration in plants also produces ethanol and heat as by-products.

—Investigation 2

Finding out about the products of alcoholic fermentation

Requirements

Two test tubes; U-shaped piece of glass tubing; one bung with single drilled hole; 20 ml lime water; 5 ml of liquid paraffin; 20 ml mixture of glucose solution and dried yeast – it is important that no oxygen should be introduced into the glucose solution, and this can be achieved by dissolving the glucose in distilled water that has been boiled and cooled; the mixture can be made up by adding 1 g of dried yeast to 25 cm^3 of a 10% glucose solution. It is important to stir the mixture thoroughly for two minutes to allow the dried yeast cells to hydrate thoroughly. The mixture should be prepared about half an hour before the lesson, and maintained at 35°C.

Practical skills

AMO 10, EXP 5.

General Comments

It is important that no oxygen should be present in the reaction mixture. You may wish to introduce an indicator into the glucose/yeast mixture to show when anaerobic conditions exist. A 0.03% solution of Janus Green B solution will become pink when oxygen is absent. The pink colour should persist throughout the experiment. The use of the indicator presents two sets of colour changes to observe (AMO 10 for the lime water and the indicator). The use of controls could also be discussed (EXP 5), since strictly speaking an experiment should be run without the use of the indicator. If the production of carbon dioxide is slow at room temperature, the apparatus can be placed in a water bath at 35°C.

—Investigation 3

To find out if yeast makes dough rise

Requirements

Plate; 50 g flour; warm water; knife; test tube; 10 g sugar; pinch of dried yeast; two 250 cm^3 beakers; margarine to grease the beakers; access to a warm cupboard (if necessary); water baths at different temperatures; apparatus for the class-designed experiments.

Practical skills

HMA 1, HMA 7, AMO 1, AMO 2, REC 2, REC 3, REC 5, INT 1, EXP.

General Comments

This experiment illustrates the need for a suitable food and temperature if yeast is to respire. If the yeast is thoroughly mixed in with the flour, then anaerobic respiration occurs deep within the dough ball and produces carbon dioxide. The gas causes the strands of dough to separate, and the dough is said to 'rise'. The investigation could be used to assess following instructions (HMA 1), handling materials (HMA 7), measuring temperature and length (AMO 1 and 2) and recording accurately (REC 3), possibly in tables (REC 2).

The experimental design exercise is an excellent one for developing the skills of experimental design (EXP). The experiment should be designed to make sensible use of the apparatus available. It is worth stating at the start of the exercise the number of water baths that are potentially available. The pupils can be encouraged to write their designs on paper. These can then be assessed after the lesson for the various EXP skills. In particular, the pupils need to find some way of measuring the increase in size of the dough, and relating this to the temperature of the water bath. Adequate replication of numbers, and the control of other variables (particularly ensuring that all the dough is mixed to the same consistency) are also important.

If the experiments are to be performed, a compromise needs to be reached as to the temperatures of the water baths! The pupils should present their results in an appropriate form (REC 5); this may include graphs, histograms, tables or scale diagrams.

—Investigation 4

To show the effect of lactic acid in our muscles

Requirements

Willing volunteers; stop watches

Practical skills

AMO 4, AMO 6, REC 2, INT 2, INT 4.

General Comments

This is a simple demonstration of the effects of the build-up of lactic acid in the human arm. Raising the arm reduces the flow of blood to the hand, and this forces the moving hand muscles to respire anaerobically. The accumulation of lactic acid is accompanied by the feeling of 'tiredness' in the muscles.

This exercise may be quantified by counting the number of clenches of the raised fist and noting the time taken for the arm to feel 'tired'. Does this time vary in the class? This group exercise involves timing (AMO 4), counting (AMO 6), and simple data interpretation (forming the appropriate tables (REC 2)), calculating the average rate of clenching (INT 4), and extracting the appropriate information from the tables (INT 2) to find the strongest and weakest arms in the class!

—Assignments

1 *Stops bacteria (*1*) which might be on the equipment (*1*) turning alcohol to vinegar (*1*).

(*3 marks*)

2 Mr Smith's wine will ferment first (*1*). The sunny place is warmer (*1*), yeast multiplies more rapidly (*1*), so there is faster fermentation (*1*).

(*4 marks*)

3 Marmalade has been infected/contaminated (*1*) by wild yeast (*1*) during bottling (*1*).
Prevention:
e.g.
(i) sterilise all equipment;
(ii) put lid on jar before marmalade cools.
Any one (*1 mark*)

(*4 marks*)

4 Sugar is only partly (*1*) broken down (*1*).

(*2 marks*)

5 (a) Whale lives in sea (*1*) and respires anaerobically during long dives (*1*).
(*2 marks*)

(b) Beef tapeworm lives in small intestine (*1*) where there is hardly any oxygen (*1*).
(*2 marks*)

(c) Threadworms are found in the rectum (*1*) where there is also little or no oxygen (*1*).
(*2 marks*)

(*Total 6 marks*)

—Discussion

1 Winemaking is more of an art than a science. Do you agree?
Note: the underlying principles of fermentation and sterilisation are certainly scientific, so too are many of the procedures (e.g. measuring specific gravity, syphoning, adding enzymes such as pectolase to prevent fruit pectin causing cloudiness, keeping fermentation at the correct temperature). However, exactly what ingredients a wine maker uses in what proportions and certain other 'personal touches' do have an element of an art rather than a science.

2 So far biogas units which have been tried on a domestic (household) level in Britain have not worked particularly well. What factors might have been responsible for this?
Note: problems in producing living sewage in these days of domestic detergents and our cool climate pose the main problems. The ease of availability of North Sea gas probably inhibits commercial developments in this area, along with the fact that biogas can be pretty smelly! In India and China community biogas vats have proved very successful.

Topic 59
Blood, The Living Fluid

Note: The DES statement on safety recommends that the use of human blood in these practicals be discontinued (see p. 6). We recommend that Investigations 1,2,3 and 4 be modified by using blood from an abattoir. Teachers should be sensitive to the needs of those pupils whose religious beliefs forbid handling certain types of blood.

—Investigation 1

Looking at blood

Requirements

Two dry microscope slides that have been washed in ethanol to remove grease; Leishman's stain; light microscope; blood from an abattoir.

Practical skills

HMA 1, HMA 3, HMA 5, HMA 7, AMO 10, REC 1.

General Comments

Using blood from an abattoir will allow pupils to see red blood cells easily. Observing white blood cells can be unpredictable, and animal blood does not, generally, give as consistent results as fresh human blood. It is important that the Leishman's stain is not allowed to dry on the slide, as it can form crystals.

An alternative procedure which may also be tried is to leave the slide with the Leishman's stain for two minutes under a petri dish lid. Then add a few drops of water and gently move the slide to mix the water and the stain together. It is important to do this gently, to avoid the stain and the water running off the edge of the slide. The slide is then left for ten minutes, after which the remaining stain is gently washed off with water. Once the slide has dried it can be viewed without a coverslip.

The indentification of the different blood cells and accurate drawings can be assessed (AMO 10 and REC 1).

—Investigation 2

The effect of gases on blood

Requirements

Two 250 cm^3 flat bottomed flasks; blood from abattoir; oxygen cylinder; carbon dioxide cylinder; vacuum pump; two rubber tubes with a fine glass pipette fitted.

Practical skills

AMO 10.

General Comments

This practical is best performed as a teacher demonstration, as it involves the use of high-pressure gas cylinders. Blood with a high oxygen content is a bright red colour. Pupils may realise that this is the colour of arterial blood. Bubbling carbon dioxide through the blood increases the acidity of the blood, and causes the haemoglobin to give up its oxygen. The blood becomes a darker, less bright colour, and this corresponds to the colour of blood in veins.

An additional experiment can be made by placing blood in a U-tube. One side arm is connected to a filter pump, whilst a cigarette is attached to the other side arm. The filter pump draws cigarette smoke through the blood. A major constituent of cigarette smoke is carbon monoxide, which forms a stable association with haemoglobin that is cherry red. Bubbling oxygen through the mixture will not cause a change in this compound. An interesting teaching point about the dangers of carbon monoxide can be made.

—Investigation 3

Separating the components of blood

Requirements

Sample of blood from an abattoir; two centrifuge tubes; centrifuge.

Practical skills

HMA 7, AMO 10.

General Comments

Abattoir blood has been diluted with water and citrate to prevent the blood from clotting. When the blood is centrifuged, it has a relatively large liquid component. This needs to be borne in mind when estimating the percentage of plasma present. An accurate estimate could be assessed (AMO 10). The sediment consists of white and red blood cells and platelets. It may also contain large plasma proteins. Safe use of the centrifuge can also be assessed (HMA 7).

—Investigation 4

The effect of osmosis on red blood cells

Requirements

Blood from abattoir; 5 cm^3 of each of the following solutions: distilled water, 0.75% salt solution, 3% salt solution; three microscope slides; three coverslips; light microscope; wax pencil.

Practical skills

HMA 5, HMA 6, HMA 7, AMO 6, AMO 10, REC 1.

General Comments

This practical can be used to assess handling apparatus skills (HMA 7) and microscopy skills (HMA 5 and 6). Acceptable results can be obtained for this practical using abattoir blood. The pupils can be encouraged to view the microscope slides under high power, and to count the number of red blood cells they can view under one field of view (AMO 6). When placed in water, the number of blood cells decreases as they burst. The accurate observation of the state of the blood cells (AMO 10), can lead to careful drawings (REC 1). It is interesting to see whether the red blood cells in water get larger *before* they burst. If so, by how much? There is potential for extended practical work here 0.75% saline is isotonic for human blood, and red blood cells should neither gain nor lose water in this solution. The importance of this fluid for blood transfusions needs to be noted.

This practical links directly with Topic 44, and could be used there.

—Assignments

1 Red blood cell:
   (i) no nucleus;
   (ii) biconcave disc shape;
   (iii) inside filled with haemoglobin;
   (iv) larger relative surface area.
   White blood cell:
   (i) nucleus;
   (ii) rounded or amoeboid shape;
   (iii) lacks haemoglobin;
   (iv) smaller relative surface area.
   Any three differences – 2 marks per difference (*6 marks*)
   Red cell – carries oxygen from lungs to all body tissues. (*1*)
   White cell – helps defend body against disease. (*1*)
   (*2 marks*)
   (*Total 8 marks*)

2 Carbon monoxide combines with haemoglobin (*1*) much (300 times) more readily (*1*) than oxygen does (*1*), so it displaces oxygen from red blood cells (*1*). Oxygen therefore cannot reach tissues (*1*). Breathing carbon monoxide therefore can be fatal (*1*).
   (*6 marks*)

3 (a) **Note:** there are two steps in the calculation:
   (i) the number of cubic millimetres per litre;
   (ii) total number of red blood cells.
   Step (i):
   1 litre = 1000 cm^3 (*1*)
   1 cm = 10 mm (*1*)
   $\therefore$ 1 cm^3 = 1000 mm^3 (*1*)
   $\therefore$ 1 litre = 10^6 mm^3 (*1*)
   Note: for very large or small numbers I use indices. Many pupils use strings of zeros, despite attempts to lure them

to easier ways of working! Indices are used in this marking scheme for brevity and convenience. You'll still have to count zeros!
Step (ii):
number of red blood cells
= number of red blood cells per cubic millimetre
x volume of blood in cubic millimetres (*1*)
$= (5 \times 10^6) \times (5 \times 10^6)$ (*1*)
$= 25 \times 10^{12}$ (*1*)
(*7 marks*)

(b) **Note:** there are three steps:
(i) total surface area in square micrometres;
(ii) number of square micrometres per square metre;
(iii) total surface area in square metres.

Step (i):
total surface area in square micrometres
= surface area of one red blood cell
x total of red blood cells (*1*)
$= 120 \times (25 \times 10^{12})$ (*1*)
$= 3 \times 10^{15}$ (*1*) square micrometres (*1*)
Step (ii):
1 micrometre $= 10^{-3}$ mm (*1*)
1 millimetre $= 10^{-3}$ metre (*1*)
$\therefore$ 1 micrometre $= 10^{-3} \times 10^{-3}$
$= 10^{-6}$ metre (*1*)
$\therefore$ 1 square micrometre $= 10^{-6} \times 10^{-6}$
$= 10^{-12}$ square metres (*1*)
$\therefore$ There are 10^{12} square micrometres per square metre (mark carried by $1\ \mu^2 = 10^{-12}\ m^2$)
Step (iii):
total surface area in square metres
= total surface area in square micrometres
÷ number of square micrometres
per square metre (*1*)
$= 3 \times 10^{15} \div 10^{12}$ (*1*)
$= 3 \times 10^3$
= 3000 (*1*) square metres (*1*)
(*12 marks*)
Note: more able pupils will not present their working exactly as in the marking scheme, nor would it be reasonable to expect them to do so. So long as the concept of the steps is there and some working is shown, award marks accordingly.

(*Total 19 marks*)

4 (a) The difference in concentration (of oxygen) (*1*) between alveolus and the blood (*1*) before diffusion occurs (*1*) is the diffusion gradient.
(*3 marks*)
Note: this answer is derived directly from the broad definition on p. 142 of *BFL*, 2nd edition.

(b) Breathing increases the concentration of oxygen (*1*) in the alveoli (*1*). Circulation decreases the concentration of oxygen (*1*) in the blood/capillary (*1*).
(*4 marks*)

(*Total 7 marks*)

5 70% (*1*) in plasma (*1*). 30% (*1*) in red blood cells (*1*).
(*4 marks*)
Actively respiring tissues (*1*) produce the most carbon dioxide (*1*) and have the greatest need for oxygen (*1*).
(*3 marks*)

(*Total 7 marks*)

6 In the mountains the air pressure has fallen with altitude (*1*)
This means less oxygen in every litre of air. (*1*)
So the body produces more red blood cells to pick up the reduced quantity of oxygen more efficiently. (*1*)

(*3 marks*)

7 Magnification = diameter of red blood cells in Figure 1 ÷ actual diameter (*1*)
diameter of red blood cells in Figure 1 = 25 mm (*1*)
= 25 000 micrometres (*1*)
Magnification = 25 000 ÷ 8 (*1*)
= 3125 (*1*)

(*5 marks*)

8 If the fluid is too dilute/weak (*1*) (endosmosis occurs (+ *1*)); the blood cells swell up and burst (*1*). If the fluid is too concentrated/strong (*1*) (exmosis occurs (+ *1*)); the blood cells shrink and crinkle (*1*).

(*4 marks*)

Note:(i) Refer to Topic 44, Figure 5.
(ii) More able pupils ought to make some comment on osmosis with respect to what happens.

—*Discussion*

1 How do you think malnutrition affects blood?
Note: consider lack of iron causing anaemia, lack of calcium causing poor clotting, lack of protein causing 'thin' blood (lack of albumen), incapable of fighting off infection (lack of globulin) or clotting (lack of fibrinogen). Thinness reduces osmotic properties, leading to failure to reabsorb water from the peritoneum, resulting in a bloated abdomen.

2 Are there any advantages to being a vampire bat?
Note: there are few competitors for food supply. Being nocturnal, the host animal sleeps while it feeds. Blood is a complete food.

Topic 60
More About Blood

—*Investigations 1 and 2*

Note: The DES statement on safety recommends that Investigations 1 and 2 be discontinued (see p. 76). Abattoir blood is not suitable as a replacement for human blood in these cases. Investigation 2 would make a suitable **theoretical** exercise, and the data presented at the end of the investigation could form the basis of a class discussion on the problems of transfusing blood.

—*Assignments*

1 (i) Reduction in blood pressure (*1*) reduces blood flow (*1*).
(ii) Reduction in number of red blood cells (*1*) reduces oxygen-carrying power (*1*).

(*4 marks*)

2 (a) So that the effects of taking blood are minimal for the donor. (*1*)
(b) Taking blood does have some effect on blood pressure (*1*) and this can lead to faintness/dizziness (*1*). Sitting down for half an hour gives body time to restore blood fluid level (*1*) and hence pressure (*1*).
(*4 marks*)
(c) Prevents clotting. (*1*)
(d) After a month too many red blood cells will have died. (*1*)
There are no blood cells in plasma so it can be kept much longer (*1*).
(*2 marks*)

(*Total 8 marks*)

3 (i) By acting as an enzyme/factor (*1*) causing fibrinogen to turn to fibrin and cause a clot (*1*).
(ii) By acting as an antigen. (*1*)
Antibodies produced by victim's blood leads to agglutination/clotting. (*1*)
(*4 marks*)

4 (a) Lack both substances A and B. (*1*)
(b) There are no substances in the red blood cells (*1*) for the patient's anti-substances to respond to (*1*), so blood can be given to anyone (*1*).
(*3 marks*)
(*Total 4 marks*)

5 (a) (i) John: A. (*1*)
(ii) David: B. (*1*)
(iii) Susan: O. (*1*)
(iv) Anna: AB. (*1*)
(*4 marks*)
(b) AB (AB Rhesus negative (+*1*)): (*1*) because it is so rare (*1*).
or O: (*1*) because it is the universal donor (*1*).
(*2 marks*)
Note: the logic of the answer matters here. AB is a universal recipient but for limited amounts of blood only. The same applies to O's universal donor status.
(c) A person's blood group is determined by certain substances (*1*) (called A and B (+*1*)) in their red blood cells (*1*).
If a patient's blood lacks either substance and receives blood containing it (*1*), anti-substances are produced (*1*), which cause the red blood cells to stick together (*1*).
(*5 marks*)
(*Total 11 marks*)

—Discussion

1 Should people be paid to give blood?
Note: it would most likely increase the supply but there are risks. Where blood is 'bought' by hospitals (e.g. in USA) many sellers are drug-addicts using their blood as a means of raising cash. This increases the risk of unsuitable and infected blood and has been partly responsible for the spread of AIDS.

2 Since more people need organ transplants than can be provided with this treatment, how should one decide who receives a transplant and who does not?
Note: does this mean deciding what a person is worth? Factors might include, value to society, tissue group, potential to survive operation and undergo healthy recovery. In exclusively private medical systems the ability to pay is also a key factor.

Topic 61 How Does Blood Move Round the Body?

—Investigation 1

Looking at the heart

Requirements

Fresh heart from abattoir, preferably sheep or pig (hearts which have the main arteries and veins are required for this exercise); sharp dissecting instruments (scalpel, scissors, forceps and blunt seeker); dissecting board or dish; soap and water.

Practical skills

HMA 1, HMA 3, HMA 7.

General Comments

It is possible for the pupils to gain an understanding of the function of the heart by exploring the internal structure using their fingers and a blunt seeker. This exercise is well suited to an enquiry-based approach, and the question in Investigation 1 and in Assignment 2 a and b provide a starting point. Pupils should have access to Topic 61, Figure 3 in *BFL*.

Although it is possible to assess a number of manipulative skills in this exercise, it might be more appropriate to spend the lesson time concentrating on the pupils' attempts to relate the complicated structure to its function. They should be challenged to work out the pathway of blood through the heart and become aware that both sides of the heart beat at once. If possible supplement the exercise with video film of the heart in action.

The coronary blood vessels supply blood to the heart muscle cells; they are the first branches of the aorta and have a narrow diameter. They can easily become blocked, and this reduces the flow of blood to the heart cells. Starved of oxygen and food, these cells die, and a heart attack occurs. Smokers are more likely to die from this condition than are non-smokers.

—Investigation 2

Finding how fast your heart is beating

Requirements

Stop watch.

Practical skills

INT 4, INT 6.

General Comments

Reliable comparisons of the sitting and standing pulse rates can be made only if the pupils are relaxed and quiet. They need to sit quietly for about two minutes before attempting to measure their resting pulse. Moving or even talking will alter the pulse rate. The exercise can be used to assess counting skills, so long as the teacher is prepared to check the result! It can also be used to assess the ability to make simple calculations (INT 4). Relating the pattern of pulse rate to exercise can be used to assess INT 6.

The standing pulse is slightly faster than the sitting pulse, and should be felt about ten seconds after standing up. This exercise can lead directly on to Investigation 4.

—Investigation 3

Listening to the heart

Requirements

Stethoscope; stop watch or clock.

Practical skills

This practical is inherently subjective, and does not make a suitable basis for assessing many of the practical skills.

General Comments

The heart sounds consist of two distinct parts: the dull thud ('lub') sound is caused by the closing of the atrio-ventricular (bicuspid and tricuspid) valves as the ventricles contract. The higher ('dub') sound is caused by the closing of the arterial (semilunar) valves in the mouth of the aorta and pulmonary artery during diastole. Blood enters the arterial system only when the ventricles contract, and the blood flows in distinct pulses.

The elastic walls of the arteries expand just before blood arrives, and contract as soon as it has passed. Thus a wave of contraction and expansion passes along the artery. This is known as the 'pulse wave'. The time between the end of the heart sound and the sensation of a pulse in the wrist is a measure of the time the blood has taken to ravel from the heart to the wrist. This time will be shorter when the heart is beating faster.

—Investigation 4—

To find the effect of exercise on the heart rate

Requirements

Stop watch, low stool or box.

Practical skills

HMA 1, INT 4, INT 6.

General Comments

The calculation of the heart rate before, during and after exercise can be assessed (INT 4). The heart responds to the requirements of exercise by increasing its rate of beating. The time taken for it to recover to its normal standing rate is a measure of athletic fitness. Comparison of class results can be made, providing it can be ensured that each person exercises equally hard. Athletes should have slower heart rate, and a faster recovery rate than non-athletes. Relating the heart rate to the effects of exercise can be used to assess INT 6.

—Assignments—

1 (a) Pressure increases when heart (ventricles (+*1*)) contracts. (*1*)
Pressure decreases when heart relaxes. (*1*)
(*2 marks*)
(b) (i) Exercise. (*1*)
(ii) Excitement. (*1*)
(*2 marks*)
(*Total 4 marks*)

2 (a) Right atrium receives blood from whole body. (*1*)
Left atrium from lungs only. (*1*)
(*2 marks*)
(b) Left ventricle pumps blood to whole body. (*1*)
Right ventricle to lungs only. (*1*)
(*2 marks*)
(c) Muscles of artery walls (*1*) press back against the blood flowing through artery (*1*), helps blood to flow quickly (*1*). In veins blood pressure is greatly reduced (*1*). Thin, less muscular walls have more give in them (*1*), easing (a gentler/more passive (+*1*)) blood flow (*1*).
(*6 marks*)
(d) Enable oxygen and other substances (*1*) to diffuse easily across (*1*)
(*2 marks*)
(e) Prevent blood slipping back. (*1*)
(*Total 13 marks*)

3 ***Note:** Two methods spring immediately to mind:
(i) 'balloon' method;
(ii) 'elastic band' method.
e.g.
(i) 'Balloon' method: Take similar sized lengths (say 5 cm) of artery and vein (*1*). Tightly seal one end with thread or a clip (*1*). Underwater attach the other end to a (1 ml) syringe (*1*). Stretchability can be measured from extent the vessel swells and/or the ease with which the plunger is pressed (*1*).
(ii) 'Elastic band' method: Take similar sized rings of artery and vein (*1*). Attach each to a clamp alongside a ruler/scale (*1*). Add weights (*1*). Stretchability can be measured by reading ruler/scale (*1*).
Either method
(*4 marks*)

Notes:
(i) Pupils may have difficulty 'translating' blood vessels into balloons and elastic bands, i.e. figuring out underlying principles, and might need cues.
(ii) Method (i) more accurately represents the type of stretching (transverse) but is not easy to measure.

4 (a) Percentage = (capillary blood speed ÷ arterial blood speed) × 100 (*1*)
= (0.5 ÷ 450) × 100 (*1*)
= 0.11% (*1*)
(*3 marks*)
(b) Although capillaries are very narrow there are so many of them (*1*) that the total cross sectional area is greater than that of arteries (*1*).
(*2 marks*).
Note: resistance set up due to a viscous liquid passing through very narrow vessels is another, though less significant, factor.
(c) To give time (*1*) for substances to diffuse across walls (*1*).
(*2 marks*)
(*Total 7 marks*)

5 Heart: engines. (*1*)
Blood cells: buses. (*1*)
Vessels: roads. (*1*)
Oxygen: passengers. (*1*)
Capillaries: bus stops. (*1*)
Bus route is obviously a circular one. (*1*) (*6 marks*)
Note: it is worth investing in a bus timetable and map of town.

6 (a) There is a regular pattern. (*1*)
Early morning (around 2 a.m.) troughs are clearly visible. (*1*)
Peaks in pulse activity are harder to tell. (*1*)
But they tend to be from midday to early afternoon (+*1*).
(*3 marks*)
Note: for checking draw lines along:
(i) each 2 a.m. line;
(ii) line corresponding with pulse rate of 80 beats per minute
(average pulse rate).
(b) The four-hourly points are joined with straight lines (*1*) and take no account of possible fluctuations during the intervening periods (*1*).
(*2 marks*)
(c) Highest = 112 beats per minute. (*1*)
Recorded = Wednesday at midday. (*1*)
Lowest = 58 beats per minute. (*1*)

Recorded = Saturday at 2 a.m. (*1*)
(*4 marks*)

(d) Highest: due to e.g. exercise/anxiety/ horror video! (*1*)
Lowest: due to deep sleep/sedation. (*1*)
(*2 marks*)

(*Total 11 marks*)

—*Discussion*

1 Before William Harvey discovered in the seventeenth century that blood circulates around the body what ideas do you think doctors had about blood, the heart, and blood vessels?
Note: blood was seen as a 'vital essence' and one of the four humours: blood, phlegm, black bile and yellow bile. Its power was elemental, i.e. it held a life force. Hence the 'vitality' of the heart mattered more than its function. Perhaps telling pupils about such a strange perception will give them an understanding of the sheer incomprehension doctors of the middle ages would have had about what appears to us to be a relatively easy to understand mechanism. Harvey's famous demonstration of pushing back on the veins so the valves appear as bumps is easily performed as part of a discussion exercise.

2 A recent survey has shown that better off people are less likely to suffer from heart disease than the not so well off. Any suggestions as to why?
Note: poor diet increasing risk of cardiac disease is at the centre of this. Perhaps it is worth getting pupils to create weekly shopping lists for a family of four (or their family) on sums of, say, £15, £30 and £45, and then look at the quality of food bought. This ties in with Discussion Question 3, in Topic 47, 'Food and diet', p. 60 in this guide.

Topic 62
Tissue Fluid and Lymph

—*Assignments*

1 (i) Blood: red and white cells (*1*), platelets (*1*) and plasma (*1*).
(*3 marks*)

(ii) Tissue fluid: plasma (*1*) minus proteins (*1*).
(*2 marks*)

(iii) Lymph like tissue fluid (*1*) but with white cells (*1*) and antibodies (*1*).
(*3 marks*)

(iv) Explanation:
Blood is the major transport medium of body. (*1*)
Tissue fluid is filtered blood. (*1*)
Tissue fluid drains back to the blood system as lymph. (*1*)
But in doing so it passes through lymph glands. (*1*)
(*4 marks*)

(*Total 12 marks*)

2 Two of the following:
(i) drains away tissue fluid;
(ii) defence against disease;
(iii) transport of fats;
away from small intestine;
(iv) filtering body fluid.
1 mark each

(*2 marks*)

3 Septic foot has become serious infection (*1*).
Germs carried in lymph to lymph glands in groin where (*1*) phagocytes and lymph cells do their best to kill them and prevent spread of infection to rest of body (*1*). In doing so lymph glands become swollen and painful (*1*).

(*4 marks*)

4 (a) Action of heart causes high arterial pressure (*1*). Loss of water/fluid across the capillary wall (*1*) lowers pressure by the time blood gets to venous end (*1*).
(*3 marks*)

(b) Water has passed across capillary wall (*1*) concentrating salt present (*1*).
(*2 marks*)

(c) Arterial pressure forces fluid into tissues (*1*); concentrating the salt draws the fluid/water (*1*) back by osmosis (*1*).
(*3 marks*)

(*Total 8 marks*)

5 e.g.
(i) High blood pressure forces more fluid into the tissues.
(ii) Old age leads to lack of exercise so body movements cannot move lymph away from legs.
Any two reasons – 2 marks per reason

(*4 marks*)

—*Discussion*

Surgeons almost always remove nearby lymph glands if they suspect a patient has cancer of a particular organ. Why do you think they do this?
Note: the same mechanism by which the lymph glands trap germs can occur for cancer cells carried from body tissue into lymph. Once lodged there, new tumours can occur which are capable of releasing cancer cells into circulatory system and setting up 'satellite cancers' all around body (i.e. metastasis).

Topic 63
What do Plants Need to Live?

—*Investigation 1*

To find out which elements are needed for plant growth

Requirements

Eight bottles; eight small pieces of cork tile, large enough to form a lid on each bottle (every tile should have a hole in the centre); eight identical seedlings (e.g. wheat, maize, barley or broad bean); access to an aquarium aerator; sufficient Knop's culture to fill each of the bottles; black paper; bucket of clean sand that has been thoroughly washed beforehand in distilled water; general liquid plant fertiliser.
1 dm^3 Knop's culture contains 0.8 g calcium nitrate, 0.2 g potassium nitrate, 0.2 g potassium dihydrogen phosphate, 0.2 g magnesium phosphate and a trace of iron(III) phosphate, 0.2 g calcium sulphate, dissolved in distilled water. Solutions deficient in nutrients can be prepared from tablets.

Practical skills

HMA 1, HMA 2, HMA 4, HMA 7, AMO 9, AMO 10, REC 3, EXP.

General Comments

This experiment needs to be set up several weeks *before* the theory of this topic is taught, in order for the pupils to draw their own conclusions from the practical work. The pupils can be assessed for their abilities in handling the delicate seedlings (HMA 1, HMA 7). Ideally, they should be encouraged to think of ways of measuring the growth of the seedlings (e.g. number of leaves, length of internodes, colour of leaves, etc.), and this could be used as a useful test of initiative (HMA 2). Accurate observations (AMO 10) of the similarities and differences between the plants (AMO 9, REC 3) are needed.

The experiment can form the basis of open-ended practical work running, for example, over a summer term. If the sand culture experiment is carried out, it is essential that the sand is thoroughly washed to remove all traces of soluble mineral ions. Designing these experiments can be used to develop the EXP skills.

—Assignments

1 *Nitrogen, phosphorus, sulphur, magnesium, potassium, calcium, iron.

(*2 marks*)

Note: some pupils are bound to include carbon, hydrogen and oxygen. This is not worth penalising, since marking should be positive, but is worthy of comment.

2 (i) Harvesting. (*1*)

(ii) Rain washes mineral nutrients out. (*1*)

(*2 marks*)

Note: link with soil, Topic 29, 'What is soil?' especially page 79.

3 (a) Some plants remove more of a particular element than others do (*1*).
Crop rotation (*1*) helps to prevent one element (*1*) from being removed altogether (*1*).
(*4 marks*)

(b) Compost puts essential minerals back into the soil (*1*) and improves texture (*1*).
(*2 marks*)

(c) Plants have a constant need for minerals (*1*) so that they can grow (*1*).
(*2 marks*)

(*Total 8 marks*)

4 *e.g. Advantages of manure:

(i) cheap;
(ii) improves soil texture;
(iii) improves water-holding ability;
(iv) stays in soil longer;
(v) benefits advantageous/desirable soil organisms, e.g. earthworms, which in long term improve the soil still further.
Any two (*2 marks*)

e.g. Advantages of artificial fertilisers:

(i) easier to store and apply;
(ii) can use to special requirements;
(iii) do not smell;
(iv) not limited by the amount available.
Any two (*2 marks*)
Note: very similar to question 6 (b).

(*Total 4 marks*)

5 *e.g.

(i) Analyse soil for minerals.
(ii) Observe farming practice.
(iii) Look for drainage problems.
(iv) Ask about whether/which type of fertiliser is used.
At least three – 1 mark each

(*3 marks*)

6 (a) Plot 2 – 63% or 64% (63.5%). (*1*)
Plot 3 – 73% (72.9%). (*1*)
Plot 4 – 121% (120.8%). (*1*)
Plot 5 – 154% (154.2%). (*1*)
Plot 6 – 161% (161.5%). (*1*)
(*5 marks*)

Notes:

(i) Ideally the percentage for Plot 2 (63.54%)should be rounded down and Plot 6 (161.46%) rounded up.
(ii) Whole number percentages are given first to encourage an accuracy limit of 1 part in 100.
(iii) Working out is not required since this task will most likely be carried out easily using a calculator.

(b) Mark as for question 4.
(*4 marks*)

(*Total 9 marks*)

7 (a) Double (*1*) the original yield (*1*).
(*2 marks*)

(b) A fallow field gets colonised by wild plants (*1*) including members of the legume family (e.g. clover) (*1*) which can turn nitrogen in the air into nitrates (*1*). This and organic matter from their decay adds nutrients to the soil (*1*). When wheat is grown, nutrients are taken out of the soil (*1*) faster than they are returned (*1*).
(*6 marks*)

(*Total 8 marks*)

—Discussion

What are the long-term environmental consequences of the exclusive use of inorganic fertilisers? How do these arise?
Note: the section 'Modern farming' in Topic 33 mentions wind erosion, but water erosion farming gulleys may also occur due to loss of texture and adhesion between particles. Other consequences include the depletion of mineral resources and leaching of mineral salts, e.g. nitrates, into rivers causing eutrophication and the harmful consequences of nitrates in drinking water.

Topic 64
How do Plants Feed?

—Investigation 1

Testing a plant for reducing sugar

Requirements

Pieces of onion bulb; scalpel; white tile; pestle and mortar; pinch of silver sand; distilled water; two test tubes; filter paper;

filter funnel; Benedict's or Fehling's solution (see p. 59 of this guide); beaker; tripod; gauze; bunsen burner (or a water bath at maximum temperature).

Practical skills
HMA 1, HMA 3, HMA 4, HMA 7, AMO 10.

General Comments
A thermostatically controlled water bath set to its maximum temperature can make an effective substitute for the rather awkward arrangement of the beaker on the tripod. This practical could form an assessment for safety (HMA 3), for general experimental techniques (HMA 1, HMA 4, HMA 7) and for observation of the colour changes (AMO 10).

—Investigation 2

Testing a plant for starch

Requirements
Geranium or hibiscus leaf; beaker; tripod; gauze; bunsen burner (or a water bath at maximum temperature); forceps; test tube; ethanol; safety spectacles; petri dish; dilute iodine solution (see p. 59 of this guide); dropping pipette.

Practical skills
HMA 1, HMA 3, HMA 4, HMA 7.

General Comments
This practical allows the pupils to investigate the presence of starch in leaves in a variety of situations. For example, the disappearance of starch from leaves that have been kept in the dark, or the absence of starch from 'non-green' parts of variegated leaves (see Investigation 2, Topic 65) could be studied further. This could lead on to a variety of photosynthesis investigations.

The safety aspects must be emphasised. No bunsen flames must be present near tubes of boiling ethanol. Safety spectacles must be worn at all times. This is an important practical that will form the basis of practicals in the next topic. It is important that the pupils can use it routinely. It can be used to assess experimental techniques (HMA 1, HMA 3, HMA 4 and HMA 7).

—Investigation 3

Testing soil for reducing sugar

Requirements
Soil; pestle and mortar; two test tubes; tap water; filter paper; filter funnel; Benedict's or Fehling's solution (see p. 59 of this guide); beaker; tripod; gauze; bunsen burner (or water bath at maximum temperature).

Practical skills
HMA 1, HMA 3, HMA 4, HMA 7, AMO 10.

General Comments
Soil should not contain significant amounts of reducing sugar and, therefore, plants cannot feed by absorbing it through their roots. This practical should help to correct a misconception that pupils sometimes have. The ability to carry out a test for reducing sugars could be assessed.

—Assignments

1 Oak tree manufacturers own food from simple substances (*1*) by photosynthesis (*1*). Human eats food (*1*), from other animals and plants (*1*).

(*4 marks*)

2 Plants use roots for uptake of water (*1*) and mineral salts (*1*). Feeding by photosynthesis does not necessitate movement (locomotion) (*2*).

(*4 marks*)

3 Protein in grass, when eaten (*1*) becomes protein in cow (*1*) which we consume as beef (*1*).

(*3 marks*)

4 *At least three valid suggestions:
e.g.
(i) brush roots carefully before weighing;
(ii) cover soil in pot (except, maybe, when watering);
(iii) use only distilled water;
(iv) water tree from underneath.
2 marks each

(*6 marks*)

5 *There are many reasons. Some might not relate directly to the quantity of plant material, but still accept these as valid. Some examples:
(i) People are not always where the plants are. (*1*)
(ii) Not all organic matter made by plants is consumable. (*1*)
(iii) To feed a large population plant growth needs to be organised (i.e. agriculture needed). (*1*)
Any two

(*2 marks*)

—Discussion

If you are capable of realising that the willow tree in Van Helmont's experiment had absorbed simple substances from the air and soil and built them up into food, why didn't Van Helmont?

Note: in 1692 there was very little understanding about the gaseous composition of the air. Adding oxygen (e.g. in burning or respiration) was believed to be taking away a mysterious 'substance' called phlogiston. Consequently the concept 'simple substances' was beyond the comprehension of even the greatest scientists in those days.

Topic 65
Photosynthesis

—Investigation 1

To find out if a plant needs carbon dioxide in order to make starch

Requirements
Two geranium plants in pots; balsam or *Coleus* plants can be used as substitutes (the plants must have been kept in a warm

dark place for 36 hours prior to the experiment); two small petri dishes; sodium hydroxide pellets; sodium hydrogencarbonate solution; two plastic bags which are large enough to cover each plant; two elastic bands; apparatus for testing leaves for starch: beaker, tripod, gauze, bunsen burner (or water bath at maximum temperature), forceps, test tube, ethanol, safety spectacles, petri dish, dilute iodine solution (see p. 59 of this guide), dropping pipette.

Practical skills

HMA 1, HMA 2, HMA 3, HMA 4, HMA 7, EXP 5.

General Comments

The success of this experiment depends entirely upon there being no starch present in the leaves of the plant *before* the experiment commences. It is well worth checking this! The plant with the enriched atmosphere of carbon dioxide should have starch in its leaves, whilst the control should not. The importance of keeping all of the other factors the same for both plants (especially light intensity and the watering regime) needs to be considered. It can be used to exphasise the correct use of controls (EXP 5) and the usual handling skills (HMA 1–4, 7).

—Investigation 2

To find out if a plant needs chlorophyll to make starch

Requirements

Potted plant with variegated leaves; drawing paper; pencil; beaker; tripod; gauze; bunsen burner (or water bath at maximum temperature); forceps; test tube; ethanol; safety spectacles; petri dish; dilute iodine solution (see p. 59 of this guide); dropping pipette.

Practical skills

HMA 1, HMA 2, HMA 3, HMA 4, HMA 7, EXP 5.

General Comments

Starch is stored close to the chloroplasts. This accounts for its absence in the non-green areas of a variegated leaf. Once again, the pre-treatment of the plant is critical, and it should have been well illuminated for several days before the experiment commences. The best control for this experiment is the green part of the leaf, and this can be used to emphasise the importance of controls (EXP 5).

—Investigation 3

To find out if a plant needs light in order to make starch

Requirements

Method a. Two geranium plants in pots (balsam or *Coleus* plants can be used as substitute plants; the plants must have been kept in a warm dark place for 36 hours prior to the experiment); access to a well-lit and a dark place.

Method b. Single geranium plant in pot (balsam or *Coleus* plants can be used as a substitute plant; the plant must have been kept in a warm dark place for 36 hours prior to the experiment); strip of black paper or foil large enough to mask part of the leaf; two paper clips; access to a well-lit place.

Both methods will require after several days: beaker; tripod; gauze; bunsen burner (or water bath at maximum temperature); forceps; test tube; ethanol; safety spectacles; petri dish; dilute iodine solution (see p. 59 of this guide); dropping pipette.

Practical skills

HMA 1, HMA 2, HMA 3, HMA 4, HMA 7.

General Comments

Once again, the use of a starch test on a leaf indicates that photosynthesis has occurred. There should be no starch in the darkened area, assuming that the plant was adequately destarched prior to the experiment.

—Investigation 4

To find out if a water plant gives off oxygen

Requirements

Two healthy specimens of *Elodea* or *Hydrilla,* each about 7 cm long (these can be obtained from streams or from a shop selling aquarium equipment); two 250 cm^3 beakers; two glass funnels; two test tubes; wooden splint; water.

Practical skills

HMA 1, HMA 3, HMA 4, AMO 10, EXP.

General Comments

The effectiveness of *Elodea* in this practical can vary. If possible, obtain a large amount of the pond weed, and keep it well illuminated before the practical. Select small lengths of the weed (preferably terminal pieces with many leaves) for the experiment. The rate of oxygen production can be increased by dissolving a small amount of sodium hydrogen carbonate in the water in the beaker. This increases the amount of carbon dioxide available to the plant. There are possibilities for project work here to determine the most effective concentration of hydrogencarbonate needed, and this could test the EXP skills.

It is unlikely that the glowing splint will give a very positive indication of oxygen. A more effective test would be to repeat the procedure of Topic 55, Investigation 3 – the J-tube gas analysis using potassium hydroxide and pyrogallol.

—Assignments

1 Interpreted as the procedures needed to be carried out to produce starch print.
De-starch geranium (*1*). Cover leaf with card with letter 'M' cut out (*1*). Put plant in well-lit place for several days (*1*). Detach leaf and remove mask (*1*). Kill in boiling water (*1*). Turn off bunsen burner (used to boil water) (*1*). Decolorise leaf in test tube of alcohol (*1*) standing in beaker of hot water (*1*). Soften leaf in (beaker of) water (*1*). Test for starch with iodine solution on white tile/petri dish (*1*).

(*10 marks*)

2 *Any well-reasoned argument, e.g.
(i) it only shows if part of a leaf needs light to make starch;

or
(ii) it lacks a control (worth considering what the control should be);
or
(iii) contact of mask with leaf may affect result.
(*2 marks*)

3 (a) Kept in dark (*1*) for 48 hours (*1*).
(*2 marks*)
(b) Presence of starch constitutes a positive result (*1*). Therefore could invalidate experiment (*1*).
(*2 marks*)
(c) Test one leaf from each plant for starch (*1*) at beginning of experiment (*1*).
(*2 marks*)
(*Total 6 marks*)

4 (i) Diagram showing:
potted plant with at least two leaves; (*1*)
two polythene bags, each around a leaf; (*1*)
each bag closed at petricle; (*1*)
soda lime in one bag; (*1*)
saturated sodium hydrogencarbonate solution in other; (*1*)
contained in a practical way, e.g. soaked in cotton wool. (*1*)
(*6 marks*)
(ii) Clarity of drawing. (*3*)
(iii) Labels:
soda lime; (*1*)
saturated sodium hydrogencarbonate solution; (*2*)
polythene bag. (*1*)
(*4 marks*)

Notes:
(i) labelling simply 'sodium hydrogencarbonate' = *1 mark*
(ii) other labels, e.g. cotton wool, small container, elastic band, may merit bonus marks.

(iv) 'Is it as good as the set up in Investigation 1?' Yes/No, dependent on reasoning. (*2*)
Note: Elizabeth's experiment would certainly yield the expected results and it eliminates effects due to differences between the plants or the soil they are grown in. However, it takes a single leaf rather than the whole plant, and the fact that the two leaves are connected might affect the results.
(*Total 15 marks*)

5 (a) Kept in dark (*1*) for 48 hours (*1*) to de-starch it (*1*).
(*3 marks*)
(b) Leaves above the cork (*1*).
(c) Remove leaves above and below cork (*1*). Kill in boiling water (*1*). Turn off bunsen burner (*1*). Decolorise leaves in test tube of alcohol (*1*) standing in beaker of hot water (*1*). Soften leaf in (beaker of) water (*1*). Test for starch with iodine solution on white tile/petri dish (*1*).
(*7 marks*)
(d) Yes/No dependent on reasoning. 'No' is more likely to be correct (*2*).

Note: expected result probably yielded by this set up, but test and control leaves come from same plant. Absence of root system probably won't affect result but mention should be considered valid with supporting teacher's comment.
(*Total 13 marks*)

—Discussion—

Sooner or later someone will be able to recreate the process of photosynthesis in a laboratory. This could have far-reaching consequences affecting us all. What do you think these consequences could be?
Note: carbohydrates could be formed as possible industrial raw material. Also it could form the means by which fuel could be produced, either ethanol via fermentation, or hydrogen (by way of platinum-treated chloroplasts). Will sunny countries get all the business?

Topic 66
What Controls the Rate of Photosynthesis?

—Investigation—

To see if raising the light intensity increases the rate of photosynthesis

Requirements

Darkened room; 5 cm *Elodea*; paper clip; 250 cm³ beaker; pinch of potassium hydrogencarbonate; drinking straw; lamp; narrow aquarium tank; water; 1 m ruler; graph paper.

Practical skills

HMA 1, HMA 2, HMA 3, HMA 4, HMA 7, AMO 4, AMO 6, REC 2, REC 3, REC 4, INT 1, INT 2, INT 3, INT 4, INT 5, INT 6.

General Comments

This is a major investigation that can be used to assess a number of skills. Most of the precautionary comments for Topic 65, Investigation 4 (p. 83 of this guide) are relevant here.

Counting the number of bubbles coming off the weed can be difficult, but could be used to assess AMO 4 and AMO 6. Note that the teacher will need to count along with the pupil, to ensure that the counting is accurate. Sometimes the bubbles do not rise to the surface, but become trapped on the side of the weed. Such bubbles can either be ignored, or can be persuaded to surface by gently waving the weed. If this latter procedure is adopted, it is important to wave the weed equally at all distances from the light source.

If the average number of bubbles are obtained for several distances from the lamp, then a graph can be plotted of the data. Note that a straight line will only be obtained by plotting $1/d^2$ against the rate of bubble formation, where d is the distance of the light source from the plant. This should probably be attempted only with the more able classes because of problems in handling inverse square distances. It could provide useful practice at simple calculations (INT 4). There are a number of skills related to data handling and graph plotting that can be assessed (REC 2, REC 3, REC 4, INT 1–3, INT 5).

There is an increase in photosynthetic rate (as measured by the number of bubbles evolved per minute) with increasing illumination. Inaccuracies in estimating the true rate of oxygen evolution will cause the graph to deviate significantly from a curve or a straight line (depending upon whether 'd' or '$1/d^2$' is plotted on the x-axis). This could form the basis of an assessment for recognising patterns in data (INT 6).

In theory, if not in practice, there is an upper limit beyond which increasing the light intensity will not increase the rate of photosynthesis further. Whether this limit will be reached in the pupils' experiment will depend upon the exact conditions of the experiment.

—*Assignments*

1 Mrs Jones (*1*). More photosynthesis (*1*) in bright light (*1*) results in more growth (*1*).

(*4 marks*)

2 (i) Grass is killed by lack of light (*1*) so cannot photosynthesise (*1*).
(ii) Yellow colour is caused by breakdown of chlorophyll (light needed for chlorophyll synthesis) (*1*).

(*3 marks*)

3 Reason: e.g. more carbon dioxide in the atmosphere (*1*).
Investigation: e.g. (i) wheat growth in different carbon dioxide concentration; (ii) survey of wheat growth near other coal-burning power stations.
Any two investigations – 2 marks each (*4 marks*)

(*Total 5 marks*)

4 (i) Sugar cane, Java: has ideal conditions for productivity. (*2*)
e.g. Characteristics:
(i) crop plant;
(ii) closely planted;
(iii) warm;
(iv) bright;
(v) wet.
At least two examples – 1 mark each (*2 marks*)
(ii) Tropical rain forest:
good conditions for productivity; (*1*)
but plants more loosely packed. (*1*)
e.g. Characteristics:
(i) lush but wild;
(ii) more loosely (naturally) planted;
(iii) warm, but cooler than cane field;
(iv) top of forest bright, lower down dimmer;
(v) wet.
At least two examples – 1 mark each (*2 marks*)
(iii) Pine forest, England:
coolness and less light reduce productivity. (*2*)
e.g. Characteristics:
(i) wild or crop;
(ii) closely packed (especially if crop);
(iii) cooler than tropics;
(iv) less light than tropics;
(v) wet;
(vi) evergreen.
At least two examples – 1 mark each (*2 marks*)
(iv) Birch forest, England:
lower density and seasonal leaf loss reduce productivity further. (*2*)
e.g. Characteristics:
(i) wild;
(ii) more spread out;
(iii) cooler than tropics (same as pine forest);
(iv) less light than tropics (same as pine forest);
(v) wet;
(vi) deciduous.
At least two examples – 1 mark each (*2 marks*)

(*Total 16 marks*)

5 (a) Rate of photosynthesis increases rapidly (*1*) with increase in carbon dioxide concentration (*1*) up to a certain limit (*1*), beyond which further increases in carbon dioxide concentration have no effect (*1*).
(*4 marks*)
(b) Rate of photosynthesis depends directly on the concentration of carbon dioxide. (*1*)
(c) e.g.
(i) The maximum rate of photosynthesis has been reached, so further increases in carbon dioxide have no effect.
(ii) Other factors such as temperature and light are limiting the rate of photosynthesis.
Any two reasons – 2 marks each (*4 marks*)
(d) e.g.
(i) Establish the maximum rate of photosynthesis by exposing plant to known 'ideal' circumstances (or by first finding these out). Does this maximum rate then match where the curve levels out?
(ii) Provide the plant with optimum (where curve flattens) concentration of carbon dioxide and raise e.g. temperature or light.
Any two experiments – 2 marks each (*4 marks*)

(*Total 13 marks*)

6 (a) (i) Correctly labelled axes. (*2*)
(ii) Accurate plotting: 7 points = 3 marks; 5 points = 2 marks; 3 points = 1 mark. (*3*)
(iii) Curve well drawn. (*2*)
(iv) Presentation. (*2*)
(*9 marks*)
(b) (a) 1.10% (± 0.02%). (*1*)
(b) 0.46% (± 0.02%). (*1*)
(*2 marks*)
(c) 3.30 p.m. (± ½ hour). (*1*)
Note: depends on pupil's graph.
(d) *At dawn (6 a.m.) there is light (*1*) phtosynthesis begins (*1*) and sugar begins to increase (*1*).
As morning progresses light gets brighter (*1*), increasing the rate of photosynthesis (*1*) so sugar continues to accumulate (*1*).
After midday the day gets less bright (*1*) so rate of photosynthesis decreases (*1*). Sugar accumulates less rapidly (*1*) until it reaches maximum in late afternoon (*1*) (3.30 p.m.)
In evening light becomes dim (*1*), greatly reducing photosynthesis (*1*). The plants need for sugar (in respiration) (*1*) means it is transported from leaves (*1*) much faster than it is made (*1*) so sugar concentration decreases. (*1*)
In the dark only respiration occurs (*1*) so sugar concentration decreases rapidly (*1*).
(*18 marks*)

(*Total 30 marks*)

—*Discussion*

Market gardeners rely on greenhouses to make a living. The overheads are high and poor decisions could result in bankruptcy. What sort of decisions would you have to take in keeping your business a success?

Note: which plant should you grow off-season? What are the means of keeping greenhouses at the right temperature without enormous fuel bills? At which scale is it economical to grow any particular crop? What outlets are there for products? Ultimately a biological understanding of what market gardener is doing underlies good financial sense. Scientific subjects are not purely academic but exist to be applied in everyday contexts.

Topic 67 Chlorophyll, The Miracle Molecule

Investigation 1

How to make a solution of chlorophyll

Requirements

Scissors; few green leaves; pestle and mortar; pinch of washed sand; 100 cm^3 ethanol or acetone; beaker; filter funnel; filter paper; water.

Practical skills

HMA 1, HMA 3, HMA 4, HMA 7.

General Comments

This technique can be used to provide sufficient chlorophyll extract to be used in Investigations 2 and 3 of this topic. The chlorophyll extract should be as concentrated as possible. Green cabbage is a ready source of chlorophyll.

Adequate ventilation should be provided in the classroom when using the solvents, which should not be inhaled.

Investigation 2

To find the effect of chlorophyll on light

Requirements

Solution of chlorophyll obtained from Investigation 1; narrow container (e.g. a colorimeter cuvette); projector; prism; screen.

Practical skills

HMA 1, HMA 3, HMA 7, AMO 10.

General Comments

It is important that the room is darkened, and that the beam of white light is as narrow as possible. It should be possible to see that red and blue light are absorbed by the chlorophyll.

Investigation 3

To separate the pigments present in a leaf

Requirements

First method. Solution of chlorophyll from Investigation 1; clean stick of blackboard chalk; 20 cm^3 ethanol or acetone; small beaker (e.g. 100 cm^3).

Second method. 20 cm^3 ethanol or acetone; large boiling tube and rubber bung; thin strip of filter paper; scissors; dressmaking pin; drawing pin.

Practical skills

HMA 1, HMA 3, HMA 4, HMA 7, AMO 10, REC 5.

General Comments

This practical is a good test of simple manipulative ability. Common errors include adding too much solvent, so that the green spot is washed off immediately, and not putting enough chlorophyll on the paper. The colour of the pigments fade in the light, and the boiling tube is best kept in the dark whilst the solvent is moving up the paper.

The different colours are due to different pigments. The green colour is chlorophyll, whilst the yellows are the accessory pigments xanthophyll and carotene, which are closely associated with chlorophyll molecules and protect them from being destroyed by the light. They may also absorb light and pass it onto the chlorophyll molecules. Carotene is the pigment near the solvent front. The different pigments have different solubilities in the solvent, and move through the paper at different rates.

Pupils could be asked to choose the most appropriate way of presenting their results (REC 5), e.g. an accurate coloured drawing or a table of measurements.

Investigation 4

Looking at chloroplasts in a moss leaf

Requirements

Pair of forceps; one small leaf of a moss plant; drop of water; light microscope; microscope slide; coverslip; dilute iodine solution.

Practical skills

HMA 1, HMA 3, HMA 5, HMA 6, HMA 7, AMO 10.

General Comments

This practical would make a good practical assessment for using microscopes (HMA 5, HMA 6). Starch is found near the chloroplast, suggesting that it has been involved in its synthesis.

Assignments

1 Leaves contain chlorophyll. (*1*)
Green light either passes straight through chlorophyll; (*1*)
or is reflected by it. (*1*)

(*3 marks*)

2 e.g. De-starch eight geraniums(*1*)
Put plants into boxes with one light source (*1*)
Box 1 – red light, (*1*)
Box 2 – orange, (*1*)
Box 3 – yellow, (*1*)
Box 4 – green, (*1*)
Box 5 – blue, (*1*)
Box 6 – violet, (*1*)
Box 7 – white light (control), (*1*)
Box 8 – total darkness, (+*1*)
Leave plants for a few days. (*1*)
Test for starch (*1*)

(*11 marks*)

3 e.g. (i) Not enough light. (*1*)
(ii) Wrong spectrum – not enough red and blue light (*1*) (Some pupils may suggest that the man forgot to water the plant! Use discretion.)
(*2 marks*)

4 Not all plants are green. (*1*)
e.g. different colours to absorb (*1*) other light colours/parts of the spectrum (*1*).
(*3 marks*)

5 (a) Chlorophyll eventually breaks down (*1*) so needs to be made all the time (*1*) and light is needed to make chlorophyll (*1*).
(*3 marks*)
(b) e.g. Take plant with yellowed leaves (*1*) and plant with green leaves (*1*) (control (+*1*)); De-starch both (*1*). Expose both to light for a few days (*1*). Test for starch (*1*).
(*5 marks*)
(c) Plant would die. (*1*)
Not light means no photosynthesis. (*1*)
Plant cannot make food. (*1*)
(*3 marks*)
(*Total 11 marks*)

6 (a) White (*1*)
(b) Splits up into spectrum (*1*)
(c) Blue and red parts of spectrum (*1*) absorbed/disappear from view (*1*).
(d) Chlorophyll absorbs blue and red light/colours (*1*).
(*5 marks*)

Discussion

It could be an advantage for us to have chlorophyll in our skin – or would it?
Note: some animals have green protists in their skin, e.g. green hydra, green sea slugs. They have the advantage of 'photosynthesising' and supplement their diet. Our problems are the thickness of our skin, presence of hair and the fact that we digest plant material and what about the wearing of clothes?!

Topic 68
More About Photosynthesis

Assignments

1 Heavy oxygen's atoms are slightly heavier than normal oxygen's. (*1*)
These atoms can be told apart by using a mass spectrometer. (*1*)
Heavy oxygen in carbon dioxide (*1*) is taken in in photosynthesis (*1*) and later found in carbohydrate made by plant (*1*).
(*3 marks*)
(*Total 5 marks*)

2 No. (*1*)
Photosynthesis has light and dark stages (*1*): light stage – water is split up into oxygen and hydrogen (*1*); dark stage – hydrogen combines with carbon dioxide (*1*) to make carbohydrate (*1*). So plant will stop making carbohydrate when its supply of hydrogen released in the light stage (*1*) runs out (*1*).
(*5 marks*)
(*Total 7 marks*)

3 Nitrogen is needed to convert (*1*) to protein (*1*).
(*2 marks*)

4 *e.g. Not certain that temperature is the same in both bottles.
2 marks for reasonable criticism plus bonus marks for others
(*4 marks*)

5 *$6CO_2 + 12H_2O \rightarrow C_6H_{12}O_6 + 6O_2 + 6H_2O$.
(*1*) (*1*) (*1*) (*1*) (*1*)
(*5 marks*)
Note: teachers might prefer to discuss this question with more able pupils rather than set it as an exercise. It serves to alert pupils to the inadequacy of the standard photosynthetic equation given in Topic 65 of *BFL*.

Discussion

By coating chloroplasts with platinum in a special way it is possible to make them carry out the light reaction but not the dark. How would you set about designing a machine which requires only sunlight, water, and modified chloroplasts? Is there any way of getting it to run on dull days or at night?
Note: I'm not sure that the idea is very practical! It works in principle though and may appeal to pupils' imagination. The light reaction uses sunlight to split water into hydrogen and oxygen. The hydrogen could be burned (in the oxygen?) to run a steam engine, or directly in a small internal combustion engine. If the engine powered a dynamo which recharged a battery it might work in the dark, or would one need to cheat and turn a light on?

Topic 69
The Leaf: Organ of Photosynthesis

Investigation 1

Looking at leaves

Requirements
Selection of leaves of dicotyledonous plants (e.g. horse chestnut, rose, ash, daisy); hand lens.

Practical skills
HMA 7, AMO 8, AMO 10.

General Comments
The pupils could be asked to describe the similarities and differences between two of the leaves, as an assessment for AMO 8 or AMO 10.

Investigation 2

Finding the leaf area of a plant

Requirements
Access to a large plant or shrub with leaves approximately the same size; graph paper; pencil.

Practical skills
AMO 6, INT 1, INT 4.

General Comments
This exercise will provide a graphic indication of the total surface area of the leaves on a bush. Opportunities exist for accurate counting (AMO 6) and simple calculations (INT 4).

—*Investigation 3*—

Looking inside the leaf

Requirements
Prepared slide of a leaf, or sections of a fresh leaf; light microscope with low power objective lens; microscope slide; coverslip; mounted needle; dropping pipette; water.

Practical skills
HMA 5, HMA 6, AMO 10, REC 1, INT 1.

General Comments
This exercise will allow microscopy skills to be assessed, and accurate observations. The adaptation question at the end can be used to assess (INT 1).

—*Assignments*—

1 A list of five features is a reasonable expectation.
e.g.
(i) Tall upright stem (but note climbers, scramblers, etc.)
(ii) many branches;
(iii) each branch may have numerous leaves;
(iv) leaves (generally) large and flat;
(v) leaves held at right angles to sunlight;
(vi) leaves spaced to catch as much sunlight as possible.
At least five – 1 mark each
(*5 marks*)

2 (a) Stomata – carbon dioxide (*1*), water (*1*) (light (+*1*)).
Vessels – water (*1*).
Chloroplasts – chlorophyll (*1*), light (*1*).
Air spaces – carbon dioxide (*1*) (water (+*1*)).
(*6 marks*)

Notes:
(i) Words in brackets constitute reasonable answers. Award bonus marks.
(ii) Chlorophyll is a plausible answer to 'stomata' but I'd like to hear the pupil qualifying it.

(b) All structures within the leaf (*1*)
(c) All necessary for photosynthesis (*1*)
(*Total 8 marks*)

3 Most chloroplasts are (*1*) in palisade layer (*1*) near upper side of leaf (*1*), so lower side appears paler (*no mark*).
(*3 marks*)

4 Palisade layer is near upper surface (*1*) so it gets more light (*1*).
(*2 marks*)

5 (a) Transports water (*1*) and mineral salts (*1*).
(*2 marks*)
(b) Allow gases to pass in and out of leaf. (*1*)
(c) Carbon dioxide can circulate freely within leaf. (*1*)
Notes:
(i) In (b) gases may be named as carbon dioxide, oxygen and water vapour.
(ii) In (c) oxygen and water vapour might be named. You might consider awarding extra marks for greater detail.
(*Total 4 marks*)

6 All arranged so each leaf gets maximum sunlight.
(*2 marks*)

—*Discussion*—

Why are leaves so many different shapes and sizes?
Note: leaves have to satisfy several requirements which vary from plant to plant. Usually they are thin with a large surface area to maximise photosynthesis. Other overriding demands can cause many variants: e.g. succulents – thick and fleshy leaves to conserve water, cacti – leaves reduced to spines for protection against browsers, water lily – large and flat leaves with air spaces for bouyancy. Some trees have many smaller leaves so light can penetrate numerous foliage layers. There are others!

Topic 70
Uptake and Transport in Plants

—*Investigation 1*—

Measuring the uptake of water by means of a potometer

Requirements
Leafy twig or shoot; access to a sink of water or a bowl; short length of rubber tubing (5 cm) attached to a straight length of capillary tube; 250 cm^3 beaker of water; ruler; retort stand and clamp; blotting paper; marker pen; stop watch; vaseline, knife.

Practical skills
HMA 1, HMA 2, HMA 3, HMA 4, HMA 7, AMO 2, AMO 4, REC 2, INT 2, INT 4, INT 5, INT 6.

General Comments
This is a major practical which can work effectively, providing satisfactory plant material can be found. Woody shoots are easier to manipulate than herbaceous ones. Sycamore is recommended. The practical is temperamental, and teachers need to consider it carefully before using it as an assessment for all but the most dextrous pupils.

Cutting the leafy twig from the parent plant will cause air to enter the xylem vessels adjacent to the cut. This will prevent any further uptake of water into those vessels. It is necessary to remove the terminal part of the shoot under water. Place the cut end of the shoot in a bowl of water, and make a diagonal cut 3 cm from the end of the shoot. Fill the capillary tube with water and attach it to the shoot. This operation should be carried out under water. It is very important that a continuous column of water exists in the plant from the leaves to the capillary tube. The junction between the rubber tubing and the plant can be sealed with vaseline. When carrying out this operation, it is also important that the leaves do not get wet, as this will significantly reduce transpiration from their surfaces.

Once working the practical provides an excellent opportunity for assessing the collection, analysis and interpretation of data (AMO 2, AMO 4, REC 2, INT 2, INT 5, INT 6). Rates of water uptake can be calculated and assessed (INT 4). The practical can be extended to consider the rate of water uptake in various environmental conditions, e.g. light and dark, still and moving air (using a hair drier with the heating element turned off).

—*Investigation 2*—

Measuring the uptake of water by the weighing method

Requirements

Herbaceous plant, with leaves and roots; 20 cm^3 measuring cylinder; 20 cm^3 water; vegetable oil; access to top-pan balance.

Practical skills

HMA 1, HMA 7, AMO 3, AMO 5, INT 5.

General Comments

The practical allows an excellent opportunity to assess the ability to weigh accurately (AMO 5). Assuming that the oil forms an effective seal on the surface of the water, the only way that water can be lost from the leaves is by evaporation from the leaf surfaces. The volume of liquid in the cylinder can be measured on two occasions (AMO 3), and the difference noted. The mass of water lost can be calculated from the volume of water lost by assuming that 1 cm^3 of water weighs 1 g. This figure ought (in theory) to equal the loss of mass measured earlier.

There are sources of error, however. A plant can take up water, and not lose it by transpiration. This is particularly likely if the plant is wilted when placed in the water. In such circumstances, the weight obtained from the volume measurements should be greater than that obtained by direct measurement. It is, of course, possible that the plant may lose certain structures (e.g. leaves, flowers or fruits) when placed in the measuring cylinder. In such circumstances, the weight loss by measurement should be greater than that obtained from the volume measurements. A consideration of the experimental variability could be used as a basis for a written assessment (INT 5).

—*Investigation 3*—

Looking at the transport tissues in a stem

Requirements

6 cm of non-woody stem (e.g. *Impatiens*); sharp razor blade; dish; water; dropping pipette; phloroglucinol stain; concentrated HCl; paintbrush; light microscope with low power objective lens; microscope slide; coverslip; mounted needle.

Practical skills

HMA 1, HMA 3, HMA 5, HMA 6, HMA 7, AMO 10, REC 1.

General Comments

Care needs to be exercised when using the razor blade and the phloroglucinol/HCl mixture, and this could form the basis of a safety assessment (HMA 3). The sections that are cut need to be about 1 mm in thickness. It is not necessary to cut completely circular sections. The cutting exercise needs dexterity, and could usefully be used to assess handling materials and apparatus (HMA 7). It also provides an opportunity to assess the microscope skills (HMA 5 and 6) and to draw the stem structures (REC 1), although the pupil needs to have access to Topic 70, Figure 3 in *BFL* for help with labelling.

The arrangement of vascular bundles differs in the stems of monocotyledons and dicotyledons, and this could form the basis of useful extension work for fast finishers.

This practical can be linked to Investigation 2 in Topic 71.

—*Investigation 4*—

Showing the passage of water through a plant

Requirements

Freshly picked herbaceous plant with leaves and roots; bowl of water; three 100 cm^3 conical flasks; eosin (or red ink dye); scalpel; cutting of balsam plant (*Impatiens*); plant with white flowers (e.g. periwinkle, deadnettle, carnation).

Practical skills

AMO 2, HMA 7.

General Comments

This is a simple demonstration that needs preparing before the lesson starts. The distance travelled by the dye can be assessed (AMO 2).

—*Investigation 5*—

Looking at the stomata in a leaf

Requirements

Plant with green leaves; paintbrush; clear nail varnish; forceps; Light microscope with low power objective lens; microscope slide; coverslip; mounted needle; water.

Practical skills

HMA 5, HMA 6, HMA 7, AMO 6, EXP.

General Comments

This practical allows assessment of microscope skills (HMA 5 and HMA 6), diagrams of the guard cells (REC 1) and counting the number of stomata on the upper and lower surfaces in one low power field of view (AMO 6). It could form the basis for a more extended investigation testing the hypothesis that the relative numbers of stomata on the upper and lower leaf vary with the angle of the leaves to the stem. (Compare stomatal densities of daffodil, maize, wheat and crocus leaves with those of horse chestnut, ash or sycamore, for example.) This could be used to develop or assess EXP skills.

It is important that the impression is completely dry before it is peeled off the leaf. If it is not completely dry, it will stretch when pulled, ruining the impression of the leaf surface.

—*Investigation 6*—

To see how quickly the two sides of a leaf lose water

Requirements

Two pieces of anhydrous cobalt chloride or thiocyanate paper; leafy twig of a tree; small pieces of sellotape; pair of scissors; clock.

Practical skills

HMA 2, HMA 7, AMO 4, AMO 6, INT 1.

General Comments

The time taken for the pink colour to appear can form the basis for an assessment (AMO 4). It is an acceptable hypothesis that the side of the leaf with the most open stomata will lose water most quickly. This can be used to assess INT 1. The pupil has formed a hypothesis that now needs to be tested. This can be done using the techniques of Investigation 5. Asking the pupil to test the hypothesis could be a good way of assessing initiative (HMA 2) and counting skills (AMO 6).

—*Assignments*—

1 Some water had evaporated from the plant (*1*) i.e. transpiration had occurred (*1*). The cold night made the glass a cold surface (*1*) on which the water vapour had condensed (*1*).
(*4 marks*)

2 (a) Watering plants in evening ensures water does not evaporate from the soil (*1*), so it can penetrate deep down to the roots (*1*).
(*2 marks*)
(b) Transplanting disturbs the roots (*1*) and reduces their ability to take in water (*1*). Removing leaves reduces transpiration (*1*) so reduces the demand on the roots for water (*1*).
(*4 marks*)
(c) Water evaporates faster on a hot dry day (*1*) so more water is lost from the leaf (*1*), resulting in water moving more quickly up stem (*1*).
(*3 marks*)
(d) Food materials are transported in the phloem – sensible place to feed! (*1*)
(*Total 10 marks*)

3 By removing a ring of bark from the trunk (*1*). This would remove phloem (*1*), so food could not be transported down tree (*1*).
(*3 marks*)

4 (a) Stomata. (*1*)
(b) Visking tubing bags take in water (*1*) by osmosis (*1*) and swell, bowing outwards (*1*).
(*3 marks*)
(c) e.g.
(i) Artificial stoma is not light sensitive. Guard cells respond to light.
(ii) Artificial stoma has a fixed amount of sugar in visking tubing bags. (By photosynthesis and respiration (+ *1*) guard cells can vary their sugar content.)
(iii) Artificial stoma needs to be entirely surrounded by distilled water/a weaker solution to work. Guard cells of real stoma surrounded by air and other cells.
(iv) The visking tubing walls do not assist the opening of the artificial stoma.
(v) The guard cell walls are different thicknesses so do assist in opening the real stoma.
Any two differences – 2 marks each (*4 marks*)
Note: answers must be functional
(*Total 8 marks*)

5 (i) Conclusions:
(a) Salt uptake involves active transport (*1*).
(b) Active transport requires energy from respiration (*1*). Respiration rate increases with temperature (*1*), but above 40°C it slows down rapidly (*1*) because enzymes involved are destroyed (*1*).
(c) Since active transport depends on respiration (*1*) it can only work in a living/metabolising cell (*1*).
(d) Respiration requires oxygen (*1*); waterlogging fills air spaces in soil so there is no soil oxygen (*1*).
(*9 marks*)
(ii) Help to farmers.
e.g.
(a) Mineral salts need not be added in large quantities (*1*).
(b) Warmth (*1*) but not extreme heat (*1*) (unlikely in Britain) is needed for cereals to grow.
(c) Be careful what poisons (*1*) (pesticides/herbicides) are used and in what quantities (*1*).
(d) Aeration of soil (*1*) and good drainage are essential (*1*) (e.g. by ploughing, earthworms (+ *1*))
(*7 marks*)
(*Total 16 marks*)

—*Discussion*—

1 The Egyptians and Israelis have found that by growing certain crops in the desert they can export off-season vegetables when the prices are high. What problems do you think the desert presents and can you suggest practical solutions?
Note: the soil being sandy and very dry, needs irrigation and mulching. Deserts are hot and dry by day. It can get very cold at night. Greenhouses are used but careful control of reflective blinds is needed to prevent overheating – opening a window loses water!

2 How does a plant's transport system differ from ours?
Note: e.g. different 'tubes' are used for water and food products; they are not pumped internally; it doesn't penetrate tissues as extensively as ours; the system is designed to lose water rather than conserve it (transpiration).

Topic 71
How do Plants Support Themselves?

—*Investigation 1*—

To find how strong a stem is

Requirements

Two retort stands and clamps; plastic protractor; a selection of freshly cut plant stems; knife; cutting board; plastic ruler; 10 g mass; strong thread.

Practical skills
HMA 1, HMA 2, HMA 4, HMA 7.

General Comments
A variety of different shoots can be tried, including herbaceous and woody ones. If direct comparisons between shoots of different species are being made, each shoot should be of the same approximate thickness and length. It is also possible to carry out experiments on twigs of different ages taken from same tree. First and second year woody shoots can be compared.

It is important that the mass be hung at the same distance from the end of every shoot. The degree of curvature of the shoot can be measured.

The practical can be developed by investigating whether the amount and distribution of the wood in the stem can be related to its flexibility. This could be a useful test of initiative (HMA 2).

—Investigation 2

To find out how much wood there is in a stem

Requirements
Short lengths of stem/branch of several different plants (including sunflower) (the shoots from the previous investigation or those from Topic 70 Investigation 4 would be appropriate); several small watch glasses; phloroglucinol/concentrated HCl; knife/scalpel.

Practical skills
HMA 1, HMA 3, HMA 7, AMO 10.

General Comments
The need for caution with the phloroglucinol/concentrated HCl mixture needs to re-emphasised, and safe working could be assessed (HMA 3). Accurate estimates of the proportion of woody tissue in the stems can also be assessed (AMO 10).

—Assignments

1 Packing cells, epidermis, fibres, xylem.
Any three – 1 mark each
(*3 marks*)

2 (a) Water is evaporating from leaves (*1*) faster than being taken up by roots (*1*). As a result packing cells lose water (*1*) and become flabby/flaccid (*1*). This is called wilting (*1*). In the evening there is less evaporation/transpiration (*1*) and watering has supplied roots with water (*1*) so uptake now greater than evaporation (*1*). Packing cells take in water (*1*) and become turgid (*1*), causing plants to stand upright again (*1*).
(*11 marks*)

(b) e.g.
(i) Plants in shade.
(ii) Localised moist soil (due to shade, drainage).
(iii) Drought-resistant plants (e.g. succulents).
(iv) Deep roots.
At least two – 1 mark each (*2 marks*)
(*Total 13 marks*)

3 e.g.Spruce: building, furniture, hardboard, paper, cardboard, packing and packaging, matches, creosote, dyestuffs, explosives, fabrics, e.g. viscose rayon, fuel.
(*5 marks*)

Note: length of answer will vary with the timber tree chosen. Marks awarded are notional.

4 (a) Harder (*1*), denser (*1*), therefore stronger (*1*) and drier (*1*) (less likely to shrink and warp (+*1*)).
(*4 marks*)

(b) Strong (*1*) and springy (*1*).
(*2 marks*)

(c) Hard (*1*) and durable (*1*).
(*2 marks*)

(d) Grow comparatively quickly (*1*); wood suitable for most purposes (*1*).
(*2 marks*)
(*Total 10 marks*)

6 (a) Water has entered packing cells (*1*), but epidermis has been cut (*1*) therefore it cannot restrain their swelling so ends splay out (*1*). (*3 marks*)

(b) Strong salt or sugar solution (*1*).
(*Total 4 marks*)

—Discussion

1 In Great Britain we could be self-sufficient in timber if we were prepared to plant enough softwood trees. Do you think this is a good idea?
Note: cultivating trees (silviculture) is seen as mixed blessing. There are advantages of cropping timber and saving natural woodlands from felling, along with economic gains; these are counterbalanced against the encroachment of monoculture forest into moorland habitats. Close planting of forestry softwood trees restricts the community to only a few species. These forests differ greatly from the more open natural conifer forests of Canada, Scandinavia and Russia which do show species diversity, and are intermixed with deciduous tress (e.g. silver birch).

2 It can take several hundred years for a rain forest tree to grow fully. The wood of such trees is very hard, durable and commercially desirable. Bearing in mind the rate at which tropical rain forests are vanishing (the area of Great Britain every year), should there be a ban on the import of tropical hardwoods?
Note: would this stop deforestation? Human developments such as urbanisation, road building and agriculture along with ill-considered planning by governments are the key elements. As a political gesture a ban might add credibility to the affluent Western world complaining that the less affluent Third World wasn't managing its affairs properly. In Britain deforestation continues, despite our comments about what happens elsewhere.

Topic 72
The Skin and Temperature Control

—Investigation 1

The effects of insulation on heat loss

Requirements
Two 250 cm^3 conical flasks; cotton wool; elastic bands; access to very hot water; a way of dispensing the hot water safely (e.g. jugs); two thermometers; clock; graph paper.

Practical skills
HMA 3, HMA 4, HMA 7, AMO 1, AMO 3, AMO 4, REC 5, INT 1, EXP.

General Comments
The ability to work safely and effectively is important in this practical, where very hot water is being moved around the class

room. A tea urn may prove to be a more suitable source of hot water than a kettle. Assessment can be made of safe working (HMA 3), the ability to use a thermometer (AMO 1) and a clock (AMO 4), graph plotting (REC 4), recording accurately (REC 3) and presentation of results in the most appropriate form (e.g. tables or suitable graphs) (REC 5).

The cotton wool acts as an insulator and slows down the rate at which the flask loses water. This conclusion could also be assessed (INT 1).

The experiment could be extended by having a third flask of hot water which is rubbed with cotton wool soaked in ethanol. This simulates the evaporating power of heat and could be used to assess the EXP skills.

—*Investigation 2*

The effect of size on heat loss

Requirements

One 500 cm^3 conical flask; one 100 cm^3 conical flask; access to very hot water; a way of dispensing the hot water safely (e.g. jugs); two thermometers; clock; graph paper.

Practical skills

HMA 3, HMA 4, HMA 7, AMO 3, AMO 4, REC 4.

General Comments

Assessment could be made of working safely with hot water (HMA 3), the use of the thermometer (AMO 3), the use of the clock (AMO 4) and graph plotting (REC 4).

The smaller beaker has a larger surface area/volume ratio, and loses heat more quickly than the large beaker. These two beakers might represent large and small mammals (e.g. an elephant and a shrew) – a shrew loses a greater proportion of its heat than does an elephant; this heat needs to be replaced by respiration and other metabolic activities, which in turn requires a regular input of relatively large quantities of food. It will need to eat a greater amount of food each day (in proportion to its body mass) than will an elephant. An elephant, on the other hand, will find it relatively difficult to lose heat, and will have problems keeping cool.

—*Assignments*

1 On a cold day the cat's erector muscles (*1*) contract (*1*), raising hairs (*1*) and trapping a layer of air (*1*) which insulates body, preventing heat loss (*1*).
On a hot day erector muscles relax (*1*), flattening hairs (*1*). This means that heat can escape from body (*1*).
(*8 marks*)

2 (a) On a hot dry day sweat evaporates more easily than on a hot humid day.(*1*)
When sweat evaporates it carries heat away from the body. (*1*)
(*2 marks*)

(b) Dogs have sweat glands only on pads of paws (*1*), which is hardly enough surface area to lose heat (+*1*)! So they cool (*1*) themselves by panting since water evaporates from their mouths and tongues (*1*).
(*3 marks*)

(c) If air temperature is lowered (*1*) more heat is lost from a naked human (*1*). The metabolic rate increases to produce extra heat (*1*).
(*3 marks*)

(d) There are three reasons:
(i) Swimming raises the metabolic activity of body.
(ii) Coldness of water reduces blood supply to skin.
(iii) Our temperature sense compares temperatures – the air is warm relative to the sea.
Any reason (*2 marks*)

(*Total 10 marks*)

3 (a) It has a large surface area relative to its body volume (*1*).
(b) Higher metabolic rate (*1*) produces extra heat (*1*).
(*2 marks*)
(c) The small mammal has a higher metabolic rate (*1*) so it respires more (*1*) and therefore uses up more food (*1*).
(*3 marks*)

(*Total 6 marks*)

4 (a) 8 hours: basking in the sun. (*1*)
14 hours: resting in the shade/its burrow. (*1*)
18 hours: foraging for food or basking in the gentler evening sun. (*1*)
(*3 marks*)
(b) Widening (dilation) of surface blood vessels. (*1*)
Sweating. (*1*)
(*2 marks*)

(*Total 5 marks*)

—*Discussion*

1 If you were to design a spray-on dressing for the skin what qualities would you want it to have?
Note: examples are: waterproof, permeable to air, impermeable to germs, won't irritate skin, no evidence of allergic response, won't hinder healing process in general, spray dries quickly. Such dressings do exist.

2 Is the skin particularly vulnerable to disease? How many skin diseases can you think of? Are they *all* caused by factors from outside the body?
Note: the intact skin is remarkably resistant to infection. The vulnerability of severe burns and open wounds to rapid infection and gangrene bears out how resistant the skin is. Some skin disorders are dandruff, eczema, impetigo, leprosy, melanoma, prickly heat, psoriasis, ringworm, scabies, shingles, skin cancer, sunburn, urticaria (nettlerash), warts. Causes may be external infection (e.g. impetigo, ringworm, scabies) or a symptom of an internal disorder (e.g. eczema, shingles, urticaria).

Topic 73
The Liver

—*Assignments*

1 (a) Bile production. (*1*)
(b) Destruction of old red blood cells. (*1*)
(c) Deamination/urea formation. (*1*)
(d) Stores food substances (e.g. glycogen) (*1*), contains many vitamins and minerals (*1*).
(*2 marks*)

(*Total 5 marks*)

2 (a) Hepatic portal vein. (*1*)
(b) Hepatic artery; (*1*)
hepatic vein; (*1*)
hepatic portal vein (especially!). (*1*) (*3 marks*)
(c) Bile duct. (*1*)
(d) Small intestine. (*1*)

(*Total 6 marks*)

3 (a) Take a small sample (say 5 cm^3) of urine in test tube (*1*). Add a few drops of Benedict's solution (*1*); put test tube into water bath at 100°C (*1*). Leave for about two minutes (*1*). If glucose is absent – stays blue (*1*); if present – turns green, yellow, orange, brown (*1*), depending on the amount (*1*).
(*7 marks*)
(b) Kidneys are trying to lower (*1*) excess blood glucose level (*1*).
(*2 marks*)

(*Total 9 marks*)

4 (a) Pepsin. (*1*) Trypsin. (*1*)
Peptidase. (*1*) Protease. (*1*)
Any two (*2 marks*)
Note: although 'Protease' is a general term it is worth a mark. If the answer is say 'Protease and Pepsin' I would be tempted to give two marks and write a note in the margin.
(b) Pepsin: into polypeptides. (*1*)
Trypsin: into polypeptides. (*1*)
Peptidase: into amino acids. (*1*)
Protease: into polypeptides/amino acids. (*1*)
Any two (*2 marks*)
(c) By injection. (*1*)
(d) e.g.
(i) Damage to blood vessel walls;
(ii) risk of taking too high a dose of insulin;
(iii) infection if syringe and needle are not sterile.
Any one danger (*1*)

(*Total 6 marks*)

—Discussion—

1 Recently, surgical implants which release insulin slowly into the blood have been developed. What advantages and disadvantages do these have over regular injections?
Note: advantages are the stopping of vein damage caused by routine insulin injection and a steady feed of insulin into the bloodstream. Unlike healthy pancreas function an implant cannot respond to blood sugar changes but relies on a 'drip feed' method – hence diet is just as restricted. Implant also needs periodic surgery for replacement (which is minor as the implant is usually subdermal). There is also a risk of mechanical injury and component failure.

2 Why do you think alcohol damages the liver in particular?
Note: alcohol is carried straight to the liver from the gut via hepatic portal vein, hence concentrations are higher here and damage is greater. Cirrhosis of the liver results from fibrous scar tissue forming where liver cells have been damaged. Abstention can halt the progress of this condition and a return to good health can result if it is checked in time.

Topic 74
How do we get rid of Waste Substances?

—Investigation 1—

To find the effect of drinking on urine production

Note: some examination boards recommend that investigations involving the use of body fluids should be discontinued (see p. 6).

Requirements

1 litre of water; clean cup; large measuring cylinder; clock; several clean test tubes; test tube rack; access to the toilets!

Practical skills

AMO 3.

General Comments

This is a simple exercise that is probably best done as a demonstration with a suitable volunteer/victim. It is probably not appropriate for practical assessment except, possibly, for the measurement of volume (AMO 3).

—Investigation 2—

Looking at the kidney

Requirements

Kidney from butcher or abattoir, preferably with blood vessels and ureter attached; sharp knife; plate.

Practical skills

AMO 10, REC 1.

General Comments

This is a simple demonstration of the major features of the kidney, including blood vessels, ureter, cortex, medulla and pelvis. A drawing could be used to assess REC 1. It is worth noting that the kidneys are normally covered with fat in the intact animal (this may be absent from cleaned specimens).

—Assignments—

1 (a) Less urine is produced (*1*) but it is more salty (*1*).
(*2 marks*)
(b) Depends on the temperature of the bath (+ *1*)! A hot bath should reduce the amount (*1*) of normal composition urine (*1*).
(**Note:** skin not normally permeable to water!)
(*2 marks*)
(c) Large quantities (*1*) of dilute (*1*) slightly alcoholic urine (*1*).
(*3 marks*)
(d) Less urine (*1*) slightly more concentrated (*1*) but low in salt (*1*).
(*3 marks*)
(e) Normal quantity (*1*); same amount of sugar as usual (*1*). (Insulin mechanism deals with excess sugar.)
(*2 marks*)

(*Total 12 marks*)

2 (i) Excretion: Getting rid of waste products of metabolism from the body. (*2*)
(ii) Osmo-regulation: Controlling relative amounts of water and salt (solutes) in the body. (*2*)
(iii) (a) Filters urea out of the blood. (*1*)
(b) Reabsorbs appropriate amounts (*1*) of salt and water back into blood (*1*).
(*3 marks*)

(*Total 7 marks*)

3 Note: order is column A: column B.
Protein:
blood entering kidney; (*1*)
blood leaving kidney. (*1*)
Glucose:
blood entering kidney; (*1*)
blood leaving kidney; (*1*)
fluid filtered into capsules. (*1*)
Note: kidney cells themselves will use glucose for respiration.
Urea:
blood entering kidney; (*1*)
fluid filtered into capsules; (*1*)
urine leaving kidney. (*1*)
Water:
blood entering kidney; (*1*)
blood leaving kidney; (*1*)
fluid filtered into capsules; (*1*)
urine leaving kidney. (*1*)

(*Total 12 marks*)

4 (a) Record daily (*1*)
temperature; (*1*)
volume of urine produced. (*1*)
Look for a connection (correlation) between temperature and volume of urine. (*1*)
(*4 marks*)
Note: controlling other factors, e.g. volume of water drunk, amount of exercise, shows a deeper insight and is worth additional marks.

(b) More water is lost as sweat on hot days; (*1*) so less is lost as urine. (*1*)
(*2 marks*)

(*Total 6 marks*)

Discussion

1 Should kidney donation be compulsory?
Note: is saving human lives more important than individual freedom?

2 Can a person survive with only one kidney?
Note: Yes, and the same applies to other paired organs, e.g. lungs, adrenal glands, etc. With a million or so nephrons in each kidney, one kidney working faster will do the work of two.

3 Suppose that there aren't enough kidney machines to go round? Who should have them?
Note: government priorities and economic factors determine supply. Should patients be selected according to their age, (potential) value to society or what? And *who* should decide?

4 Which is preferable for a patient, to be given a kidney machine or a kidney transplant?
Note: the inconvenience of periodic sessions on the kidney machine must be weighed against the possibility that the transplanted kidney may be rejected.

Topic 75
Water Balance and Waste Removal in Other Organisms

Assignments

1 The salts in amoeba's cytoplasm (*1*) are at a higher concentration (*1*) than the surrounding water (*1*) and the amoeba's cell membrane (*1*) is a selectively permeable membrane (*1*). As a result water enters by osmosis (*1*).

(*6 marks*)

2 (i) Produce uric acid – solid waste. (*1*)
(ii) Waterproof cuticle. (*1*)
(iii) Spiracles closed as much as possible. (*1*)

(*3 marks*)

3 (i) Produce solid waste – calcium oxalate. (*1*)
(ii) Waterproof (waxy) cuticle. (*1*)
(iii) Stomata closed as much as possible. (*1*)

(*3 marks*)

4 (a) Amoeba takes in more water (*1*) when in fresh water (*1*) so contractile vacuole fills up and empties more frequently (*1*).
(*3 marks*)

(b) e.g.
(i) Vary the salt concentration of the surrounding water.
(ii) Make a more concentrated solution than seawater (will the number of emptyings go to zero?).
(iii) Sample contents of contractile vacuole.

At least three – 2 marks each (*6 marks*)

(*Total 9 marks*)

Discussion

1 Why do you think we don't produce solid excretory waste? If we did what body changes would there have to be?
Note: we don't need to conserve water. Excretory waste would possibly pass out with faeces as in reptiles, birds and insects if we did.

2 What sort of organisms live in estuaries? Are they seawater or freshwater organisms, both, or neither? And how do they come to terms with the ever changing saltiness of the water?
Note: most are varieties of marine organisms capable of 'pumping' sodium in and out to maintain salt and water balance.

Topic 76
Adjustment and Control

Assignments

1 Heater: raises the temperature of the oven (*1*).
Thermostat: keeps the temperature of the oven constant (*1*) by switching heater on if it is too cold and off if too hot (*1*).
It is extremely difficult to cook anything properly if the oven temperature cannot be kept more or less constant (*2*).

(*5 marks*)

2 Information about certain conditions in the body (*1*) is fed back to the organs and systems creating them (*1*).

(*2 marks*)

Note: the oven analogy is likely to be used – this is acceptable.

3 Raising metabolic rate (especially in liver (+*1*)). (*1*)
Shivering. (*1*)
Raising hairs on body. (*1*)
Diversion of blood away from skin. (*1*)
Brought into action when outside temperature becomes cold. (*1*)

Slight drop in body temperature; (*1*)
acts on special centre in brain. (*1*)

(*7 marks*)

4

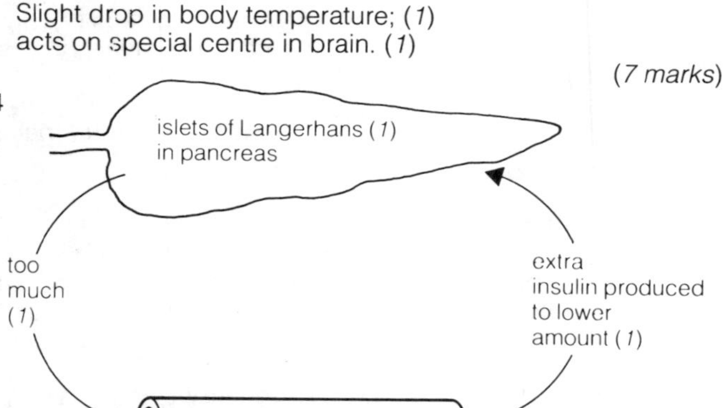

Add on 1 mark for the diagram (*5 marks*)
The above mechanism depends on the blood glucose fluctuating, albeit very slightly: that's why the glucose concentration can never be *absolutely* constant (*2*).

(*Total 7 marks*)

5 (a) The warming mechanisms (*1*) and cooling mechanisms in body (*1*) are alternately switched on and off (*1*) by centre in brain (*1*).
(*4 marks*)

(b) Two reasons:
(i) the design of the clinical thermometer, i.e. it is a 'maximum' thermometer; it takes about two minutes to get a reading.
(ii) the slight fluctuations in blood temperature are 'evened out' by passage of heat through the mouth lining and presence of saliva.
Either reason – 2 marks if well explained
(*2 marks*)

(*Total 6 marks*)

6 *(i)

Concentration increases (1) due to water loss (1) in sweat (1)

Pituitary secretes water-retaining hormone (1), kidneys reabsorb more water (1) – feel thirsty and drink (1), this lowers concentration (1)

blood concentration (1)

Add on 1 mark for diagram (*9 marks*)
(ii) Drinking a lot of water will replace the water which has been lost in sweat (*1*) but not the salt (*1*). So blood becomes diluted (*1*).
(*3 marks*)
so:
(iii) Eat some salt or take salt tablets. (*1*)

(*Total 13 marks*)

7 e.g.
(i) Automatic pilot;
(ii) rocket guidance system;
(iii) governor on lift;
(iv) industrial robot;
(v) torque converter in automatic car;
(vi) anti-locking brakes (and other responsive features of modern cars);
(vii) carburettor.

Differences:
1. Usually results in controlling movement i.e. (i) to (vi).
2. Results in controlling a fuel–air mixture 'on demand' i.e. (vii).
3. Although (i), (ii), (iv) and (vi) are electrical ('like nerves') none uses chemicals as messengers.

Any two examples: 1 mark for example, 1 mark for difference

(*4 marks*)

Note: I have deliberately tried to avoid other thermostats, e.g. car thermostat, central heating thermostat, electrical kettle 'cutout'.

—*Discussion*

1 During the Second World War pilots flying over the desert in North Africa were advised to drink lots of water before setting off on a mission. Was this good advice?
Note: desert heat encourages the pituitary to secrete ADH (anti-diuretic hormone/water retention hormone) which suppresses urine production. A pilot who bales out has a larger reserve of water to cover water loss by sweating. But salt tablets should be carried.

2 Modern jet fighter aircraft are aerodynamically unstable. If not under constant control they would literally fall out of the sky. Does their instability have parallels in the way that homeostasis works in our own bodies?
Note: the instability improves the performance and manoeuvrability of modern fighters and they need to be in a state of constant computer control. The parallel is valid. Homeostatic mechanisms too need to be in a state of constant control. Loss of control soon results in major physiological disorders, e.g. diabetes (Topic 73), thyroid conditions (Topic 80).

Topic 77
The Nervous System and Reflex Action

—*Investigation 1*

Some human reflexes

Requirements
Table; chair; heavy metal rod; cup; drinking water.

Practical skills
AMO 10.

General Comments
This simple exercise to illustrate human reflexes is not really suited to the assessment of practical skills, although it might allow one or two pupils to demonstrate consistently reliable observations (AMO 10).

The swallowing reflex involves the movement of the epiglottis upwards to cover the trachea. The epiglottis needs to return to its original position before swallowing can commence again.

—Investigation 2—

Measuring your reaction time

Requirements

Metre ruler.

Practical skills

AMO 2, EXP.

General Comments

The exercise with the ruler allows a crude form of reaction time to be assessed, also measuring length (AMO 2).

It is possible to use this technique to investigate the hypothesis that a person learns to anticipate when the ruler is dropped. Pupils could design an experiment to test this hypothesis. It could be a useful exercise in designing an experiment with standardised procedures. As such it could be used to develop many of the EXP skills.

—Investigation 3—

Looking at nerve cells in the spinal cord

Requirements

Prepared slide of TS spinal cord; light microscope with low and high power objective lenses; drawing paper.

Practical skills

HMA 5, REC 1.

General Comments

Pupils can be encouraged to compare their microscope slide with Topic 77, Figure 4 and to find the cell bodies of the axons. Drawings (REC 1) and microscopy skills (HMA 5) can be assessed.

—Assignments—

1 Receptor in foot (*1*) receives stimulus (*1*). Sensory nerve fibre (*1*) carries impulse from foot to spinal cord (*1*). Intermediate nerve fibre in spinal cord (*1*) carries impulse to brain (*1*). Motor nerve fibres (*1*) carry impulses to lungs and larynx (*1*) and person lets out a cry.

(*8 marks*)

2 (a) Receptors on dog's tummy (*1*) when stimulated by tickling (*1*) trigger off a reflex action which causes the dog's hind leg to 'scratch'. (*1*)
(*3 marks*)

(b) Synapses (*1*) (gaps) between nerve fibres in reflex arc (*1*) only allow impulses to travel in one direction (*1*).
(*3 marks*)

(c) In multiple sclerosis myelin sheaths don't work (*1*) so impulses don't reach muscles (*1*), which weaken through lack of use (*1*).
(*3 marks*)

(d) In polio a germ/virus (*1*) attacks some of the motor nerve cells (*1*) in spinal cord (*1*). As a result impulses cannot reach muscles (*1*) so patient loses use of legs (*1*). (In this case the part of the spinal cord with spinal nerves to legs was infected (+*1*).)
(*5 marks*)

(*Total 14 marks*)

3 (a) B (receptor/sensory nerve ending in muscle). (*1*)
(b) E (motor nerve fibre). (*1*)
(c) A (thigh muscle/leg extensor/rectus femoris!). (*1*)
Note: questions 3(a), (b), (c) imply responding with a single letter, but the instruction is not explicit. It is likely that pupils will offer either – with the possible exception of the rectus femoris!
(d) About one metre. (*1*)
(e) Time = distance ÷ velocity (e.g. answer to (d) is one metre, so there and back is two metres) (*1*).
= 2 ÷ 100
= $\frac{1}{50}$ second (*1*)
(*2 marks*)
(f) (i) Receptor in muscle, not in skin. (*1*)
(ii) Sensory fibre lacks cell body. (*1*)
(iii) No dorsal root ganglion. (*1*)
(iv) Not intermediate nerve fibre. (*1*)
Note: it is worth discussing which of the above are real and which are due to deficiencies in the diagram! (ii) and (iii) are the latter.
(*4 marks*)

(*Total 10 marks*)

—Discussion—

1 Much of what we know about how nerves work is based on research on much simpler animals, for example a mollusc called a sea hare. How relevant do you think such research is to humans?
Note: much biological knowledge is based on research which has been carried out (initially) on lower organisms. This approach is valuable, although there are exceptions. Our nervous system is highly complex, so it is much easier to understand the mechanisms and pathways occurring in a simpler system. Such studies, obviously, don't occur in isolation, e.g. studies on brain-damaged humans also play a significant role in research on the nervous system.

2 There is a lot of research going on at the moment in trying to help faulty nervous systems with electronics. How far could such research go? How far *should* it go?
Note: the key interest here is damaged spinal cords. There is a degree of compatibility between electrical systems and nerves. The wiring involved has to be inert and a power source always available. Whether bionic people are justified depends on social values rather than technology.

Topic 78
The Brain and Behaviour

—Investigation 1—

Short-term and long-term memory

Requirements

Clock; ten assorted objects (e.g. apple, magazine, gardening gloves, car foot pump, shoe horn, plastic shopping bag, LP record, light bulb, wine glass, can opener); drawing paper.

Practical skills

Since this practical is designed to test the effects of memory, it would be inappropriate to test practical skills with it.

—Investigation 2—

Recognising things

Requirements

Large grocery box, containing ten mysterious objects (e.g. sea shell, comb, raw sausage covered in clingfilm, match, flower, metal spring, piece of carpet, plastic ruler, 'conker', carrot); photographs of objects taken from unusual angles.

Practical skills

Since this practical is designed to test the effects of memory, it would be inappropriate to test practical skills with it.

—Assignments—

1 (a) Shock absorber. (*1*)
(b) Either : balance; or : co-ordinating precise and accurate movements. (*1*)
(c) Protection. (*1*)
(d) Contains control centres (*1*) keeping body temperature/blood concentration constant (*1*).
(*2 marks*)
(e) Sorts out impulses from various sense organs (*1*) and sets off appropriate responses/memory/intellect (*1*).
(*2 marks*)
(*Total 7 marks*)

2 By observing the behaviour of people (*1*) who have had a certain part of their cerebrum damaged (*1*).
(*2 marks*)

3 e.g.Take a small sample (e.g. 1 mm^3) of brain tissue (*1*) and cut it into many (100) thin slices/sections (*1*). Using a microscope (*1*) count the number of cells in each slice/section (*1*) and add up the total for the sample (*1*). Multiply this figure by the ratio brain : sample (*1*). (The volume of the entire brain can be worked out by fluid displacement (*+2*).)
(*6 marks*)
Note: this model outlines the means by which scientists can arrive at such a figure. This question is likely to be answered at different levels by pupils of different abilities.

4 (a) Similarities:
e.g.
(i) learning required;
(ii) association has occurred;
(iii) reward is given.
At least two – 1 mark each (*2 marks*)
(b) Differences:
e.g.
(i) chimpanzee shows exploratory behaviour;
(ii) no cue/trigger stimulus is given; instead chimp learns to associate reward with his own behaviour;
(iii) chimpanzee's behaviour results from problem solving and decision making.
At least two – 1 mark each (*2 marks*)
(*Total 4 marks*)

5 *(i) Unlearned behaviour/behaviour animal is 'born with' (*1*).
(ii) e.g.Raise a puppy in isolation from cats (*1*). Present pup/dog with a cat (*1*) and observe response (*1*).
(*3 marks*)

Note: the answer to (ii) is the most likely. A good discussion would be 'how could it be refined?'.
(*Total 4 marks*)

—Discussion—

1 Suppose you were to have a brain operation and you discovered that the operation had first been practised on cats and monkeys in order to develop the necessary new techniques. Would you go through with it?
Note: this is probably true of most operations. The alternatives, i.e. to experiment new techniques with human guinea pigs, not to operate, or to operate without having first practised the techniques involved need careful consideration.

2 How does a biologist's idea of behaviour differ from most other people's?
Note: most people's idea of behaviour involves a code of social morality. Biological behaviour simply describes all the activities of an organism without ascribing human values.

Topic 79 Drugs and Mental Illness

—Assignments—

1 Cannabis – hallucination;
morphine – pain killer;
caffeine – stimulant;
barbiturate – anaesthetic;
nicotine – tobacco.
1 mark each
(*5 marks*)

2

	Drug	Effects	Uses	Withdrawal symptoms
(i)	Caffeine	Stimulant/ speeds up brain/makes more alert (*1*)	In hot drinks e.g. coffee & tea (*1*)	Possiblefall in blood pressure headaches/ irritability (*1*)
(ii)	Alcohol	Sedative/ slows down brain (*1*)	Social drinking (*1*)	Emotional problems (*1*)
(iii)	Nicotine	Stimulant (*1*)	In cigarettes and tobacco (*1*)	Irritability (*1*)
(iv)	Valium	Sedative/ calming (*1*)	To treat anxiety (*1*)	Increased inability tocope(*1*)
(v)	Heroin	Pain-killer/ feeling of well-being (*1*)	To treat pain/ used illegally in drug habit and addiction (*1*)	Fever, sickness, cramps(*1*)

(*Total 15 marks*)
Note: this table is by no means comprehensive.

3 e.g.
(i) Barbiturates are highly habit-forming (and can be addictive).

(ii) Patients might become too dependent.
(iii) Over a period of time you have to increase dose to get effect.
Any reason

(*2 marks*)

4 (i) Sedative: drug slowing down brain (*1*);
Makes you feel calm/sleepy (*1*);
e.g. tranquillisers (valium), barbiturates, alcohol (*1*).
(*3 marks*)
(ii) Hallucinogen: drug causing hallucinations (*1*), i.e. sensing something that doesn't exist (*1*), e.g. cannabis, LSD (*1*).
(*3 marks*)
(iii) Neurosis: fairly mild mental illness (*1*), it often takes form of obsession (*1*) (e.g. phobia: obsessive fear (+*1*)).
(*2 marks*)
(iv) Nervous breakdown: intense depression (*1*) brought on by stress, worry or overwork (*1*).
(*2 marks*)

(*Total 10 marks*)

5 e.g. Take a group of coffee-fiend volunteers (*1*). Ensure they are well doused with the brown nectar (*1*) for a reasonable period of time (*1*). Then stop the supply of coffee (*1*). Monitor withdrawal symptoms (*1*), e.g. by questionnaire and blood pressure checks (*1*).
(Control group – bonus mark.)

(*6 marks*)

6 e.g.
(i) There are more stresses nowadays;
(ii) less family support;
(iii) greater awareness of mental problems;
(iv) less stigma attached to psychiatric care;
(v) GPs tending to refer more patients for psychiatric treatment.
At least three reasons – 2 marks each

(*6 marks*)

Discussion

1 Do people generally have a poor attitude toward mental illness? Is it because mental illness is something whose possibility worries us all?
Note: the difference between normal thoughts and feelings and mental illness is really a matter of degree. Feeling down or 'blue' is a mild version of depression; determination is a mild form of obsession; worrying about something is mild anxiety. It is only when these thoughts and feelings override all else that mental illness can be said to occur. This narrow borderline, since everyone has strong thoughts and feelings at times, is what tends to frighten people.

2 What would you do if you discovered that your best friend had developed a drug habit?
Note: does it matter which drug? Do all drugs have the same hazard factor? The risk of branding drugs 'soft' and 'hard' conveys a degree of condonement at the 'soft end'. The risk of failing to discriminate lacks credibility with more 'street-wise' pupils who tend to be more exposed to potential danger from drugs. To what extent does a pupil tolerate illegal or self-damaging behaviour in a friend? Does there come a point when the drug user's health holds greater significance than simple loyalty? There are no easy answers and such issues are better treated with sensitivity than piety. Try to keep the discussion impersonal.

Topic 80
Chemical Messengers

Assignments

1 To make sure that the hormones (*1*) are secreted into the bloodstream (*1*).

(*2 marks*)

2 (a) The part which secretes insulin (*1*)
(Islets of Langerhans (+*1*)).
(b) Hormone (*1*) which regulates blood sugar/glucose (*1*).
(*2 marks*)
(c) Short term. (*1*)
(d) Enzymes (*1*) (e.g. amylase, trypsin/protease, lipase (+*1*)).
(e) Into the duodenum/small intestine (*1*) (via pancreatic duct (+*1*)).

(*Total 6 marks*)

3 (a) Adrenaline/Thyroxine/Thyroid stimulating hormone. (*1*)
(b) Male sex hormone/Gonad-stimulating hormone. (*1*)
(c) Adrenaline. (*1*)
(d) Thyroxine. (*1*)
(e) Female sex hormone/Gonad-stimulating hormone. (*1*)

(*Total 5 marks*)

4 Nerves: e.g.:
(i) send impulses (electrical);
(ii) fast;
(iii) effect short-lived;
(iv) interconnected;
(v) local effect.
Ductless glands: e.g.:
(i) secrete hormones (chemicals);
(ii) slow;
(iii) effect long-lasting;
(iv) separate;
(v) general effect.
Any four comparisons – 2 marks each

(*8 marks*)

Note: (i) – (v) match in each case.

Discussion

1 How far do you think hormones affect human behaviour? Are we 'victims of the chemicals our bodies produce'?
Note: there is no reason to suppose that nerve cells and hence brain should not be affected by hormones. Adrenaline, for example, bears a very close resemblance to the neurotransmitter noradrenaline. Thyroid disorders have behavioural consequences (see 'Thyroxine' in this topic). A relationship exists between testosterone (male sex hormone) level and male aggressiveness. A decline in progesterone at end of menstrual cycle (Topic 96, 'The menstrual cycle') leading to pre-menstrual tension, and 'maternal feelings' during pregnancy when female sex hormones are at high level, are other examples of hormone-influenced behaviour, as are the changes which occur at the menopause.

2 Can you think of any medical uses for the hormones listed in Table 1?
Note: the obvious use is to supplement endocrine gland deficiencies, but there are others. Adrenaline is a powerful stimulant used in emergencies (e.g. a severe attack of bronchial asthma). Female sex hormones are used in contraceptive pill (Topic 98, 'Personal aspects of sex').

Topic 81
Feeling, Smelling and Tasting

—Investigation 1—

Which parts of the skin are sensitive to touch?

Requirements
Each group of two should have: plastic ruler; fine ballpoint pen; bristle mounted on a wooden holder; blunt needle.

Practical skills
AMO 2.

General Comments
This practical involves recognising stimuli. This is inherently subjective, and does not make a suitable basis for assessing many of the practical skills. It could, however, be used to assess the use of a ruler (AMO 2).

—Investigation 2—

Getting used to a stimulus

Requirements
Mounted needle.

Practical skills
This practical involves recognising stimuli. This is inherently subjective, and does not make a suitable basis for assessing the practical skills.

—Investigation 3—

To find out the localising power of the skin

Requirements
Each group of two should have: two fine-tipped felt pens.

Practical skills
This practical involves recognising stimuli. This is inherently subjective, and does not make a suitable basis for assessing the practical skills.

—Investigation 4—

Reading with your fingers

Requirements
Braille: available from Royal National Institute for the Blind, Braille House, 338 Goswell Road, London EC1 (Tel. 01 837 9921). Moon: available from Royal National Institute for the Blind, Holmesdale Road, Reigate, Surrey (Tel. 0737 244701).

Practical skills
This practical is inherently subjective, and does not make a suitable basis for assessing experimental practical skills.

General Comments
This is an interesting exercise which allows sighted people to begin to understand how blind people use the sensitivity of their fingers to receive written information.

—Investigation 5—

An interesting aspect of our temperature sense

Requirements
Three bowls; ice-cold water; hot (but **not** scalding) water; water at room temperature; thermometer.

Practical skills
AMO 1.

General Comments
It is important that the hot water is not too hot, since there is a danger of scalding. The use of the thermometer can be assessed (AMO 1).

—Investigation 6—

Looking at the tongue

Requirements
Mirror; torch; paper tissue; two lumps of sugar.

Practical skills
AMO 10.

General Comments
The close examination of the tongue could be assessed through drawing, written or verbal report, or used to assess AMO 10. The second part illustrates that substances can only be tasted in solution.

—Investigation 7—

Which parts of your tongue respond to different tastes?

Requirements
All apparatus used in this practical should be clean, and the experiment should be carried out under close supervision. Each group of two should have: four small beakers containing a dilute solution of sugar, salt, vinegar (ethanoic acid); 10% solution of quinine; four small paintbrushes; two or three paper tissues; drawing paper; cup; drinking water.

Practical skills
This practical involves recognising stimuli. This is inherently subjective, and does not make a suitable basis for assessing the experimental practical skills.

General Comments
It is important that the liquids are not allowed to spread over the surface of the tongue, since this will cause problems when interpreting where the different substances are tasted. A tasting diagram like the one following should be prepared:

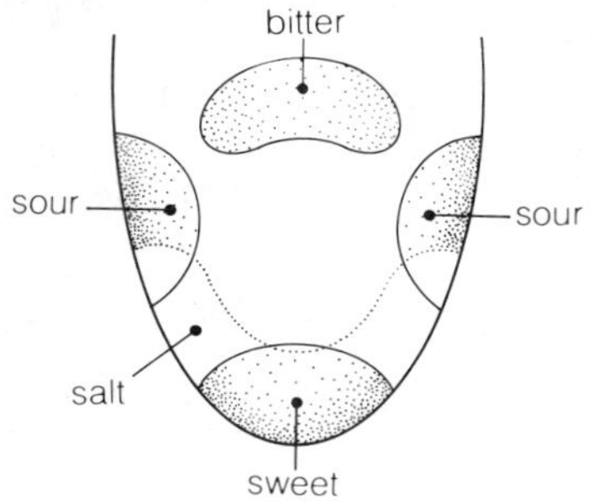

The importance of the sense of smell in 'tasting food' could be discussed at this point.

—Assignments—

1 (a) Touch. (*1*)
(b) Pain. (*1*)
(c) Touch. (*1*)
(d) Touch (*1*), temperature (*1*).
(2 marks)
(e) Touch (*1*), taste (*1*).
(2 marks)

(*Total 7 marks*)

2 (i) When sense organs are constantly receiving stimuli (*1*) they stop sending impulses to brain (*1*), so sensation stops being noticeable (*1*). (*3 marks*)
(ii) e.g. Putting on a coarse shirt (*1*), you feel it at first, but eventually don't notice it (*1*). (*2 marks*)
(iii) A continuing sensation would be distracting (*1*). Adaptation leaves the senses with the job of detecting changes (*1*). (*2 marks*)

(*Total 7 marks*)

3 e.g.
(i) Informs brain that damage has occurred;
(ii) prevents person unwittingly increasing damage;
(iii) learning experience to avoid source of pain in future.
1 mark each

(*3 marks*)

4 (i) Referred pain:felt at some distance from its true origin (*1*), caused by nerves from different parts of body going to same part of spinal cord/brain (*1*).
(2 marks)
(ii) Phantom pain: felt from an amputated limb ('still there') (*1*), caused by healing nerves sending impulses to brain (*1*).
(2 marks)

(*Total 4 marks*)

5 (a) Cold results in blocked nose. (*1*)
Can't smell. (*1*)
Smell and taste closely linked. (*1*)
(3 marks)
(b) e.g. Train dog to be fed directly into oesophagus (*1*) (using a tube (+ *1*)). Feed on variety of food(*1*), some pleasant, some unpleasant (*1*). Observe dog's reaction (*1*).
Note: not to be done at home!
(4 marks)

(*Total 7 marks*)

6 Disadvantage (*1*). Injuries would go unnoticed (*1*) and could lead to more serious damage (*1*).

(*3 marks*)

7 (a) The relationship (*1*) between temperature and the number of pain sensitive people (*1*).
(2 marks)
(b) (i) Temperature pain threshold is much the same for all people (approximately 3°C range).
(ii) Some people are more sensitive than others.
(iii) Most are around the average (45°C)
At least two conclusions – 2 marks each
(4 marks)

(*Total 6 marks*)

—Discussion—

1 Why hasn't your body developed sensory adaptation against prolonged acute pain?
Note: sensory adaptation works well in eliminating low level stimuli. Acute pain tends to override other stimuli because of the sheer intensity of the sensory impulses. Other protective mechanisms are disabled, leaving the brain in a state of total confusion. Blacking out and becoming unconscious is the only way of cutting out severe pain. Shock might prevent a severe injury (e.g. battlefield wound) from being felt at the time it occurs. Children born with the inherited condition of not sensing pain at all face much greater risk of serious injury than normal children.

2 How reliable are your senses of smell and taste?
Note: in comparison with other mammals (e.g. dogs) we have a very poor sense of smell. Smell and taste are closely connected; this is likely to be true for taste too. This can be worsened when we have a cold and our nose gets blocked. It is worth asking pupils what tastes and smells put them off eating food. Does this ever avert the risk of food poisoning?

Topic 82
A Look at the Eye

—Investigation 1—

Looking at the outside of the eye

Requirements
Mirror

Practical skills
REC 1.

General Comments
A careful labelled drawing of an eye could make a suitable assessment for REC 1.

—Investigation 2—

Dissection of the eye

Requirements
Sheep's or cow's eye; dish; scalpel; scissors; plastic bag for the remains.

Practical skills
HMA 7.

General Comments

The arrangement of the muscles into antagonistic pairs on opposite sides of the eye might be apparent. A careful dissection of the eye ought to reveal the pale grey retina, overlying the black choroid, through which blood vessels run. The retina is easily detached from the choroid. Any pupil successfully revealing the lens, retina and choroid could be assessed for using materials and apparatus (HMA 7).

—Investigation 3—

The pupil reflex

Requirements

Each group should have a torch.

Practical skills

This practical is inherently subjective, and does not make a suitable basis for assessing the practical skills.

General Comments

The size of the pupil automatically accommodates to the amount of light entering the eye.

—Investigation 4—

Demonstrating the blind spot

Requirements

Copy of *BFL*.

Practical skills

This practical involves recognising stimuli. This is inherently subjective, and does not make a suitable basis for assessing the practical skills.

General Comments

No rods or cones are found on the blind spot, which is the point at which the optic nerve leaves the eye. When an image falls on the blind spot, it cannot be seen. The ghost disappears only when its image falls on the blind spot.

—Assignments—

1 (i) Optic nerve – sending messages to brain.
(ii) Tear gland – protecting the cornea.
(iii) External eye muscle – moving eyeball.
(iv) Retina – sensitivity to light.
(v) Iris – preventing too much light entering eye.
1 mark each

(*5 marks*)

2 A

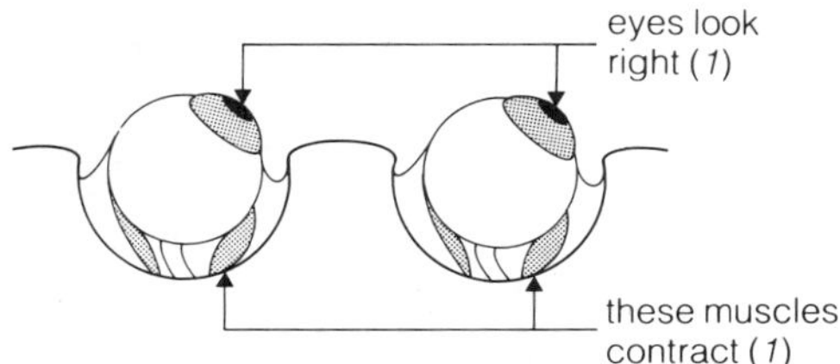

Drawing shows eyes looking **right** not left. (*1*)
Clarity of drawing. (*2*)
(*5 marks*)

B

eyes look inwards (*1*)

these muscles contract (*1*)

Clarity of drawing. (*2*)
(*4 marks*)

(*Total 9 marks*)

3 (i) Pink eye (conjunctivitis (+*1*)): infection (*1*) and inflammation of conjunctiva (*1*).
(ii) Stye: infection of eyelids (*1*). Edge of lid becomes red and sore (*1*).

(*4 marks*)

4 (a) Contraction of circular muscles (*1*) of iris (*1*).
(*2 marks*)
(b) A narrower pupil (*1*) makes eye like a pinhole camera (*1*) (light goes through centre of lens) so it is easier for the eye to focus (*1*).
(*3 marks*)
Note: pupils generally find this idea difficult and the question almost always needs following up.

(*Total 5 marks*)

—Discussion—

1 How much of the human way of life relies on vision?
Note: this is becoming more pronounced since the advent of TV and recently video. Reading, driving, operating machinery, using a computer, many crafts, clothes design, recognising each other, all depend on vision. At both extremes astronomy and microscopy are extensions of vision.

2 Would you be able to explain the idea of colour to someone who has never been able to see?
Note: this is obviously extremely difficult. Analogies of temperature, e.g. red for hot, blue for cold, can work to a limited degree. Only by imagining what it must be like to be blind can the extent and value of vision be fully appreciated.

3 How similar is the eye to a camera?
Note: this is an 'old favourite' in both physics and biology lessons. Similarities are: diaphragm/aperture, lens, inverted real image on a photosensitive layer. However, the eye is much more refined, being smaller, one of a pair for 3D images, round (i.e. multidirectional), with a rapidly adapting iris, space-saving flexible lens – a photosensitive layer processing moving images, and a sensitivity to a million-fold increase in light intensity. Perhaps a comparison with a hand-held video camera is better in some respects, but these are complex machines and difficult to describe.

Topic 83
How Does the Eye Work?

—Investigation 1—

How good is your eyesight?

Requirements

Access to a white card (about 30 cm square) upon which is drawn two black lines 1 mm apart (the lines should be drawn in ink and the card should be hung on the classroom wall); metre ruler.

Practical skills
REC 3, REC 4.

General Comments
This practical measures the ability of the eyes to resolve objects that are close together. It is possible to extend this practical by collecting the class results and plotting a bar-chart of the minimum distance needed to see the lines. This is an example of human variation, see Topic 2 (REC 3 and REC 4).

Investigation 2
Seeing in the dark

Requirements
Dimly lit room; bench lamp; any object (e.g. red travelling blanket, or a small piece of pottery); clock.

Practical skills
This practical is inherently subjective, and does not make a suitable basis for assessing the practical skills.

General Comments
It is possible to hold up a variety of objects to see if the pupils can recognise them. After a while the eyes become used to the dark, and the objects will be seen more easily.

Investigation 3
Seeing colours

Requirements
Two cards, red and green; colour blindness cards (obtainable from biological suppliers).

Practical skills
This practical involves recognising stimuli. This is inherently subjective, and does not make a suitable basis for assessing the practical skills.

Assignments
1 (i) Long sightedness. (*1*)
(ii) When looking far ahead, looks above spectacles. (*1*) When reading, looks down through spectacles. (*1*)
(*2 marks*)

(*Total 3 marks*)

2 It enables you to see in three dimensions (*1*), and thus to judge distance (*1*).

(*2 marks*)

3 (a) Dark adaptation (*1*). All visual purple is broken down (*1*) by bright sunlight (*1*), and it takes a while for rods to re-make it (*1*) and start working (*1*).
(*5 marks*)
(b) There are more rods at edge of eye (*1*), so you can see faint light more easily (*1*).
(*2 marks*)
(c) Cones are sensitive to colour (*1*) and they don't work well in dim light/dark (*1*).
(*2 marks*)
(d) The breaking down and re-formation of visual purple (*1*) happens quickly (*1*) (hence the flicker).
(*2 marks*)
(e) Normally both eyes point at the same object (*1*) so see one object in three dimensions (*1*). But push eyes means they point at different objects (*1*), so see double (*1*).
(*4 marks*)

(*Total 15 marks*)

4 (i) Wide pupils: enable maximum amount of light into eye. (*1*)
(ii) Lots of rods: rods are very sensitive to low light intensity. (*1*)

(*2 marks*)

5 (i) Top covered – no. (*1*)
(ii) Bottom covered – yes. (*1*)
(iii) Brain sees patterns and interprets them; (*1*)
or more clues given by tops of the letters.

(*3 marks*)

Discussion
1 The brain makes up much of what we see. Can you think of any cases in your life when your brain has made a mistake and you've seen the wrong thing?
Note: vision is a very complex sense involving several centres in the brain – for moving the eyes in a coordinated fashion, projecting the retinal image, identifying patterns (Topic 78, Figure 5) and associating the 'reconstructed' image with past memory. Sometimes all this image-processing goes a bit wrong!

2 How limited is our eyesight? If you were designing a human would you make any improvements?
Note: pupils might suggest all sorts of improvements e.g. more rods to see in dark, more cones to see greater detail (greater acuity), eyes on stalks for 360° vision. Looking at the natural world reveals eyes as particular adaptations (e.g. owl for darkness, hawk for acuity, fish for seeing underwater). Each eye is a compromise between varying requirements. Ours is too. Able pupils might be introduced to the idea of the inverted retina with its functional consequences (e.g. blind spot).

Topic 84
The Ear and Hearing

Investigation 1
How well can you hear?

Requirements
Each group of two must have: metre ruler; cotton wool; ticking watch.

Practical skills
This practical involves recognising stimuli. This is inherently subjective, and does not make a suitable basis for assessing the practical skills.

General Comments
The room must be absolutely quiet, and this can form the basis of a restful lesson! Once the brain has registered that a sound exists, it can concentrate on it, and can monitor its fall in volume until it is below the threshold sound level normally needed to detect it.

—Investigation 2

Finding an object by sound

Requirements
Blindfold; ticking clock; cotton wool.

Practical skills
This practical is inherently subjective, and does not make a suitable basis for assessing many of the practical skills

General Comments
This is a variation on a well known party game, and is fun to play in a classroom. Careful observation of the subject is needed, particularly watching for movements of the head. The brain relies on the differences in time at which sound from an object strikes the two ears. It is much more difficult to locate a sound with one ear blocked.

—Assignments

1 Sound waves vibrate eardrum (*1*), which passes the vibration on to the ear ossicles (*1*). If damaged, the eardrum won't vibrate (*1*) so ossicles don't vibrate (*1*) and hearing difficulty results (*1*).

(*5 marks*)

2 Middle ear is air filled (*1*). It is important to have the same pressure on both sides of eardrum (*1*). Up in an aeroplane air pressure outside eardrum drops (*1*) and the Eustachian tube (*1*) opens to equalise pressure (*1*).

(*5 marks*)

3 (a) They catch sound waves (*1*) and direct them into the auditory canal (*1*).
(*2 marks*)
(b) They carry vibrations to the inner ear. (*1*)
(c) It enables free flow of liquid in inner ear (*1*) so that the stirrup can move the oval window (*1*).
(*2 marks*)
(d) They keep the same pressure (*1*) between (air-filled) middle ear and outside (*1*).
(*2 marks*)

(*Total 7 marks*)

4 (a) The frequency of a sound (*1*)
(b) Damage to sensory cells (*1*) in the cochlea (*1*).
(*2 marks*)

(*Total 3 marks*)

5 e.g. Blindfold subject (*1*). Expose to sounds from all directions (*1*). Covering one ear (*1*), and with both ears uncovered (*1*). Subject to point at source of sound (*1*). Record successes and failures in pointing (*1*).

(*6 marks*)

—Discussion

1 Why are some people more musical than others?
Note: this is an unanswerable question! Some people are more acutely aware of pitch than others, but music includes other features such as volume and rhythm. The refinements probably are in the auditory and other centres of the brain rather than the ear itself, although cochlear sensitivity must be significant.

2 Do you always hear everything around you? When do you fail to hear sounds and why?
Note: refer to Topic 81, 'Sensory adaptation'. Sensory adaptation applies to all senses. In the case of hearing it is possibly daydreaming in class that will be mentioned. It can't be your lesson, can it? Of course not – it must be one of your colleagues!

Topic 85
How do we Keep Our Balance?

—Investigation 1

The importance of the eyes in balance

Requirements
—

Practical skills
This practical involves recognising stimuli. This is inherently subjective, and does not make a suitable basis for assessing the practical skills.

—Investigation 2

To see how the semicircular canals work

Requirements
Circular trough (e.g. ring-shaped cooking mould); water; matchstick; record player.

Practical skills
AMO 10.

General Comments
The water in the trough moves when the trough is spun. It takes a short time for the fluid to start to move, and it will continue to move for a time when the trough stops moving. Sudden changes in movement of the head will be detected by the fluid moving in a semicircular canal pulling on the sense organ in the ampulla. Accurate observation of the movement of the fluid can be assessed as AMO 10.

—Investigation 3

The part played by pressure and stretch receptors in balance

Requirements
—

Practical skills
This practical involves recognising stimuli. This is inherently subjective, and does not make a suitable basis for assessing the practical skills.

—Assignments

1 (i) Eyes: see passing objects.
(ii) Pressure receptors: feel movements while sitting.
(iii) Semicircular canals: slight side to side movements.
(iv) Ear sac: acceleration and deceleration of bus.
At least three – 2 marks each
(*6 marks*)

2 One for each plane of motion.
(*1 mark*)

3 (i) Stretch receptors (*1*): tell which muscles are stretched (*1*).
(*2 marks*)
Pressure receptors (*1*): tell us where contact is made with bed (*1*).
(*2 marks*)
(ii) Importance in balance: maintaining posture (*1*).
(*Total 5 marks*)

4 Fluid in semicircular canals continues to move (*1*), stimulating receptors in ampulla (*1*).
(*2 marks*)

5 e.g. Put subject in large room. (*1*)
Tell to walk along line on floor. (*1*)
Repeat, but this time with subject blindfolded. (*1*)
(*3 marks*)

6 Alcohol is a sedative so it slows the brain down (*1*), so information from the semicircular canals (*1*) 'arrives late' (*1*). (The brain is acting out of phase to what's really happening.)
(*3 marks*)

—Discussion

In which human activities is balance critically important?
Note: consider maintaining posture, walking (a process of continuously falling forward and putting a foot forward to prevent disaster!, running, skating (Topic 85, Figure 1), riding a bicycle, flying an aircraft, climbing, etc.! Sometimes subtle information can be used in activities which don't seem to be balance related (e.g. driving a car around a bend at a speed that won't throw it off the road, even though the driver is seated).

Topic 86
Introducing the Skeleton

—Investigation 1

Looking at the human skeleton

Requirements
Access to a human skeleton; hands and feet if available.

Practical skills
AMO 8, AMO 10.

General Comments
The questions in this section are designed to allow a pupil to examine a human skeleton carefully. AMO 10 can be used to assess accurate observations. The practical can be linked with Investigation 4 of this topic. Together they could form the basis of a comparison exercise between the skeleton of a human and a rabbit which could be assessed as AMO 8. Figures 1 and 7 could help the pupil to recognise the names of the various structures.

—Investigation 2

To find the effect of taking the calcium out of a bone

Requirements
Bone with the flesh and marrow removed; 100 cm^3 3% HCl solution, with 0.5 g sodium chloride dissolved in it; suitable container.
To remove flesh and marrow from bone: saw bone in two transversely. Remove marrow with a spoon or spatula; remove as much flesh as possible with sharp knife. Boil gently in water for sufficiently long to remove remaining marrow and flesh.

Next day. Forceps, cloth.

Practical skills
HMA 3, HMA 7, INT 1.

General Comments
This practical allows the role of calcium in the bone to be investigated. The HCl/NaCl mixture replaces the calcium in the bone by sodium. As a result the bone becomes flexible and rubbery. INT 1 could be used to assess the conclusions.

—Investigation 3

Looking inside a bone

Requirements
Fresh limb bone, sawn in half lengthways; dry limb bone, sawn in half lengthways.

Practical skills
AMO 10, EXP 2, EXP 3, EXP 4, EXP 7.

General Comments
Bone marrow is a soft fatty material in the centre of the bones. Its presence could be tested using fat test (Topic 47 in *BFL*). Pupils could be asked to design an experiment to test the hypothesis that marrow contains a fat, which could be used to test certain EXP skills.

—Investigation 4

Looking at other skeletons

Requirements
Skeleton of a quadruped mammal (e.g. rabbit), and other vertebrates (e.g. bird, frog or fish).

Practical skills
AMO 8, AMO 10.

General Comments
Investigation 1 of this topic outlines a possible comparison exercise using human and quadruped skeletons. There are other comparison exercises that could be made. The wing of a bird could be compared with the human hand. The homology between the bones of several mammalian forelimbs is illustrated in Topic 25, Figure 5. There are also similarities between the forelimbs of mammals and birds. The structure of the wing of a bird is shown in Topic 89.

—Assignments

1 Tarsals – ankle;
rib – chest;
pelvis – hip;
carpals – wrist;
femur – leg.
1 mark each
(*5 marks*)

2 (a) Tarsals; (*1*)
pelvis; (*1*)
femur. (*1*)
(*3 marks*)
(b) Carpals. (*1*)
(c) Rib. (*1*)
(d) Rib. (*1*)
(e) Femur; (*1*)
pelvis. (*1*)
(*2 marks*)
(*Total 8 marks*)

3 (i) Gristle; (*1*)
(ii) Lower jaw; (*1*)
(iii) Knee cap; (*1*)
(iv) Spine; (*1*)
(v) Shoulder blade. (*1*)
(*5 marks*)

4 Marrow is rich in nutrients (*1*), especially fat for energy (yellow marrow) (*1*) and iron for blood-formation (red marrow) (*1*).
(*3 marks*)

5 *Skyscraper, like backbone, is articulated for movement (*2*). (The Tower of Pisa is rigid.) On the other hand the Tower of Pisa leans, as does the backbone at least on occasions. (*2*)
Either answer (*2 marks*)

6 (a) Shark skull is made of cartilage. (*1*)
(b) Ligaments, although tough (*1*) are elastic (*1*).
(*2 marks*)
(c) Calcium (*1*), the hard material in bone (*1*), dissolves in acid (*1*).
(*3 marks*)
(d) Bony fibres form a lattice frame (*1*) for strength (*1*).
(*2 marks*)
(*Total 8 marks*)

—Discussion

1 Which features of the human skeleton would an engineer consider to be good design? Are there any 'weak spots'?
Note: the skeleton is an upright, mobile structure capable of both movement and support; each bone is moulded to the muscles attached to it as well as other bones with which it articulates; there is a flexible rib cage enabling simultaneous protection and movement, freedom of motion of ribs; a lattice-frame in heads of bones for strength, cartilage as a shock absorber; and synovial fluid as an ideal lubricant enabling bones to glide smoothly against each other. The most notable weak spot is the lower spinal column; evolutionary history shows a design for a horizontal structure now adapted to vertical conditions. That's one of the reasons we like to lie down!

2 In how many ways does our skeleton differ from that of a rabbit?
Note: refer to Topic 86, Figure 1 (human) and Figure 7 (rabbit).

Topic 87
How Do We Move?

—Investigation 1

Looking at muscles in relation to the skeleton

Requirements
A pig's trotter; dissecting instruments; dissecting board.

Practical skills
HMA 4, AMO 10.

General Comments
This exercise can be used to assess handling materials and apparatus (HMA 4) and careful observation (AMO 10). Tendons are tough inelastic structures that do not stretch when pulled. Further information can be obtained from *Teaching Biology Today* by Dorothy Dallas, Hutchinson (1980).

—Investigation 2

Finding out about the structure of a muscle

Requirements
Small piece of muscle from the leg of a frog, rat or chicken; light microscope with low power objective lens; microscope slide; coverslip; mounted needle; 5 cm^3 of salt solution.

Practical skills
HMA 5, HMA 6, EXP.

General Comments
This practical affords an opportunity to assess microscope skills (HMA 5 and 6) and accurate observations (AMO 10). It should be possible to see fibrils inside the muscle fibres.

A 1% solution of ATP can cause fresh muscle fibres to contract; 1% glucose solution or water will not. It is possible to ask pupils to design an experiment to test the hypothesis that ATP causes muscle contractions. This could be used to assess the EXP skills.

—Investigation 3

Studying joints

Requirements
As many joints as possible from a butcher (including shoulder, knee, hip).

Practical skills
AMO 10.

General Comments
The examination of joints (for example from a boned leg of pork), can be used to illustrate the features of a synovial joint in Topic 87, Figure 5, in *BFL*. AMO 10 assesses accurate observations.

—Assignments

1 (a) Attach muscles to bones (*1*).
(b) Lubricant (*1*) so bones can slide smoothly against each other (*1*).
(*2 marks*)
(c) Passes messages (*1*) from nerve to muscle (*1*) making it contract (*1*).
(*3 marks*)

(d) Bony fibres in spongy bone (*1*) form a frame-lattice (*1*) for strength (*1*).
(*3 marks*)
(e) Act as shock absorbers between vertebrae. (*1*)
(*Total 10 marks*)

2 e.g.
(i) Human is bipedal, so not designed for speed.
(ii) Other animals on list are four-legged, so more limbs to provide movement.
(iii) Other animals on list arch spine in running, which increases speed.
(iv) Muscles of the other animals developed for endurance or speed.
At least three reasons – 2 marks each
(*6 marks*)

3 The energy released by the muscle (*1*) to move the joint (*1*) would otherwise be used up stretching the tendon (*1*). (When muscle contracts it would stretch the tendon rather than move the bone.)
(*3 marks*)

4 (a) Raised. (*1*)
(b) Relaxes. (*1*)
(c) Contracts. (*1*)
(d) Not sent. (*1*)
(e) Force exerted by muscle X × distance of muscle from joint = force of bucket × distance from joint (*1*)
Force (X) × 2 = 20 × 28 (*1*)
Force (X) = 280 kgF (2800 Newtons) (*1*)
Note: in early printings of *BFL* it must be assumed that muscle X is 2 cm from the elbow joint.
(*3 marks*)
(*Total 7 marks*)

5 (a) e.g.
(i) First class: vertebra (moving side to side).
(ii) Second class: pressing down on fingertips.
(iii) Third class: bending leg at knee.
1 mark per example
(*3 marks*)
(b) e.g.
(i) First class:
advantage – load and effort balanced evenly; (*1*)
disadvantage – muscle has to be as far away as load, therefore not suitable for limbs. (*1*)
(ii) Second class:
advantage – enables springyness in movement; (*1*)
disadvantage – muscle always under tension. (*1*)
(iii) Third class:
advantage – enables practical limb design; (*1*)
disadvantage – considerable force needs to be exerted by flexor. (*1*)
(*6 marks*)
(*Total 9 marks*)

Discussion

How does the structure of forelimbs vary between different mammals? In what ways are they structurally adapted to carry out their functions?
Note: refer to Topic 25 on adaptation and survival, particularly Figures 5 and 6. Guides to mammals are easily available from most bookshops, and a thumb through one of these should give all sorts of further ideas (e.g. mole, short and powerful for digging).

Topic 88
Aches, Pains and Broken Bones

Assignments

1 For bone to mend properly the ends must be correctly positioned (*1*) so bones are held properly in place by plaster (*1*).
(*2 marks*)

2 e.g.
(i) Arthritis;
(ii) rheumatism/lumbago;
(iii) slipped disc;
(iv) cracked vertebra.
Any two – 1 mark each
(*2 marks*)

3 Cartilage pads in knee act as shock absorbers (*1*). These sometimes slip out of place (*1*) and can 'lock' the knee (*1*).
(*3 marks*)

4 (i) Sprained ankle: wrenched joint (*1*), sprained ligament/tendon (*1*).
(*2 marks*)
(ii) Water on knee: in front of knee cap in small sack containing synovial fluid (*1*), which gets inflamed (*1*).
(*2 marks*)
(iii) Dislocated hip: head of femur comes out of socket. (*1*)
(iv) Cramp: muscle spasm (*1*) making contraction so forceful it hurts (*1*).
(*2 marks*)
(v) Rheumatism: aches and pains (*1*) (possibly) resulting from swollen connective tissue in muscle (*1*), pressing on nerve endings and blood vessels (*1*).
(*3 marks*) (*Total 10 marks*)

5 Water on knee (*1*): small sack containing synovial fluid in front of knee cap (*1*) gets inflamed (*1*).
(*3 marks*)

6 X-rays cannot pass through bones (*1*) but can pass easily through all other tissues (*1*).
(*2 marks*)

7 e.g.
(i) Bone degenerates with age.
(ii) Intervertebral discs gradually compress.
(iii) Stooping posture.
Any two reasons – 1 mark each
(*2 marks*)

8 In order that the bone returns to its original shape (*1*) (and therefore function (+ *1*)).
(*1 mark*)

Discussion

1 Bones deteriorate during weightlessness. How would you tackle this problem in long distance spaceflight? Give the pros and cons of each solution you suggest.
Note: there are three main solutions. Exercise reduces loss of calcium from bones, but does not stop it altogether. Rotating the spacecraft creates 'artificial gravity' by way of rotational force, but it involves major design problems in the design of the spacecraft and would make it veer off course unless this was taken into account. Suspended animation would dramati-

cally slow down calcium loss but techniques for achieving this have not been developed, nor have possible consequences been understood.

2 What would you do if your best friend had a severe fracture and you were the only person immediately at hand?
Note: pupils will vary widely in their knowledge of first aid unless it is part of your institution's personal and social education/health education programme. General advice would be:
(i) make your friend as comfortable as possible and avoid moving injured area as much as possible;
(ii) if there is an open wound, cover it with clean piece of lint and try to pack the wound so that bandages won't make contact with it;
(iii) bandage the wound carefully;
(iv) immobilise the fracture, either by tying it to an improvised splint, or, if the leg, strapping to the other leg.

It is also important to treat for shock, to keep the person warm and to arrange assistance once the immediate problem is dealt with.

Topic 89 How do Other Organisms Move?

An excellent video tape on movement in a variety of organisms (called Biovideo) can be obtained from BBC Enterprises (see Topic 6 for address). It could provide a useful additional source of information on this topic.

—Investigation 1—

Watching the earthworm moving

Requirements
Live earthworm; dish; piece of rough paper; white tile or a sheet of glass.

Practical skills
HMA 7, AMO 10, INT 1.

General Comments
This practical requires careful observation (AMO 10) and interpretation (INT 1). Sounds are made by the bristles scraping against the paper. The bristles help the worm to grip the soil, and this assists locomotion. A worm does not move as readily on a smooth surface.

—Investigation 2—

How does the arthropod leg work?

Requirements
The leg of a large (dead!) crab (e.g. *Carcinus*); scalpel; fine forceps.

Practical skills
HMA 7, AMO 10, REC 1.

General Comments
Accurate observation and interpretation can be assessed (AMO 10 and INT 1).

The tendons attach the muscles to the exoskeleton. Since muscles can only contract, different antagonistic muscles are involved flexing and extending the limb. Arthropod limbs have 'peg and socket' joints, which permit movement in only one plane. If a limb is to move in several different planes, then several joints need to be located at specific sites on the limb.

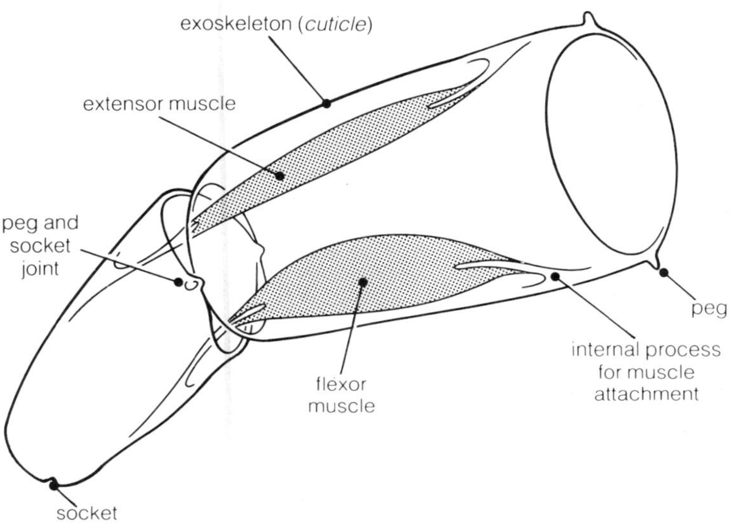

—Investigation 3—

Watching a fish swimming

Requirements
Fish swimming in a tank.

Practical skills
AMO 10, INT 1.

General Comments
Close observation of the movement of a fish can reveal the function of the fins, particularly when viewed in conjunction with Figures 8 and 9 of this topic. Assessment can be made of detailed observation (AMO 10) and the ability to interpret those observations successfully (INT 1).

—Investigation 4—

Watching a frog or toad moving

Requirements
A live frog or toad; cardboard box; tank of water.

Practical skills
HMA 7, AMO 10, INT 1.

General Comments
This practical can assess detailed observation (AMO 10) and the ability to interpret those observations successfully (INT 1).

Pupils need to be shown how to handle living animals, and only those who feel confident should be allowed to. The cardboard box should be large enough to allow the animal free movement. The movement of a frog's legs when walking and swimming is shown in Figures 10 and 12. A human swimmer uses his/her arms and legs, whilst a frog swimming only uses its legs.

—Investigation 5—

Looking at the bird's wing

Requirements
Two birds wings of equal size – one with feathers, the other without; graph paper.

Practical skills
HMA 7, AMO 6, INT 1.

General Comments
This is an exercise in measuring the surface area of the bird's wing. It is a particularly good opportunity to assess counting skill (AMO 6). The feathers increase the surface area of the wing exposed to the air, greatly enhancing its action as an aerofoil.

—Assignments—

1 (i) Exoskeleton: hard cuticle (*1*) on outside of body (*1*) serving as skeleton (*1*).
(*3 marks*)
(ii) Endoskeleton: bones (*1*) inside body (*1*) serving as skeleton (*1*).
(*3 marks*)
(*Total 6 marks*)

2 For a bulge (*1*) to travel along the worm (*1*), localised pressure changes must occur (*1*) and this can only happen if segments are watertight (*1*).
(*4 marks*)

3 (a) Longitudinal muscles contract. (*1*)
Circular muscles relax. (*1*)
(*2 marks*)
(b) If threatened by a bird (*1*) it rapidly withdrew into burrow (*1*).
(*2 marks*)
(*Total 4 marks*)

4 (i) Fish: swings tail from side to side (*1*); as tail swings back (*1*) water pushes against tail (*1*) resulting in forward thrust (*1*).
(Increased by large surface area of tail fin (+*1*).)
(*4 marks*)
(ii) Toad: pushes back (*1*) with alternate hind legs (*1*) resulting in walking motion (*1*).
(*3 marks*)
(iii) Bird: flight muscles move wings (*1*). When wing moves down feathers close (*1*) and air presses against underside of feathers (*1*), providing lift (*1*) (and thrust (+*1*)). When wing moves up feathers open (*1*) and air passes through (*1*) so minimal drag occurs (*1*).
(*7 marks*)
(*Total 14 marks*)

5 (i) *Hydra:* muscle tails on alternate sides of body.
(ii) Earthworm: longitudinal muscles contract circular muscles relax (and vice versa).
(iii) Insect: *either* muscles either side of ball and socket joint *or* longitudinal and vertical muscles in flight.
(iv) Fish: muscle blocks either side of backbone in sweeping tail.
(v) Frog: muscles either side of leg joint.
(vi) Bird: pair of flight muscles between sternum and wing.
Any four – 2 marks each
(*8 marks*)

—Discussion—

1 How many different ways can you think of animals moving?
Note: this topic covers movement in *Amoeba, Hydra,* earthworm, insect (walking and flying), fish, frogs and toads, and birds. Topics 86 and 87 cover bipedal and quadrupedal mammalian limbs and movement. Topic 25, Figure 5 shows forelimb adaptation in human, seal, bat and pig. Other ways of moving include flagellar and ciliary movement in protists (Topic 6), waves of muscular contraction in snails, hydraulic tube feet in sea urchins and starfish, jet propulsion in clams, squids and octopi, and sidewinding in snakes.

2 The diagrams and text for fish and bird movement only outline general principles. How many ways can you think of either fish or birds being specialised in the way they swim or fly? How are these special adaptations suited to their lifestyle?
Note: fish are adapted for cruising (e.g. tuna, shark), accelerating (e.g. pike) or manoeuvrability (e.g. butterfly fish). Cruisers have very streamlined bodies; accelerators are particularly muscular, using much of their body for propulsion; manoeuvrable fish have large fin surfaces, their bodies being slender in the vertical plane (flatfish are 'accelerators'). Common freshwater fish such as carp and perch are generalists, combining these qualities but excelling in none of them.

Similarly, birds are adapted for gliding (e.g. birds of prey, seagulls, storks), speed (e.g. swallows, ducks (!)) or manoeuvrability (e.g. sparrows). Gliders have large outstretched wings which ride thermals (and are hard work to flap for any length of time); speed is achieved by a small wing surface area to reduce drag and give powerful forward thrust on downbeat of the wing; manoeuvrability is achieved by small wing span without necessarily sacrificing too much surface area.

Topic 90
Producing Offspring

—Investigation 1—

Looking at yeast budding

Requirements
Two dropping pipettes; suspension of live yeast in sugar solution; methylene blue stain or lactophenol; light microscope

with low and high power objective lenses; microscope slide; coverslip.

Practical skills

HMA 5, HMA 6, REC 1.

General Comments

This practical can be used to assess microscopy techniques (HMA 5 and 6) and drawing skills (REC 1).

The yeast suspension needs to be made up about an hour beforehand, and kept in a warm place.

—Investigation 2

To see if a mushroom produces spores

Requirements

A mushroom with a flat top; scalpel; white tile; sheet of white paper; dish; light microscope with low power objective lens; microscope slide.

Practical skills

HMA 5, EXP.

General Comments

This practical allows the size of spores to be observed. It can be used to assess the use of the microscope (HMA 5). These spores could be used to form the basis of an open-ended investigation to study the environmental conditions needed for spore germination, which could be used to develop the EXP skills.

—Assignments

1 Bacterial cell splits once every 20 minutes, i.e. three times per hour, or thirty times in ten hours. (*1*)
Number of cells after ten hours:
= 2^{29} (or equivalent calculation) (*1*)
= 537 million (5.37×10^8) (*1*).

(*3 marks*)

2 The chance of any spore forming a fungus (*1*) (i.e. germinating (+ *1*)) is very small (*1*) so vast numbers are produced (*1*).

(*3 marks*)

3 (a) Internal fertilisation – sperms fertilise egg inside female's body. (*1*)
External fertilisation – sperms fertilise egg outside female's body. (*1*)
(*2 marks*)
Note: give credit for examples even though these are not specifically requested.

(b) Self-fertilisation – the same organism has testes and ovaries, male and female sex organs. (*1*)
They are called hermaphrodites. (*1*)
If eggs of hermaphrodite fertilised by own sperm, this is called self-fertilisation. (*1*)
Cross fertilisation – in order to fertilise egg sperms must swim to a different organism. (*1*)
(*4 marks*)
Note: a pupil relying on using this topic to answer this question is more likely to use the terms 'ovary' and 'testes' than 'male and female sex/reproductive organs'.

(*Total 6 marks*)

4 Sperms only need to swim to the egg (*1*) (and millions need to be produced (+ *1*)), whereas an egg needs food reserves (*1*) for development of offspring (*1*).

(*3 marks*)

5 e.g. (i) *Hydra* – testes and ovaries mature at different times. (*1*)
(ii) Earthworm – copulation with another worm enables partner's sperms only to reach eggs. (*1*)

(*2 marks*)

—Discussion

1 Eggs show all the features of quality craftsmanship, whereas sperms are like mass-produced disposable goods. Do you agree?
Note: eggs are produced in small numbers, and contain food reserves as well as the female gamete. For the offspring to be healthy the quality of the egg is critical. Sperms are produced by the million, are short-lived and have a high wastage rate.

2 Did sexual reproduction make evolution possible?
Note: sexual reproduction involves gamete production, which in turn involves meiosis (refer to Topic 107, 'Chromosomes, genes and cell division'). The two key features of meiosis are free assortment and crossing over (refer to Topic 110,'Variation'). This leads to variation, from which natural selection can occur (refer to Topic 111 'How do new kinds of organisms arise?').

3 A scientist claims that it is possible to reproduce humans asexually by cloning. What problems can you see cropping up as a result?
Note: cloning can be carried out with amphibians, so why not with humans. Whether society is willing to open such an ethical can of worms is another matter; one can only speculate on this (and hope common sense will prevail!).

Topic 91
How do Living Things Grow?

—Investigation 1

Measuring the growth of an animal

Requirements

Small mammal (e.g. mouse or gerbil); ruler with centimetre scale; access to weighing balance; cradle for placing mammal on balance; graph paper.

Practical skills

HMA 3, HMA 7, AMO 2, AMO 5, REC 3, REC 5, REC 4, INT 3, INT 4.

General Comments

This practical allows a number of different skills to be assessed on a number of occasions. It is, therefore, particularly suited to the demands of practical assessment. The correct procedure of handling the animal must be explained before the pupils start the investigation, and working safely can be assessed (HMA 3).

Measuring length (AMO 2), mass (AMO 5), accurate recording of the results (REC 3), graph plotting (REC 4), extracting information from graphs (INT 3) and simple calculations (INT 4) can also be assessed. The pupils could be asked to write about the growth of the animal, selecting those results that seem most relevant (REC 5).

—Investigation 2—

Measuring the growth of a plant

Requirements

Twenty dry seeds (either maize, wheat or oat seeds); water at 30°C; moist soil; seed trays; plastic rulers; graph paper.

Practical skills

HMA 1, HMA 7, AMO 2, AMO 8, AMO 10, REC 2, REC 3, REC 4.

General Comments

Each pupil or group of pupils should study the growth of one type of seed, and should sow about 20 of them in a seed tray. Pupils should soak their seeds in warm water (30°C) for about 30 minutes before sowing them. Different groups of pupils could study the growth of different seeds, and comparisons of the growth of a variety of seeds could be made.

This Investigation allows repeated opportunities to assess making accurate observations (AMO 10) and measuring length (AMO 2). Pupils should be encouraged to record their observations accurately (REC 3) in tables they have prepared themselves (REC 2). Graph plotting skills can be assessed as REC 4. The Investigation also asks pupils to compare the growth of the plants with the growth of a mammal (Investigation 1) and an insect (Investigations 1 and 2, Topic 100). This could be developed into an exercise involving observing major similarities and differences (AMO 8).

—Investigation 3—

To find where growth takes place in a root

Requirements

Bean seedling, with root about 2 cm in length; Indian ink; wire bent into an arc with a piece of cotton stretched across it (see Topic 91, Investigation 3 in *BFL*); ruler; flat piece of cork; jar water; sheet of glass.

Practical skills

HMA 7, AMO 2, AMO 10.

General Comments

This practical requires a certain amount of manual dexterity, and can be used to assess the handling skills (HMA 7), measuring length (AMO 2) and accurate observations (AMO 10).

The region of cell expansion occurs just behind the root tip, and the gap between the ink marks should be greatest in that region.

—Investigation 4—

Examining the inside of a young root

Requirements

Prepared slide of an LS of a young root; light microscope with low and high power objective lenses; drawing paper.

Practical skills

HMA 5, AMO 10, REC 1.

General Comments

This practical can be used to assess the use of the microscope (HMA 5), drawing skills (REC 1) and accurate observation (AMO 10).

The cells behind the tip are small and were in the process of dividing. If a suitable magnification is chosen, chromosomes in various stages of mitosis can be seen. This observation can be recalled later, during Topic 107 on cell division. The cells further back are larger, because they have expanded in size. This change is irreversible. Cell division in plants is localised to specific meristematic regions, and the cells produced undergo expansion and differentiation. This contrasts with the growth of humans, where cell division occurs all over the body, and produces cells that can, in principle, grow throughout their existence.

—Investigation 5—

Secondary growth in a plant

Requirements

Prepared TS of twigs of different ages; sheet of white paper; hand lens.

Alternative requirements: Razor blade; watch glass; acidified phloroglucin; twigs of different thicknesses; sheet of white paper; hand lens.

Practical skills

HMA 3, HMA 7, AMO 10.

General Comments

If the pupil prepares the sections, working safely and handling materials can be assessed (HMA 3 and HMA 7). The sections can be compared with Topic 91, Figure 7 in *BFL*.

Each annual ring of a tree consists of two parts. Xylem vessels produced in the spring tend to be larger than those of the summer, and are found nearest to the centre of the trunk. The later vessels (the summer wood) are laid down on the outside of the spring wood. The extent of the xylem produced will depend upon the weather conditions (especially temperature) during the growing season.

—Assignments—

1 (a) Divide;
(b) materials and energy;
(c) food;
(d) differentiate;
(e) position.
One mark each

(5 marks)

2 In animals:
(i) growth occurs all over the body;
(ii) growth occurs all the year round;
(iii) cells are replaced;
(iv) growth occurs primarily by cell division;
(v) there is more extensive differentiation.
In plants:
(i) growth in localised (in meristems);
(ii) growth occurs mostly in summer;
(iii) more cells are added to existing number;
(iv) growth occurs by both division and expansion;
(v) there is less extensive differentiation.
Match (i) – (v) for animals and plants.
Any three – 2 marks each

(6 marks)

3 At the tip of the stem (*1*) cells are continually dividing (*1*). The young cells then draw in water by osmosis (*1*) and expand (*1*). This lengthens the shoot/growing stem (*1*).
Later there is secondary growth/thickening (*1*). Cambium cells divide (*1*) to make more xylem and phloem (*1*) so stem increases in width (*1*).

(*9 marks*)

4 *Measurements:

Age (years)	*Length of head(mm)*	*Length of legs (mm)*
Birth/0	6	10
2½	7	12
5	7	16
15	9	29
20	10	35

1 mark per measurement
(*10 marks*)

Note: a table of measurements prior to constructing a graph is strongly recommended, otherwise determining accuracy of measurement from reading the graph is extremely time consuming. Furthermore, it is good practice to construct a table before drawing a graph.

Graph:
(i) Correctly chosen and labelled axes. (*2*)
(ii) Accurate plotting. (*2*)
(iii) Well drawn curves. (*2*)
(iv) Presentation. (*2*)
(*8 marks*)

Questions
(a) Legs. (*1*)
(b) There are three ways in which this question can be interpreted. A good analogy would be the way politicians and journalists interpret economic growth!
(i) Comparing absolute increase:
= difference in leg size ÷ difference in head size
= 25 ÷ 4
= 6.21 times.
(ii) Comparing proportional increase:
= (35 ÷ 10) ÷ (10 ÷ 6)
= 2.10 times.
(iii) Comparing net percentage gains:
Legs show a 250% gain in length.
Head shows a 67% gain.
Comparing gains:
= 250 ÷ 67
= 3.73 times.

Note: it is worth discussing how best to compare how much two things have grown.
For each method: 2 marks for working, 1 mark for answer
(*3 marks*)

(*Total 22 marks*)

5 (i) Advantages and disadvantages in methods (a), (b) and (c):
(a) e.g. Advantages:
easy/quick/doesn't harm plants.
At least two – 1 mark each (*2*)
e.g. Disadvantages:
height is not a reliable indicator of size;
for example, it doesn't take roots into account.
Both – 1 mark each (*2*)
(*4 marks*)
(b) e.g. Advantages:
measures entire plant;
mass indicates amount of plant material.
Either – (*1*) *mark*
e.g. Disadvantages:
water content of plants varies;
destroys plant sample.
Both – 1 mark each (*2*)
(*3 marks*)
(c) e.g. Advantages:
measures plant material accurately;
most careful and methodical approach.
Either – 1 mark (*1*)
e.g. Disadvantages:
destroys plant sample;
sample of five is too small.
Both – 1 mark each (*2*)
(*3 marks*)

(ii) Periodically remove plants from oven and weigh them (*1*) until there is no further loss of mass (*1*).
(*2 marks*)
Note: there are other plausible explanations and possible experimental designs. Use discretion.

(iii) Method (c) (*1*). It is the only method which measures the increase in plant material (*1*) and nothing else (*1*).
(*3 marks*)

(*Total 15 marks*)

—*Discussion*

1 Why do some organisms continue growing throughout their lives, while others, including ourselves, stop at a certain age?
Note: giant tortoises, snakes and fish are some organisms I can think of that grow continuously throughout their lives, although the growth rate is most rapid when young. In humans there is an optimum maximum size of about two metres, above which problems occur such as acromegaly (enhanced growth of hands, feet and chin) and scoliosis (curvature of the spine). This is probably true for other animals as well. Plants continue growing with age, but then the bulk of a tree trunk's girth is wood and largely non-living (in the strictest sense).

2 How can the age of a medieval building be calculated from its timbers? Other than points of architectural interest, what additional information might be revealed?
Note: each year has different weather during the growing season so tree rings have different widths from year to year. The sequence of relative tree ring size is the same for all trees and is unique for any historical period. Tree ring sizes can be compared with recently felled trees of the same species, so not only can the age be told, but also what the general climate was like in those days.

Topic 92
How Is Growth Controlled?

—*Investigation 1*

To find the effect of growing a seedling in darkness

Requirements

Two potted bean seedlings whose shoots have just appeared; cardboard box; watering can.

Practical skills
AMO 8.

General Comments
This exercise could form the basis for a comparison exercise for assessing major similarities and differences between the two shoots (AMO 8). Etiolated plants have long internodes and are yellow in appearance. Their leaves are probably also smaller than those of the control shoot.

—Investigation 2—
To find the effect on growth of cutting off the tip of a shoot

Requirements
Petri dish containing twelve germinating seedlings (e.g. wheat, maize, or barley); small scissors; access to a uniformly lit place.

Practical skills
HMA 1, AMO 10, INT 1.

General Comments
This practical could provide an appropriate way of assessing following instruction skills (HMA 1), accurate observations (AMO 10) and drawing appropriate conclusions (INT 1) from the answer to the question in the text.

It is important that the tip is removed, leaving the remainder of the shoot intact. The control shoots ought to have grown in length, whilst the cut ones should not.

—Investigation 3—
To find the effect of removing the apical bud from a plant

Requirements
Two identical potted plants with no side branches; small scissors.

Practical skills
AMO 10, INT 1.

General Comments
As the previous practical, this can be used to assess accurate observations (AMO 10) and drawing appropriate conclusions (INT 1).

Removing the apical shoot removes the dominance of the apex over the side buds. Once broken, side shoots grow from the axillary buds.

—Investigation 4—
To find the effect of a growth substance on cuttings

Requirements
Two healthy side branches from *Coleus* or geranium plants; hormone rooting powder; pruning knife; two small beakers; access to a warm, evenly lit place; distilled water.

Practical skills
HMA 1, HMA 7, EXP.

General Comments
This experiment can be used to see if certain cuttings can be induced to develop roots if the correct combination of growth hormones are applied to their cut ends. It can assess following instructions and handling apparatus skills (HMA 1 and 7). The questions in the text lead the pupil to think about the limitations of this experimental design. The levels of replication are inadequate, and this will affect the validity of the conclusions that can be drawn. It might be possible to extend this practical to allow the pupil to design more rigorous experiments. Additional investigations might include testing a variety of plant hormones, a hormone at different concentrations, or different parts of the same plant (e.g. will leaves or flowers form roots?).

—Assignments—

1 Plants: auxin; (*1*)
from shoot/root tip. (*1*)
Animals: e.g.:
(i) growth hormone, from pituitary gland;
(ii) throxine, from thyroid gland;
(iii) moulting hormone, from cells in insect brain;
(iv) juvenile hormone, from gland in insect thorax.
Any one – 2 marks

(*4 marks*)

2 (a) Removing apical bud removes source of auxin (*1*), this stimulates axillary buds (*1*) so (lateral) branches develop (*1*) and hedge gets 'bushier' (*1*).
(*4 marks*)
(b) Rooting powder contains a growth substance (*1*) which is similar to auxin (*1*) so the cutting is encouraged to form roots (*1*).
(*3 marks*)

(*Total 7 marks*)

3 (a) Auxin (*1*) from shoot tip (*1*) promotes growth (*1*).
(*3 marks*)
(b) A – stops growing (*1*); no auxin can pass from tip to shoot (*1*).
B - bends to left (*1*); auxin can only pass down right-hand side (*1*) so only right-hand side grows (*1*).
C – bends to right (*1*); auxin can only pass down left-hand side (*1*) so only left-hand side grows (*1*).
(*8 marks*)

(*Total 11 marks*)

4 (i) A benign tumour stays in one place (*1*) and does not harm surrounding tissue (*1*).
(*2 marks*)
(ii) A malignant tumour spreads (*1*) since cells from it detach (*1*) and are carried by blood or lymph to other parts of body (*1*) where they invade and destroy tissue (*1*).
(*4 marks*)

(*Total 6 marks*)

5 *The second (lower) experiment. (*1*)
e.g. explanation:
(i) It shows that bending resulted from a substance (hormone) which must have passed from tip into the agar.
(ii) It eliminates any effect resulting from the physical presence of the shoot tip.
Either – 2 marks

(*3 marks*)

Note: is the second experiment invalid because it lacks a control? Is it worth discussing?

—*Discussion*—

1 Is it right to use hormones to improve agricultural production?
Note: plant hormones are sprayed on crops for various reasons, e.g. as weedkiller, to develop seedless fruit. The use of animal hormones (steroids) in developing animals for meat is somewhat more suspect.

2 How would you set about lowering your personal risk of developing cancer?
Note: cancer high-risk activities include smoking and excessive sunbathing. Other risks are exposure to radioactivity, chemical irritants, asbestos, and some heavy metals, particularly zinc and cadmium. Chemicals in the drinking water and sprayed on food are suspected of having caused cancers but evidence is not comprehensive.

Topic 93
Growth Responses In Plants

—*Investigation 1*—

To find which part of a shoot responds to light

Requirements
Dish containing twelve seedlings (e.g. maize or oats) (each seedling should have a shoot that is about 10 mm long); aluminium foil (about 5 cm square); small scissors; box with a hole in one side; lamp.

Practical skills
HMA 1, HMA 4, HMA 7.

General Comments
It is important that the foil caps cover only the tip of the shoot. It requires a degree of manual dexterity to make a good foil cap. This exercise could be used to assess following instructions and handling materials and apparatus (HMA 1 and HMA 7). The cardboard box should be light proof, apart from the hole in the side, since it is important that the shoots are exposed to directional light only. This experiment shows that it is the tip of the shoot that is light sensitive.

—*Investigation 2*—

To find if a seedling responds to gravity

Requirements
Six bean seeds, each with a root that is just emerging; six pins; piece of cork; small aquarium tank; sheet of glass to fit the aquarium; cardboard box; access to water; drawing paper.

Practical skills
HMA 1, HMA 4, HMA 7, REC 1.

General Comments
It is important that the roots of the seedlings are placed in a dark environment, so that the effects of phototropic responses are eliminated. This investigation can be used to assess the usual instruction and handling skills (HMA 1, 4 and 7), and drawings (REC 1).

—*Investigation 3*—

Experiments with a klinostat

Requirements
Klinostat; two young bean seedlings whose roots are about 1 cm in length; piece of cork large enough to cover the bottom of a beaker; retort stand and clamp; beaker; cardboard box; cotton wool; water.

Practical skills
AMO 8, AMO 10.

General Comments
This exercise is probably best performed as a demonstration, because it is unlikely that sufficient numbers of klinostats are available. This should not prevent pupils examining the seedlings carefully. Their descriptions of the similarities and differences between the two seedlings could be assessed (AMO 8 or AMO 10); complete answers should include observations about the lengths of the two roots as well as observations about their orientation.

It is important that the control seedling is initially placed at the same orientation as the seedling in the klinostat.

—*Assignments*—

1 e.g. Support a bean seedling in a darkened chamber (*1*) with a window or lamp on one side to illuminate seedling from one direction only (*1*). Make sure that the root points downwards at the start of the experiment (*1*). Leave for several days (*1*). Observe direction root grows (*1*) daily (*1*).
(*6 marks*)

2 No it doesn't matter (*1*); roots are positively geotropic (*1*) so they always grow downwards (*1*).
(*3 marks*)

3 Drawing(s) should show shoot bending away from side on which the auxin has been painted. Root should be straight or bending towards side on which the auxin has been painted (see note below).
   (i) Accurate representation of events. (*2*)
   (ii) Clear drawing(s). (*2*)
   (iii) Labelling of root, shoot and seed. (*2*)
   (iv) Indication where auxin was applied. (*2*)
(*8 marks*)
   Note: current theory of geotropism is that a growth inhibitor is produced by the root cap (see Topic 93 in *BFL*). Use discretion in marking.

4 Drawing should show undulating root and shoot.
   (i) Accurate representation of events. (*2*)
   (ii) Clear drawing. (*2*)
   (iii) Labelling of root, shoot, seed and klinostat ' base'. (*2*)
   (A pupil might mention that if the klinostat rotates rapidly the shoot and root will grow straight.)
(*6 marks*)

5 e.g. Cut off tip of shoot (*1*) and shoot stops growing (*1*). Put tip on divided (*1*) agar block (*1*) and illuminate from one side (*1*). Put agar block on cut end of shoot (*1*) and shoot will bend towards the previously illuminated side (*1*).

(*7 marks*)

(See Topic 93, Figure 3 in *BFL*.)

Discussion

1 Growing plants in space might prove to be the only way of producing oxygen economically over long periods of time. What problems might you, as an astronaut – horticulturalist, be faced with in growing your plants and what solutions might you come up with?
Note: if there is no gravity then getting the shoots and roots to grow in a particular direction is the problem. Overriding phototropism and hydrotropism (how do you handle water in weightless conditions?) could get the plant orientated. It would be easier to simulate gravitational force by rotating the space station. Also see Topic 31 on decay, and Topic 22, Assignment 4.

2 How might the Venus flytrap shown in Topic 93, Figure 9, close when an insect lands on it?
Note: the text on that page states that no one knows for certain how it is brought about. However, certain principles can be applied. For example, nerve cells transmit membrane potentials, but the membrane potential itself is a feature of many cells, both animal and plant. The active pumping of salts is also well known and will be expected to have osmotic effects. Giving the pupils some additional underlying principles such as those above might make it possible for them to suggest possible mechanisms. A plausible hypothesis is the desired end-product.

Topic 94
The Human Reproductive System

Investigation 1

Looking at the male reproductive system

Requirements
Male rat, dissected to show the reproductive structures; blunt seeker; sharp scissors.

Practical skills
HMA 1, HMA 3, HMA 7, AMO 10, REC 1.

General Comments
The pupils will need to follow the instructions carefully, if all of these structures are to be seen; this skill can be assessed (HMA 1). Normal precautions of hygiene are required for a dissection. Safe working practices, are assessed as HMA 3. The pupil will need to examine the animal carefully in order to see the various structures properly. Some degree of initiative will be required (HMA 3). The pupil ought to have access to dissection diagrams if required.

Useful reference books are: H.G.Q. Rowett, *Dissection Guides: III The Rat*, John Murray, and *BAFA Student's Manual*, 2nd edition.

Investigation 2

Looking at the female reproductive system

Requirements
Female rat, dissected to show the reproductive structures; blunt seeker.

Practical skills
HMA 1, HMA 3, HMA 7, AMO 10, REC 1.

General Comments
(These are the same as the general comments for Investigation 1 above.)

Assignments

1 Raises the chance of one of them reaching the egg. (*1*)
Because many die on the way. (*1*)

(*2 marks*)

2 (i) Advantage: slightly cooler than rest of body; (*1*) testes make sperm more rapidly in cool conditions. (*1*) (*2 marks*)
(ii) e.g. Disadvantages:
(i) more vulnerable;
(ii) could become too cool for sperm making;
(iii) testes need to descend – can lead to complications;
(iv) obstructive/get in the way.
At least three – 1 mark each (*3 marks*)

(*Total 5 marks*)

3 (a) Urethra. (*1*)
(b) (i) Carries sperm. (*1*)
(ii) Carries urine; (*1*)
(*2 marks*)
(c) (i) Intercourse/copulation/ejaculation. (*1*)
(ii) Urination. (*1*)
(*2 marks*)
(d) Fills with blood (*1*) to make penis stiff and hard/erect (*1*) (called an erection (+*1*)).
(*2 marks*)
(e) Makes it possible for penis to enter vagina during sexual intercourse. (*1*)

(*Total 8 marks*)

4 (a) Either:
(i) Clitoris. (*1*)

Both become erect during sexual excitement. (*1*)
or
(ii) Vagina. (*1*)
Both make intercourse possible. (*1*)

Either equivalent and reason (*2 marks*)

(b) Ovaries. (*1*)
Makes sex cells (eggs); testes make sex cells (sperms). (*1*)
(*2 marks*)

(c) Oviducts. (*1*)
Carries eggs away from the ovaries; sperm ducts carry sperms from the testes. (*1*)
(*2 marks*)

(d) Urethra. (*1*)
Both carry urine. (*1*)
(*2 marks*)

(*Total 8 marks*)

—*Discussion*

1 Which features of the male and female reproductive systems raise the chances of fertilisation?
Note: in the male reproductive system, up to 500 million sperms at a time are made by the testes; the seminal vesicles and prostate gland ensure sperms are in an activating fluid, the shape and erectile nature of penis ensure that sperm is deposited deep in the female reproductive system. In the female system, the shape, length and angle of the vagina guarantee reception of the penis and semen; fluid secretion (lubricant) enables intercourse to occur without injury. Mammalian reproductive structures are generally advanced when compared with the cloacal openings of other classes of vertebrate.

2 In which ways are the male and female reproductive systems similar?
Note: both are Y-shaped tracts leading from paired gonads. During the first two months or so of foetal development the sexes are indistinguishable, even though most other anatomical features are clearly defined. For example, the foetus in Topic 97, Figure 2 is not necessarily a boy. Post-natal development into boys and girls, indistinguishable initially, has been recorded.

Topic 95 Eggs, Sperms and Sexual Development

—*Investigation 1*

Looking at sperms

Requirements

Freshly killed male rat that has been dissected; sharp scissors; dropping pipette; 5 cm³ 0.9% saline solution; light microscope with low and high power objective lenses; microscope slide; coverslip.

If possible, bull sperm from an artificial insemination centre (a local veterinary surgeon or cattle breeder can probably give information on the nearest centre); 5 cm³ 0.9% saline solution; light microscope with low and high power objective lenses; microscope slide; coverslip.

Practical skills

HMA 4, HMA 5, HMA 7, AMO 10.

General Comments

This practical can be used to assess microscope skills (HMA 4 and 5). There are probably many reasons why the sperms on the microscope slide are not moving. If the rat is not freshly killed, the sperms may have died. It may be that sperms do not start swimming until they are mixed with seminal fluid, or it may be that the sperms extracted from the testes are immature. The important thing is for the pupils to suggest hypotheses. Testing them is beyond the scope of most GCSE pupils, though they could make an interesting topic for discussion.

—*Investigation 2*

Looking inside the testis

Requirements

Prepared slide of a mature mammalian testis; light microscope with low power objective lens.

Practical skills

HMA 5, AMO 10, REC 1.

General Comments

This exercise can be used to assess the use of the microscope (HMA 5) and accurate observations (AMO 10), or REC 1 if drawings are required.

—*Investigation 3*

Looking inside the ovary

Requirements

Prepared slide of a mature mammalian ovary; light microscope with low power objective lens.

Practical skills

HMA 5, AMO 10, REC 1.

General Comments

This exercise can be used to assess the use of the microscope (HMA 5) and accurate observations (AMO 10), or REC 1 if drawings are required.

—*Assignments*

1 Five differences between sperm and egg (numbers (i) – (viii) match):
e.g. Sperm:
(i) extremely small;
(ii) nucleus at end/head;

(iii) swims;
(iv) tadpole shaped;
(v) not surrounded by jelly;
(vi) formed all the time;
(vii) made in testes;
(viii) male gamete.
e.g. Egg:
(i) much larger;
(ii) central nucleus;
(iii) static;
(iv) ball shaped;
(v) surrounded by jelly;
(vi) already formed at birth;
(vii) made in ovaries;
(viii) female gamete.
Any five differences – 2 marks each
(*10 marks*)
e.g. Why far more sperms are produced than eggs:
Sperms have to swim to the egg (*1*) and most don't succeed (*1*) so large numbers improve the chances of fertilisation (*1*).
(*3 marks*)

(*Total 13 marks*)

2 (i) Ovary – oestrogen. (*1*)
(ii) Testis – wet dreams; (*1*) androgen. (*1*)
(iii) Both – sex hormones; (*1*) pituitary gland. (*1*)

(*5 marks*)

3 (a) Puberty: change which occurs (*1*) between ages of twelve and fourteen (*1*) when sex organs become active (*1*).
(*3 marks*)
(b) Sex hormone: hormones which bring about puberty. (*1*)
(c) Menstruation: 'periods' (*1*) bleeding from vagina (*1*) resulting from breaking down of womb (uterus) lining (*1*).
(*3 marks*)
(d) Secondary sexual characteristics:
physical changes, other than those to the sex organs themselves, occurring during puberty. (*1*)
e.g. In boys:
(i) voice breaks;
(ii) facial and body hair.
Either, or others – 1 mark (bonus for others?)
e.g. In girls:
(i) breasts develop;
(ii) fat laid down on thighs.
Either, or others – 1 mark (bonus for others?)
(*3 marks*)
(e) Menopause: at about the age of 45 to 50 (*1*) ovaries stop producing eggs (*1*). Sex hormones also stop being produced in large amounts (*1*), which results in feelings of tiredness or being run-down (*1*) for several months (*1*). It is also called the 'change of life' (*1*).
(*6 marks*)

(*Total 16 marks*)

4 Children are growing taller now than 30 years ago (*1*) due to better diet (*1*) and health care (*1*).

(*3 marks*)

5 *e.g. (i) Mother – run down and irritable due to menopause.
(ii) John and Wendy – emotional swings due to adolescence.
(iii) Father's and/or mother's desire for sexual activity declines so father and mother less 'close'.
(iv) John and Wendy showing interest in girlfriends and boyfriends with resulting stresses (e.g. from parents – 'be back home not a minute later than eleven'!).
Any three reasons – 2 marks each

(*6 marks*)

6 (i) Graph shows how growth rate (*1*) changes with age (*1*) from birth to 20 years (*1*) in brain, in general and in reproductive organs (*1*).
(*4 marks*)
(ii) Differences between curves:
(a) Brain:
growth rate decreases from birth; (*1*)
there is virtually no further growth after 20 years. (*1*)
(*2 marks*)
(b) Body:
growth in two stages: (*1*)
(i) 0 – 8 years, (*1*)
(ii) 11 – 20 years. (*1*)
(The second stage coincides with puberty (+ *1*).)
(*3 marks*)
(c) Reproductive organs:
little growth until 12 – 14 years; (*1*)
then develop rapidly. (*1*)
(*2 marks*)
Note: it is worth advising pupils to consider the features of each curve individually before giving reasons for the differences. This should avoid 'blanket' answers which tend to be vague.

(*Total 11 marks*)

Discussion

1 There is a condition when a person is genetically male (see Topic 107, Figure 7) but their testes produce female sex hormones by mistake. What do you think happens?
Note: the testes never descend and the person is, by all outward appearances, female. However, because a uterus doesn't develop there are no periods and the 'woman' is infertile. This condition is rare – I've needed to stress this point in the past myself! A chromosome test verifies genetic masculinity.

2 What forms of development, other than sexual changes, occur during adolescence?
Note: rely on pupils' own perceptions of their experience. To what extent sexual development has a bearing on their social development is an interesting point.

3 Is there a male menopause?
Note: theoretically we wouldn't expect there to be a menopause in males; testosterone secretion and sperm production continue into old age and there are no hormonal changes comparable to those of the female. And yet some authorities claim that some males go through psychological/behavioural and physiological changes at around the age of 50. It is interesting to speculate why.

Topic 96
The Menstrual Cycle

Assignments

1 Cycle starts with menstruation (*1*), which means 'having a period' (*1*).

(*2 marks*)

2 (a) Heals (*1*) and builds up (*1*).
(*2 marks*)

(b) Breaks down (*1*) and menstruation occurs. (*1*)
(*2 marks*)
(c) Continues to develop (*1*), thickens (*1*) and blood vessels grow into it (*1*).
(*3 marks*)
(d) (i) Follicle stimulating hormone (*1*): results in uterus lining healing (*1*) and building up (*1*).
(ii) Luteinising hormone (*1*): uterus lining continues to develop (*1*), thickens (*1*) and blood vessels grow into it (*1*).
(*7 marks*)
(e) Uterus lining continues to develop (*1*), thickens (*1*) and blood vessels grow into it (*1*).
(*3 marks*)

(*Total 17 marks*)

3 (a) Oestrogen, (*1*)
progesterone. (*1*)
(*2 marks*)
(b) Both in ovary. (*1*)
Oestrogen: Graafian follicle. (*1*)
Progesterone: yellow body. (*1*)
(*3 marks*)
(c) In bloodstream. (*1*)
(d) Oestrogen: shortly before ovulation. (*1*)
Progesterone: shortly after ovulation. (*1*)
(*2 marks*)
(e) During menstruation. (*1*)

(*Total 9 marks*)

4 (i) So the embryo is not lost (*1*) when the uterus lining breaks down (*1*).
(*2 marks*)
(ii) Presence of embryo in uterus (*1*) preserves yellow body (*1*) so it keeps on producing progesterone (*1*).
(*3 marks*)

(*Total 5 marks*)

5 (a) Oestrogen is increasingly produced (*1*) as the Graafian follicle develops (*1*) until the time of ovulation (*1*) when its production declines (*1*). Progesterone levels remain low (*1*) since there is no yellow body present at this stage (*1*).
(*6 marks*)
(b) Progesterone level will increase (*1*) since the Graafian follicle (*1*) has changed into a (progesterone producing (+*1*)) yellow body (*1*).
(*3 marks*)

(*Total 9 marks*)

—*Discussion*

1 How would society differ if men and boys had periods too?
Note: don't worry about *why* men and boys should have periods. Possible social consequences matter more than biological logic!

2 Redesign the human body so that sexual reproduction can take place without the necessity for menstruation.
Note: this is an exercise in creative imagination! It is amazing the extent to which our inventiveness is limited by what we know and experience. More seriously, is menstruation an inevitable result of viviparity with placentation?

Topic 97
Pregnancy and Birth

—*Assignments*

1 (a) Pushes the baby out at birth. (*1*)
(b) Cushions the foetus (*1*) protecting it from being bumped and damaged (*1*).
(*2 marks*)
(c) Brings food and oxygen (*1*), removes carbon dioxide and excretory waste (*1*).
(*2 marks*)
(d) Secrete milk (*1*) – food for the baby for first few months of its life (*1*).
(*2 marks*)

(*Total 7 marks*)

2 (i) Supplies food.
(ii) Supplies oxygen.
(iii) Removes carbon dioxide.
(iv) Removes excretory waste (urea).
(v) Allows antibodies to pass from mother to protect foetus.
(vi) Produces hormones (oestrogen and progesterone) which prevent menstruation and ovulation.
Any five – 1 mark each (*5 marks*)
e.g. Why placenta is ideally suited:
(i) mother's and baby's/foetus blood flow very close to each other;
(ii) plate-like structure and villi provide large surface area for exchanges;
(iii) well supplied with blood from both mother and foetus.
Any reason (*2 marks*)

(*Total 7 marks*)

3 e.g. Advantages for a head-first birth:
(i) head has largest diameter, so if it emerges first it is less likely for baby to get stuck;
(ii) less likely to get strangled by own umbilical cord;
(iii) baby can start breathing very soon after birth.
Any reason (*2 marks*)
e.g. Changes shortly after birth:
(i) breathes;
(ii) feeds;
(iii) excretes;
(iv) egests;
(v) cries.
At least three – 1 mark each (*3 marks*)

(*Total 5 marks*)

4 (a) Extra energy needed for growth of foetus/carrying foetus around. (*1*)
(b) Carbohydrates (starch, sugar). (*1*) Fats/oils/lipids. (*1*)
(*2 marks*)
(c) Growth of foetus. (*1*)
(d) Development of foetal bones (prevent mother's bones and teeth from being stripped of calcium as a result of foetal demands (+*2*)). (*1*)
(e) Energy – 16.3% (*1*)
protein – 31% (*1*)
vitamin D – 300% (*1*)
calcium – 140%. (*1*)
(*4 marks*)

(f) Vitamin A; (*1*)
Vitamin C. (*1*)
(*2 marks*)

(g) e.g. Vitamin A:
(i) foetal retina is not used and vitamin A is needed for retina formation;
(ii) 750 mg is more than enough;
(iii) there are vitamin A reserves in mother's liver.
Any one (*2*)
e.g. Vitamin C:
(i) vitamin C does good as it passes through the system;
(ii) there are vitamin C reserves in mother's liver.
Any one (*2*)
(*4 marks*)

(h) Development of foetal red blood cells. (*2*)

(*Total 17 marks*)

—Discussion

1 Why are human babies so much more helpless than the newborn of other animals?
Note: e.g. newborn foals are capable of walking; newborn dolphins can swim freely. Non-human primates are more dependent on the mother than other mammals, but at least they are limited in the degree to which they limit her feeding activities since they cling to her fur. Even in primitive human societies e.g. the Kung (bushmen) of the Kalahari and Australian aborigines, babies are extremely dependent on their mothers and limit her food gathering activities. The most likely reason is the time it takes to learn complex motor skills such as bipedal movement (balance and walking) and manual dexterity. Humans also lack enough fur to cling to (is this a cause or an effect?). It is probably worth extending this discussion into the need for food sharing and division of labour (by gender), for which there is some evidence, both from observation of 'primitive' societies and palaeoanthropological (e.g. fossil evidence for food sharing in East African hominid ancestors). Is food sharing the basis for the family, extended family (i.e. tribe) and ultimately the type of society we live in? Has the sheer dependence of infants given rise to our traditional perceptions of gender and social role? The implications of very dependent offspring are far reaching both in the nature of our evolution and in social values that still persist in contemporary society, which is so far removed from the families and extended families of our ancestors.

2 Is mother's milk always best for the baby?
Note: see Topic 98, Figure 10. What happens if a mother cannot breast feed her baby, as is frequently the case? Breast and bottle feeding have both had periods of fashion. Colostrum, which is produced in the first few days after birth, is now considered to be so protective against diseases and allergies that many maternity wards in hospitals encourage mother to provide this even if they find it difficult to breast feed when milk is produced later on. However, a few hundred years ago suckling on colostrum was avoided at all costs! Advantages of bottle feeding include convenience (what if mum works and someone else looks after the baby?), the fact that the nutrients are well thought out by professional nutritionists and the fact that fathers too can be involved with feeding their children. Perhaps the most significant disadvantage of bottle feeding has occurred in the Third World where major food companies have actively promoted bottle feeding by advertising and appealing to 'being modern'. Poverty leading to mothers overdiluting the milk powder has caused infant malnutrition, and poor sanitation leads to gastrointestinal problems (see Topic 51, Discussion Question 1, 'How do we digest our food?', page 67 in this guide). This is generally not true of bottle feeding in Europe or North America.

Topic 98
Personal Aspects of Sex

—Assignments

1 (i) Contraception: any procedure preventing conception. (*1*)
(ii) Reliable: can be depended upon to prevent conception (*1*) when used properly (*1*).
(*2 marks*)
(iii) Sheath is reliable because it forms a barrier to sperms. (*1*)
(iv) Disadvantages:
e.g.needs to be used properly;
thought about in advance;
needs to be used with spermicide.
At least two disadvantages – 1 mark each (*2*)

(*Total 6 marks*)

2 Advantages:
e.g. (i) very reliable;
(ii) easy to use.
Both, or others – 1 mark each (*2 marks*)
Disadvantages:
e.g. (i) need to take regularly;
(ii) possible long-term effects;
(iii) won't stop AIDS.
At least two – 1 mark each (*2 marks*)

(*Total 4 marks*)

3 (a) The part of the menstrual cycle (*1*) during which fertilisation/conception cannot occur (*1*) (usually the very beginning of the cycle (days 5 and 6) and the end (after day 20)).
(*2 marks*)
(b) e.g.
(i) length of menstruation;
(ii) overall length of menstrual cycle;
(iii) time of ovulation;
(iv) survivability of sperm/egg in oviducts.
At least two – 1 mark each (*2 marks*)
(c) e.g.
(i) sperm survive menstruation because they are in oviduct;
(ii) early ovulation;
(iii) late ovulation;
(iv) mentruation occurs before embryo implants, so it is still in oviduct.
Any two reasons – 1 mark each (*2 marks*)

(*Total 6 marks*)

Note: pregnancy probably occurs as a result of more than one unusual circumstance. Nature can be quite mischievous and if it humanly can happen, it probably has already!

4 *e.g.
(i) Sperms are poor swimmers.
(ii) There are insufficient sperms.
(iii) There are no sperms at all.
(iv) Sperms are defective so cannot fertilise egg.
(v) Sperms have poor survival in woman's body fluids.

(vi) Ovary doesn't make eggs.
(vii) Oviduct is blocked.
(viii) Eggs are defective.
(ix) There is an immune reaction between woman's body and presence of sperms.
(x) Eggs not entering oviduct funnel.
Any five – 1 mark each

(*5 marks*)

5 Why pregnancies increased 1948–68:
e.g.
(i) social pressures;
(ii) changing moral values;
(iii) effect of advertising;
(iv) influence of television, movies, etc.
At least two reasons – 1 mark each (*2 marks*)
Why data may be misleading:
e.g.
(i) it shows the increase but not the overall scale of the problem; only *recorded* cases of pregnancy included;
(ii) it doesn't include unrecorded terminated (aborted) pregnancies;
(iii) it does not indicate a breakdown by age, or relate it to over 16s.
Any two reasons – 2 marks each (*4 marks*)

(*Total 6 marks*)

—Discussion

1 To what extent are the following morally acceptable?
(a) abortion;
(b) embryo research;
(c) surrogate motherhood.
Note: (a) At the time of writing, the legal grounds for abortion are that two doctors recommend the pregnancy be terminated within the first 28 weeks because in their opinion the health or life of the mother may be jeopardised. Psychological problems are the commonest basis for claiming a threat to health. (b) Embryo research is strictly limited to the first 14 days. (c) Surrogacy contracts are illegal in the United Kingdom.

2 'Ultimately only the mother can decide the fate of the embryo/foetus she is carrying.' Do you agree?
Note: the law is not exactly clear here, but the principle that a woman should have the ultimate right over her body is upheld.

3 In California women can choose to be artificially inseminated by an unknown, but successful, father in order to have bright and capable children. Are you in favour of this?
Note: what are the implications? There is a trade in paternity, a form of human artificial selection, and there may be identity crises in the offspring. However, it does seem to produce bright and capable children.

4 How has AIDS affected people's attitudes towards sex and contraception?
Note: prophylaxis is now more prominent, in terms of publicity, than contraception. What will happen when a vaccine and a treatment for AIDS are found?

5 Artificial insemination, extra-uterine fertilisation (i.e. 'test tube babies'), surrogacy and adoption are all measures which an infertile couple might take. Consider the advantages and disadvantages of each from both the parent's and the child's point of view.
Note: artificial insemination and extra-uterine fertilisation may be seen as modern aids to overcome infertility. Surrogacy raises complex problems, especially with respect to the developing child's identity. (For whose benefit is a child brought into the world?) Adoption has been going on for years and is acceptable throughout society, but is it problem free?

6 Would a pill which completely suppressed the menstrual cycle be popular amongst women?
Note: it would avoid some of the problems of the conventional pill, e.g. dysfunctional menstrual bleeding (heavy or irregular periods), dysmenorrhoea (painful periods) and menorrhagia (excessively heavy bleeding). Two disadvantages could be that uterine problems might remain concealed, and that such a pill might have long-term side effects. Some contraceptive pills can suppress the menstrual cycle completely – courses of such contraceptives are usually stopped if this occurs.

Topic 99
Sexually Transmitted Diseases

—Assignments

1 Initial symptoms are often mild (*1*) and then disappear (*1*). However, the person remains infectious (*1*) and if untreated much more severe symptoms (*1*) and eventually death (*1*) occur much later (*1*).

(*6 marks*)

2 Gonorrhoea:
Caused by bacterium. (*1*)
It can be destroyed with an antibiotic. (*1*)
Herpes:
Caused by virus. (*1*)
This remains in body for life. (*1*)

(*4 marks*)

3 (a) Promiscuity resulting from war. (*1*)
(b) Use of penicillin on a wide scale. (*1*)
(c) More promiscuous social attitudes (*1*)
(d) Trend upwards from 1970 to 1987 (*1*) due to increased casual sexual activity (*1*), then downwards from 1987 (*1*) due to reduction in casual sex (*1*) resulting from fear of AIDS (*1*). (*5 marks*)

(*Total 8 marks*)

4 Non-sexual acquisition of AIDS:
(i) shared needles by addicts;
(ii) infected transfused blood.
Both, or others – 1 mark each (*2 marks*)
Precautions e.g. in cases (i) and (ii):
(i) needles supplied to addicts to prevent shared use;
(ii) blood screening for AIDS virus.
Both, or others – 1 mark each (2 marks)

(*Total 4 marks*)

—Discussion

1 What advice would you give to a friend who confided in you that he/she thought that he/she had contracted a venereal disease?
Note: tell them to see a doctor as early as possible – delay will only make matters worse. They should also let anyone else that they might have infected know the truth - if untreated the disease can be fatal. They should follow doctor's prescription regularly and completely.

2 What impact do you think the early, mild stages of AIDS make on the sufferer's life?
Note: when the symptoms are mild, a normal life can be led. Care must be taken with any cuts or other possible sources of infection. Much prejudice still exists.

References on AIDS are:
AIDSFACTS. Educational Material on AIDS for Teachers and Students, Ian Harvey and Michael Reiss. Cambridge Science Books, 1987. This is a very thorough series of fact sheets covering all aspects of the disease. Regular updates are planned. Copyright has been waived and unlimited photocopying is permitted by educational establishments.
Understanding AIDS, a Self-defence Manual, Christopher Rouan. Ryburn Publishing, 1987. This is a short, concise booklet on AIDS, which is scientifically sound and easy to read.

Topic 100 How Do Insects Reproduce?

Investigation 1

The life cycle of the locust

Requirements

A cage of locusts mating (they normally need little encouragement to do this!); cage of live locust nymphs; preserved nymph material for each of the five stages; ruler with centimetre scale; drawing paper.

Pratical skills

AMO 2, AMO 10, REC 1, REC 4, INT 3.

General Comments

The female locust is usually underneath the male when mating, and is recognisable by the ovipositor; accurate observations can be assessed (AMO 10). There are five nymph instars, each one of increasing size; measuring skills (AMO 2) and drawing skills (REC 1) can be assessed. The length of a large number of nymphs can be measured, and a bar chart of length (along the *x*-axis) against number of individuals on the *y*-axis can be plotted (REC 4). The data should be divisible into five discrete groups, corresponding to the five instars. INT 3 can be used to assess this conclusion.

Investigation 2

The life cycle of the cabbage white butterfly

Requirements

Preserved specimens of the eggs, larva, pupa and adult cabbage white butterfly; hand lens; white tile; video or film material of caterpillars moving/feeding, of butterflies on flowers if available; drawing paper.

Practical skills

AMO 10.

General Comments

This is a simple observation exercise which is dependent upon having the correct material available. If living material or preserved is available, then this can be used. Video film or Super-8 film loop material can also be used. Budleia plants, if available locally, are an excellent source of butterflies.

There are a number of butterfly 'farms' around the country, and a visit to one of these could be recommended. An hour in one of these farms will be far more instructive than any amount of preserved or video material. This exercise could be used for assessment purposes; careful observation of the movement of mouthparts of larvae could be assessed (AMO 10).

Assignments

1 e.g.
(i) Overheat;
(ii) dehydrate;
(iii) damage by sun's ultraviolet rays.
Any two – 1 mark each (*2 marks*)

2 (i) Moulting: shedding cuticle (*1*) in order to grow. (*1*) (*2 marks*)
(ii) Mating: process by which male puts sperm into female's body (*1*) to fertilise her eggs (*1*). (*2 marks*)
(iii) Metamorphosis: change in body form. (*1*)
(iv) Instar: stage between one moult and next (*1*) during development of locus nymph (*1*). (*2 marks*)
(v) Cocoon: when larva changes to pupa (*1*) it spins a cover of fine threads around itself (*1*), which protects developing pupa (*1*). (*3 marks*)
(*Total 10 marks*)

3 (i) Nymph: like miniature version of adult (*1*) but lacking wings (*1*). (*2 marks*)
(ii) Larva: differs completely from adult. (*1*)
(*Total 3 marks*)

4 Larval tissues break down into a kind of cream (*1*) which then reorganises into adult form (*1*).
(*2 marks*)

5 Small nymph emerges from egg (*1*). As it grows it moults at least five times (*1*) until a mature adult emerges (*1*).
(*3 marks*)

6 (i) Larva: worm-like (*1*) to crawl among leaves (*1*). Powerful mandibles (*1*) to chew leaves (*1*). Soft body (*1*) enables rapid growth (*1*). (*6 marks*)
(ii) Pupa: pad and silk thread (*1*) for anchorage (*1*). Cover of fine threads (*1*) for protection while tissues reorganise inside (*1*). (*4 marks*)
(iii) Adult: sex organs (*1*) to reproduce (*1*). Wings (*1*) to find mate (*1*) and reach flowers for nectar (*1*). Proboscis (*1*) to such nectar from flowers (*1*). (*7 marks*)
Note: the proboscis is not in this topic, but it may be found in Topic 54, Figure 9.
(*Total 17 marks*)

7 e.g. Make life-sized models of female butterfly (*1*) with and without movable feelers (*1*).
Expose model females to trial males (*1*), and count the number of attempted mountings (*1*).
(*4 marks*)
Note: removing feelers from females is an alternative requiring less observation since production of offspring would be evidence of a successful mounting. Would pupils consider this to be ethically acceptable? It is worth discussing.

Discussion

1 Suppose you discovered a chemical that would do no harm to larvae but disrupted the events inside the pupa. What commercial value might it have? What tests would have to be carried out before it could be used commercially?
Note: it would be particularly good for treating insect pests whose life cycle showed complete metamorphosis. Tests on harm to other animals, food chain effects, effects of trace

quantities on sprayed/treated foods when eaten by humans and degradation time would have to be carried out.

2 If biologists understood fully what happened inside the pupa would such knowledge have value above and beyond academic research?
Note: there is a strong likelihood that much could be learned about development in general. How a highly organised animal can degenerate into a creamy soup-like state, then reorganise into something else, might provide clues about repairing damaged tissue and cancer control. The relevance of pure research with unforeseen applications is a point worth making.

3 Is it plausible that an alien life form, as intelligent as humans, could undergo complete metamorphosis? What circumstances might make metamorphosis necessary and what might be its disadvantages?
Note: I suppose all things are possible, but I find the notion rather incredible. The question is really meant as a mind-stretcher.

Topic 101
How Do Amphibians Reproduce?

—Investigation

Watching tadpoles develop

Requirements

Three tanks of tadpoles, each with an aquarium aerator, pond weed and stones; thyroxine tablets; iodine crystals (typical concentrations of thyroxine are 1 p.p.m. – 0.1 g thyroxine in 10 cm^3 0.1 M sodium hydroxide and 90 cm^3 distilled water – and those of iodine are a few crystals of iodine in 1 dm^3 water).

Pratical skills

AMO 8.

General Comments

This exercise could form the basis of an interesting observation exercise based on observing and comparing major features for the tadpoles in the three tanks (AMO 8). These observations can be expressed in a short report, using drawings and written descriptions. At least three differences need to be observed between the tadpoles in the three tanks at any one stage. Frog or toad spawn should be brought from a local pond. Ideally the tanks should be filled with water from the same pond, and aerated continually. At an early stage tadpoles eat vegetation, and later they become carnivorous. For conservation reasons use as little spawn as possible.

Information on the hormonal techniques for *Xenopus* referred to in this investigation can be found in *Biology, A Functional Approach, Students' Manual*, 2nd edition, Nelson, 1987.

—Assignments

1 (a) Voice box: air forced through (*1*) causes croaking (*1*). Males croak to attract mates (*1*). (*3 marks*)

(b) Nuptial pads: enlarged thumbs, covered with tough black skin, like warts (*1*). During mating they (*1*) enable the male to grip (*1*) female's slippery skin (*1*) when he climbs on her back (*1*). (*5 marks*)

(c) Albumen: jelly-like protein (*1*) which swells up on contact with water (*1*) and surrounds each frog egg (*1*). Protects egg from damage (*1*) and drying out (*1*), and clumps eggs together in a mass (*1*) which sticks to weeds and stones (*1*), called frog spawn. (*1*) (*8 marks*)

(d) Thyroxine: hormone (*1*) produced by thyroid gland (*1*), which brings about metamorphosis (*1*). (*3 marks*)

(*Total 19 marks*)

2 e.g.
(i) Frog spawn must be kept moist.
(ii) Tadpoles need to develop in water.
(iii) External fertilisation means sperms need water to swim through.
Any two reasons – 1 mark each

(*2 marks*)

3 e.g.
(i) Eggs are less likely to be eaten by predators.
(ii) Frogs are adapted to life in trees and therefore this choice is easier than the unfamiliar (and dangerous!) forest floor.
Any reason

(*2 marks*)

4 (a) e.g.
(i) Protection from predators.
(ii) Always moist.
(iii) Can be transported to suitable habitat (when developed into froglet.)
(iv) Parent can seek and provide food.
Any four possible advantages – 1 mark each (*4 marks*)

(b) e.g.
(i) More protected environment.
(ii) Less likely to be accidentally swallowed.
(iii) Tadpoles don't interfere with parent eating.
At least one reason (*1 mark*)

(*Total 5 marks*)

—Discussion

A few species of frogs and toads live in very dry surroundings. What adaptations might they make to their life cycle?
Note: pupils might suggest *Rhinoderma* (see Question 4) but its habitat is hardly arid. The African tree frog's foam nest is useful in a region where aquatic habitats are limited and competition or predation is high. A West African species of *Nectophrynoides* retains the complete tadpole stage within the female's oviduct – the tadpoles actively feeding on white flakes shed from the mother's walls. The Australian desert frog *Cyclorana* spends most of its life in a dormant state in a burrow. Mating occurs after infrequent desert rain; the tadpoles develop extremely quickly before the shallow pools dry up. The frogs then bloat with water, secrete a waterproof membrane and retire to their burrows! What a life!

Topic 102
How Do Birds Reproduce?

—Investigation

Looking at a chick embryo

Requirements

A fertilised hen's egg (that *must not* be more than three days old); plasticine; sharp scissors; dropping pipette; magnifying glass.

Pratical skills
AMO 10, REC 1.

General Comments
This exercise needs to be handled sensitively, since it raises emotive issues about vivisection and the use of embryos for research. Both of these issues can be discussed at length.

It is essential that the egg is less than three days old when this practical is attempted. The embryo corresponds to the one in Topic 102, Figure 5. At this stage there is no nervous system, and the limb appendages have not yet appeared. The heart can be seen beating, and the embryo is 'alive'. Assessment can be made of accurate observations (e.g. correctly identifying the structures seen in Figure 5) (AMO 10), and any drawings made (REC 1).

—Assignments

1 e.g.
(i) Shelter while egg hatches and chick develops.
(ii) Source of food for birds and offspring.
(iii) Prevents overpopulation which results in reduced chances of successful rearing of young.
Any good explanation – 2 marks (2 marks)

2 (a) e.g. Advantages:
(i) concealment;
(ii) chicks can learn to feed themselves sooner;
(iii) learning to fly not critical to leaving the nest so mother can leave young unattended while foraging for food;
(iv) usually well sheltered from wind.
e.g. Disadvantages:
(i) vulnerable to ground (and other) predators;
(ii) can be accidentally trampled, ploughed, etc.;
(iii) ground can get wet, cold, snow-covered, etc.

(b) e.g. Advantages:
(i) out of reach to most predators;
(ii) parents have lookout.
e.g. Disadvantages:
(i) generally easier to see;
(ii) usually fatal if chick leaves nest prematurely;
(iii) exposed to wind, rain, etc.

(c) e.g. Advantages:
(i) excellent shelter from predators;
(ii) excellent shelter from wind, rain, etc.;
(iii) relatively warm (if occupied).
e.g. Disadvantages:
(i) vulnerable to human whims;
(ii) usually fatal if chick leaves nest prematurely.
Marking Question 2(a), (b) and (c): Each advantage – 1 mark, each disadvantage – 1 mark
(6 marks)

Note: it is reasonable to expect one advantage and one disadvantage for (a), (b) and (c), but award additional mark for others. The mark given is therefore a notional minimum.

3 e.g.
(i) Courtship.
(ii) Lining nest.
(iii) Keeping eggs warm during incubation.
(iv) Keeping chicks warm when alone in nest.
At least two explanations – 1 mark each (2 marks)

4 It lets expanding (*1*) air escape (*1*) from the air space (*1*) without cracking egg (*1*).
(4 marks)

—Discussion

1 To what extend is bird reproduction similar and different from our own? What are the advantages and possibly disadvantages in the bird's method of reproduction?
Note: similarities are: the involvement of both parents, provision of a home, internal fertilisation and care of young. Differences lie in the laying and hatching of eggs. This gives the female bird more mobility than a pregnant mammal and enables both parents to provide care of the developing embryo. The absence of mammalian-type genitalia makes internal fertilisation harder to achieve. Also temporarily left eggs are vulnerable to predators.

2 How many nest designs can you think of? What factors do you think give rise to this wide diversity?
Note: some birds have no nest at all – plovers lay eggs on ground(well camouflaged), and gulls on cliff ledges with little material. Other nests are: woodpecker – holes in trees; kingfisher – holes in river banks; weaver birds – hollow ball; some swifts – spittle nests (used for bird's nest soup); thrush – cup woven grass. There are many more. Factors to consider are: avoiding predators at vulnerable times, materials available, nesting density (e.g. in seabird colonies), availability of suitable nesting sites.

Topic 103
Sexual Reproduction In Flowering Plants

An opportunity exists within these topics to undertake an observation exercise based on AMO 8 and AMO 9 'observing major and detailed features'. It would require three of the investigations to be incorporated into a single exercise. (Alternatively, each investigation can be carried out and assessed separately.)

Requirements
If this exercise is carried out, then the requirements are those of the separate investigations.

General Comments
Investigation 1 prepares the pupil for the exercise with a preliminary exercise in the appearance of floral parts. Investigations 2, 3 and 5 could then be combined into a single exercise.

If several wind- and insect-pollinated flowers were provided, the pupil could be told that the specimens were either insect-pollinated or wind-pollinated flowers. A first step would be to separate them into the two categories (an activity which could be assessed separately (AMO 7). The teacher should check that the pupils' classification was correct *before* allowing the next stage of the activity to begin.

The pupil could then be asked to produce an illustated report comparing insect- and wind-pollinated flowers; this could involve producing a table (similar to that in Topic 103, Table 1) listing the similarities and differences between them (if so, it would be essential that it were covered before the pupils encountered Table 1).

For assessment purposes, major features could include: differences in colour, size, orientation of the flower (i.e. flower facing upwards or hanging down) and the arrangement of flowers on the stem (AMO 8). Detailed features could include: the position of the stamens and stigmas, the relative numbers of pollen grains, and the appearance of the stigma and pollen grains (AMO 9).

—Investigation 1

Looking at the structure of a basic flower

Requirements

Flowers from a cherry or a hawthorn tree; hand lens; white tile; drawing paper.

Practical skills

AMO 10, REC 1.

General Comments

This pratical will allow accurate observations (AMO 10) and drawing skills (REC 1) to be assessed. A pupil will score highly on AMO 10 if the correct floral parts are observed, irrespective of the quality of the final drawing. Teachers should check that pupils whose drawings are unrecognisable are in fact seeing the correct features by talking to them and asking for an oral description of the features.

—Investigation 2

Looking at other flowers

Requirements

Hand lens; white tile; drawing paper; a variety of flowers (at least six) depending upon the seasonal availability (e.g. daisy, buttercup, sweet pea, rose, tulip, crocus, horse chestnut, cow parsley, etc.) (if the wind-pollinated flowers are presented, then this investigation should be combined with Investigation 5 of this topic); ideally, a length of stem should also be provided, enabling Investigation 3 to be completed on the same materials.

Practical skills

AMO 10, REC 1.

General Comments

This practical can be completed in conjunction with Investigation 1, and can be used to assess the same skills in the same way (see comments above).

—Investigation 3

Looking at how flowers are arranged on the stem

Requirements

A variety of different flowers attached to their stems (see Requirements for Investigation 1 of this topic); drawing paper.

Practical skills

AMO 10, REC 1, INT 1.

General Comments

This practical can be completed in conjunction with Investigation 1, and can be used to assess the same skills in the same way (see comments above).

—Investigation 4

To find out what makes pollen grains send out a tube

Requirements

225 cm^3 of pollen tube medium – 15% sucrose solution (0.01 g boric acid and 0.01 g yeast could also be added); 50 cm^3 distilled water; a ripe flower with pollen (e.g. nasturtium, *Impatiens,* hyacinth); paintbrush; dropping pipette; light microscope with low power objective lens; microscope slide; coverslip; access to a warm, dark place (e.g. a cupboard).

Practical skills

HMA 1, HMA 4, HMA 5, AMO 10, INT 1.

General Comments

This practical provides a good opportunity to assess microscopy skills (HMA 5 and HMA 6). The pollen growth medium can be unpredictable, and needs to be made freshly before the practical begins.

—Investigation 5

Exploring the differences between wind- and insect-pollinated flowers

Requirements

One insect-pollinated flower (e.g. daisy, buttercup, sweet pea, rose, tulip, crocus, horse chestnut, cow parsley, depending upon seasonal availability); one wind-pollinated flower (e.g. maize, wheat, barley, grasses); hand lens; access to a garden with flowering plants being visited by insects.

Practical skills

AMO 10, REC 1.

General Comments

Assessment can be made of the detailed observation of the two flowers (AMO 10) and of drawings, if made (REC 1).

—Assignments

1 Sepal – leaflet.
Petal – colour.
Pollen – sperm.
Nectary – sugar.
Ovule – egg cell.
(*1 mark each*)

(*5 marks*)

2 (i) Pollination: transfer of pollen (*1*) from another to stigma (*1*).
Fertilisation: fusion (*1*) of pollen male nucleus (*1*) with egg cell (*1*). (*5 marks*)
(ii) There is a high risk (*1*) of pollen failing to reach stigma (*1*), so many are produced to raise chances of success (*1*). (*3 marks*)

(*Total 8 marks*)

3 (i) Large (*1*) hanging anthers (*1*) make sure wind carries the pollen away (*1*). Large (*1*) feathery stigma (*1*) raises the chance of catching airborne pollen (*1*). (*6 marks*)
(ii) Stigma is held upwards (*1*) and anthers hand downwards (*1*) so a flower is unlikely to catch its own pollen (*1*). (*3 marks*)
(*Total 9 marks*)

4 Pollen from a flower of different design (*1*) ends up on a different part of bee (*1*) so pollen is less likely (*1*) to be passed on to a flower's own stigma (*1*).
(*4 marks*)

5 Make sure it has female flowers (*1*) and there is the chance of it being pollinated (*1*) by a nearby male-flowered tree (*1*).
(*3 marks*)

—Discussion—

Early spring flowers are sometimes white but are usually yellow. Why are they these colours in particular?
Note: a possible explanation is that in early spring there are both few flowers and few insects. Yellow is the colour most likely to attract insects. Population of flowers and insects increase as summer progresses so different colours appear as a means of identifying particular flowers.

Topic 104 Seeds And Germination

—Investigation 1—

Looking at seeds

Requirements
A pod of a bean plant, containing seeds; broad bean seed that has been soaked in water for 24 hours prior to the experiment; iodine solution (see Topic 47, p. 58).

Practical skills
AMO 10, INT 1.

General Comments
Relating the colour of the iodine to the storage of starch in the cotyledon can be used to assess drawing conclusions (INT 1). It might be an interesting extension to this practical to examine the storage of foods in endospermic seeds (e.g. maize or wheat) where the cotyledons are relatively small. Accurate description of the parts can be assessed (AMO 10) – for this to be effective, it is necessary to ask the pupil to describe the seed before studying Topic 104, Figure 1A, or to find identical structures in other seeds (e.g. peas or lupins or kidney bean pods).

—Investigation 2—

How do seeds germinate?

Requirements
A variety of seeds (e.g. cress, wheat, maize, broad bean); blotting paper; dishes for germinating each type of seed; water.

Practical skills
AMO 10, EXP 5, EXP 6.

General Comments
The simple instructions for this practical can be developed in a number of different ways. The pupils can be asked to investigate a number of different hypotheses, e.g.:
Do different types of seeds take the same length of time to germinate? Within each dish of seeds, how long does it take for all of the seeds to show signs of germinating?
Do each of the different types of seed germinate faster at higher incubation temperatures?
Do tomato seeds germinate better in distilled water or in tomato juice?

These hypotheses can be used to develop the EXP skills, particularly the use of controls (EXP 5) and appropriate levels of replication (EXP 6).

—Investigation 3—

The effect of water on a seed

Requirements
Several dry broad bean seeds; top pan balance; blotting paper.

Practical skills
AMO 5, INT 4.

General Comments
This practical allows the assessment of mass (AMO 5), and simple calculations (INT 4).

The % uptake in water is calculated using the formula: second weight/first weight × 100. It might be interesting to calculate the percentage uptake of different seeds, to see which are the 'most thirsty's. Could this be related to whether the seed stores food in enlarged cotyledons?

—Investigation 4—

Watching broad bean seeds germinating

Requirements
Jam jar, or other suitable container; water; sheet of blotting paper; several broad bean seeds (pre-soaked in water for 24 hours before the experiment starts).

Practical skills
HMA 1, HMA 7, AMO 10, REC 3, INT 1.

General Comments
This exercise can be used to assess following instructions and assembling apparatus. Although apparently simple, the scope for error is large, particularly if the instructions are not followed precisely. Fortunately, failure will only result in wet seeds and torn blotting paper, and this makes it appropriate for this type of assessment. The observation of the germinating seeds will have a greater immediate relevance to a pupil if they have been sown personally.

The pupil could be asked to keep a short diary describing the day-to-day appearance of the seed, which could be assessed (AMO 10 and REC 3).

—Investigation 5—

To find out the conditions needed for germination

Requirements

Cotton wool; five large test tubes; water; 2 g of cress seeds; vaseline: potassium pyrogallol (see p. 70 of this guide); cardboard box; one bung; 5 cm of cotton; muslin bag; access to refrigerator.

Practical skills

HMA 1, HMA 3, HMA 4, INT 1, EXP 3, EXP 4, EXP 5.

General Comments

This practical work can be used to assess safe practices (using the pyrogallol), assembling apparatus (HMA 4) and following instructions in the textbooks (HMA 1). The results of the experiments can be used to assess drawing appropriate conclusions (INT 1). This experiment could also form the basis of an experimental design exercise, before the instructions are read. The hypothesis could be to design experiments to test that water, oxygen, light and temperature are needed for germination. It is a particularly good exercise to assess apparatus, sequence, and controls skills (EXP 3, 4 and 5). If the experiments are designed prior to starting the practical, the written work can be collected in before copies of *BFL* are opened.

—Assignments—

1 (a) Either: level in beaker has fallen.
Or: level in neck of retort flask has risen. *Either* (*1*)
(b) Reduction in/no carbon dioxide. (*1*)
Reduction in/no oxygen. (*1*) (*2 marks*)
(c) Germinating (*1*) peas respire (*1*). (*2 marks*)
(d) Two diagrams (*1*), well drawn (*2*) almost identical to that in the question (*1*), but with the following changes:
(i) first diagram – water instead of potassium hydroxide solution (*1*),
(ii) second diagram – no peas (*1*). (*6 marks*)
(*Total 11 marks*)

2 e.g.
(i) Shoot has too far to grow upwards .(*1*)
(Before runs out of energy reserves (+ *1*).)
(ii) Not enough oxygen for seed to respire. (*1*) (*2 marks*)
e.g. Experiment to test suggestion (i):
Germinate seeds in total darkness (*1*) (so cannot make own energy reserves by photosynthesis (+ *1*)) and measure shoot/plumule length (*1*) until no further growth occurs (*1*).
Plant (same species) seeds at various depths in soil (*1*). If the maximum length of dark-grown plumule (*1*) shows a relationship (*1*) with maximum depth of successful planting (*1*), there is a (likely) connection (*1*) between plumule growth and planting depth (*1*). (*9 marks*)
(*Total 11 marks*)

3 (a) Many seeds are planted (*1*). Samples of germinating seeds/seedlings (*1*) are taken at given intervals (e.g. daily) (*1*), dried in an oven at 100°C (*1*) and weighed (*1*). The average dry masses then plotted against time (*1*). (*6 marks*)
(b) A: germinating seed uses up energy reserves (*1*) to grow into seedling (*1*) so loses dry mass (*1*).
B: emerging shoot is exposed to light (*1*), so can photosynthesise (*1*), so gains dry mass (*1*). (*6 marks*)
(*Total 12 marks*)

—Discussion—

1 What advice would you put on a packet of seeds?
Note: you need to detail the seed viability, whether to sow in a greenhouse, frame or open garden, when to sow, type of soil, closeness, depth, aspect of garden (light/shade, open/sheltered), care of seedlings and details about their re-planting/thinning when relevant and, in the case of vegetables, when to harvest crop.

2 What proportion of your diet is made up of seeds and seed products? Do seeds have other uses?
Note: examples are breakfast cereal, bread, crackers, spaghetti, rice, beans, peas. Cereals and pulses provide a high proportion of dietary starch – almost all if you exclude potatoes. Pulses can also be the major source of protein in a vegetarian diet. The main importance of seeds is in extracting oils, chiefly for food industry (e.g. linseed oil, castor oil), but other applications exist.

3 How have seeds helped in making plants so successful?
Note: for example, they enable propagation and variation to occur together, and help them to survive adverse conditions and to produce an offspring only where conditions likely to be suitable. It could also be argued that cereals have ensured their success by making their seeds highly nutritious to a certain consumer – ourselves.

Topic 105
Fruits And Dispersal

—Investigation 1—

Looking at fleshy fruits

Requirements

Kitchen knife; two ripe tomatoes; one apple; if possible, tomato plants bearing fruit; other fleshy fruits.

Practical skills

AMO 8, AMO 10, INT 1.

General Comments

This exercise could be used to assess accurate observations (AMO 10) and drawing correct conclusions (INT 1). It could be developed by later providing a variety of fruits for a comparison exercise to be carried out for detailed similarities and differences (AMO 8).

The small leaf-like structures at one end of the tomato are sepals. The seeds are arranged around the central tissue, (called the placenta). They are embedded in a clear jelly which is produced by the seeds. Only the seeds and jelly have formed directly as a result of the fertilisation; the flesh, skin and stalk have all been formed from the ovary tissue of the maternal plant. The seeds are dispersed by animals eating the fruits; they are resistant to destruction in the guts of the animals and germinate freely in the excreta.

The seeds of the apple are found in the core; this is the structure formed from the ovary tissue of the maternal plant. The sweet outer part of the fruit is formed from the receptacle tissue of the flower, and so the fruit is called a 'false fruit'.

Rose hip, strawberry, plum and orange could make an interesting comparison exercise. The juicy part of the orange is an outgrowth of the ovary wall, and it is a 'true fruit'.

—*Investigation 2*—

Looking at dry fruits

Requirements

Pea or bean pod; if possible, a plant bearing pods; a variety of examples of dry fruits (e.g. the pods of gorse, broom, laburnum, lupin, poppy heads, sycamore 'wings'); white tile; lamp.

General Comments

This exercise could be used to assess accurate observations (AMO 10) and drawing correct conclusions (INT 1).

The structure of a bean pod is shown in Topic 105, Figure 3E. The pod is formed from the ovary of the plant, and contains several seeds. The pod splits open lengthways, and the seeds are thrown to the ground. They may be propelled through the air and land some distance from the parent plant.

—*Assignments*—

1 (i) Fruit: part of plant surrounding seeds (*1*) which helps to disperse them (*1*). (*2 marks*)
(ii) Seed: part of plant containing embryo (fertilised ovule) (*1*) and food reserves (*1*) from which new plant (offspring) grows/germinates/develops (*1*). (*3 marks*)
(*Total 5 marks*)

2 (a) e.g. sycamore, dandelion.
Either, or other (*1*)
(b) e.g.Plum, tomato, strawberry, apple, burdock, goosegrass.
Any one (*1*)
(c) e.g. Coconut. (*1*)
Wide dispersal enables species to colonise new areas (*1*) and prevents overcrowding and competition (*1*). (*2 marks*)
(*Total 5 marks*)

3 (a) e.g. Plum/tomato. (*1*)
(b) e.g. Strawberry/apple. (*1*)
(c) e.g. Pea; (*1*)
pod. (*1*) (*2 marks*)
Note: the above examples can be found in this topic.
(d) e.g. Runner beans. (*1*)
(*Total 5 marks*)

4*(a) Longest distance:
e.g.dandelion; (*1*)
parachute-like fruits are very light and can be carried by air currents. (*2*) (*3 marks*)
Note: animal dispersed fruits that rely on adherence to fur are limited to the range of that particular mammal. Bird-dispersed fruits have a much greater chance of travelling long distances.
(b) Shortest distance:
e.g. sycamore (*1*);
quite heavy so their flight path (unlike dandelion's) tends to be downwards (*2*). (*3 marks*)
Note: the limited range of some furry animals is possibly a good argument for burdock or goosegrass. The best answer can arise from discussion. What matters is the reasoning.
(*Total 6 marks*)

5 e.g.
(i) Protects seed (*1*) inside an animal's digestive system (*1*). (*2 marks*)
(ii) Protects seed in soil (*1*) against fungal attack prior to germination (*1*). (*2 marks*)
(*Total 4 marks*)

6 (i) In seed: carbohydrate is concentrated as starch (*1*), an energy reserve (*1*) for germination (*1*). (*3 marks*)
(ii) In fleshy fruit: carbohydrate is diluted as sugar in solution (*1*), to taste sweet (*1*) and attract animals (*1*). (*3 marks*)
(*Total 6 marks*)

—*Discussion*—

1 The tomato is not particularly rich in nutrients, yet it is a major contributor of minerals and vitamins in the western diet. What features of the tomato have helped it to exploit humans successfully as agents for their dispersal?
Note: it was brought over from Central and South America in the sixteenth century. It was popular in Italy but avoided elsewhere until this century because of its relationship with deadly nightshade (same family). It is the prime consumed food in USA, possibly because of its attractive colour, flavour and versatility. The idea of an exploited plant exploiting humans is a way of showing interdependence. Tomato plants can be seen growing in sludge from sewage works!

2 What advantages are there for a seed to enter an animal's digestive system?
Note: apart from dispersal, there is possibly activation of the seed. An example is the relationship between the dodo and a large tree, *Calvaria major,* whose seeds have not germinated since the dodo's demise. *Calvaria* seeds needed to be ground by the dodo's gizzard before they could germinate. Grinding *Calvaria* seeds in turkey gizzards has also resulted in germination.

Topic 106
Vegetative Reproduction

One approach to teaching this topic is to consider perennating organs as structures for storing food. A variety of organs can be tested for the presence of starch, reducing sugars and non-reducing sugars, using the techniques learned in Topic 64. Many of these plants are native to woodlands, where there is a need for rapid growth during early spring, so that flowering and seed formation can occur before the leaves develop on the trees. Perennation can be developed as an adaptation to this type of environment.

—Investigation 1

Looking at bulbs

Requirements

Kitchen knife; onion bulb; onion bulb that is starting to sprout into a new plant.

Practical skills

AMO 10.

General Comments

This is a simple investigation of the inner leaves of an onion bulb. It is sometimes difficult for pupils to appreciate that the food is stored in non-photosynthetic leaves. The bulb is a swollen underground bud. This concept, although difficult to visualise, is the reason why a green shoot can emerge from the depths of the bulb.

—Investigation 2

Looking at potatoes

Requirements

Two potato tubers with 'eyes', one of which has been left in a warm, dark place for several weeks and is sprouting; a complete potato plant with tubers present.

Practical skills

AMO 10.

General Comments

The potato is a swollen extension of a stem. It cannot be root tissue, since the 'eyes' of a potato are buds, from which stems and leaves arise.

—Investigation 3

Taking cuttings

Requirements

Test tube of water; healthy specimen of *Impatiens* (Busy lizzie); access to a warm, well-lit place, scalpel.

Practical skills

HMA 1, HMA 7, AMO 10.

General Comments

This simple exercise can be developed into a series of attempts to propagate plants vegetatively. It can be linked to the use of rooting hormones, which are chemicals that control the development of root tissue (Topic 92, Investigation 4).

—Assignments

1 Perennating organs contain food reserves (*1*) for the new plant to grow (*1*).

(*2 marks*)

2 (a) Potatoes are *stem* tubers. (*1*)
(b) Grafting gives rise to one new plant (*1*) growing from a single stock (*1*). Budding gives rise to several new plants (*1*) (growing from a single stock). (*3 marks*)
(c) True remark (*1*).

(*Total 5 marks*)

3 Each eye is a bud (*1*) giving rise to a new shoot (*1*). The fewer shoots there are (*1*) the stronger they grow (*1*) since they have more access to food reserves (*1*).

(*5 marks*)

4 e.g.
(i) Generally reliable.
(ii) Don't need to rely on insects or other means of pollination.
(iii) Can produce identical offspring.
(iv) Don't need to depend on germination.
(v) No seeds for birds to eat.
At least three – 1 mark each

(*3 marks*)

5 (a) Flower takes up a lot of food reserves (*1*), reducing chances of cutting taking (*1*). (*2 marks*)
(b) Leaves increase water loss (*1*) and cutting lacks roots to take up water (*1*). (*2 marks*)
e.g. Other ways of helping:
(i) Putting cutting in rooting powder before planting (see Topic 92, Investigation 4).
(ii) Stand cutting in water so rootlets develop, *then* plant in soil.
(iii) Initially raise cutting in warm, sheltered place, e.g. greenhouse.
Any one (*2 marks*)

(*Total 6 marks*)

—Discussion

1 What perennating organs do we include in our diet? Is it likely to vary much world-wide?
Note: examples are: potatoes, carrots, onions, beetroot, swede, parsnip, and radish. This does vary world-wide, e.g. yams, mooli, jerusalem artichoke, are eaten more in other countries. Many larger supermarkets now display a wide variety of fresh international vegetables; this could form the basis for a follow-up in which pupils visit local supermarket(s) and survey the range of perennating organs available.

2 Cloning is a form of artificial vegetative reproduction by which hundreds of identical daughter plants can arise from a single parent. Suppose you were in this line of business, which plants would you clone and why?
Note: the ideal candidates would most likely be crop plants which would be slow to propagate by other means, e.g. fruit trees. Whether attractive flower hybrids, e.g. tea rose, would be viable commercially from cloning is worth discussing.

Topic 107 Chromosomes, Genes and Cell Division

—Investigation

Looking at chromosomes in dividing cells

Requirements

Light microscope with low and high power objective lenses; microscope slide; coverslip; mounted needle; prepared microscope slide of LS of a young root; watch glass; warm hotplate; acidified acetic orcein stain (50% mixture of dilute HCl and acetic orcein stain); blotting paper; young healthy root tips (e.g. broad bean).

Practical skills

HMA 1, HMA 3, HMA 4, HMA 7, REC 1.

General Comments

This practical is often temperamental, and it is wise to have prepared slides at hand in case of emergency, or during times that are spent waiting for the stain to work. It is best to have as many root tips present as possible, so everyone can have more than one go at the practical, if necessary. The cell walls of the root need to be softened before the stain can penetrate the nuclei. Acidified acetic orcein stain on a warm watch glass begins to penetrate the cells. An alternative method is to warm the root tips in dilute HCl for about 2 minutes, and then to add the stain. The stain penetrates more quickly if it is warm, and the hot plate (or other hot surface) is important. If no such surface is available, then passing the slide through a bunsen flame (but **not** keeping it there!), will suffice.

It is important to separate the many cells in the root tip, so that they form a layer one cell thick on the slide. The treatment with acid helps this process, but the way in which the slide is squashed is essential. It is possible to wrap the slide in blotting paper, and to press evenly (but firmly) on the coverslip with a thumb. Rotating the thumb through 360° whilst holding onto the slide, will separate the cells. Interpreting the patterns of chromosomes in the cells requires practice, and it is unreasonable to expect the pupils to be able to identify all the stages of mitosis. Nevertheless, it could be possible to assess the drawing of two cells from the squash (REC 1). The skill of manipulating the techniques (HMA 1, 3 and 7) and using a microscope (HMA 5) could also be assessed.

—Assignments—

1 (i) Chromosome: threadlike structure in nucleus (*1*) visible under light microscope (*1*). (*2 marks*)
(ii) Gene: small part of chromosome (stretch of DNA) (*1*) determining a characteristic (*1*). (*2 marks*)
Note: see question 2 (c)

(*Total 4 marks*)

2 (a) A pair of chromosomes (*1*) looking exactly alike (*1*). (*2 marks*)
(b) Original chromosome (*1*) and its replica (*1*). (*2 marks*)
(c) Single instruction in chromosome (*1*) determining a characteristic (*1*). (*2 marks*)

(*Total 6 marks*)

3 (a) 12. (*1*)
(b) 6. (*1*)
(c) 12. (*1*)
(d) 6. (*1*)
(e) 4. (*1*)

(*Total 5 marks*)

4 Cell just about to divide (*1*) (note: i.e. prophase). Chromosomes have become (*1*) shorter and more visible (*1*).

(*3 marks*)

Note: there might be a case for a pupil putting 'just after dividing into daughter cells' (i.e. telophase). The photographs in the investigation of Topic 107 show prophase to be a better choice. Use discretion and consider the pupil's ability level.

5 (a) 46. (*1*)
(b) 23. (*1*)
(c) 23. (*1*)
(d) 46. (*1*)
(e) 46. (*1*)

(*Total 5 marks*)

6 No. (*1*)
For each child (*1*) there is a 50 per cent chance it will be a girl (*1*).

(*3 marks*)

—Discussion—

1 Nearly all our characteristics are coded in our genes. Does this mean, as some people have suggested, that we are robots run by computer programmes?
Note: physiologically our cells do follow instructions, and a good thing too! Whether the decisions our brains make are based on environment, cumulative memory, or inherited properties of our nerve cells is highly contentious and frequently argued about. All three factors are involved, of course; it's just a matter of degree.

2 What advantages are there in chromosomes being in pairs?
Note: paired chromosomes enable characteristics to be passed on from both parents. It encourages variation (see Topic 110), prevents mutated disorders being passed on too easily (see Topic 108), and enables sexual reproduction by providing a sex-determining mechanism (see Topic 107, Figure 7).

3 We are just the means by which our genes live on forever. What do you think?
Note: this idea was entertained in the book *The Selfish Gene* by Richard Dawkins. However, genes themselves don't remain immutable forever – see text on mutations, 'Sharp differences', in Topic 110.

Topic 108 Heredity

In genetics, the terms 'gene' and 'allele' are not synonymous, and the distinction between them is often not fully appreciated. A gene is a specific length of DNA that carries precise instructions for the production of a polypeptide or a protein. Diploid cells have two copies of each gene, located on similar (homologous) chromosomes. An allele is as particular sequence of bases that makes up the length of DNA that is the gene. The sequence of bases in one gene need not be the same as in the other gene in the pair, and may therefore produce different proteins. The result is an individual heterozygous for the the alleles.

Biology for Life *does not emphasise the distinction between gene and allele. Teachers who wish to introduce their pupils to the concept could do so by using the explanation that 'a gene is involved in controlling the development of a particular characteristic and that there may be different forms of that gene, called alleles. Different alleles may alter the way in which a characteristic develops in the organism'.*

—Investigation 1

How are genes sorted out in heredity?

Requirements

Two beakers; beads (e.g. poppit beads) – 75 beads of one colour and 25 beads of a second colour (e.g. black and white).

Practical skills

AMO 6, INT 1.

General Comments

This investigation works only if the pupils appreciate what the model represents. Each coloured bead represents two genes that control the same character (i.e. two alleles). The beaker of black beads represents a homozygous parent. The beaker of black and white represents a heterozygous parent.

When a single bead is selected from each beaker, we are choosing which genes will appear in the offspring of that cross. We are, in effect, determining the genotypes of the gametes. Since it is chance that determines which of the two gametes are involved in fertilisation, it is important that we choose beads randomly from each beaker. Joining the two beads together (see below) after we have selected them makes the final counting simpler, and also emphasises that the two genes have now been brought together in the new individual. This cross should give a 1:1 ratio of black/black, black/white genotypes, and is equivalent to the backcross between the F_1 generation and one of its parents.

This simple exercise can be used to assess counting skills (AMO 6) and drawing correct conclusions (INT 1).

Plastic beads that can be joined together are available from biological suppliers. These beads have the advantage that they can be joined together to form pairs.

—Investigation 2

How are the genes sorted out in heredity?

Requirements

Five beakers; beads (e.g. poppit beads) – 50 beads of one colour and 50 beads of a second colour (e.g. black and white).

Practical skills

AMO 6, INT 1.

General Comments

This cross represents the formation of an F_2 generation from a cross between two F_1 organisms. The same comments apply as in Investigation 1 (see above).

—Investigation 3

Inheritance in the fruit fly

Requirements

Tubes of *Drosophila* made up in advance: one bottle of vestigial winged males, a second bottle of wild type females (if the flies are sorted some days before the practical they should be placed in bottles containing food and filter paper (see diagram, Investigation 3 in *BFL*); *Drosophila* food (can be obtained from suppliers); filter paper; anaesthetising apparatus; filter funnel with cotton wool soaked in ether or 50% ether/ethanol mixture; two specimen tubes; white tile; paintbrush: unused *Drosophila* bottle containing food and filter paper; marker pen; incubator at 25°C.

Practical skills

HMA 1, HMA 3, HMA 7.

General Comments

Handling *Drosophila* flies at this level can be very difficult. This practical simplifies the process, but requires extensive preparation. Space does not permit detailed discussion of the techniques of *Drosophila* genetics. The students' manual of *Biology: A Functional Approach* gives full details. Teachers need to be experienced at handling flies before commencing this practical, and plenty of time needs to be given for it.

It is essential that the wild type female flies are virgins. This will require collecting the flies within six hours of their emerging from pupae. Sufficient female flies need to be collected to allow each group to have between five and ten each. Male flies do not need to be virgin.

Ether is dangerous. Have the room well ventilated, and do not allow the pupils to keep the flies in the etheriser for any longer than necessary. If the flies start to move during the examination, they need to be tipped back into the etherising tube. There is no need to panic since it takes a few minutes for the flies to become strong enough to fly. A ripe apple in the room will soon collect any flies that do manage to escape!

The F1 flies that emerge will have long wings, since the gene for short wings is recessive. The pupils can be encouraged to cross several F1 flies together to produce an F2 generation. This is easier to achieve, since it does not require the flies to be virgins before they are handled (since an F2 generation is produced by randomly mating an F1 generation). It does, however, require that the pupils know how to sex fruit flies, which will need to be taught beforehand. Once again, the students manual of *Biology: A Functional Approach* gives full details.

This exercise is so problematical that it is probably too difficult for assessment at this level, although several handling skills could be attempted (e.g. HMA 1, 3 and 7).

—Assignments

1 Black gene is dominant (*1*), brown gene is recessive (*1*). The offspring have both black and brown genes (*1*), i.e. are heterozygous/hybrids (*1*) and show only the dominant (black) coat colour (*1*).

(*5 marks*)

2 Parents are from the offspring in Question 1. (+*1*)
Gene for black mouse – B
Gene for brown mouse – b. (+*1*)

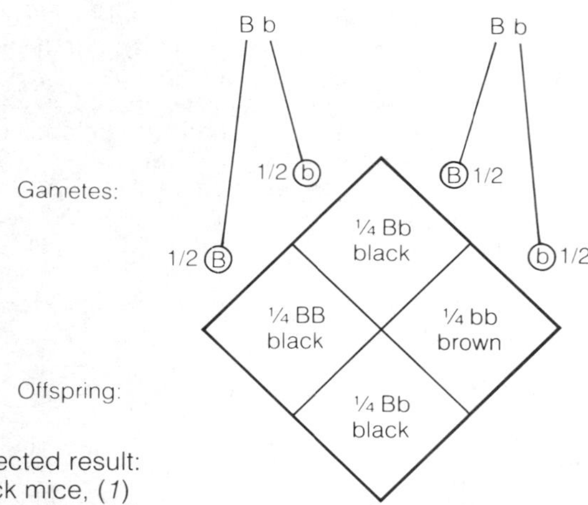

Expected result:
¾ black mice, (*1*)
¼ brown mice. (*1*)
Marking the diagram:
(i) parents' phenotypes; (*1*)
(ii) parents' genotypes; (*1*)
(iii) gametes; (*1*)
proportions; (*1*)
(iv) table/grid. (*2*)

(*8 marks*)

3 (a) Mother's genotype is homozygous recessive (*1*) since other genotypes would hide (*1*) the blue-eyed phenotype (*1*). (*3 marks*)
(b) Father's genotype is heterozygous (*1*), since the recessive phenotype (blue eyes) (*1*) appears in the offspring (*1*). (*3 marks*)
(c) The three brown-eyed children are heterozygous (*1*) since they express dominant (*1*) brown-eyed phenotype (*1*), but must have acquired a recessive gene from their mother (*1*).
The two blue-eyed children are homozygous recessive (*1*), since other genetypes would hide (*1*) the blue-eyed phenotype (*1*) (i.e. 'same reason as mum'). (*7 marks*)

(*Total 13 marks*)

Note: some pupils are likely to use diagrams. These should count as adequate explanations.

4 (i) There is a 50% (½ chance that the first child will be albino. (*1*)
(ii) Since one of woman's parents was albino and was homozygous recessive for this gene (*1*) then one of her genes must be albino gene (*1*). Since she is normal the other gene must be for normal skin colour (*1*) (i.e. she is heterozygous (+*1*). There is a 50% chance therefore (*1*) that one of her eggs will have albino gene (*1*), and all her husband's sperm contain albino gene (*1*). (*6 marks*)
(iii) Those appearing normal (*1*) (for skin colour).
(iv) A heterozygous (normal appearing) individual (*1*) who can pass on a recessive gene. (*1*) (*2 marks*)

(*Total 10 marks*)

Note: the use of a diagram to answer this question is perfectly acceptable as an explanation.

5 (a)

1 – Bb;	2 – bb;	3 – bb;
4 – bb;	5 – Bb;	6 – bb;
7 – bb;	8 – Bb;	9 – bb;
10 – Bb;	11 – bb;	12 – bb;
13 – Bb;	14 – bb;	15 – Bb.

1 mark each (*15 marks*)

(b) Must be heterozygous since gene for night-blindness is dominant (*1*) and the recessive phenotype (*1*) appears in some of the offspring (*1*) (alternatively: if number 1 was homozygous dominant all the offspring would be night-blind – they're not). (*3 marks*)

(c) Cousins. (*1*)

(d) Number 13: must be heterozygous because he expresses dominant night-blindness (*1*) and his mother has normal vision (*1*) and is therefore homozygous recessive (*1*). (*3 marks*)
Number 15: must be heterozygous, for the same reasons as number 13 (only father has normal vision this time). (*3 marks*)

(e) ¾ (75%) chance. (*1*)
Explanation:
Let N - gene for night blindness
n - gene for normal vision } (+*1*)

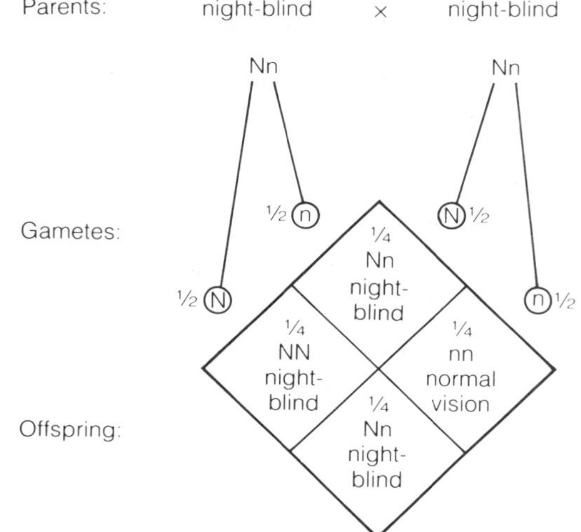

Expected result:
¾ night-blind. (*1*)
¼ normal vision. (*1*)
Marking the diagram:
(i) parents' phenotypes; (*1*)
(ii) parents' genotypes; (*1*)
(iii) gametes; (*1*)
proportions; (*1*)
(iv) table/grid. (*2*)
(*9 marks*)

Note: this answer is only really possible if a diagram is used.

(f) ½ (50%) chance. (*1*)
Let N-gene for night blindness
n - gene for normal vision } (+*1*)

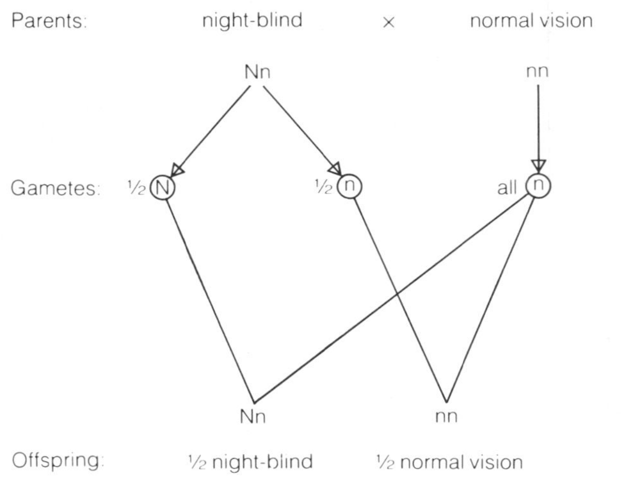

Marking the diagram:
(i) parents' phenotype; (*1*)
(ii) parents' genotypes; (*1*)
(iii) gametes; (*1*)
proportions; (*1*)
(iv) combination lines (*1*)
(v) offspring; (*1*)
proportions. (*1*) (*8 marks*)

(*Total 42 marks*)

—Discussion

1 Should we all be monitored for the chances of passing inherited disorders to our offspring and, if so, should 'high risk' parents be forbidden from having offspring?
Note: this idea has been seriously proposed, but the whole idea of eugenics (genetic control) is still treated with unease. Where there are family histories of some heritable disorders, prospective parents are advised by their family doctor or a genetic counsellor. Examples are spinal bifida, muscular dystrophy, cystic fibrosis, haemophilia, thalassaemia and sickle cell anaemia.

2 What traits have you noticed running through families?
Note: examples are: eye colour, hair colour, shape of face, size of nose, etc. It is interesting to talk about what the pupils see in their own families.

Topic 109 More About Genes

—Assignments

1 Genetic code is set of instructions (*1*) in DNA (*1*) which tell organism how to develop (*1*).

(*3 marks*)

2 So that when a cell divides by mitosis (*1*) the daughter cells have exactly the same genetic code as the parent (*1*).

(*2 marks*)

3*(a) There was not enough human growth hormone to go round (*1*) and only *human* growth hormone would work (*1*). (*2 marks*)
Note: award additional mark(s) for deducing that dead people's pituitaries were needed and not every dead person has their brain removed to get at it! Referring pupils to Topics 78, 80 and 92 should hint at this.

(b) Gene which makes growth hormone (*1*)
taken out of human cell (*1*)
and put into a bacterium. (*1*)
Bacteria reproduce rapidly (*1*)
replacing human DNA along with its own (*1*)
so a continual supply of growth hormone
can be produced. (*1*) (*6 marks*)

(*Total 8 marks*)

4 e.g. Dangers:
(i) genetically engineered killer germ might wipe out all humans;
(ii) genetic engineering might be used to modify people;
(iii) artificial organisms might severely disrupt the environment.

e.g. How to avoid:
(i) strict laws controlling genetic engineering;
(ii) using genetic engineering only with weakened strains of bacteria.

Any plausible danger – 2 marks, any plausible avoidance – 2 marks

(*4 marks*)

—Discussion

What do you think the chances are for the following happening as a result of genetic engineering: designer pets, particularly nasty germ warfare agents, gene injections to cure diseases, or modified people?
Note: genetic engineering opens up limitless possibilities which no longer rest securely in the realm of science fiction. Viruses as well as bacteria can act as gene vectors – indeed in some viruses the viral genetic material becomes incorporated into human chromosomes to wreak havoc at a later stage (e.g. AIDS, shingles, herpes). Designer pets could seem like a frivolous piece of free enterprise – but are there implications if such pets are intelligent? So little is known about germ warfare that a sense of caution must be taken. Gene injections are being developed for dealing with brain degenerative disorders, e.g. Parkinson's disease. Modified people – this is pure mischief and speculation! However, a massive medical genetics programme has already begun with the objective of determining the entire sequence of human DNA.

Topic 110 Variation

—Investigation

Looking at an example of variation

Requirements

Rulers or tape measures suitable for measuring the heights of pupils in the class; graph paper.

Practical skills

AMO 2, REC 2, REC 3, REC 4, INT 2, INT 3, INT 4, INT 6.

General Comments

This simple exercise can be used to assess a variety of skills: data is collected by measuring the heights of each person in the class (AMO 2); it needs to be recorded accurately (REC 3) in tables designed by the pupils (REC 2); and then plotted on a bar chart (REC 4). The average height of the class can be calculated (INT 4) from the data extracted from the table (INT 2). It can be compared with the modal class of the graph (INT 3) and can introduce the concept of different ways of summarising data.

The answer to the question about the interpretation of the shape of the curve should include the idea that most people fall into the category of 'average' height, with relatively few people at the extremes. This can be used to assess recognising patterns in data (INT 6). Height is ultimately controlled by genes, but in adolescents the variation in the timing of puberty can also have a profound effect on the heights of the members of the class.

Even though most of these skills can be assessed from written product, the teacher might be advised to select a few of the skills for assessment with any particular pupil, since it is unfair to assess too many skills in a single investigation.

Assignments

1 (a) Free assortment (*1*) means it is chance (*1*) which determines which chromosomes (*1*) (and therefore genes (+*1*)) of each homologous pair (*1*) end up in each gamete (*1*); and crossing over (*1*) during meiosis (*1*) results in genes being exchanged (*1*) between homologous (*1*) chromosomes (*1*). (*10 marks*)

(b) Identical twins occur when a single fertilised egg (*1*) divides into two separate embryos (*1*) so their genes are identical (*1*). (*3 marks*)

(*Total 13 marks*)

2 (i) Continuous variation: gradual transition between the two extremes of a feature/characteristic. (*2*)
e.g. Height, weight (i.e. body mass), intelligence, hair colour.
Any example (*1*)
(*3 marks*)

Note: although examples are not specifically asked for it is reasonable to expect an example to form part of any good explanation.

(ii) Discontinuous variation: there is sharp difference between two or more contrasting characteristics (i.e. no in-betweens). (*2*)
e.g. Tongue-rolling, blood groups, flower colour, colour blindness, haemophilia, sickle-cell disease, wing length (etc.) in fruit flies.
Any example (*1*)
(*3 marks*)

(*Total 6 marks*)

3 (i) Mutation: sudden change (*1*) in genetic make-up of an organism (*1*). It may be either a change to a whole chromosome (*1*) or to a single gene (*1*). (*4 marks*)

(ii) Whereabouts: testes and ovaries (*1*) during egg and sperm formation (*1*). (*2 marks*)

Note: 'whereabouts' could have a different meaning, e.g, 'in a nuclear disaster area'. Use your discretion.

(iii) Consequences: may be harmful. (*1*)
e.g. Downs syndrome, sickle cell disease, cystic fibrosis.
Any one example (*1*)
May be neither harmful nor helpful (*1*)
e.g. Extra fingers and toes (*1*)
May be helpful (*1*).
e.g. Penicillin resistance in bacteria, DDT resistance in mosquitoes, warfarin resistance in rats, black colour in peppered moths (in industrial areas).
Any one example (*1*)
(*6 marks*)

(*Total 12 marks*)

Note: all these helpful mutations can be found in Topic 111.

4 A. Inherited features:
e.g.
(i) hair colour;
(ii) skin colour;
(iii) eye colour;
(iv) straight/wavy/curly hair;
(v) shape of nose.

B. Environmental features:
e.g.
(i) body mass;
(ii) hair style;
(iii) physical fitness.

C. Could be either (an interaction of inherited and environmental factors):
e.g.
(i) height;
(ii) intelligence;
(iii) agility.

At least three inherited features (*i.e. from list A and/or C*) *– 1 mark each* (*3 marks*)
At least three environmental features (*i.e. from lists B and/or C*) *– 1 mark each* (*3 marks*)

Environment:
e.g. everything we have experienced from our surroundings (*2*)

Note: wording will vary a lot, but the above *idea* should earn the marks.

(*Total 8 marks*)

5*e.g. Find sets of identical twins (*1*) who have been orphaned (*1*) and then adopted (*1*) by different families (*1*). Carry out basic tests for intelligence (*1*) and try to see if differences in performance (*1*) relate to differences in environment (*1*).

(*7 marks*)

Note: there are probably other more inventive answers! Research of this type has been carried out for several decades, and is still inconclusive!

Discussion

1 To what extent to do you think the following are inherited?
(a) intelligence;
(b) creativity;
(c) agility;
(d) criminality.

Note: this is referred to as the 'nature versus nurture' argument about which even the most eminent psychologists disagree.

2 Why do some species show more variation than others?
Note: where there is a wide range of niches available and a limited number of competitors there we would expect adaptive radiation and a wide degree of variation (e.g. Galapagos finches). Variation is narrowest where an organism becomes highly adapted to a particular niche (e.g. crocodile). Even then there will be variation in length, body mass, etc., among similarly aged individuals.

3 The Nazis in Germany wanted to reduce human variation by selecting a 'master race'. Apart from being morally unacceptable, what was the biological weakness of such thinking?
Note: despite current popular belief the idea of human selection was not exclusively a Nazi idea in the 1920s and 30s; it was a widely held idea and one of the classic examples of 'pseudo science'. Aldous Huxley's *Brave New World* was published in 1932. Two problems present themselves in wanting human genetic uniformity. First, who selects what is meant by desirable, since people's opinions vary widely? Secondly, what evidence is there that uniformity is preferable to variation? Nature seems to favour the latter!

Topic 111
How Do New Kinds Of Organisms Arise?

Assignments

1 Vestigial structures have no use (*1*), although the same basic structures (*1*) are useful in other organisms (*1*) which suggests ancestors did use these structures (*1*) (suitable e.g. – appendix, coccyx in humans (+ *1*)).
(*4 marks*)

2 (i) Homologous structures (*1*) are found in different animals (*1*) but have the same basic design (*1*). (*3 marks*)
(ii) Suggest common ancestry. (*1*)
(*Total 4 marks*)

3 Process of natural (unwittingly artificial?) selection (*1*). Those immune to warfarin (*1*) survive to produce immune offspring (*1*).
(*3 marks*)

4 (i) Similar: selection of features has occurred. (*1*)
(ii) Different: selection is artificial (*1*) for human tastes/pleasure (*1*) rather than survival of fittest (*1*). (*3 marks*)
(*Total 4 marks*)

5 (a) e.g.
Disadvantages to being short:
(i) cannot run fast to escape;
(ii) vulnerable to smaller and therefore more predators;
(iii) reduced grazing range;
(iv) greater energy required to travel distances (therefore need to eat more);
(v) competition from other small grazers.
At least three reasons – 2 marks each (*6 marks*)

(b) e.g.
Disadvantages to being very tall:
(i) there is an optimum leg length for running fast – very tall antelopes are therefore 'handicapped';
(ii) more conspicuous to predators;
(iii) require more food;
(iv) harder to graze.
At least three reasons – 2 marks each (*6 marks*)
(*Total 12 marks*)

Discussion

1 Could the formation of human beings be a mistake in evolution in much the same way that cancer is a mistake in cell development?
Note: this hypothesis has been seriously proposed by some of the world's leading ecologists. Geological time is so long that we cannot judge if previous mistakes have been made and erased – this idea too has been suggested. Our geologically catastrophic impact on the biosphere suggests that this might be the case. Personally, I'm an optimist! This is well worth discussing (is evolution fallible?)

2 Some politicians argue that human society ought to follow the same basic rules as natural selection. Do you agree?
Note: this is case for and against what is referred to as 'Social Darwinism'. No society functions fully this way, although some are more biased towards survival of the fittest than others. Do we really understand why we are social animals to sufficient a degree to put forward simplistic models for how our social organisation ought to function?

3 How have distasteful insects become brightly coloured?
Note: bright colouration could have appeared suddenly via a selected mutation or gradually via a 'biased preference', that is, those which are slightly more coloured are slightly more likely to warn would-be predators that they are distasteful. Failure to warn means failure to pass on genes – even if you're distasteful, for if you're chewed up and spat out you're still dead!

4 As medicine succeeds in treating and curing diseases will we be forever selecting more virulent (i.e. nastier) germs?
Note: the mechanism of developing disease resistance works by natural selection. Germs which fail to 'beat the cure' become eradicated (e.g. smallpox). Whether certain viruses can always stay one step ahead by means of rapid reproduction remains to be seen. The chances are that we'll be selecting 'smarter' germs, though not necessarily nastier ones. After all, syphilis was every bit as nasty as AIDS until a method of treatment was found.

—Introduction to the worksheets

Ten worksheets are provided in this section. Each one is copyright-free so that it can be photocopied for distribution to pupils. It is suggested that the sheets be used either as the basis of exercises for the formal assessment of skills or in the course of normal teaching to supplement the Investigations in *Biology for Life*.

Teacher's notes are also provided. These give lists of equipment requirements and general comments for teachers to indicate how the worksheets can be used to assess each of the 37 skills on at least one occasion.

The worksheets are **not** intended to be a complete skills assessment package. They merely provide examples of the type of practical investigations which can be used by teachers to assess practical skills. It is hoped that teachers will use these as the starting point for the development of their own ideas.

If the worksheets are to be used for assessment purposes, pupils must be given ample opportunity to learn and practise the required skills beforehand. It is recommended that the investigations in *Biology for Life* be used for this purpose. It should also be noted that whilst some skills can be assessed several times, others are only represented once in the worksheets. Teachers will need to plan their use of the worksheets carefully to make maximum use of the opportunities for assessment found in them.

The worksheets are entitled:

1 A key to identify some tree leaves
2 Comparing organisms
3 Osmosis and potatoes
4 To find out how fast an enzyme works
5 To find out if potatoes produce carbon dioxide
6 Measuring the temperature of your body
7 Fields of vision
8 Trotting and galloping
9 Counting fruit flies
10 Designing experiments to test hypotheses

The skills are distributed as follows:

	Worksheet									
Skill	**1**	**2**	**3**	**4**	**5**	**6**	**7**	**8**	**9**	**10**
HMA 1			+	+	+	+			+	
HMA 2				+	+					
HMA 3				+	+	+			+	
HMA 4					+					
HMA 5		+								
HMA 6		+								
HMA 7		+	+	+	+				+	
AMO 1						+				
AMO 2			+							
AMO 3				+		+				
AMO 4				+						
AMO 5			+							
AMO 6									+	
AMO 7	+									
AMO 8		+								
AMO 9		+								
AMO 10	+	+	+		+			+		
REC 1		+								
REC 2			+	+		+	+	+		
REC 3			+	+					+	
REC 4						+				
REC 5			+							
INT 1			+		+		+		+	
INT 2						+	+	+		
INT 3						+				
INT 4						+		+		
INT 5			+						+	
INT 6				+			+	+	+	
EXP 1–9										+

—Notes on Worksheets 1 to 10—

—Worksheet 1—

A key to identify some tree leaves

Requirements
A variety of leaves from the trees included in the key.

Practical Skills
AMO 7, AMO 10.

General Comments
This key has been designed to include trees that are common to many localities, but it may be that some leaves are absent from a particular area. In such circumstances teachers should provide leaves from those local trees that are included in the key. It is unfair to include leaves that are not mentioned in the key. Some teachers might like to adapt the key to suit the trees that are present in their locality.

This exercise can be used to assess AMO 7, assigning objects to groups. If a pupil can use the key to correctly identify most of the leaves, but has problems with one or two of them, then the highest level of achievement should still be awarded. This is because the exercise is testing whether a pupil can use a key, rather than identify each of the leaves correctly. An alternative skill that could be assessed is AMO 10.

—Worksheet 2—

Comparing organisms

Requirements
For each pupil: Pairs of specimens (e.g. snail/slug, earthworm/millipede, watershrimp/waterflea, woodlouse/centipede, iris/foxglove, bracken/daisy plant, *Chlamydomonas/Paramecium, Elodea/Cladophora, Elodea/Spirogyra, Euglena/Amoeba*—each pair of organisms should be presented to the pupil in the most appropriate way. The microscopic protists, for example, could be presented in small volumes of water inside dropping pipettes); hand lens; where appropriate, light microscope with low and high power objective lenses, microscope slides, cavity slides, coverslips, mounted needle, water; drawing paper, sharp pencil.

Practical Skills
HMA 5, HMA 6, HMA 7, AMO 8, AMO 9, AMO 10, REC 1.

General Comments
This worksheet is designed to allow teachers to assess observation skills (AMO 8, 9, 10) in a way that they feel to be most appropriate. The choice of pairs of organisms mentioned above is meant to be illustrative rather than prescriptive. Some teachers may wish to give the whole class the same organisms to study, or to give each pupil different ones. Teachers should bear in mind that it is easier to observe similarities and differences between some pairs of organisms than others. Pupils are not necessarily expected to find five similarities and differences, and it is better if the teacher informs the pupils of how many to look for in the light of the choice of organisms.

Teachers can assess how well pupils can handle the materials (HMA 7), and those who wish to assess microscopy skills (HMA 5, 6) can select microscopic organisms, or can ask pupils to compare parts of macroscopic organisms. The pupils will be expecting to be informed whether or not to use a microscope.

At the end of the exercise, the pupils could be given drawing paper and a sharp pencil and be asked to draw one (or both) of the specimens. This will enable REC 1 to be assessed. It is important that an indication of scale should be included with the drawing.

Teachers need to be careful that pupils are not hampered by a lack of suitable vocabulary. The worksheet tells pupils not to mind if they do not know the name of part of an organism, and pupils should be encouraged to describe in their own words what they see.

—Worksheet 3—

Osmosis and potatoes

Requirements
For each pupil: a cork borer; three petri dishes with lids; marker pen; one medium-sized potato; plastic ruler; a sheet of absorbent paper; a knife; a plate or tile upon which cut; about 20 cm^3 of each of these liquids—water, 5% sucrose solution, 50% sucrose solution; access to a weighing balance.

Practical Skills
HMA 1, HMA 7, AMO 2, AMO 5, AMO 10, REC 2, REC 3, INT 1, INT 5.

General Comments
This exercise can be used to assess 'following instructions' (HMA 1), since it will be apparent from the appearance of the chips on the following day whether or not the instructions have been followed carefully. HMA 7 assesses the ability to use materials and apparatus correctly. Obviously there is considerable overlap between these two skills, and teachers ought not to assess both of them in the same exercise. Measuring length and mass accurately can be assessed as AMO 2 and AMO 5. Assessing mass can be a time consuming activity (since one has to observe the pupils carefully, they have to queue to use a single balance), and it is probably better to assess a few pupils on the first day and a few more on the second day. The description of the textures of the chips can be used to assess accurate observations (AMO 10).

Pupils should be told to read the worksheet carefully and to work out a suitable data table in advance of starting. This will ensure that they have thought about the procedure before starting the activity, thus helping the assessment of HMA 1, and allowing REC 2 to be assessed properly.

The interpretation of the results is important (INT 1), as is the discussion on possible sources of variation in the experiment (INT 5). One of the major causes of variation is probably the extent to which the potato has moisture squeezed out of it, particularly during the second lesson. It is possible that different potatoes will be stored in different places and will contain different amounts of water to start with.

Worksheet 4

To find out how fast an enzyme works

Requirements

For each pupil: three small beakers—one empty, one containing at least 30 cm^3 hydrogen peroxide, one containing at least 30 cm^3 of water (the beakers should be clearly labelled); forceps; 20 cm^3 plastic syringe; a piece of fresh liver; a stop clock; a paper towel.

Skills

HMA 1, HMA 2, HMA 3, HMA 7, AMO 3, AMO 4, REC 2, REC 3, INT 6.

General comments

This exercise is a development of an Investigation in *Biology for Life* (Topic 46, 'Enzymes') which will allow the measurement of volume (AMO 3) and time (AMO 4) to be made. Pupils need to exercise caution in using hydrogen peroxide, which is an oxidising agent. Safety reminders are included in the worksheet, and should be assessed as HMA 3. The practical could also be used to assess 'following instructions' (HMA 1).

It would be a good idea to check that the liver does break down hydrogen peroxide before starting the practical. Excellent results have consistently been obtained with fresh liver, but not with liver that is frozen. Some butchers freeze liver overnight if they have some left over at the end of the day.

This practical will also enable REC 2 (designing tables) and REC 3 (accurate recording) to be assessed. The answer to step 8 can be used to assess recognising patterns in data (INT 6).

The final part of the investigation (step 9) is open-ended and will test the initiative of the pupils. Some will use up all their hydrogen peroxide at once, whilst others will use smaller volumes, and obtain more than one result. It could be used to assess pupil initiative (HMA 2).

Worksheet 5

To find out if potatoes produce carbon dioxide

Requirements

For each pupil: 20 cm^3 syringe, delivery tubes and split bungs assembled as shown in the worksheet diagram; 20 cm^3 hydrogen carbonate indicator; marker pen; two small pieces of rubber tubing to connect the delivery tubes together; retort stand and clamp; two boiling tubes, one of which is sealed by a bung—this tube should contain a piece of potato, which has been placed in the tube for at least 24 hours. The potato should be fresh, and it is best to put a large piece in the boiling tube.

Skills

HMA 1, HMA 2, HMA 3, HMA 4, HMA 7, AMO 10, INT 1.

General comments

The tube containing the potato should be set up well in advance to allow time for CO_2 to accumulate (see 'Requirements' above). The potato is respiring, producing carbon dioxide, which accumulates in tube A. Pupils need to remove the bung from A and replace it with the split bung containing the delivery tubes. This needs to be performed quickly. Provided that tube A is kept upright and not tilted, the carbon dioxide should stay in the tube. This exercise is a good opportunity to assess 'following instructions' (HMA 1) and/or 'assembling and handling apparatus' (HMA and HMA 7). It will be clear from the result of the experiment whether the pupils have assembled and handled the apparatus correctly. Pupils need to be careful when connecting the delivery tubes together, and should be reminded of this in advance. This could be used as a basis for assessing safe working (HMA 3).

Pupils are asked to use the apparatus to design a control, and this can be used to assess the handling of apparatus with initiative (HMA 2). The correct observation of the colour changes could be used to assess accurate observations (AMO 10). The response to the last question could be used to assess INT 1 (drawing appropriate conclusions).

Worksheet 6

Measuring the temperature of your body

Requirements

For each pupil: clinical thermometer (ideally one per pupil); antiseptic solution for sterilising thermometers (e.g. cetrimide solution or dilute TCP); graph paper; writing paper.

Practical Skills

HMA 1, HMA 3, AMO 1, AMO 3, REC 2, REC 4, INT 2, INT 3, INT 4.

General Comments:

Ideally, each pupil should be provided with a clinical thermometer. Otherwise pupils will have to wait to use them, particularly if they are being assessed for their ability to use a thermometer (AMO 1). The teacher may wish to set additional work for pupils to do whilst they are waiting to start the practical. If pupils do have to share thermometers, it is essential that the thermometers are sterilised very thoroughly between use.

The answer to step 1 should provide an indication as to whether they can read the scale on the thermometer, but should not be used to assess AMO 1. The instructions for using a thermometer could be used to assess following instructions (HMA 1). Pupils need to exercise caution in using the thermometer, and must be made aware of the danger involved in biting the thermometer and breaking it. A safety reminder is included in the worksheet, and should be assessed as HMA 3. Recording the result accurately (including units) on the worksheet and on the blackboard can be used to assess recording accurately (REC 3). The data table can be assessed as REC 2, and should be headed with units and a title. The bar chart can be assessed as REC 4. The questions at the end of the worksheet are designed to allow pupils to extract information from tables (INT 2) and graphs (INT 3), and perform simple calculations (INT 4).

Worksheet 7

Fields of vision

Requirements

For each pupil: protractor

Practical Skills

REC 2, INT 1, INT 2, INT 6.

General Comments

This exercise can be used to assess the ability to extract relevant information from the pie diagrams (INT 2), and the ability to interpret it (INT 1 or INT 6). The table in step 4 of the worksheet can be used to assess REC 2 (completing prepared tables).

Humans can see a range of 200° with both eyes, when looking straight ahead: 120° of this vision is seen by both eyes simultaneously. This enables stereoscopic vision to occur, which is important in judging distances and in gripping and manipulating objects.

Animal	Left eye	Right eye	Extent of overlap of both eyes	Field of vision not covered by either eye
Human	160°	160°	120°	160°
Rabbit	195°	195°	30°	0°
Cat	210°	210°	130°	70°

A rabbit needs to be aware of movements in the grass around it, because of the threat of predation. A wide field of vision helps it to be vigilant.

A cat is a hunter, and needs to be able to pounce upon its prey. Stereoscopic vision is an important part of this. The extent of the overlap between the left and right eyes is even greater than in humans.

The second part of the exercise may not be appropriate for all pupils, in which case it can be blanked off when photocopying.

—Worksheet 8—

Trotting and galloping

Requirements

For each pupil: calculator.

Practical Skills

AMO 10, REC 2, REC 3, INT 2, INT 4, INT 6.

General Comments

It is important that pupils realise that when a dog trots and gallops it is repeating a sequence of movements over and over again. By analysing one complete sequence of movements they can compare how a dog trots and gallops. Observations of which legs are on the ground can be assessed as AMO 10, and accurate recording in tables can be assessed as REC 2 or REC 3.

Pupils are then asked to identify patterns in the data (INT 6). When trotting, the dog either places its LB and RF legs on the ground or the LF and RB legs. In other words, it moves alternate legs at the same time. When galloping, the LF and RF legs move together as do the LB and RB legs. The calculation of the average length of time a leg stays on the ground when trotting or galloping can be assessed as INT 4. The answers are 0.24 s and 0.074 s, respectively.

Pupils are then asked to summarise their observations in the form of a comparison between trotting and galloping. This can be used to assess INT 2. Answers should indicate how the pattern of movements for trotting and galloping differ. Accurate observations of the diagrams should also reveal that other parts of the body are also involved, especially the bending and stretching of the back during galloping. This enables dogs to move faster, with longer strides.

—Worksheet 9—

Counting fruit flies

Requirements

Tube containing a mixture of *Drosophila* with normal wings and vestigial wings, in an approximate 3:1 ratio. The tube should contain at least 40 flies; etheriser for flies; white tile; paintbrush; well ventilated room.

Practical Skills

HMA 1, HMA 3, HMA 7, AMO 6, REC 3, INT 1, INT 5, INT 6.

General Comments

Drosophila breeding experiments have a great importance in genetics, but can be difficult to perform in schools. One reason for this is the difficulty in preserving the momentum of pupil interest over the time required to produce an F_2 generation. This exercise is designed to allow the pupils to undertake the final scoring exercise, without necessarily working on the whole programme. Some teachers might like to demonstrate the procedures involved in producing the F_2 generation; others might prefer just to use the results of the F_2 generation.

Although it takes time to make up the tubes containing flies, once made up they can be used for several different classes over a few days, providing a small amount of food medium is placed in the bottom of each tube. The ratio of flies should be approximately 3:1, although some pupils could be presented with ratios that are not exactly 3:1 so that they begin to appreciate the idea of sampling variation.

The teacher should demonstrate the correct etherising procedures for the flies, and the pupils should then try it for themselves. This is an important part of the exercise, and can be used to assess HMA 1 (following instructions) or HMA 3 and 7 (working safely, using materials and apparatus correctly). Care over safety is important both for the flies and for the pupils. Pupils should not sniff the ether, and should work in a well-ventilated room.

Counting skills can be assessed as AMO 6. This is particularly easy if each tube contains the same number of flies. Teachers using the NEA scheme who are assessing counting ought to ensure that there are at least 100 flies in each tube. REC 3 assesses accurate recording of the results onto the worksheet. INT 5 can be assessed if the ratios of flies in the tubes are not exactly 3:1. The breeding diagrams produced at the end of the exercise can be assessed as INT 1.

—Worksheet 10—

Designing experiments to test hypotheses
(i) Experiments with amylase
(ii) Experiments with destarched plants

Requirements

As specified by pupils.

Practical Skills

EXP 1–9.

General Comments

Pupils should be given the opportunity to perform the experiments which they design, so that they can evaluate their design afterwards. It is important that pupils realise that the evaluation should be in terms of how well their experiments tested the original hypothesis. This is more important than collecting large quantities of data.

The assessment of experimental design skills is fraught with logistical problems, particularly if very different problems are given to each pupil. The amount of apparatus needed to support all of the experiments can be enormous, and this can place a great burden on the technical resources of the department.

One way round this problem is to prepare a series of hypotheses on a particular topic, the testing of which require similar pieces of apparatus. It is not necessary for every member of the class to work on a different hypothesis, but there should be a sufficient number of hypotheses to prevent two pupils sitting close to each other being given the same one.

Two sheets have been prepared listing a number of hypotheses. One set involves the enzyme amylase, whilst the other involves photosynthetic experiments with destarched plants. The worksheets can be cut up, so that each pupil is given only one hypothesis.

The exercises will be most effective if they are presented at the right point in the course. It is important that the pupils are familiar with the background to the problem, and the range of techniques available to solve it—but they should not have rehearsed the actual experiment. Some of these hypotheses are more difficult to test than others, and require different amounts of preliminary knowledge. Teachers should therefore allocate them to pupils carefully.

Pupils should know what is required of them when designing an experiment. The EXP skills provide an excellent list of points to consider, which can be useful to both teachers and pupils. It is recommended that pupils design their experiments and make a list of apparatus in class time. The teacher can then assess the plan (modifying it where necessary). The apparatus list can form the basis for the apparatus needed for the next lesson, when pupils receive back their plans and perform the experiment. A third lesson will be needed for evaluating the experiment.

For the amylase hypotheses, all pupils should be familiar with the idea that amylase breaks down starch to maltose, that I_2/KI is blue-black in the presence of starch, and that the presence of maltose can be detected using Benedict's solution. Individual hypotheses may need some additional information (e.g. that starch and maltose can be separated by a selectively permeable membrane such as visking tubing; and that there are different types of starch). One of the hypotheses involves the explicit use of saliva, and some teachers may prefer to omit it. All the other hypotheses can be tested using powdered amylase. A 0.5% solution of amylase of bacterial origin can successfully digest an equal volume of 1% starch in less than 1 minute.

The photosynthesis hypotheses demand that pupils know that destarched leaves contain no starch, that starch is a product of photosynthesis that can be detected using a standard procedure (given in Investigation 2, *BFL*, 'How do plants feed?'). They should not have seen Investigations 1–4, BFL, 'Photosynthesis'. Coloured filters, placed on the leaves in the manner of Investigation 3, can be used as a basis for some of the designs.

—Permission to copy the worksheets—

A key to identify some tree leaves

Diagram 1

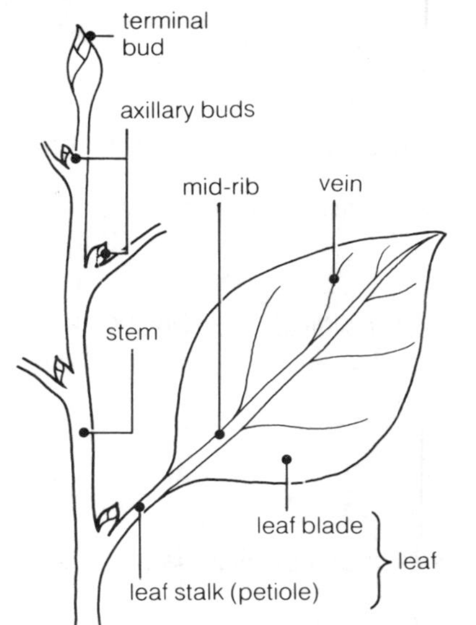

Diagram 2

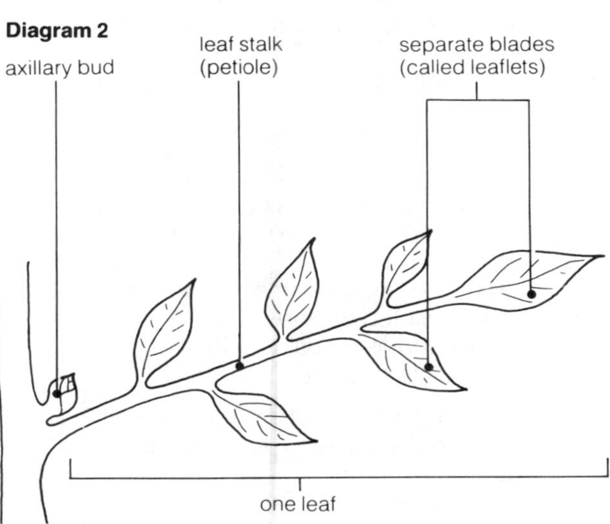

1	–Leaves shaped like needles, single or in groups.	**2**
	–Leaves with a flat blade or blades.	**3**
2	–Leaves in groups of three, quite long, 7–11 cm.	*Pinus radiata*— Monterey pine
	–Leaves in pairs, quite short, 4–7 cm.	*Pinus sylvestris*—Scots pine
3	–Leaves consisting of several separate blades either with each blade attached to a central stalk (diagram 2) or all meeting at one point.	**4**
	–Leaves consisting of a single blade either lobed, toothed or cut (diagram 3)	**5**
4	–Leaves with approximately five pairs of leaflets on a central stalk, and with a single leaflet at its end.	*Fraxinus excelsior*—Ash
	–Leaves with approximately five separate blades attached at the end of a leaf stalk. Leaves often large.	*Aesculus hippocastanum*—Horse Chestnut
5	–Leaves with a smooth (or only slightly toothed) or wavy outline.	**6**
	–Leaves distinctly lobed or toothed.	**7**
6	–Leaves oval but pointed. Veins going straight from the central mid-rib to the edge and sometimes projecting as a slight tooth.	*Fagus sylvatica*—Beech
	–Leaves with a smooth edge.	*Populus* sp.—Poplar
7	–Leaves with toothed edge, not cut or lobed.	**8**
	–Leaves are deeply cut, possibly with deeply lobed margins.	**10**
8	–Leaves small, 4–6 cm long with the leaf stalk about half the length of the blade. Rather triangular in outline with the stalk in the middle of one curved side.	*Betula* sp.—Silver Birch
	–Leaves rather larger, oval or distinctly rounded in outline. Leaf stalk ¼ or less that of the length of the blade. (*Beware:* the separate leaflets of Ash are long, narrow and spear-point shaped.)	**9**

A key to identify some tree leaves continued

9 –Leaves oval but pointed, about twice as long as broad. They have straight veins branching off the mid-rib. — *Carpinus betula*—Hornbeam

–Leaves distinctly pointed but very wide. The leaf blade is about as long as wide. — *Tilia x europaea*—Common lime

–Leaves very large, 13 cm or more long. Three or more times as long as wide. — *Castanea sativa*—Sweet chestnut

10 –Leaves with a toothed edge, but deeply cut one to four times at least halfway to the mid-rib. Leaf stalk about as long as blade. — *Crataegus monogyna*—Hawthorn

–Leaves with a lobed edge with each lobe smooth or with a slightly pointed outline. — **11**

–Leaves with a 'hand-like' outline with five major lobes each with distinct points. — **12**

11 –Leaves with smooth edged lobes. The base of the blade joining the leaf stalk with a small folded-back region on each side. — *Quercus robur*—English oak

–Leaves rather narrower than English oak, with each lobe distinctly pointed, and lacking the 'folded-back region'. — *Quercus cerris*—Turkey oak

12 –Leaves with a leaf stalk as long as the blade. The cuts between the 'fingers' or lobes reach less than halfway to the mid-rib. There are one or two side teeth on each lobe. — *Acer platanoides*—Norway maple

–Leaves with a leaf stalk about ⅓ the length of the blade. The cuts between the fingers reach at least halfway to the mid-rib. There are two, three or more side teeth on each lobe. — *Platanus x platanoides*—London plane

Diagram 3

edge of a lobed leaf

edge of a cut leaf

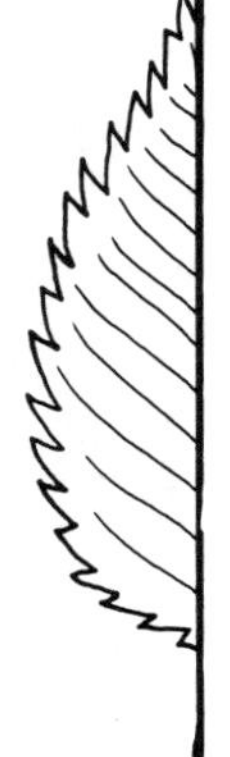

edge of a toothed leaf

Comparing organisms

You will be given two organisms which have a number of features in common, as well as a number of differences. Look at the organisms carefully using a hand lens.

If your organisms are very small, or if you are meant to look for small differences between the organisms, your teacher will tell you to use a microscope. If so, you will need to put the organism on a microscope slide, with a drop of water, and place a coverslip on top of the slide. *Biology for Life* reminds you how to do this, and how to use a microscope (see the section on 'Studying Living Things').

Look for as many similarities and differences between the two organisms as you can and write them down in the table below. Your teacher will tell you how many similarities and differences to look out for. Describe the similarities and differences as carefully as you can, but do not worry if you do not know the names of the various parts of the organism. You can make drawings if it helps you to explain what you can see.

Similarities between the two organisms	Differences between the two organisms

Osmosis and potatoes

Make sure you have these things in front of you:
a cork borer,
three petri dishes with lids,
marker pen,
one medium-sized potato,
plastic ruler,
a knife and a plate or tile upon which you can cut.

You will need about 20 cm³ of each of these liquids: water, 5% sucrose solution and 50% sucrose solution. You will also need to be able to use a weighing balance.

1 Write your initials and the name of one of the liquids (water, 5% sucrose solution or 50% sucrose solution) on the base of each petri dish.

2 Fill each of the petri dishes with the appropriate solution. Make sure that the solution you add is the same as the name on the outside of the dish. Fill each dish as full as you can, but bear in mind that you will need to put a piece of potato in the dish before you put the lid on it, so don't overfill it!

3 Use the cork borer to cut three cylinders of potato. Remove the skin from each one, and trim them until they are all of the same size. We will call these pieces of potato 'chips'. Make each chip about 5 cm in length.

4 Measure the length and mass of each chip. Write down these measurements in a suitable table. You should try to invent your own table, but first read the rest of this sheet to find out what measurements you will be taking.

5 Put a potato chip into each of the solutions. Place the lid on the dish, and leave the dishes until the next lesson.

The next lesson

Make sure you have these things in front of you: the petri dishes containing the potato chips, a sheet of absorbent kitchen paper, plastic ruler. You will also need to use a weighing balance.

6 Remove each chip from the solution, and dry it with the kitchen paper. This is best done by patting the chip **gently** with the paper. Don't squeeze it. Measure the length and the mass of each chip. Add these new figures to your results table. Feel each chip, and write a description of how it feels.

7 Calculate the **change** in length and mass. Increases should be given a + sign, decreases a − sign. Write these figures in your table.

8 Your teacher will collect the results from the whole class so that you can compare them. Are they the same? If not, why not? Why should this experiment produce a variation in results?

9 Osmosis is the movement of water from a weak solution into a strong one across a selectively permeable membrane. All potato cells are surrounded by membranes of this type. Explain your results in terms of osmosis.

10 *For fast finishers:*

Calculate the percentage (%) change in length and mass for each of your potato chips. Why is it better to express the results this way?

How could you use this technique to find out the concentration of solution **inside** the potato cells?

To find out how fast an enzyme works

This exercise involves using an enzyme called catalase, which is found inside liver. Catalase turns hydrogen peroxide into water and oxygen. The oxygen is released as bubbles of gas. We can use these observations to find out how quickly the enzyme works. Read the instructions before you start the experiment.

1 Check that you have all these things in front of you: a beaker labelled 'hydrogen peroxide', a beaker labelled 'water', an empty beaker, a plastic syringe, a pair of forceps, a piece of fresh liver, a stop clock, a paper towel.

2 Use the syringe to measure out exactly 5 cm^3 of hydrogen peroxide into the empty beaker. Be careful not to spill any of the hydrogen peroxide on your skin or on the bench. If you do spill any of it on your skin wash it off **immediately** with lots of water, and tell your teacher.

3 Draw a table that will be suitable for recording the results.

4 Get ready to switch on the stop clock. Using the forceps, drop the piece of liver into the hydrogen peroxide. Switch on the clock as soon as the liver touches the hydrogen peroxide. You should see bubbles of oxygen gas being given off. If you do not, tell your teacher straight away.

5 Swirl the contents of the beaker gently, and watch for the point at which no more bubbles are formed. Immediately switch off the clock, and record the time in the results table.

6 Reset the clock, and use the forceps to drop the liver into the beaker of water. Wash out the beaker which contained the hydrogen peroxide, and dry it with the paper towel.

7 Use the syringe to measure 10 cm^3 hydrogen peroxide into the clean dry beaker, and repeat stages **4** and **5** with the same piece of liver. Record the new result in your table.

8 Do you think that there is a link between the volume of hydrogen peroxide used, and the time taken for no more bubbles to be formed? If so, what is it?

____

____

____

____

____

9 Use the remaining hydrogen peroxide to obtain more results to see whether your answer to **8** is correct.

To find out if potatoes produce carbon dioxide

In this exercise you will assemble a piece of apparatus and use it to find out if a piece of potato produces carbon dioxide. Study the diagram below the instructions very carefully.

1. Use the items provided to set up this apparatus exactly as shown in the diagram.
2. When you remove the bung from the boiling tube containing the potato (tube A), make sure that you keep the tube upright. Replace it with the bung with the glass tubing as quickly as possible.
3. Push in the syringe plunger as far as it will go **once**. This will move air from tube A to tube B.
4. Record any change in colour of the hydrogen carbonate indicator:

   ____

5. **Let your teacher check your apparatus.**
6. This experiment is designed to show that potatoes produce carbon dioxide. At the moment this experiment is not a fair test because there is no control.
7. Use the apparatus provided to set up a control experiment.
8. **Let your teacher check your apparatus.**
9. Push in the syringe plunger as far as it will go **once** to move air from tube A to tube B.
10. What evidence is there to suggest that potatoes produce carbon dioxide?

    ____

    ____

    ____

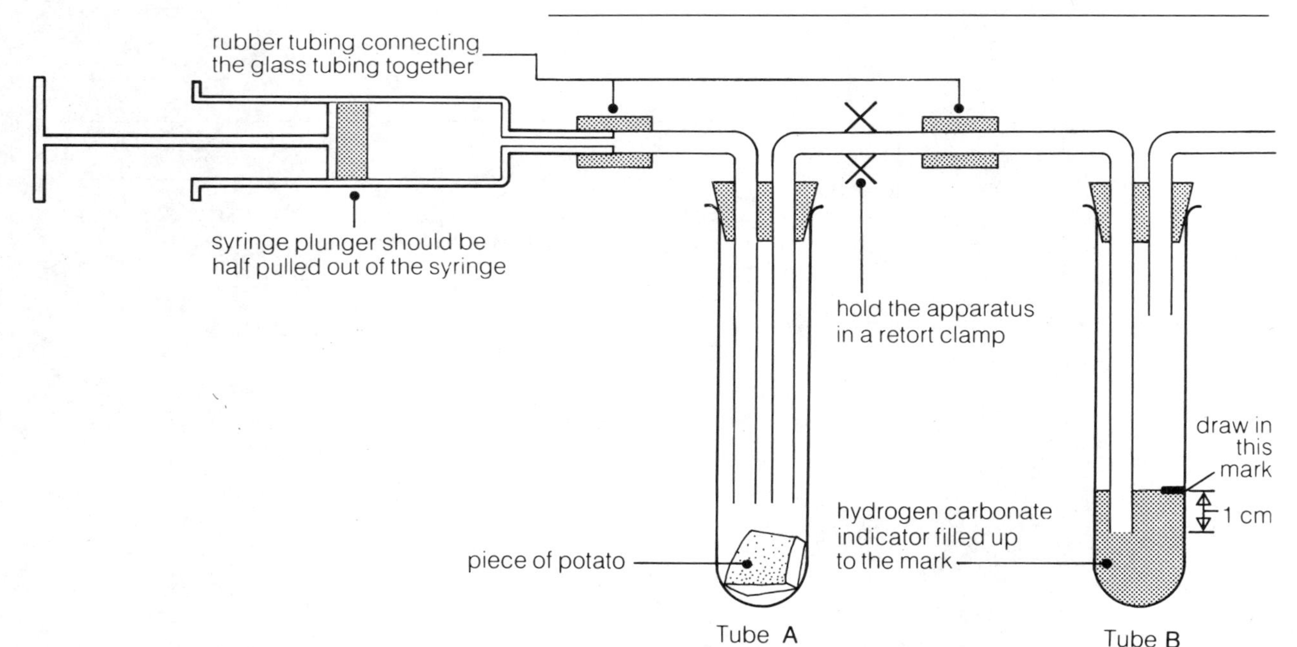

Measuring the temperature of your body

In this exercise you will be asked to measure your temperature using a clinical thermometer, and write the result on the blackboard. You will then use the class results to plot a bar chart like the one in Biology for Life *('Studying Living Things', Figure 3).*

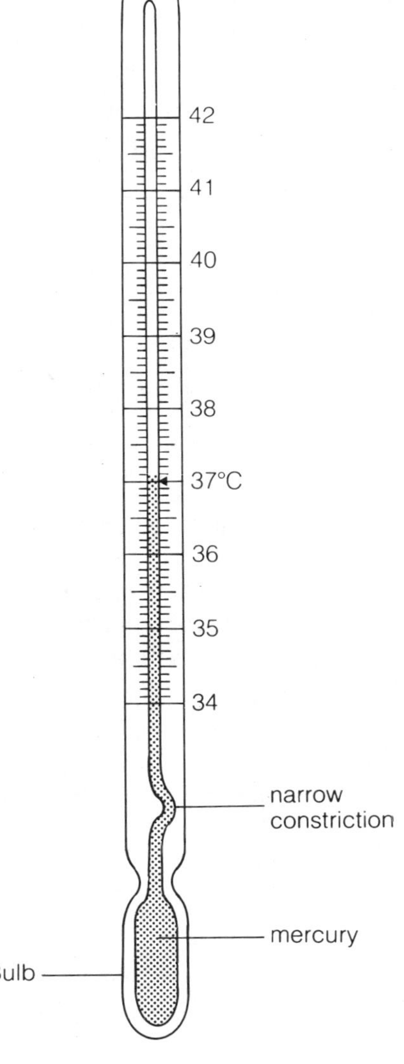

1 The diagram shows a clinical thermometer. What temperature does it indicate?

____

2 You should use the thermometer properly if you are to obtain an accurate measure of the temperature of your body. Read these instructions carefully, and make sure that you understand them:

a The bulb end of the thermometer should have been placed in a dilute antiseptic solution to sterilise it before you use it. Check that this has been done.

b Hold the middle of the thermometer firmly between your finger and thumb, and shake it by flicking your wrist sharply. This moves the mercury back into the bulb of the thermometer.

c Sit down and place the bulb of the thermometer underneath your tongue, and close your mouth. **Be very careful not to bite on the thermometer, and do not talk!** Leave the thermometer in your mouth for at least 2 minutes.

d Remove the thermometer, and turn it slowly until you can see a thick line of mercury. Read the farthest point on the scale which is touched by the mercury. This is the temperature inside your mouth.

e Replace the thermometer in the antiseptic solution.

f Your thermometer may have measured the temperature in degrees Fahrenheit (°F) rather than degrees Centigrade (°C). If this is the case then you can convert your result to °C by subtracting 32 from it and then multiplying by $5/9$.

g Write your result here and on the blackboard.

____

3 When all of the results are on the blackboard you will have to sort them into equal sized groups so that you can plot a bar chart. Show your teacher the table containing the grouped results before you start to plot the bar chart.

4 Use the bar graph and your table of results to answer these questions:

a What are the maximum and minimum temperatures found in the class?

____

b Which group of temperatures contained the largest number of individuals?

____

c What is the mean (average) temperature of the class? How does it compare with the national average of 37.0°C?

____

d People sometimes talk about a 'normal' body temperature. Do you think that this is a useful idea?

____

Fields of vision

Can you see what is happening behind you? Some animals can! This worksheet will help you find out how much different animals can see.

Human

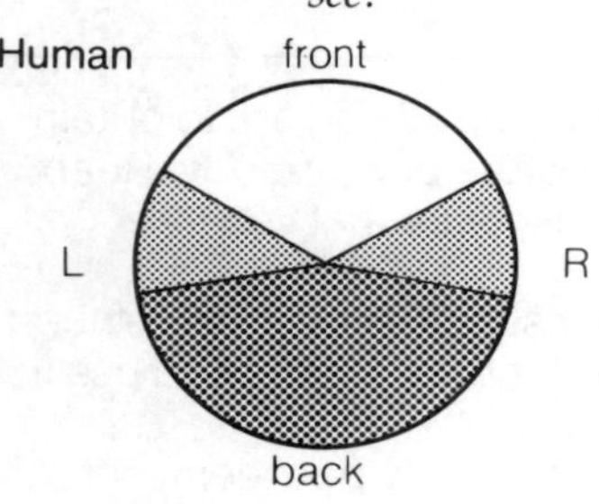

Rabbit

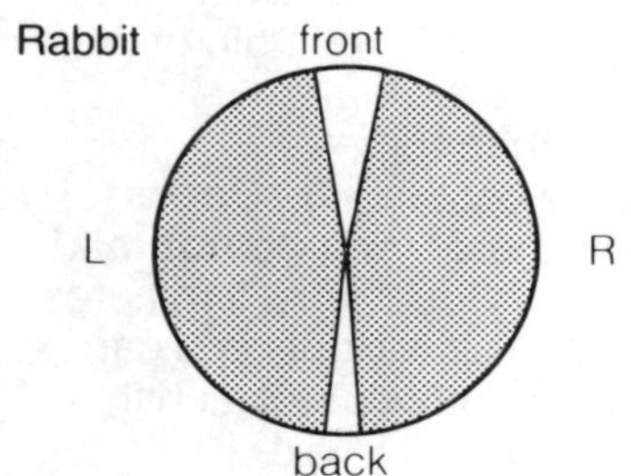

Cat

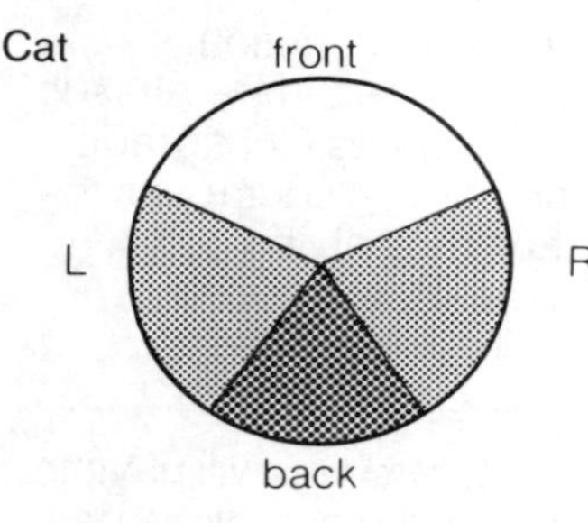

The **field of vision** is a measure of how wide an area you can see with each eye, when looking straight ahead. The top pie diagram shows how wide the **fields of vision** are for both eyes in a human.

field of vision of both eyes

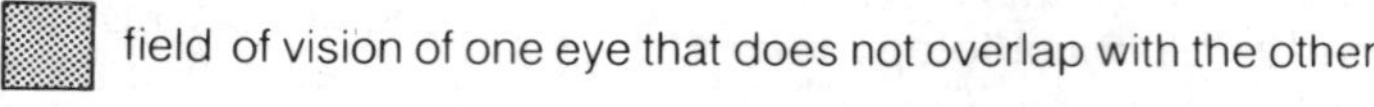
field of vision of one eye that does not overlap with the other

field of vision not seen by either eye

The white segments are the fields of vision that both eyes see. The shaded segments are the fields of vision of one eye only. The darkest segment is the area that neither eye can see.

1 How wide are the fields of vision for each eye?

____

2 The fields of vision of each eye overlap to some extent. How many degrees of overlap are there?

____

3 Why are overlapping fields of vision useful to us?

____

(**Hint:** Look at an object held 10 cm from your eyes. Close one eye and look at it. Then view the object through the other eye.)

4 Pie-diagrams of fields of vision for a rabbit and a cat are shown below that of a human.

Measure the angles of each portion of the 'pie' in each diagram. This gives you the size of the fields of vision for each eye, for the overlap between each eye and the extent of the field of view not seen by either eye. Write down the angles in the following table:

Animal	**Left eye**	**Right eye**	**Extend of overlap of overlap of both eyes**	**Field of vision not covered by either eye**
Human				
Rabbit				
Cat				

5 Why do you think it might be advantageous for a rabbit to have 'all-round vision'?

____

6 The cat is good at seeing objects in depth. Why might this be advantageous to it?

____

Trotting and galloping

When dogs trot they move slowly, and when they gallop they run quickly. In this worksheet, we are going to study how dogs trot and gallop.

It may be that when a dog trots it moves its legs in a different way from when it gallops. Trotting and galloping involve a sequence of movements that are repeated over and over again. It is possible to film a dog moving and examine the way that it moves its legs. The diagrams below were drawn from a film of a dog trotting and galloping. Each set of diagrams makes up a complete sequence of movements.

The left side of the dog is nearest to you, and we can call each leg by an abbreviation:

LB is the left back leg
LF is the left front leg
RB is the right back leg
RF is the right front leg

Trotting dog

1
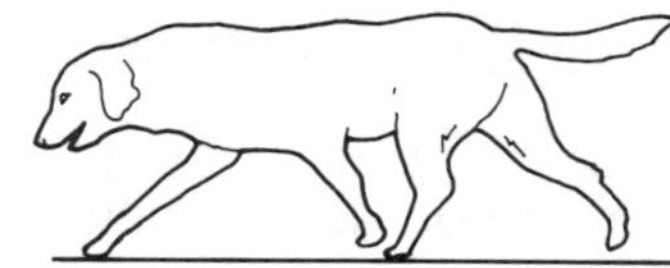

2
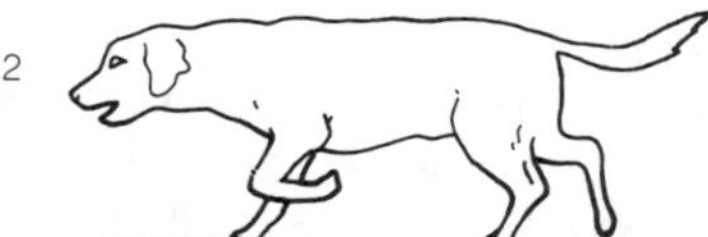

3
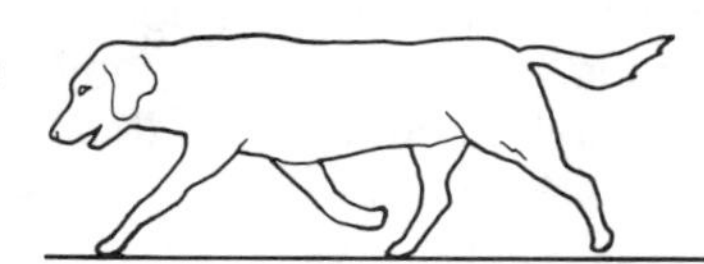

4
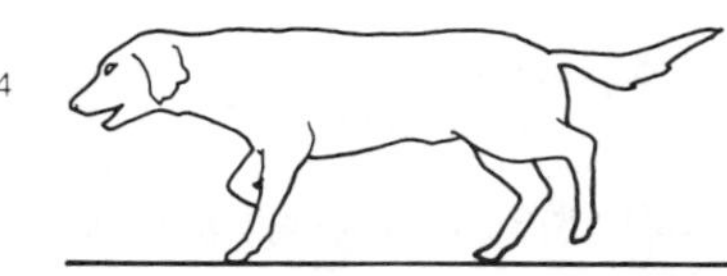

5
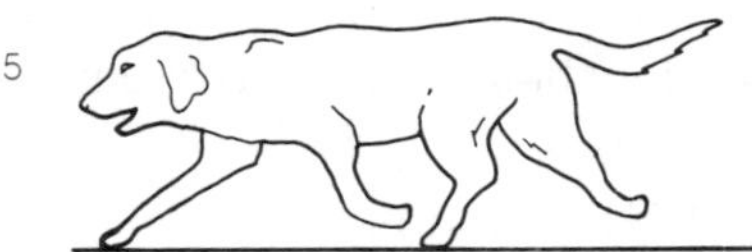

Galloping dog

1
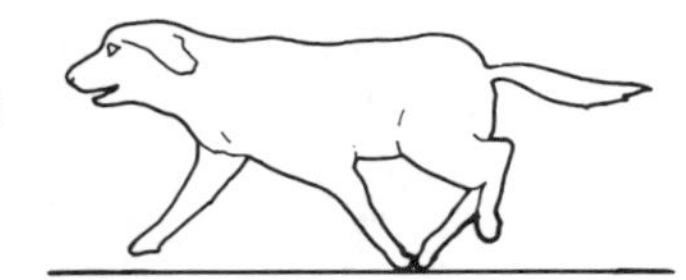

2

3
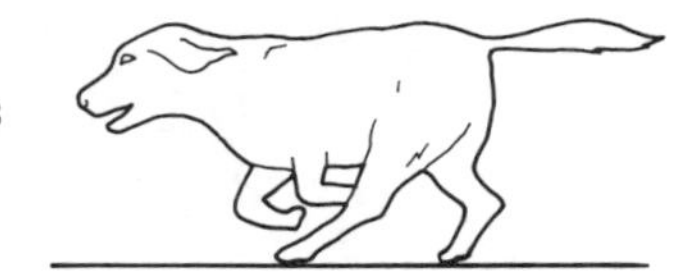

4
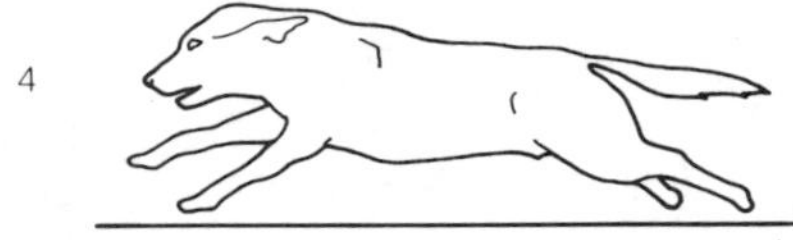

5
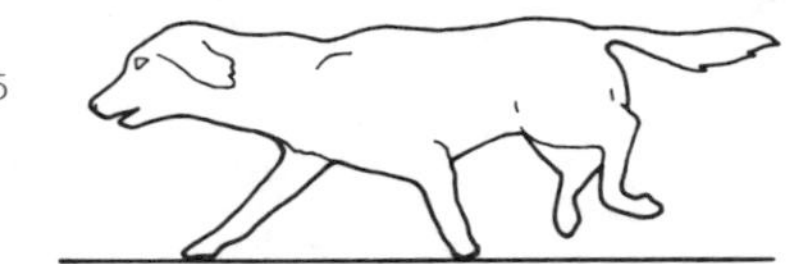

1 Look at each of the drawings carefully, and observe which legs are touching the ground. Here is a table in which you can record your observations. If you need help, ask your teacher.

Trotting		**Galloping**	
Diagram number	**Legs touching the ground**	**Diagram number**	**Legs touching the ground**
1		1	
2		2	
3		3	
4		4	
5		5	

Trotting and galloping continued

2 Study the observations in your tables, and work out which legs move together when the dog trots and gallops.

3 When the dog trots, which pairs of legs move together?

____

When the dog gallops, which pairs of legs move together?

____

When trotting, the dog took 0.5 seconds to complete one sequence of movements, but when galloping it took only 0.4 seconds to complete one sequence. In addition, the dog moved 3 times further in one sequence of galloping movements than it did in one sequence of trotting movements.

Looking at this information, you might think that the average length of time that a leg is on the ground is different when the dog trots or gallops. Use the figures below to find out whether this idea is correct:

4 The total length of time each leg touches the ground in one trotting sequence is:

LB 0.23 seconds **LF** 0.25 seconds
RB 0.26 seconds **RF** 0.23 seconds

Work out the average length of time that a leg stays on the ground:

____

The total length of time each leg touches the ground in one galloping sequence is:

LB 0.078 seconds **LF** 0.078 seconds
RB 0.078 seconds **RF** 0.063 seconds

Work out the average length of time that a leg stays on the ground:

____

When a dog trots it always keeps at least one leg on the ground. This is not the case when galloping. For 0.063 seconds in each galloping sequence there are no legs on the ground. When some animals gallop their feet rarely touch the ground! Film of cheetahs and greyhounds galloping show that all of their feet may be in the air for up to 50% of the time.

5 Look carefully at the diagrams and the results in this worksheet, and summarise the major differences between trotting and galloping.

____

____

____

____

Counting fruit flies

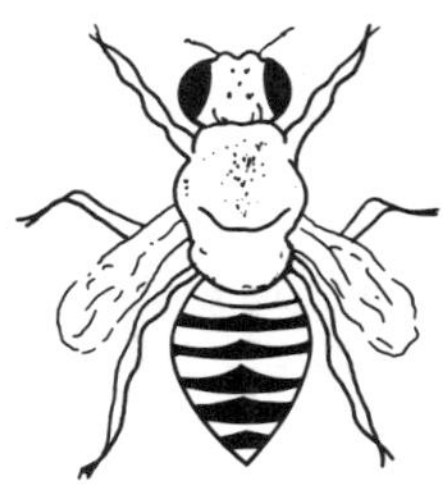

Vestigal wing

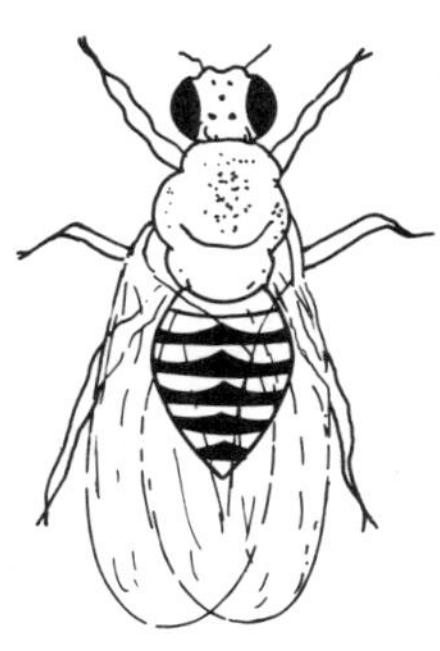

Normal wing

1 You will be given a tube containing a population of *Drosophila* fruit flies. They are all members of one family that have been produced by mating a male fly with a virgin female fly.

2 Your teacher will show you how to anaesthetise the flies in an etheriser. Now repeat the procedure with your tube of flies. You should remove them as soon as they stop moving. Be careful not to leave the flies in the ether for any longer than is necessary. Do not inhale the ether fumes.

3 Put the anaesthetised flies on a white tile. Examine them carefully. If at any time the flies 'come round' from the ether, use a paintbrush to put them back gently into the etheriser for a few moments until they stop moving.

4 Count the number of flies and write the answer below.

There are __________ flies in this tube.

5 The flies in this family are of two types: flies with normal wings and flies with vestigial wings.

Count the number of normal and vestigial winged flies in the family.

There are ____________ flies in this family with normal wings.

There are ____________ flies in this family with vestigial wings.

6 Now put all of the flies back into the original tube, and answer questions **7** and **8**.

7 The ratio of normal wings to vestigial wings in this family is:

____

8 These flies are part of an experiment to show how a gene which controls wing shape is inherited.

A male with normal wings and a virgin female with vestigial wings were mated. Eventually 150 flies emerged, all of which had normal wings. Two of these flies were separated and allowed to mate. They produced the family that you have in front of you today.

Draw a breeding diagram in the space opposite (like the ones in *Biology for Life* (see the section on 'Heredity')), to explain what has happened in this experiment. Your teacher will help you if you have difficulties.

Is the gene for vestigial wings dominant or recessive?

____

Designing experiments to test hypotheses

Experiments with amylase

Boiling destroys the activity of amylase.

Cigarette smoke reduces the activity of amylase.

Acid affects the activity of amylase.

Salt affects the activity of amylase.

The concentration of amylase affects the time it takes to digest a known volume of starch.

The concentration of starch affects the time taken for the starch to be digested by a fixed volume of amylase.

The molecules of maltose produced by amylase digestion are smaller than the starch molecules.

Temperature affects the activity of amylase.

The saliva produced before tasting food differs from that produced when food is in the mouth.

The presence of sugars (e.g. maltose) slows down the activity of amylase.

Amylase is equally effective in breaking down different types of starch.

Designing experiments to test hypotheses continued

Experiments with destarched plants

Plants do not produce starch in the absence of light.

Plants produce starch in green light.

Plants produce starch in red light.

Plants produce starch in blue light.

Plants produce starch in white light.

Plants produce more starch in bright light than in dim light.

Plants do not produce starch in bright light in the absence of carbon dioxide.

Plants produce reducing sugars when they photosynthesise.

Only the green part of a variegated leaf produces starch.

A leaf doesn't photosynthesise if its stomata are blocked by vaseline.

Notes